MARRIAGE BY FORCE?

MARRIAGE BY FORCE?

Contestation over Consent and Coercion in Africa

EDITED BY ANNIE BUNTING,
BENJAMIN N. LAWRANCE,
AND RICHARD L. ROBERTS

Foreword by Doris Buss
Afterword by Emily S. Burrill

OHIO UNIVERSITY PRESS • ATHENS, OHIO

Ohio University Press, Athens, Ohio 45701
ohioswallow.com
© 2016 by Ohio University Press
All rights reserved

Printed in the United States of America
Ohio University Press books are printed on acid-free paper ⊗ ™

26 25 24 23 22 21 20 19 18 17 16   5 4 3 2 1

Library of Congress Cataloging-in-Publication Data
Names: Bunting, Annie, 1964– editor. | Lawrance, Benjamin N. (Benjamin
  Nicholas), editor. | Roberts, Richard L., 1949– editor.
Title: Marriage by force? : contestation over consent and coercion in Africa
  / edited by Annie Bunting, Benjamin N. Lawrance, and Richard L. Roberts ;
  foreword by Doris Buss ; afterword by Emily S. Burrill.
Description: Athens, Ohio : Ohio University Press, 2016. | Includes
  bibliographical references and index.
Identifiers: LCCN 2016005089| ISBN 9780821421994 (hc : alk. paper) | ISBN
  9780821422007 (pb : alk. paper) | ISBN 9780821445495 (pdf)
Subjects: LCSH: Forced marriage—Africa. | Child marriage—Africa. | Marriage
  customs and rites—Africa. | Women's rights—Africa.
Classification: LCC HQ691 .M354 2016 | DDC 306.84096—dc23
LC record available at http://lccn.loc.gov/2016005089

Contents

PART THREE: CONTEMPORARY PERSPECTIVES

Foreword

DORIS BUSS

Marriage, perhaps more than any other social institution, highlights the complexity of violence against women. As this volume demonstrates, both marriage and violence are situated in a complex spectrum of practices and classifications. Their intersection at the point of forced marriage—and its association with violence in armed conflicts on the African continent—has brought to the fore difficult questions about how sexualized forms of harm, as well as their enmeshment in social practices such as marriage, should be understood *as harms* and *as wrongs*. These questions are difficult because they require disentangling the complicated relationships between social structures, particularly those presumed to be essential and foundational, and the continuum of violence against women. At what point is marriage forced? What constitutes coercion? How do physical, cultural, and economic relations structure the ways in which some forms of coercion are visible and others are not?

Feminists have long made the case that violence against women, particularly in the context of war, needs to be seen as part of a continuum where the spectacular forms of violence—such as rape in war or the targeting of schoolgirls in Nigeria, Uganda, or Pakistan—are linked to "mundane" daily acts of violence—such as street harassment, employment inequality, or intimate partner violence. But the continuum of violence is surprisingly difficult to see. This volume highlights some reasons why. The chapters assembled here provide close readings of different country contexts and varied historical periods to tease out the ways in which "the spectacular hides the mundane." The analyses in these chapters help to reveal the ways in which social structures and norms are positioned as so essential and enduring that we lose sight of just how variable, changing, and historically contingent they actually are.

This collection provides the sort of historically informed and finely grained analysis needed to go beyond the spectacle of contemporary imaginings of forced marriage, to disentangle the very ideas of *force* and *marriage* and the conditions needed for the two terms to be brought together in a single sentence. Issues of consent and conjugal union emerge here as long-standing preoccupations of colonial rulers; as social dramas in which changing expectations about labor and control, both within and outside the "family," are worked out; and as contexts for the contestation of different discourses about girls, women, and the meaning of justice.

A historical focus provides a rich unpacking of consent and conjugal union, where both emerge as dynamic, multivalent concepts over multiple country-specific case studies. The complex historical approach also insists that we pay attention to the moments of stasis, the legal and social dramas where ideas about marriage and rightness seem to fix and cohere. If we want to understand specifically *how* the spectacular hides the mundane, then we need to look at these moments that often appear in the form of legal disputes. The "frozen in time" quality of law, for all its limits, also provides a productive vantage from which to examine some of the currents, tensions, and discourses through which the wrongs of forced marriage materialize at some moments and in particular ways. Attending to social dramas and their legal contexts provides a basis from which to explore the why and why now questions. Why and in what terms are marriage and consent emerging as issues of concern, at this point in time and in this way?

It is significant that international criminal law is a key site where contemporary concerns and framings of forced marriage are unfolding. International criminal law, though it tends to offer a comparatively ahistorical understanding of conflict and its harms, is also an important arena for expressing the hopes of a more (gender-) equal future and one that might be secured through transitional justice. The various legal and bureaucratic institutions built around securing this transition make the task of unraveling the harms of forced marriage particularly urgent.

Naming and officially recognizing gendered forms of harm are essential to any postconflict transition, one where political, social, and economic institutions are reconstituted.[1] International criminal courts have become prominent sites where this process of recognition (or misrecognition) unfolds.[2] Identifying gendered harms is necessarily linked to the ways in which the postconflict future is imagined and the terms of public life and citizenship established. In this context, it is more imperative than ever that we bring a complex, historically informed, close reading to the terms by which concepts of force and marriage are understood.

NOTES

1. Doris Buss, "Performing Legal Order: Some Feminist Thoughts on International Criminal Law," *International Criminal Law Review: Special Issue on Women and International Criminal Law* 11 (2011): 409–23; Fionnuala Ní Aoláin, "Emerging Paradigms of Rationality: Exploring a Feminist Theory of Harm in the Context of Conflicted and Post-conflicted Societies," *Queen's Law Journal* 35, no. 1 (Fall 2009): 219–44; Aoláin, "Advancing Feminist Positioning in the Field of Transitional Justice," *International Journal of Transitional Justice* 6, no. 2 (2012): 205–28.

2. Nancy Fraser, "Rethinking Recognition," *New Left Review* 3 (May–June 2000): 113.

Acknowledgments

As is always the case, this edited volume is much more than the sum of its parts. Fresh on the heels of the completion of *Trafficking in Slavery's Wake* (Ohio University Press, 2012), coeditors Benjamin Lawrance and Richard Roberts first conceived of a joint project examining the intersection of slavery and forced marriage at an annual meeting of the African Studies Association in Washington, DC, in November 2011. In conversations with coeditor Annie Bunting, we soon found shared interests and concerns and began to plan our collaboration.

The majority of papers in this volume were assembled from a symposium examining forced marriage practices in Africa, convened as part of the third Conable Conference in International Studies at the Rochester Institute of Technology (RIT), in Rochester, New York. The symposium and publication of this volume were made possible with a generous grant from the Social Science and Humanities Research Council of Canada (SSHRC), and additional funding for the symposium and conference came from the Harriet Tubman Institute for Research on Africa and Its Diasporas at York University; the Avon Global Center for Women and Justice at Cornell Law School; the Susan B. Anthony Center for Women's Leadership at the University of Rochester; the Department of History at Stanford University; and the Department of Criminal Justice, the Program in Women's and Gender Studies, the Program in International and Global Studies, and the Department of Sociology and Anthropology, all part of the College of Liberal Arts at RIT. Maps and photographs were made possible with support from the Department of History at Stanford University. Proofreading and indexing by Meridith Murray were underwritten with a grant from RIT's College of Liberal Arts.

The editors deeply appreciate the remarkable talents of the staff at Ohio University Press, particularly Gill Berchowitz, Ricky Huard, Nancy Basmajian, Jeffrey Kallet, Sebastian Biot, Samara Rafert, John Pratt, Kristi

Goldsberry, Rebecca Welch, and the anonymous reviewers. We are grateful for the excellent work of Philip Schwartzberg in preparing the maps included in this volume and for the index expertly prepared by Meridith Murray. And we are most indebted to January Mvula, the executive director of Sustainable Rural Community Development in Malawi (SURCOD), for granting permission to use his photograph on the cover of this volume. SURCOD is part of a consortium of nongovernmental organizations working to improve the lives of girls and women throughout the world, affiliated with Safe World for Women alliance.

The editors would like to thank many individuals who were involved at various stages in the collaborative process leading to the publication of this book, including (alphabetically) Penny Andrews, Ramatu Bangura, Deb Blizzard, Leigh Blomgren, Israel Brown, Elizabeth Brundige, Charlie Bush, Kate Cerulli, Barbara Cooper, Steven Fabian, Jeremy Haefner, Dorothy Hodgson, Saida Hodžić, Ann Howard, Bonny Ibhawoh, Rachel Jean-Baptiste, Tabitha Kanogo, Christine Kray, Uli Linke, Jennifer Lofkrantz, Yael Machtinger, LaVerne McQuiller Williams, Chesiche Mibenge, John Osburg, Jason Polito, Joel Quirk, Marie Rodet, Karlee Sapoznik, Jody Sarich, Jane Schmeider, Debbie Steene, Robert Ulin, Judith van Allen, Bruce Whitehouse, and James Winebrake.

We would like to thank our families for their patience, generosity of spirit, and limitless support. Richard Roberts thanks the John Simon Guggenheim Memorial Foundation for a fellowship that enabled him to devote the time needed to develop and complete this project and to the African Studies Center seminar at Emory University, where participants engaged seriously with the issues raised in this volume and provided many useful insights. Benjamin Lawrance thanks the invaluable support of his invincible assistant, Cassandra Shellman. Annie Bunting thanks her colleagues at the Tubman Institute for their intellectual and institutional support, and in particular, she thanks Yael Machtinger and Karlee Sapoznik, who provided vital research assistance and worked as rapporteurs for the forced marriage symposium.

We are very grateful for such a fruitful collaboration throughout this process.

Annie Bunting
Benjamin N. Lawrance
Richard L. Roberts

Something Old, Something New?

Conceptualizing Forced Marriage in Africa

ANNIE BUNTING, BENJAMIN N. LAWRANCE, AND RICHARD L. ROBERTS

FORCED MARRIAGE features prominently in historical and contemporary accounts of gender relations throughout sub-Saharan Africa. Forced marriage—also known by a variety of other terms, including, but not limited to, marriage by capture, servile marriage, forced conjugal associations, war brides, and marriage in absentia—affects millions of Africans, predominantly women and girls. In some popular accounts, forced marriage is depicted as a new and urgent human rights violation demanding immediate action from national governments and the international community. In these accounts, ironically, forced marriage is both a fresh crisis and an ancient tradition.[1] The accounts of contemporary "marriage without consent" or "enslavement in war for forced marriage" are often put in uncritical comparison with historical marriage practices, which were the subject of colonial debate, intervention, and regulation. These comparisons are often made in the absence of empirical data and knowledge. Such uncritical analogous thinking runs the risk of doing a disservice to both historical understanding of African marriage practices and contemporary advocacy to address violence in marriage. And like other pressing contemporary human rights struggles, ranging from trafficking to domestic violence, forced marriages in Africa defy many attempts at interpretation and analysis.

This collection of new research places African forced marriages in broader social structures and historical contexts that shape gender, marriage, and human rights. The authors in this volume investigate dimensions of gender subordination, the diversity of sexualities and sexual identities, sociolegal regulation, resistance, and liberation in the context of conjugal relationships of the past and the present. The collection focuses on the role marriage plays in the mobilization of labor, the accumulation of wealth, the prevalence of dependent status, and slippage between marriages and other forms of gendered violence, bondage, slavery, and servile statuses. The chapters presented here also investigate the continuities, ruptures, and inventions of forced marriage practices of the colonial and postcolonial eras and the contemporary period. Although forced marriage has, since the mid-2000s, been the subject of scholarly inquiry and popular attention, it has received inadequate attention in the fields of African studies, law and society, and slavery studies. Where scholars do engage with these issues, few speak to audiences outside their fields.[2] As Jean Allain and others have argued, servile marriage has been a neglected dimension of slavery studies, and forced marriage has only recently emerged as a scholarly topic in legal studies.[3] Here, we bring together legal scholars, anthropologists, historians, gender equity activists, and development practitioners to examine forced marriage, consent, and coercion across time and place in Africa.

As with so many human rights issues, the spectacular hides the mundane, and the popular discourse misses the range of experiences and changes over time. In the case of "child, early, and forced marriage," the focus of policy and academic discussion is often reduced to "child marriage." And even "child marriage" is further reduced to "girl brides." Thus, though a lack of capacity to consent to marriage due to age is a dimension of forced marriage, the concentration on girls obscures analysis of the limitations on consent more generally. We hear much less about forced marriage than we do about girl brides married to much older men in India, Afghanistan, and Ethiopia, sometimes in group weddings.[4] Photographer Stephanie Sinclair, who documented child marriages over a decade, produced the exhibit Too Young to Wed.[5] In an interview, she compares the fight against child marriage to the anti-apartheid movement:

Just like every other human rights issue, like apartheid or civil rights, it is real and important to the people who are going through it. And the only reason it's happening to these girls is because they are girls. . . . Their lives are being held back because they are girls. This issue isn't going to be resolved in a couple years. Maybe in our lifetime. Just like we fought for civil rights 50 years ago and racism is still a huge issue in our country, no single thing will solve this. People are just figuring out it's an issue. We've started, but we have a long way to go.[6]

Early and forced marriages have been on the human rights agenda since before the contemporary human rights movement and the Universal Declaration of Human Rights (UDHR), but today, we are seeing an unprecedented level of international attention given to the issue. Like all human rights issues, change will come when the depth and complexity of the problem are realized and when policies and programs address changes at both the international level and in local communities.

FRAMING FORCED MARRIAGE IN LAW AND POLITICS

Forced marriage has been framed in a variety of ways in law, politics, and popular advocacy over its long documented history. Forced marriages are often represented as matters of slavery, crimes against humanity, women and children's rights, or human trafficking. The issue was an object of concern in Africa for missionaries, colonial administrators, anthropologists, social reformers, and antislavery activists. These concerns were articulated first in the context of civilizing missions that sought to change African marriage practices. Both before and after World War I, as examined in this volume in the chapters by Brett Shadle and Richard Roberts, colonial administrators debated whether bridewealth and early marriage were akin to slave trading and slavery. The lack of consent to marriage was historically clustered in debates over "native marriage" in Africa—concerns that included age and capacity to consent, polygyny, seclusion, and violence in marriage. In addition to framing forced marriage as a matter of colonial social engineering, with the establishment of the League of Nations forced marriage was seen as slavery or a practice similar to slavery. The debates on the ground in Africa regarding bridewealth, consent in marriage, and age of consent resonated with debates in European capitals and emerging international organizations.[7]

Though not explicitly included in the 1926 Slavery Convention, child marriage in particular was referred to by antislavery activists as a form of slavery. The drafters of the convention, having considered native marriage practices, concluded that forced marriage or dowry ought not be included in the 1926 convention. In his analysis of the debates within the Temporary Slavery Commission, Jean Allain writes that the commission concluded both customary law and Muslim law do not regard marriage as involving the purchase of a wife or an act of enslavement even if the situation may approximate slave dealing.[8] Nonetheless, after discussion of practices similar to slavery including forced and child marriage, the League of Nations adopted the 1926 Slavery Convention, of which article 1(1) states, "Slavery is the status or condition of a person over whom any or all of the powers attaching to the right of ownership are exercised."[9]

Significant debate remained as to whether servile forms of marriage ought to be included in the definition of slavery. Whether these marriages could be considered slavery depended on the conditions at the time of the marriage and also on whether "the powers attaching to the right of ownership" were exercised over the spouse, as required by the 1926 definition.[10] It is important to note that marriage without consent of one of the spouses does not generally meet the convention threshold for servile status. However, as we will discuss and as was discussed throughout the colonial period, bridewealth—as the transfer of goods and services for rights in persons—may meet this measure. Clearly, the framers of the 1956 Supplementary Convention on the Abolition of Slavery, the Slave Trade, and Institutions and Practices Similar to Slavery thought so. The post–World War II era experienced the development of a much more robust framework for international human rights and human rights conventions.

The 1956 Supplementary Convention includes child exploitation and marriage without the right to refuse where consideration (in legal terms this applies to anything of value promised to another when entering into a contract) is exchanged as forms of slavery as defined in the Slavery

Convention of 1926.[11] Article 1(c) of the 1956 Supplementary Convention calls for the suppression of

> any institution or practice whereby:

> (i) A woman, without the right to refuse, is promised or given in marriage on payment of a consideration in money or in kind to her parents, guardian, family or any other person or group; or

> (ii) The husband of a woman, his family, or his clan has the right to transfer her to another person for value received or otherwise; or

> (iii) A woman on the death of her husband is liable to be inherited by another person.[12]

Here, the language is "given in marriage" for money or consideration, "transferred" or "inherited," indicating that this prohibition was targeted at families treating girls and women as chattel. In other words, the 1956 Supplementary Convention developed a critique of familial and community practices, some of which came to be referred to as "harmful traditional practices." In current child marriage advocacy, for the most part only Anti-Slavery International, Walk Free Foundation, and Free the Slaves frame the issues of forced and child marriage as a matter of "modern slavery."[13] The nomenclature of slavery operates as a powerful rhetorical and symbolic tool in efforts to combat severe exploitation in marriage.

In international human rights law and many national legal regimes, forced marriage refers broadly to cases where one or both spouses are married without their full and free consent. This is wider in scope than servile marriage and is a matter of state responsibility. The Universal Declaration of Human Rights states that

> (1) Men and women of full age, without any limitation due to race, nationality or religion, have the right to marry and to found a family. They are entitled to equal rights as to marriage, during marriage and at its dissolution.

> (2) Marriage shall be entered into only with the free and full consent of the intending spouses.[14]

Shortly after the UDHR and the 1956 Supplementary Convention, the United Nations (UN) passed a treaty on age and consent to marriage. The 1962 Convention on Consent to Marriage, Minimum Age for Marriage and Registration for Marriage mandates that national governments pass laws that prohibit child marriage and require full and free consent to marriage.[15] The 1979 Convention on Elimination of All Forms of Discrimination against Women (CEDAW) reiterates this prohibition on child marriage and marriage without consent in article 16.[16]

Age and consent have figured prominently but paradoxically in the international law of marriage rights. Although consent and the capacity to consent are assumed to be requisite elements of legitimate marriage, international human rights law has deferred to States Parties to determine when young people have the requisite age of maturity. The UDHR notes in article 16 that men and women of full age have the right to marry, but it does not specify what "full age" means. Even the 1962 Convention on Consent to Marriage and CEDAW do not specify a minimum age at marriage or how to ascertain what constitutes meaningful consent. In its preamble, the 1962 convention calls on states to

> take all appropriate measures with a view to abolishing such customs, ancient laws and practices by ensuring, *inter alia,* complete freedom in the choice of a spouse, eliminating completely child marriages and the betrothal of young girls before the age of puberty, establishing appropriate penalties where necessary and establishing a civil or other register in which all marriages will be recorded.[17]

Article 2 of the convention calls on States Parties to set national marriageable ages in law and to establish marriage registries.

In 1965, the United Nations passed a nonbinding recommendation on marriageable age that included in Principle II that "Member States shall take legislative action to specify a minimum age for marriage, which in any case shall not be less than fifteen years of age."[18] The 1989 Convention on the Rights of the Child defines a child as anyone under the age of eighteen years. This standard is now read into the definitions of child marriage. The debates today take up children's rights not to be married and women's rights to fully and freely consent to marriage. Most recently, the African Union passed the Protocol to the African Charter of Human and Peoples' Rights on the Rights of Women in Africa (2003).[19] In article 6 of the protocol, States Parties are called on to enact legislation to guarantee a minimum marriage age of eighteen years and free and full consent to marriage. The article also instantiates monogamy as the "preferred form of marriage."

Notwithstanding international efforts to concretize terminology, in the first decade of the new millennium forced marriages in conflict situations ushered in new challenges. Notably, in 2008 the Appeals Chamber of the Special Court for Sierra Leone (SCSL) determined in the trial of rebel soldiers affiliated with the Armed Forces Revolutionary Council (AFRC) that the practices described as forced marriage constituted a separate crime against humanity, as another and distinct inhumane act.[20] The Trial Chamber found the practice of sexual slavery to constitute a crime against humanity.[21] The International Criminal Court (ICC) issued indictments in Uganda for similar practices as "sexual enslavement." In the Democratic Republic of the Congo, the ICC indictments include the war crimes of "sexual slavery and rape." In the Extraordinary Chambers in the Courts of Cambodia, lawyers for civil parties requested in February 2009 that the prosecutor conduct a supplementary investigation with the aim of amending the indictments in a case to include forced marriage.[22]

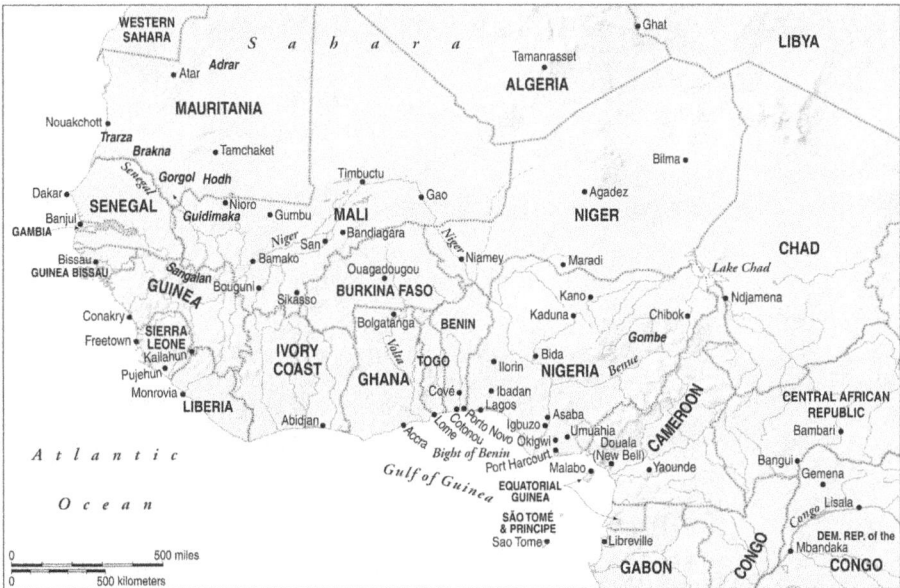

MAP I.1. Contemporary West Africa, by Phil Schwartzburg, 2015

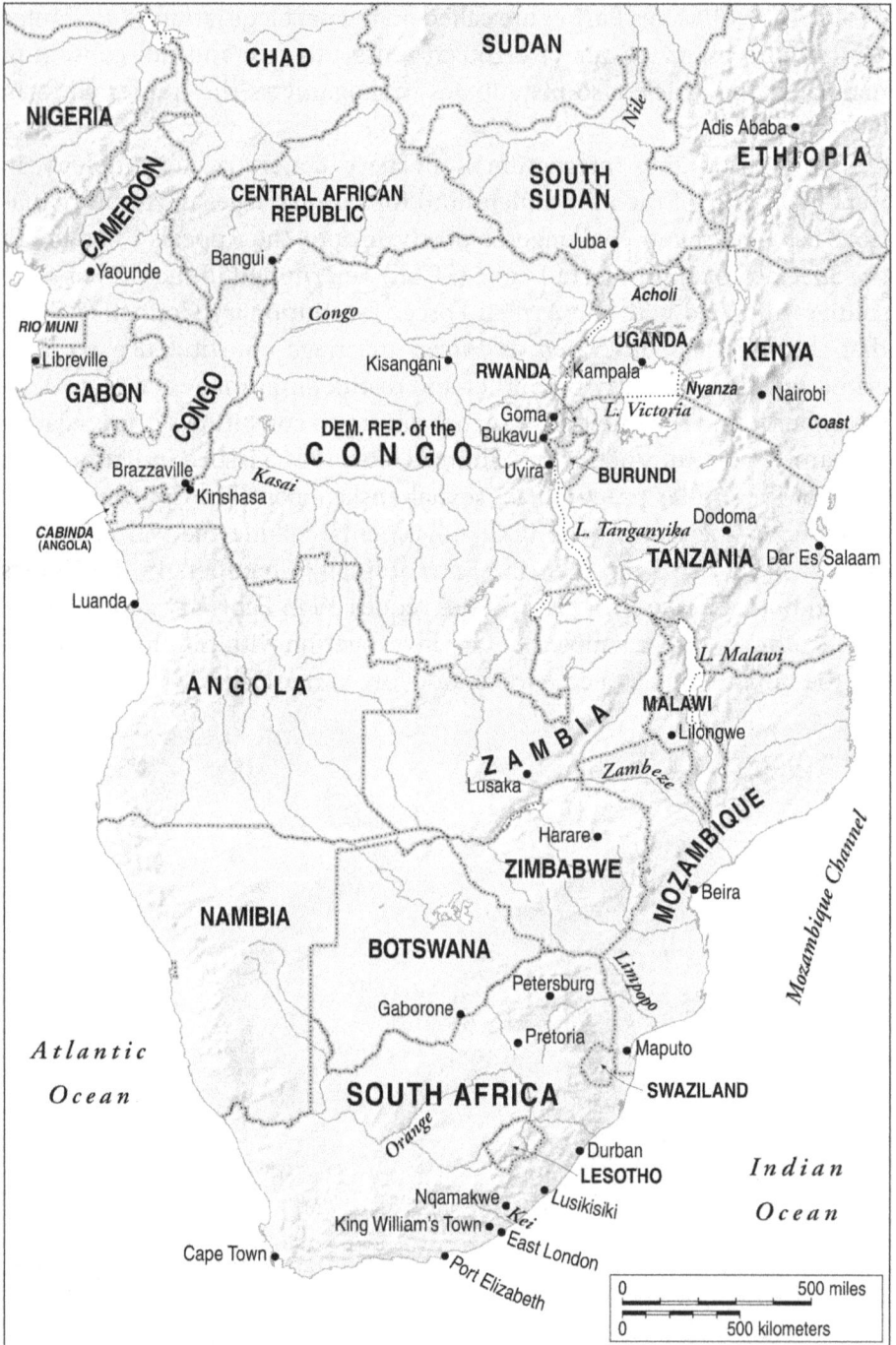

MAP I.2. Contemporary Central and Southern Africa, by Phil Schwartzburg, 2015

MAP I.3. Contemporary East Africa, by Phil Schwartzburg, 2015

The former UN special rapporteur on systematic rape, sexual slavery, and slavery-like practices during armed conflict, Gay J. McDougall, reported in 1998 that sexual slavery "also encompasses situations where women and girls are forced into 'marriage,' domestic servitude or other forms of labor that ultimately involve forced sexual activity, including rape by their captors."[23] The SCSL established the new crime against humanity of "other inhumane act (forced marriage)" in the Appeals Chamber decision regarding the AFRC to hold commanders responsible for the harms described as the "bush wife phenomenon." In that case, the legal precedent was set, but convictions on this ground were not entered. But the SCSL's prosecution of commanders of the Revolutionary United Front (RUF), another rebel army in Sierra Leone, resulted in a conviction for committing crimes against humanity.

In the RUF appeals decision, the court laid out the elements according to the SCSL statute as follows:

> With respect to forced marriage, the Appeals Chamber recalls that the offence "describes a situation in which the perpetrator[,] . . . compels a person by force, threat of force, or coercion to serve as a conjugal partner." The conduct must constitute an "other inhumane act," which entails that the perpetrator: (i) inflict great suffering, or serious injury to body or to mental or physical health; (ii) sufficiently similar in gravity to the acts referred to in Article 2.a through Article 2.h of the Statute; and that (iii) the perpetrator was aware of the factual circumstances that established the character of the gravity of the act. As a crime against humanity, the offence also requires that the acts of the accused formed part of a widespread or systematic attack against the civilian population, and that the accused knew that his crimes were so related.[24]

According to Valerie Oosterveld, this new definition of the crime of forced conjugal association substantially adds to the recorded history of gender-based violence within the conflict in Sierra Leone and thereby contributes to transitional justice in that country.[25] This definition may also have a substantial impact on future indictments from the ICC. With the conclusion of its work in Freetown, the SCSL moved on to the legacy stage of its mandate. The two most important precedents from the perspective of the offices of the prosecutor and registrar of the Special Court for Sierra Leone are its decisions on recruiting children into soldiering and forced marriage.

However, there appears to be no universal agreement on whether forced marriage under wartime is a human rights crime. The 2012 SCSL case involving Charles Taylor revisited the matter and found that the new crime against humanity of forced marriage was flawed and inaccurate.[26] The *Taylor* decision held that the term *marriage* should be avoided and that *conjugal form of enslavement* more accurately described the experience of women and girls who were abducted and held by rebels for long periods of time for sexual and other labor. The earlier Appeals Chamber decision for the AFRC did not enter fresh convictions because the court was "convinced that society's disapproval of the forceful abduction and use of women and girls as forced conjugal partners," being "part of a widespread or systematic attack against the civilian population," was "adequately reflected" insofar as "such conduct is criminal and that it constitutes an 'Other Inhumane Act' capable of incurring individual criminal responsibility." The 2012 *Taylor* decision upended this.[27] It focused initially on the enslavement and then on the sexual aspect, and in so doing, it addressed the "linguistic camouflage" critique of the use of the term *forced marriage*.[28] The *Taylor* verdict also recognized that enslavement through forced labor can be a gendered crime, leading Oosterveld to opine that "conjugal slavery" may have "clear expressive benefits" over the "forced marriage" formulation.[29] The term *conjugal slavery* signals the organization of labor in war and the severity of the crime, while also distinguishing it from peacetime marriage without consent.

Despite the legal recognition that servile marriage is a form of slavery, the prosecution strategies and judicial decisions of the ICC and the SCSL do not yet show a coherent approach or theory for holding perpetrators responsible for practices of forced marriage. Although the international legal standards make it clear that the constituent elements under the rubric of forced marriage—such as torture, rape, and forced impregnation—are distinct crimes against humanity, it remains unclear whether the totality of crimes amounts to slavery, sexual slavery, or some "other inhumane act." The academic commentary is also mixed in assessing the relative merits of charging forced marriage as slavery or as a new and separate crime. On the one hand, when forced marriage is framed as a form of slavery, it is recast as the most serious crime against humanity, one with the longest and richest history of global prohibition. On the other hand, to successfully prosecute forced marriage as a form of slavery, the court must find that the perpetrator had "powers attaching to ownership over a person" (1926 Slavery Convention) or "a similar deprivation of that person's liberty" (Rome Statute of 1998).

The Rome Statute of 1998, establishing the ICC and its Elements of Crimes, expands the 1926 definition of slavery—"any or all of the powers attaching to the right of ownership" over a person—with the additional phrase "or similar deprivation of liberty." Enslavement in the Rome Statute explicitly signals analogous situations. Thus, there is good reason to argue that the practice described variously as the "bush wife phenomenon" or "forced marriage" in Uganda or Sierra Leone would meet this definition of enslavement (see the chapters by Mariane Ferme and Stacey Hynd in this volume). Nonetheless, any effort to designate contemporary practices as forms of slavery may provoke charges of analytical overreach and rhetorical excess. Even if we accept that some practices can legitimately be described as a form of slavery or enslavement, it does not necessarily follow that the relevant *actus reus* (criminal act), such as exercising the powers of ownership, can be easily applied to specific cases of forced marriage in either wartime or peacetime.[30] Some observers will be very concerned that prosecuting practices referred to as forced marriage in conflict situations as forms of slavery will lead to higher standards of proof for forced marriage in nonconflict situations. The context and conditions of war are substantively different from times of relative peace, and therefore, forced marriage in nonconflict zones would not necessarily meet the definition of *slavery*, nor would it be required to do so. The Supplementary Convention of 1956 defines *servile marriage*, and not all forms of marriage without consent meet this definition.[31]

Survivors of forced marriage in Sierra Leone and elsewhere and their advocates may or may not agree with this characterization as slavery or the distinctions drawn between sexual slavery and forced marriage. Indeed, the language of sexual slavery is very provocative and powerful. Joel Quirk writes that the "key question here is not so much whether specific practices are identical to slavery, at least in part because slavery can be defined in a number of ways, but instead *whether they share sufficient features in common with slavery to be rendered illegitimate as a result of prior anti-slavery commitments.*"[32] It is important to underline that international criminal law holds individuals responsible for crimes against humanity, genocide, and war crimes.

In the cases before the ICC, the SCSL, and their predecessors—the International Criminal Tribunal for Rwanda (ICTR) and the International

Criminal Tribunal for the Former Yugoslavia (ICTY)—the highest-ranking officials were indicted for crimes against humanity. However, international customary law includes the prohibition on slavery and calls on states, not individuals, to be responsible for compliance and breaches.[33] International human rights law is also a matter of state responsibility. When states enact penal laws against slavery, individuals may be prosecuted under such provisions, as demonstrated in 2008 in Australia in the case of *The Queen v. Tang*. The legal field of action against forced marriages is only part of a wider campaign against these practices.

ARRANGED MARRIAGES AND FORCED MARRIAGES

The 2008 decision of the Appeals Chamber of the SCSL in its judgment of the *AFRC* case raised significant but vague distinctions between forced marriages and arranged marriages. Justice Julia Sebutinde's separate concurring opinion in the case compared forced and arranged marriages in Sierra Leone. According to Neha Jain, the opinion argued that forced marriages "mimicked peacetime situations of gender-stereotyped roles of women, where they were forced to perform all kinds of domestic labour and have sexual relations (and as a consequence, children) against their will. However, arranged marriages were characterized by the consent and participation of the families of the parties and accompanied by rituals and religious ceremonies."

Both of these situations were different from forced marriages during conflict situations, where "girls were forcefully abducted and held against their will in order to render sexual services to and perform conjugal duties for the rebels, had no protection and security of their families and were completely at the mercy of the rebels." The crucial distinction between forced marriage during conflict and the customary practice of arranged marriage was the "lack of involvement of the spouses and the absence of rituals in the case of the former."[34] In this volume, Mariane Ferme explores the differences between arranged and forced marriages from her two decades of fieldwork experience in Sierra Leone. If, as Ferme argues, forced marriages mimic customary arranged marriages, how do we account for the fundamental and irremediable social changes to the character of such customary practices as a consequence of war?

Building on the legal issues raised in the 2008 *AFRC* judgment, Kim Thuy Seelinger has explored the ambiguities of differentiating between arranged and forced marriages as they apply to asylum cases in the United States and the United Kingdom. Reflecting on the SCSL's definition of forced marriage under combat conditions as a crime against humanity, Seelinger asserts that "most forced marriages are . . . quieter, subtler affairs: fathers settle debts by selling their daughters; uncles promise their young nieces to their friends; or rapists avoid punishment by marrying their victims."[35] These quieter forms, Seelinger argues, remain distinct from arranged marriages: "The former is a violation of human rights, while the latter is generally not."[36] Seelinger supports her argument—at least insofar as it applies to claims of persecution in asylum cases—with reference to the UK Foreign and Commonwealth Office document entitled "Forced Marriage: A Wrong, Not a Right."[37]

In arranged marriages, the families of both spouses take a leading role in choosing the marriage partner, but the choice of whether to accept the arrangement remains with the potential spouses. They must give their full and free consent. The UK document describes this as a "consensual model of arranged marriage." Crucial to the UK policy on arranged marriages is the assumption that the individuals to be married give their "full and free consent."[38] In a forced marriage, by contrast, one or both spouses do not consent to the marriage or consent is extracted under duress, as examples in Benjamin Lawrance and Charlotte Walker-Said's chapter demonstrate. Duress includes both physical and emotional pressure. In some societies, the tradition of arranged marriage is a deeply entrenched practice, and it may be very difficult for potential spouses to resist pressure to accept the parental choice of marriage partner. Ferme argues persuasively that within the totality of forced and arranged marriages, we should be attentive to a spectrum ranging from forced subjection to something akin to consent, which suggests that the boundaries separating arranged and forced marriages are much more ambiguous. Francesca Declich, Bala Saho, and Judith-Ann Walker explore these ambiguous boundaries later in this volume.

Those seeking to make a distinction between arranged marriages and forced marriages are implicitly invoking "custom" as age-old practice. In an important argument about the politics of custom in both colonial and contemporary Africa, Liz Thornberry, in chapter 5, examines debates about abduction as a form of marriage in South Africa. Thornberry is especially interested in determining in whose interests claims of "custom" are being made and how these claims invoke history. In his discussion of the challenges of reforming forced marriages in the Gambia, Saho also asks in whose interests the claims of "endless tradition" are being made. These are vital issues to examine precisely because claims of custom and tradition are often invoked to shield practices from international human rights conventions and because students of custom in Africa have long understood that custom is unstable, flexible, and often subject to robust debate.

Although Seelinger generally accepts the distinction between arranged and forced marriages, she notes that "as the amount of input parents accept from their child and the degree to which parents allow their child to make the decision decrease, and the pressure to marry a certain individual rises closer and closer to the level of duress, the marriage moves along the continuum from 'arranged' to 'forced.'" In such a situation, Seelinger admits that "full and free consent" may be difficult to measure.[39] This was especially true in marriages of young girls arranged by their kin, as Saho and Roberts discuss in this volume. Many of the contributors to Aisha Gill and Sundari Anitha's volume on forced marriages in the United Kingdom and the European Union point to the range of coercion that girls and young women experience in the arranged marriages that still take place within some immigrant communities.[40] Gill and Anitha argue effectively that the coercion involved in arranged marriages is actually gendered violence and thus addressable under the legal sanctions of violence against women. Such coercion rises to the level of violence against women and sexual minorities precisely because of both the psychological harm and the actual harm the individuals fear if they say no to an arranged marriage. This coercion thus forms the basis of a "diminished capacity to consent."[41] As we will discuss next, the ability to consent to marriage or to think otherwise about marriage has been deeply constrained by ideologies and social practices linked to personhood and bridewealth in Africa.

PERSONHOOD, BRIDEWEALTH, AND CONSENT: CONSTRAINTS ON CHOICE

Marriage is a central institution in African societies, but its forms and meanings have changed over time. Marriage was and remains linked to personhood, although the instability of marriages in Africa raises key questions about gender, status, and social vulnerability. Bridewealth and early female marriage, long core components of marriage, have changed dramatically since the 1960s. The arrival of statutory same-sex marriage in sub-Saharan Africa adds a new dimension to a constantly changing set of traditions and practices. This section explores the linked nature of personhood, marriage, bridewealth, and consent.

Personhood in Africa is a process. Becoming a person depends in part on participating fully in social relations. John Comaroff and Jean Comaroff have described this process as "becoming rather than being." They contend that the Tswana social construction of the person should be understood as "nobody existed or could be known except in relation and with reference to, even as part of, a wide array of significant others." Moreover, "the identity of each and every one was forged, cumulatively, by an infinite, on-going series of practical activities."[42] Personhood should therefore be considered a process through which social relations generate social identity, but social identity itself changes with statuses achieved. Jane Guyer refers to this as "stages in social maturation."[43]

In a major assessment of personhood in Africa, J. S. Fontaine has compared the concepts of personhood in four African societies. She concludes that "the completed person . . . is the product of a whole life. By conferring personhood on the individual such societies also, though implicitly, distinguish between person and individual, conferring moral worth not on the individual but on the social form."[44] Fontaine's distinction between person and individual illuminates the process through which individuals attain the rights and privileges of personhood. Personhood thus carries the quality of social authority and indicates that the individual has achieved such a status. Along the way to this status, the individual gradually accrues more qualities of personhood. Marriage and having children usually play significant roles in this process, thereby ensuring the reproduction of the social unit. But personhood does not adhere evenly to men and women. Gender was historically a central part of the social construction of personhood, and in many African societies during the precolonial and colonial periods, women were considered jural minors and could not attain political office or titles, even if they could exert significant influence on kin and community.[45]

The concept of rights-bearing individuals, so central to the international human rights conventions, maps uneasily on the more fluid and complex African concepts of personhood, in which different sets of rights adhere to individuals during different stages of their lives. Concepts of personhood are often framed in processual terms about changes through status, but they do not account for social and historical change. Concepts of personhood are shaped by specific cultures, but cultures are hardly static and are most often sources of considerable debate among members of societies. Historical change, including the multiple encounters with other cultures, religions, and colonialism, merely accelerated these debates. Moreover, the context of the social relations that generate social identity has never been static and is linked to broader changes in the wider political economy in which the social unit generating social relations is embedded. Social identities are shaped by deep inequalities in terms of gender, generation, and access to economic and political resources. Personhood thus emerges out of what Anitha and Gill call "a matrix of intersecting inequalities."[46] These intersecting inequalities shape an individual's consciousness and agency, particularly in his or her abilities to consent or to think otherwise about socially sanctioned passages to personhood.[47]

The forces that have shaped social relations and personhood in Africa include the slave trade, conversion to Islam and Christianity, the redefinition of ideas of "custom" and "tradition" under colonial rule, new colonial legal systems, the end of slavery, male labor migration and the resulting feminization of poverty in rural areas, increasing commoditization of things and social relationships, the emergence of new forms of property and new means of accumulation in the colonial and postcolonial economies, rapid urbanization, the HIV/AIDS pandemic, rising heteronormative discourse and homophobia, and international human rights conventions. Each of these forces has influenced the constitution of personhood through its impact on households and communities and their relations with their members. Each of these influences has spurred intense debates about culture, obedience, and belongingness.[48] Many of the influences also have exerted deeply contradictory pressures on these debates. For example, colonial efforts to end slavery enhanced the debates about rights adhering in persons at the same time that colonial indirect rule policy strengthened the authority of male household heads over female and junior male members of their domestic units.[49] Bridewealth and age of marriage practices were essential parts of the "matrix of intersecting inequalities" that influenced colonial and postcolonial debates about forced marriage in Africa (see the chapters by Roberts and Shadle in this volume).

In much of Africa, marriage was legitimated through bridewealth. Bridewealth was a strategic investment that built and maintained webs of kinship and organized and controlled labor. Bridewealth often involved the transfer over a number of years of goods (grain, livestock, and cash) and services (weaving, herding, and occasional farmwork) from the husband's kin to those of the bride. In return, the husband and his kin group received the rights to the bride's labor (at least for that portion of the day customarily devoted to household chores and other activities that contributed to the well-being of the household, such as farming, weeding, spinning, and the like), as well as her reproductive power and her domestic services.[50] The value of bridewealth changed over time as African regional economies were drawn ever more fully into colonial and global ones. Many regions of colonial Africa experienced a "marriage crisis" when the value of bridewealth increased as rural and urban incomes increased, only to collapse again in the face of economic reversals such as the Great Depression. As Olatunji Ojo argues in this volume, changes in the value of bridewealth often resulted in waves of litigation in African native courts, as promises of betrothal and value of bridewealth were broken.[51]

Colonial administrators consistently failed to understand the complex flow of goods and obligations involved in bridewealth transfers. The shift in terminology is indicative of this: in the early colonial period, the term *bride-price* was widely used by colonial officials, which implied a sale or transfer of the bride to the husband's kinship group. As colonial anthropologists began to study African social practices more fully in the interwar period, the term *bridewealth* gained currency by suggesting that marriage involved more than a commercial transaction.[52] But the transfer of wealth from the groom's kin to the bride's guardian was often only one part of a much more complicated flow of goods and value between the groom's and bride's kin. In her discussion of Muslim Hausa in Niger, Barbara Cooper prefers the term *gift exchange* to *bridewealth,* in part because the female kin of the bride and groom actively engaged in gift giving that enhanced both the value of the marriage and the social networks of the women. Among these gifts were portions of a dowry, which were gifts given to the bride to carry into marriage.[53]

Cooper's analysis complicates the generalized binary between bridewealth and dowry marriage systems. Jack Goody and Stanley Tambiah have laid out the bold distinctions between these systems for sub-Saharan African and north Indian societies and the implications for women's social positions. They stress the separate nature of these systems rather than a more complex interrogation into the multiplicity of cross-flowing transfers of gifts, wealth, and labor. In general, dowry is a means to enhance the attractiveness of a bride in marriage and is provided by the bride's kin. The dowry, as Tambiah argues, consisted of several different portions that were used to support the "joint" family of the new couple within the groom's kin, to enhance the bride's well-being in her new home, and to provide a fund to support the bride if she became a widow. In bridewealth systems, Goody asserts, most of the value flowed from the groom's kin to the bride's kin in order to secure unambiguously the affiliation of her children.[54] In African Muslim communities, bridewealth, dowry, and dower often coincided. As the bridewealth flowed from the groom's kin to the bride's, the bride's father sometimes provided a dowry to ease her entry into her new home. The groom also gave presents directly to the bride, which formed the dower. Upon divorce, the wife retained the dower and often the dowry, especially if it was not commingled with the household's general assets.[55] As the value of bridewealth increased in many places throughout the subcontinent during the colonial period, some husbands also understood the higher value of bridewealth to confer on them both fuller control over their wives' labor and sexuality and enhanced patriarchal authority. At the same time, economic pressures often limited the ability of husbands to pay bridewealth and contributed, particularly in the postcolonial period, to a rise in long-term domestic relationships that did not attain the status of marriage.[56]

Starting in the colonial era, European administrators sought to engineer changes to African societies, especially in areas where they considered African practices to be contrary to civilization. Age of marriage was one such area for significant colonial intervention. Colonial administrators faced considerable pressure from missionary societies, activist groups in the metropole, and the liberal press to prohibit child marriages. The signal imperial precedent for legislating against child marriages was the Indian Government Age of Consent Act of 1891, which was part of a revision of the Indian Penal Code and Code of Criminal Procedure. The Age of Consent Act did not prohibit child marriages, but it made sexual intercourse with girls and the consummation of marriage with child brides under the age of twelve illegal. This 1891 act revised an 1882 law that had permitted sexual intercourse with girls at age ten. The debates surrounding the 1891 act were precipitated by the death of a child bride of eleven due to massive hemorrhaging following sexual intercourse with her much older husband. The 1891 Age of Consent Act had nothing to say about consent, but it did intervene in Indian child marriage and religious practices by adding another element to the social construction of biological sexual difference in assuming a uniform age at which Indian girls reached menarche. Child marriages remained common, and girls were often betrothed as infants even if they did not move to their husbands' homes until puberty. But there was another side to the controversies in India surrounding the 1891 Age of Consent Act, and that had to do with the bride's obligation to fulfill her wifely duties even if she did not consent to the marriage.[57] Age, consent, and coercion were thus deeply entwined in debates about both Indian and African marriages precisely because the Indian Penal Code was received into British colonial East Africa with the establishment of colonial rule. In this volume, Shadle explores the periodic expressions of debates about the age of majority, sexual development, and consent in marriage in colonial Kenya. As discussed by Declich in her chapter, forms of forced marriage in which the consent of the brides was deemed unnecessary existed in postemancipation colonial Somalia, where Italian settlers and administrators sought to mobilize labor by forcing women to marry male laborers.

With mounting intensity since World War II, human rights activists have also targeted child marriages as human rights violations. Organizations such as the United Nations Children's Fund (UNICEF) and the International Women's Health Coalition have argued that early marriage harms the child in several overlapping ways: it forces the girl to leave school, it imposes sexual activity that may be physically and psychologically harmful, it may result in pregnancy that can cause obstetric fistulas associated with long and obstructed labor, it increases a girl's dependence upon her husband, and it can raise rates of sexually transmitted infections (STIs) and HIV among young married girls.[58] Crucial to the argument about why child marriages constitute forced marriages is that children may not be capable of giving their full and free consent or at the very least what one US asylum judge called "meaningful consent."[59]

The age of consent in marriage was one of the fraught areas in this broad transformation of law and society.[60] Changing notions of childhood, contract, and age of reason in seventeenth-century England led to changes in marriage laws governing the minimum age of consent. In the sixteenth century, children as young as seven were considered able to enter into legally binding marriages, although they could seek a divorce if they had not consummated the marriage by the time they turned twelve. Marriages were directly linked to status, and marrying was a means of maintaining status endogamy. The major change occurred between the seventeenth and nineteenth centuries when parental control over children was strengthened. Holly Brewer points to a link between an increasing sense that valid contracts "should be based on intentional choice" that only comes with age and experience and that "binding marriages, once linked to puberty, shifted upwards, and parental consent for marriages began to be enforced."[61] Brewer also argues that children's ability to choose marriage partners was more constrained when they were seen as property. Children as property, in which rights in their persons could be exchanged or transferred, was most pronounced in societies where patriarchal ideology was most enshrined. The society Brewer has in mind was antebellum Virginia, where masters' control over slaves and servants and parents' control over their children were most fully elaborated in law. But the same process prevailed in many African societies where bridewealth marriages were common. Within this context, what does it mean to talk about consent in marriage?

Consent in marriage has a distinctive history. It is linked to fundamental changes in marriage and the family and in conceptions of childhood, personhood, and individual agency that have occurred over the past three centuries and accelerated with late nineteenth-century imperialism and with the trajectories of twentieth-century globalization and religious conversion. It is also linked to the development of international human rights and the international women's movement that has its roots in the early and mid-twentieth-century North American, European, and Soviet worlds.[62]

The concept of consent in our contemporary debates about forced marriages takes as its starting point a "robustly self-sufficient notion of responsibility" that associates freedom with the ability to separate oneself from others and assumes a significant distinction between free choice, arranged, and forced marriages. The concept of consent is linked to freedom more generally, which has a long and tortured intellectual history. Few scholars would agree that freedom is simply equated with "not being physically constrained." Many would want to introduce a more complex notion of constraints on freedom to consent because of the varied pressures to conform and the lack of viable alternatives. Thus, consent is always in conversation with the capacity to imagine and to implement alternative visions of society and social relations.[63]

Herein lie the important contributions of Carole Pateman to liberal theories of democracy and contract. These theories assume that political obligations derive from voluntary acts made by free and equal individuals. These voluntary acts are linked to free consent. Pateman contends that such liberal theories fail to recognize how liberal theorists have constructed women as men's natural subordinates and thus incapable of exercising consent that would give them the status of full citizens. Pateman draws attention to the cultural and structural constraints on real autonomy and meaningful consent under conditions of social, economic, and gender inequality. To consent freely also means to be able to say no. As such, consent needs to be distinguished from "habitual acquiescence, assent, silent dissent, submission, or even enforced submission. Unless refusal of consent or withdrawal of consent are real possibilities, we can no longer speak of 'consent' in any genuine sense." [64] Much of Pateman's original concern related to the legal issues of rape, wherein submission was often construed as consent unless resistance could be proved. Pateman's argument raised the broader issue of what she identified as "the special problem of women and consent" in a world shaped by deep inequalities of all kinds.

The status of full and free consent is central to issues raised by child marriages, which have been included within the growing corpus of forced marriages. Pateman has recently elaborated her theories of consent, contract, and subordination with a more precise linking of subordination to rights in persons. She argues that the "specific form of contracts about property in the person constitute relations of subordination, even when entry into the contract is voluntary." [65] Pateman is not necessarily thinking about bridewealth, but certainly bridewealth as the transfer of rights in persons is linked to marriage, subordination, and lack of consent.

International human rights instruments dating from the time of the UDHR have reiterated again and again certain basic assumptions about rights to marry, and over time, they have established a universal standard for the age of consent at eighteen. [66] In a major challenge to the proponents of a mandated minimum age of marriage, Annie Bunting argues that a human rights strategy to protect girls based on a uniform age of marriage of eighteen "obfuscates the diversity of childhoods" throughout the world. Bunting calls instead for analysis of "the complexity of both marriage and age" in different societies in which "cultural constructions of childhood need to be considered." [67] Bunting is not arguing for cultural relativism in demanding that scholars and practitioners pay attention to culture and especially the cultural construction of childhood. Nor does she deny the very real physical and psychological harm that can result from early marriage. Instead, she asserts that early marriage is more often than not directly related to social and economic conditions and to strong cultural biases against premarital sex.

Countries that have the lowest average age of marriage for girls and adolescents also have the lowest social indicators such as socioeconomic development, maternal and infant mortality, literacy, and life expectancy. Early marriage, Bunting argues, is directly correlated with a lack of schools, gender inequality, and deteriorating economic conditions, and as a result, many families seek to marry off adolescent girls in order to have one less mouth to feed or fewer school fees to pay. Cultural factors, such as social shame associated with out-of-wedlock pregnancy, contribute to the pressure to marry off young daughters. Islam, Bunting admits, also influences early marriage. Gender inequality, often leading to significant age disparities between spouses, is both a cause and a consequence of early marriage.

In calling for the analysis of socioeconomic conditions as well as cultural constructions of childhood in the practices of early marriage, Bunting wants international human rights advocates to be attentive to problems that adhere to what she terms "facile universalism" and an "inflexible legal standard." In challenging "simplistic portrayals of 'child brides' and 'child marriage,'" Bunting calls for enlarging the intellectual and political space between facile universalism and facile relativism in order to promote productive conversations about change.[68] Bunting's argument, however, does not address the place of consent in marriages and thus the agency and relative autonomy ("the ability to say no") of the girls or adolescents who enter into early marriages. In many African contexts, the boundary between consent and coercion is a gray area marked by social, economic, gendered, and cultural constraints on a girl's, boy's, man's, or woman's consent to marry. In this volume, Roberts explores the interplay of consent and coercion, especially in first marriages in colonial French West Africa, and Muadi Mukenge discusses how programs funded by the Global Fund for Women (GFW) are empowering mothers and girls to resist significant pressures for early marriages and to develop their human capital through schooling.

LOCATING FORCED MARRIAGES

A central contention in this volume is that although forced marriages lie at the fraught intersection of intimacy and labor, they are difficult to theorize because they constitute "continuing crimes" in the sense first interdicted in the 2012 *Taylor* decision pertaining to sexual slavery.[69] As Jeffrey R. Boles explains, within the criminal law crimes may be classified according to their nature as instantaneous or continuing; as its name implies, an instantaneous offense is a discrete action at a single, immediate period of time. The harm caused occurs in the moment (as, for example, with battery) and does not continue beyond the moment. A continuing offense, by contrast, "embodies a special legal meaning" and covers conduct over an extended period of time, and the harm it generates continues uninterrupted until the course of conduct ceases.[70] Previous scholarship on forced marriages has often framed such unions as intimate, domestic, or familial sites of struggle, but our collection blurs the lines between domestic, familial, public, and state by shifting attention to what is actually at stake when a union is forcibly established. The contributors to this volume argue that control over labor is a central dimension in contestation, as much as control over sexuality and the physical body.

At its core, forced marriage reflects ongoing struggles in Africa over patriarchy, patrimonialism, power, and control over labor and bodies. The difficulties encountered when investigating and narrating forced marriage speak to its role as part of a continuous and much broader drama. The public website of the Greater Manchester Police describes forced marriage as "a form of domestic abuse [that] is primarily, but not exclusively, an issue of violence against women."[71] Mirroring British legal formulas wherein forced marriage is not a crime per se but the associated offenses are criminal acts, officials in Sierra Leone or Ghana, for example, routinely advise women fleeing forced marriages to first seek assistance from domestic violence teams in urban police departments.[72] And as Lawrance and Walker-Said's chapter demonstrates, lawyers representing asylum claimants alleging forced marriage often compensate for social prejudices by reframing claims within more recognizable and documented forms of persecution, such as gender violence or state-sponsored homophobia.

A central element in the definition of domestic violence is controlling behavior on the part of the abuser. Forced marriages are always the result of controlling behavior, but the abuser may well be the household head who is eager to marry off his child. Clearly, the receiving groom or groom's kin also have a significant interest in controlling the new spouse's labor and sexuality. Physical and psychological violence and threats thereof serve to maintain control over the new bride and occasionally the new groom.

Yet domestic violence is only a part of the wider phenomenon of forced marriage. As a "continuing crime," the violence of forced marriage often begins long *before* the establishment of the conjugal union that becomes the site of domestic violence. In terms of refugee law, an individual fleeing a planned or imminent forced marriage may fear violence even before aspects of the threatened violence take place. But as the chapters by Saho, Ojo, Declich, and others demonstrate, the violence of forced marriages may originate with a father, an uncle, an imam, or a colonial state official. Indeed, as the essays in this volume attest, control over labor resides at the heart of many forms of forced marriage.

Building on such debates, the essays presented in this volume offer new perspectives on the nexus of coerced productive and reproductive labor and patriarchy. The authors examine a variety of contexts, historical and contemporary, that collectively reveal how attempts to coerce individuals into marriage are linked to struggles over labor and how labor demands have manifested themselves in the form of new ways of coercing individuals into marriage. During the colonial era, coercing women into marriage operated as a powerful mechanism for the expansion of political, social, and economic power in complex and contradictory ways. Ojo explores how, in the wake of the official abolition of slavery by the British, men in western Igboland revisited and resurrected various form of labor coercion through marriage as means to enhance household labor. And though slavery had already been abolished, the British colonial officers had an ambivalent attitude toward many practices they viewed as traditional, whether benign or not. Pawnship, for example, reemerged during the colonial period through child betrothal and bridewealth exchanges because wealthier men sought wives to contribute to their social aggrandizement. Bridewealth exchanges conveyed to prospective grooms certain rights to women (even as it deprived the women of consent), including sexual access, power to commandeer a woman's labor, and custody of children and the children's labor, even if the woman had had children by another man. Shadle's discussion of colonial Kenyan policies demonstrates that colonial ambivalence toward tradition, the age of consent, and the appropriate labor expectations for children extended across the colonies.

Similar patterns are discerned by Roberts in the French Soudan in the wake of the abolition of slavery during the first decade of the twentieth century. African societies were dynamic and rapidly changing, in spite of the imaginings of French colonial officers who documented customs and practices as if they were static. But unlike the British, the French colonial authorities were constrained by metropolitan pressures to civilize. Bridewealth contracts were viewed by many Europeans as little more than disguised purchases of women and girls, yet facilitating female emancipation by refusing to enforce such contracts threatened to destabilize the continuity and supply of labor that were essential to the colonial economy. Bridewealth operated as a bond, and the women subjects of bridewealth were bondswomen. Though the French wanted to enforce minimum ages of consent to marriage, they also realized that their colonial economic and political interests were best served when patriarchy—and female labor as a form of "patrimony"—remained undisturbed.

African men sought to "capture" women and the labor of women via marriage, in some cases with the tacit acquiescence of Europeans. Thornberry's discussion of the Xhosa practice of *ukuthwala* (bride abduction) reveals a complicated and contested site of labor coercion. Some South Africans insist that the practice of seizing a woman, which often included the sexual assault and rape of a girl, has become corrupted in the present era. The contemporary practice has spread beyond the Xhosa of the Eastern Cape, and the term has entered South Africa's legal lexicon and lingua franca.[73] The historical practice, however, was a mock experience of abduction, whereby a young man indicated the woman he wanted as his wife. But the historical record does not support the idea that the southern African practices once existed in a benign form. Instead, Thornberry demonstrates that the ukuthwala concept emerged to describe "irregular" marriages without consent, which men used to exert pressure over a woman's parents in order to release her and her labor into a marriage that was not necessarily of her own choosing.[74] Whereas the British South African authorities were confounded in their attempts to explain the practice or legislate the matter, Declich finds that the Italian government in Somalia deliberately restructured marriage to attend to labor considerations. In Somaliland, a variety of arranged marriage practices safeguarded the interests of women and children, as well as particularly vulnerable dependents. As the Italians sought to expand industrial agricultural production, they used marriage as a means to mobilize male *and* female labor. To this end, they enacted a policy of forcible monogamous marriage to supply plantation labor to Italian settlers.

The use of marriage as a vehicle to control labor is not confined to the colonial period. Examples from western, central, eastern, and southern

Africa show that in the postcolonial era and the contemporary period, a coerced conjugal union is often the most reliable and accessible form of labor control. Ann McDougall's analysis of *hartaniyya* (freed slaves) in Mauritania demonstrates that as slavery was abolished, elite Muslim men resorted to concubinage and "secret marriages" to safeguard their interests in women and their labor. Just as research on human trafficking has revealed how slippery terminology contributes to the persistence of coercive labor practices, McDougall focuses on the emergence of amorphous parallel marital norms. But concubinage also creates complex kinship relations that foster increased interdependence and provide access to labor for patriarchal family heads. In contemporary Gambia, Saho describes how labor considerations are at the heart of many nonconsensual marriages and why forced marriages persist to this day. Betrothals of girls permit parents to access the labor of potential grooms through preconjugal bridewealth payments in the form of labor. Girls or boys who resist these "customary" obligations risk violence at the hands of family elders.

Violently coerced labor is at the core of some of the most infamous forms of forced marriage in contemporary African sites of conflict. Stacey Hynd examines evidence of forced marriage from Sierra Leone, Liberia, Uganda, the Democratic Republic of the Congo, Somalia, and other countries, and she highlights how labor considerations paralleled the increasing militarization of girls' and women's lives in conflict zones. Marital frameworks and marital simulacra are routinely used by men to ensure domestic and sexual labor in conflict situations. In civil and ethnic conflicts, forced marriage combines sexual abuse with domestic labor and inverts the socially desirable status of marriage and motherhood. Ferme, however, argues that with international attention to forced marriage—and the drive to criminalize the practices attendant to so-called bush wives in Sierra Leone—traditional and customary marital practices are misinterpreted. Although forced marriages operated as a mechanism to secure the necessary labor and logistic support to maintain the war effort, particularly among nonregularized, mobile forces such as the RUF, Ferme contends that the new crime of forced marriage undermines one explicit goal of international transitional justice institutions—namely, to use war crimes courts as models for the return to the rule of law in postconflict settings—by criminalizing and thus undercutting traditional marital practices.

Early marriage has significant economic, social, and health consequences. Mukenge investigates efforts to combat girl marriage in Burkina

Faso, Benin, Uganda, and the Democratic Republic of the Congo. Evidence supports the view that deeply vested patriarchal interests in sub-Saharan Africa resist efforts to combat sexual violence and safeguard the rights of girls and protect them from illegal demands on their labor. But her research ties the struggle against forced marriage to the expansion of educational opportunities for girls and demonstrates an equally, if not more, powerful emerging resistance against patriarchy led partly by mothers who want for their daughters the equality they themselves never experienced.

The authors herein explore a variety of innovative legal strategies that emerge from the contestation over marriage. Lawrance and Walker-Said's experiences as expert witnesses in asylum claims provide the insight for an examination of how lawyers representing both heterosexual and homo-sexual clients seeking protection often choose to dismantle and reassemble their clients' narratives to privilege particular forms of persecution. In cases where women flee forced marriages and traditional gendered expectations, asylum claims are framed as defensively resisting patriarchy and "tradition." When lesbians, gay men, and bisexual individuals escape heteronormative marital regimes, their claims are often reframed as affirmatively contesting homophobia. Judith-Ann Walker's chapter discusses an innovative but problematic Islamic solution to widowed, abandoned, destitute, and vulnerable young women. In Kano State, government-sponsored mass marriages have ushered in thousands of unions of young women to men of all ages. Deciphering the degree of consent and coercion is difficult because of the complex process involved in the required written application and because of the powerful role of the quasi-judicial Hisbah Board in overseeing the program; further, the labor dimensions are concealed in the discourse of "welfare" efforts to ease the social burden of visibly destitute women. Young women, some of them divorcées or unwed mothers, find themselves in domestic labor situations as a result of these marriages, and many male spouses find second, third, or even fourth wives through the program.

THE (IN)VISIBILITY OF FORCED MARRIAGE

We began this book with the observation that forced marriage has emerged as one of the more critical human rights challenges in twenty-first-century sub-Saharan Africa. Domestic mobilizations and transnational human rights activism have spawned organizations, charities, newsgroups, and other entities devoted to elevating public awareness of forced marriage far beyond Africa.[75] Sensational stories about forced marriage circulating in the media, in the annual reports of gender equity advocacy organizations, or at film festivals capture the violence, horror, and injustice of this practice throughout the continent. Such narratives have added to the public debates about the persistence of forced marriages.[76]

Beyond continental Africa, international awareness of the global dimensions of forced marriage has never been greater. Mukenge documents US-led and UN-led advocacy and shows how international norms are reshaping domestic African statutes and curbing customary norms. Vigilance for indicators of compulsion and coercion has never been higher, and forced marriages are uncovered with increasing frequency in a broad swath of contexts, including as a vehicle for immigration fraud.[77] Growing international migration from the Global South to the North is one of several factors thrusting debates about forced marriage into public consciousness.[78] Many jurisdictions have promulgated new statutes prohibiting a plethora of practices, many of which are perceived to be "new," "deviant," or curiously "persistent."[79] And new rulings across the globe abound, expanding protections and giving rise to important legal novelty and neologism. One has only to consider UK Justice J. Parker's 2013 description of the Islamic and civil marriage of a woman of diminished mental capacity as "incapacitous marriage" and therefore a "forced marriage" under the United Kingdom's 2007 Forced Marriage Act.[80] Forced marriage has never before garnered such intense political, juridical, or public interest throughout the world.

Notwithstanding the value of greater visibility and accessibility, such scandalous representations of forced marriages are often monocausal, simplistic, heteronormative, and reflective of vested interests. What may be gained in terms of public visibility may actually be to the detriment of a richer and more nuanced understanding of the sociocultural habitus of forced marriage in Africa. Very few of the developments discussed previously are demonstrably tied to empirical fieldwork or synthetic scholarly analysis of forced marriage practices or patterns. The chapters in this volume by contrast offer a variety of perspectives that move beyond the representation of forced marriage as "scandal" and increase the visibility of forced marriage in Africa's historical past and its persistence, often in different guises, into the contemporary present.

The historical dimensions of contemporary forced marriage confusion are embedded in colonial archival records, where they became visible in social and official contestations and court struggles. Shadle demonstrates that in the first half of the twentieth century, Kenya colonial officials, missionaries, and elite African men wrestled with the question of early marriage, specifically regarding the appropriate minimum age for marrying Kenyan girls. Although marrying prepubescent girls appeared to have been universally rejected, establishing a "marriageable" age was next to impossible. Because of a reluctance to define the terms *puberty* and *sexual maturity,* no legislation was enacted. Instead, customary practices prevailed, giving rise to the context for the contemporary struggles we see today. By contrast, Declich observes, the Italian colonial rulers of Somali identified "monogamous" marriage as a mechanism for managing male and female labor. As Italian officials in the early twentieth century sought to establish plantations in the riverine regions of Gosha and the Juba Valley, they co-opted marriage practices, which they viewed as mere economic arrangements, and forced young women into unions with men who had no connection with their familial lineages or clans—affiliations that often protected women from domestic abuse. These women were deeply traumatized by the experience of forced marriage, which conveyed to the new husbands complete control over their bodies and sexuality in a manner entirely unrecognizable to prevailing cultural practices.

In a variety of contexts in sub-Saharan Africa, what precisely constitutes "custom" and "forced marriage" is a rich site of historical and contemporary struggle. Forced marriages often conceal conflicts over resources. In his exploration of forced marriage in the Gambia, Saho argues that when individuals, families, communities, or nations act in a "traditional way," we ought to ask precisely whose interests are reflected in the invocation of "tradition." In his study of historical and contemporary forced marriage incidents, Saho finds that the sociocultural, economic, and traditional norms and values as well as rural livelihood practices continue to be controlled by elderly men.

Ideas of custom, tradition, and religion inform contemporary northern Nigerian policies of organized mass marriages, as discussed by Walker. She describes how the paternal power to give consent or select a husband for a Hausa daughter is mostly legitimated using the doctrine of *Ijbar* under the Maliki school of Islamic law. But in Kano State, the Hisbah Board, a quasi-legal government entity, has taken over this responsibility for women considered "vulnerable," including young widows, divorcées, single mothers, and destitute individuals, and created a program of mass marriage. Although advocates claim to be finessing a traditional legal *practice*, many of the components, such as mandatory testing for sexually transmitted diseases and application forms, have been rejected by more conservative Islamic clerics as un-Islamic corruptions of tradition. And flight from custom or tradition is often the foundation of an asylum claim alleging forced marriage.

Such struggles over what constitutes custom are mirrored in southern Nigeria and South Africa. Ojo examines an epidemic of *isinmo,* or "hair cutting," in Igbo communities in the 1930s. Isinmo involved a man cutting a lock of a girl's hair, putting an eagle feather on her head, or throwing an egg at her in order to coerce her into marriage. Historically, isinmo was associated with the creation of a regal mate for the most senior Western Igbo chief (*eze*), but by the 1920s, it had become a tactic for forcing woman into marriage and maintaining sexual fidelity even if the husband was not a chief. Isinmo increased sharply during the Depression because young men had fewer resources for bridewealth. Thornberry observes similar changes over time in her discussion of the South African practice of bride abduction, or *ukuthwala*, prevalent in the Eastern Cape and KwaZulu-Natal Provinces. Thornberry interrogates the changing meaning of the practice of ukuthwala and how traditions surrounding this practice are invoked in the present. In today's postapartheid South Africa, men participating in ukuthwala marriages may be criminally charged with abduction, kidnapping, assault, or rape, but the first public discussions of marriage by abduction date to the 1880s in both civil and criminal court cases. In the nineteenth and early twentieth centuries, people used the word to refer to a variety of irregular forms of marriage that took place without the prior consent of a woman or her father or both; ukuthwala included both consensual mock abductions, which South African commentators today assert are the "proper" form of the custom, and truly violent abductions.

Ojo and Thornberry find a proliferation of marriage disputes in Nigeria and South Africa, respectively, to be a rich source for studying contestation over marriage, divorce, and consent to a union, reflecting how local patterns are challenged by international and global transformations and the emergence of new standards. Formal court disputes also speak to the widespread social mobility and household instability that erupted during the colonial period. Roberts, examining French colonial polices in French Soudan, finds considerable ambivalence about marriage, divorce, and consent in the early twentieth century. The French harbored conflicting opinions regarding women's consent to marriage, likening bridewealth payments either to "disguised purchases" of people and thus contrary to French antislavery policies or to the foundation of family stability and patriarchal households. Women and men went to court with increasing frequency because at the core of the "murky separation" between arranged and forced marriage was the problem of bridewealth. Particularly in first marriages, bridewealth constrained females' capacity both to consent to marriage and to envision alternatives to those unions arranged by kinsmen or lineage heads.

Contemporary forced marriage struggles continue to play out in courts and tribunals. Court testimonies often provide open-ended discussions of how gender violence, rape, and women's victimhood all contribute to forced marriages. In the privileged spaces of courtrooms and tribunals, such discussions can lead to a better understanding of the longer-term structural violence that gives rise to the wartime concepts of forced marriage, such as the so-called bush wife. Testimonies recorded by truth and reconciliation commissions in Sierra Leone, Liberia, Uganda, Rwanda, and elsewhere, as investigated by Hynd, demonstrate how tribunals situate forced marriage narratives within emerging international humanitarian discourses and in so doing validate such discourses in sub-Saharan Africa. Furthermore, she documents how the contemporary conceptualization of forced marriage owes much to the confluence of emerging concerns about child rights, child soldiering, and human trafficking. The Hisbah Board of Kano State operates as an autonomous quasi court, and Walker explains how it vigorously defended itself against charges that the girls comprising mass marriage cohorts are compelled by documenting the support of parents, even in cases where girls are below eighteen, the age of consent. Both McDougall and Declich cite examples of how forced marriage features as an aspect of contemporary refugee claims, specifically in Canada and the Netherlands.

The chapters in this volume also demonstrate how African forced marriages continue to spill out of courts and refugee tribunals into new international legal contexts, contributing to the reshaping of debates and the emergence of new norms and even customs. Mukenge documents how grassroots women's organizations in Benin, Burkina Faso, Uganda, and the Democratic Republic of Congo address the complex factors that perpetuate child and early marriage. They adopt emerging international norms, many of which originated from court-based struggles, and turn them into community-based initiatives that are subsequently integrated into higher-profile, broader regional and global campaigns seeking to bring about transformations in the everyday lives of girls. Ferme studies the impact of the SCSL and focuses on notions of individual and collective consent, which in some instances mimic the gender biases of local customary law. She argues that the criminalization of forced marriage at the SCSL has a paradoxical consequence for women's rights because it appears predicated on establishing certain forced relations as crimes against humanity, whereas others practices are accepted as "customary." She highlights how a transformative impact is being wrought by what she describes as the "legal empowerment" movement, which arrived in postconflict Sierra Leone simultaneously with the SCSL but remained beyond its control. In one sense, this nongovernmental organization (NGO) community is an aspect of the transitional and international justice apparatus, but it often operates in tension with the criminalization paradigm.

Even if the 2008 SCSL Appeals Chamber finding that forced marriage in wartime is a human rights crime has not yielded widespread legal agreement, it has generated public awareness and significant new scholarship on the issues of forced and arranged marriages. The chapters in this volume bring historical and contemporary perspectives to these issues and provide much-needed context to the discussions. Taken together, the chapters demonstrate how important it is for legal practitioners and community development experts to be aware of the historical precedents and wide variations in forced and arranged marriages practices we see today. Similarly, historians need to be mindful of how pressing legal and development issues influence the ways in which both historical actors and historians define problems.

As the contributors to this volume argue, coercion and consent play major but complex roles in marriages. The interplay between coercion and consent is mutable and changes dramatically in the face of contemporary pressures, including violent conflict, economic conditions, panics regarding status and culture, gender and sexuality, and international legal norms. Coercion and consent are also linked to the changing character of patriarchy, patrimonialism, heteronormativity, and the demand for labor. As discussed in the chapters ahead, any analysis of forced and arranged marriages must examine the wider social, cultural, economic, and legal contexts in which the debates occur. The chapters presented here underscore the three central themes of this volume: analysis of continuities and ruptures in forced marriage practices in the colonial and postcolonial era, the place of forced marriage as coerced labor, and the value and limitation of the new legal decisions on forced marriage in relationship to the longer history and ongoing efforts to prohibit it.

This book is organized into three parts. The first section explores colonial debates about forced marriage. The case studies in this section address colonial anxieties about African customary practices and the conflicts that erupted as European colonial officials attempted to control, alter, and reshape African lives and families. The second section focuses on what we call postindependence transformations. These chapters investigate complex indigenous idioms, practices, and traditions contested in the colonial past and reshaped and revalidated in the postcolonial present. The third section examines contemporary perspectives on prevailing practices in the present day, concentrating on the legacy of recent conflicts, attempts to rebuild and reconcile, refugee mobilities, and the lived experiences of day-to-day struggles between local attitudes and the imposition of international legal norms and standards.

The new research presented here suggests directions for future work on marriage, consent, and coercion. Studies of contemporary forced marriage in Africa are not often linked to marriage practices and debates in the diaspora, whether within corresponding immigrant communities or elsewhere. Thus, we see a tendency to study early and forced marriage in Africa in isolation from the debates in Europe and North America on the same topic. Refugee claims on the basis of fleeing forced marriage is one site of intersecting debates on violence and resistance in marriage. There is also rich potential for comparative work on forced marriage in Asia and Africa, while remaining ever attentive to the local sociohistorical context. Further, there is an urgent need for qualitative research on the ways in which people living with disabilities as well as gay, lesbian, and nontraditionally gendered young people are vulnerable to forced marriage. Finally, although there is a recognition among development workers and legal practitioners that men need to be engaged in programs to prevent and redress early and forced marriage, little research exists on the perspectives of traditional and religious leaders, heads of families, and others implicated in the institution of marriage.

1. In an address on October 24, 2013, Canadian foreign minister John Baird stated: "Today's introduction of this [UN] resolution marks a symbolic day for the millions of women and girls subjected to the inhumane practice of child, early and forced marriage. It reaffirms our commitment to protecting children's rights and calls for further action in the UN General Assembly to address this barbaric practice."

2. Claire C. Robertson and Martin A. Klein, eds., *Women and Slavery in Africa* (Madison: University of Wisconsin Press, 1983); Aisha K. Gill and Sundari Anitha, eds., *Forced Marriage: Introducing a Social Justice and Human Rights Perspective* (London: Zed Books, 2011).

3. Jean Allain, "*Hadijatou Mani Koraon v. Republic of Niger*," *American Journal of International Law* 103 (2009): 311–17; Allain, *The Legal Understanding of Slavery: From the Historical to the Contemporary* (Oxford: Oxford University Press, 2012); Annie Bunting, "Forced Marriage in Conflict Situations: Researching and Prosecuting Old Harms and New Crimes," *Canadian Journal of Human Rights* 1, no. 1 (2012): 165–85.

4. See Girls Not Brides, www.girlsnotbrides.org; Plan International, http://plan-international.org/girls/; ICRW, http://www.icrw.org/media/news/icrw-strategies -end-child-marriage-shared-un-general-assembly. accessed February 9, 2014.

5. See http://tooyoungtowed.org/, accessed February 7, 2014.

6. See http://www.thedailybeast.com/witw/articles/2014/01/24/too-young-to-wedo .html, accessed February 9, 2014.

7. J. P. Daughton, "Behind the Imperial Curtain: International Humanitarian Efforts and the Critique of French Colonialism in the Interwar Years," *French Historical Studies* 34, no. 3 (2011): 503–28; Susan G. Pedersen, "Back to the League of Nations," *American Historical Review* 112, no. 4 (2007): 1097–1117; Michael D. Callahan, *Mandates and Empire: The League of Nations and Africa, 1914–31* (Brighton, UK: Sussex Academic Press, 1999).

8. Jean Allain, "Servile Marriage as Slavery and Its Relevance to Contemporary International Law," paper, 2009, on file with authors. See also Allain, *The Slavery Conventions* (Leiden: Nijhoff, 2008).

9. League of Nations, 1926; entered into force on March 9, 1927, in accordance with article 12. The convention was amended by the protocol done at the headquarters of the United Nations, New York, on December 7, 1953; the amended convention entered into force on July 7, 1955.

10. For discussion of the criteria of slavery and interpreting the "powers attaching to ownership," see the "Bellagio Principles" in Allain, *Legal Understanding of Slavery*.

11. UN Economic and Social Council, Resolution 608 (XXI) of April 30, 1956, and done at Geneva on September 7, 1956; entered into force on April 30, 1957. "Consideration" in a contractual agreement is anything given or promised in exchange for the performance or promise of the other party.

12. Ibid.

13. The Modern Slavery Index 2013 includes child marriage in the prevalence Index, Walk Free Foundation; Anti-Slavery International, "Out of the Shadows:

Child Marriage and Slavery," report, 2013; and Free the Slaves website, http://www .freetheslaves.net/.

14. UN General Assembly, Resolution 217 A (III) of December 10, 1948.

15. UN General Assembly, Resolution 1763 A (XVII) of November 7, 1962, entered into force in 1964; full text available at http://www.ohchr.org/EN/ProfessionalInter-est/Pages/MinimumAgeForMarriage.aspx, accessed February 9, 2014.

16. Some of the same countries currently championing the UN resolution on child, early, and forced marriage have not signed or ratified the 1962 Convention on Consent to Marriage.

17. UN General Assembly, Resolution 1763 A.

18. UN General Assembly, Resolution 2018 (XX) of November 1, 1965.

19. African Union, Protocol to the African Charter on Human and Peoples' Rights on the Rights of Women in Africa, July 2003, entered into force on November 25, 2005. See http://www.achpr.org/instruments/women-protocol/, accessed February 10, 2014.

20. Cite to AFRC Appeals decision, 2008.

21. Cite to Trial decision, 2007.

22. 001/18–07–2007-ECCC/TC.

23. UN Sub-commission on the Promotion and Protection of Human Rights, *Systematic Rape, Sexual Slavery and Slavery-Like Practices in Conflict.* Final report submitted by Gay J. MacDougall, Special Rapporteur, UNESCOR, 50th session, UN doc E/CN.4/Sub/2/1998/13 (1998).

24. Prosecutor v. Issa Hassan Sesay, Morris Kallon, Augustine Gbao, SCSL-04-15-A, Appeals Judgment (October 26, 2009) (Special Court for Sierra Leone), available online at UNHCR, http://www.unhcr.org/refworld/docid/4ae9b31c2.htm, at para 735 [RUF Appeal Decision].

25. Valerie Oosterveld, "The Special Court for Sierra Leone's Consideration of Gender-Based Violence: Contributing to Transitional Justice?" *Human Rights Review* 10 (2009): 88.

26. Prosecutor v. Taylor, Case No. SCSL-03–01-T, Trial Chamber II, Sentencing Judgement, 40 (May 30, 2012).

27. 200, 202.

28. Patricia Viseur Sellers, "Wartime Female Slavery: Enslavement?" *Cornell International Law Journal* 44 (2011): 115, 130n97, 137, 142.

29. Valerie Oosterveld, "Gender and the Charles Taylor Case at the Special Court for Sierra Leone," *William & Mary Journal of Women and the Law* 19, no. 1 (2012): 22.

30. Ibid., 17.

31. UN Economic and Social Council Resolution 608 (XXI); also see the prior discussion.

32. Joel Quirk, "Ending Slavery in All Its Forms: Legal Abolition and Effective Emancipation in Historical Perspective," *International Journal of Human Rights* 12, no. 4 (2008): 529–54; emphasis added.

33. See Helen Duffy, "*Hadijatou Mani Koroua v. Niger:* Slavery Unveiled by the ECOWAS Court," *Human Rights Law Review* 9, no. 1 (2009): 151–70.

34. Neha Jain, "Forced Marriage as a Crime against Humanity: Problems of Definition and Prosecution," *Journal of International Criminal Justice* 6 (2008): 1018–19.

35. Kim Thuy Seelinger, "Forced Marriage and Asylum: Perceiving the Invisible Harm," *Columbia Human Rights Law Review* 42, no. 1 (2010): 59.

36. Ibid., 60.

37. UK Foreign and Commonwealth Office, "Forced Marriage: A Wrong, Not a Right," 2005, available at www.gov.uk/forced-marriage, accessed December 5, 2015. See http://collections.europarchive.org/tna/20080205132101/fco.gov.uk/files/kfile /05062006%20final%20fm%20report%20nja,0.pdf, cited in Seelinger, "Forced Marriage and Asylum," 61.

38. Seelinger, "Forced Marriage and Asylum," 60–61.

39. Ibid., 61.

40. Gill and Anitha, *Forced Marriage.*

41. Especially Geeranjali Gangoli, Khatiddj Chantler, Marianne Hester, and Ann Singleton, "Understanding Forced Marriage: Definitions and Realities," in Gill and Anitha, *Forced Marriage,* 25–45.

42. John L. and Jean Comaroff, "On Personhood: An Anthropological Perspective from Africa," *Social Identities* 7, no. 2 (2001): 268, 271.

43. Jane Guyer, "Comment," in Stanley Tambiah, "Bridewealth and Dowry Revisited: The Position of Women in Sub-Saharan Africa and North India," *Current Anthropology* 30, no. 4 (1989): 429.

44. J. S. Fontaine, "Person and Individual: Some Anthropological Reflections," in *The Category of the Person: Anthropology, Philosophy, History,* ed. Michael Carrithers, Steven Collins, and Steven Lukes (Cambridge: Cambridge University Press, 1985), 132.

45. See Jean Allman, Susan Geiger, and Nakanyike Musisi, eds., *Women in African Colonial Histories* (Bloomington: Indiana University Press, 2002), and Dorothy Hodgson and Sheryl McCurdy, eds., *"Wicked Women" and the Reconfiguration of Gender in Africa* (Portsmouth, NH: Heinemann, 2001).

46. Sundari Anitha and Aisha Gill, "Reconceptualising Consent and Coercion within an Intersectional Understanding of Forced Marriage," in Gill and Anitha, *Forced Marriage,* 46.

47. These issues lie at the heart of the debates surrounding the social reproduction of domestic groups and the problem of agency more generally. See Claude Meillassoux, *Maidens, Meal and Money: Capitalism and the Domestic Community* (Cambridge: Cambridge University Press, 1981), and Anthony Giddens, *The Constitution of Society* (Berkeley: University of California Press, 1984), for various positions on these debates. We attribute the concept of the "ability to think otherwise" to Giddens, *Constitution,* 9, 14.

48. For how these debates played out in colonial and early postcolonial East Africa, see Derek Peterson, *Ethnic Patriotism and the East African Revival: A History of Dissent, c. 1935–1972* (New York: Cambridge University Press, 2012).

49. See the invention of tradition debates for insights into how these pressures may have operated. In particular, see Terence Ranger, "The Invention of Tradition in Colonial Africa," in *The Invention of Tradition,* ed. Eric Hobsbawm and T. O. Ranger

(New York: Cambridge University Press, 1992); Martin Chanock, *Law, Custom and Social Order: The Colonial Experience in Malawi and Zambia* (Cambridge: Cambridge University Press, 1985); Thomas Spear, "Neo-Traditionalism and the Limits of Invention in British Colonial Africa," *Journal of African History* 44, no. 1 (2003): 3–27.

50. There is a significant body of work on bridewealth in Africa. Major works that influenced this study are John Comaroff, ed., *The Meaning of Marriage Payments* (New York: Academic Press, 1980); Camilla Toulmin, *Cattle, Women, and Wells: Managing Household Survival in the Sahel* (Oxford: Clarendon Press, 1992); Brett Shadle, *"Girl Cases": Marriage and Colonialism in Gusiiland, Kenya, 1890–1970* (Portsmouth, NH: Heinemann, 2006).

51. See in particular Jane Guyer, "The Value of Beti Bridewealth," in *Money Matters: Instability, Values and Social Payments in the Modern History of West African Communities*, ed. Jane Guyer (Portsmouth, NH: Heinemann, 1995), 113–32; Richard Roberts, *Litigants and Households: African Disputes and Colonial Courts in the French Soudan, 1893–1912* (Portsmouth, NH: Heinemann, 2005), chap. 6; Shadle, *"Girl Cases"*; Rachel Jean-Baptiste, *Conjugal Rights: Marriage, Sexuality, and Urban Life in Colonial Libreville, Gabon* (Athens: Ohio University Press, 2014).

52. Stanley Tambiah credits E. E. Evans-Pritchard with coining the term *bridewealth* in 1931. See Tambiah, "Bridewealth and Dowry Revisited," 414.

53. Barbara Cooper, "Women's Worth and Wedding Gift Exchange in Maradi, Niger, 1907–89," *Journal of African History* 36, no. 1 (1995): 121–40.

54. Jack Goody and S. J. Tambiah, *Bridewealth and Dowry* (Cambridge: Cambridge University Press, 1973).

55. Elke Stockreiter, *Islamic Law, Gender, and Social Change in Post-abolition Zanzibar* (New York: Cambridge University Press, 2015); see also Roberts, *Litigants and Households*, 219–23.

56. See Anne O. Griffiths, *In the Shadow of Marriage: Gender and Justice in an African Community* (Chicago: University of Chicago Press, 1997); Jennifer Cole and Lynn Thomas, eds., *Love in Africa* (Chicago: University of Chicago Press, 2009).

57. For a sample of these debates, see Charles Heimsath, "The Origin and Enactment of the Indian Age of Consent Bill, 1891," *Journal of Asian Studies* 21, no. 4 (1962): 491–504; Dagmar Engels, "The Age of Consent Act of 1891: Colonial Ideology in Bengal," *South Asian Research* 3 (1983): 107–31; Padma Anagol-McGinn, "The Age of Consent Act (1891) Reconsidered: Women's Perspectives and Participation in the Child-Marriage Controversy in India," *South Asian Research* 12 (1992): 100–118. For a discussion of this act in regard to the issue of consent, see Tanika Sarkar, "A Prehistory of Rights: The Age of Consent Debate in Colonial Bengal," *Feminist Studies* 26, no. 3 (2000): 601–22.

58. UNICEF, *Early Marriage: A Harmful Traditional Practice; A Statistical Exploration* (2005), available at http://www.unicef.org/publications/index_26024.html.

59. The unnamed judge in the Gao v. Gonzales case of 2006 is quoted in Seelinger, "Forced Marriage and Asylum," 70.

60. Holly Brewer, *By Birth or Consent: Children, Law, and the Anglo-American Revolution in Authority* (Chapel Hill: University of North Carolina Press, for the Omohundro Institute for Early American History and Culture, 2005), 8, 48–49, 96,

139. For an assessment of the long history of this debate in England, see T. E. James, "The Age of Majority," *American Journal of Legal History* 4, no. 1 (1960): 22–33.

61. Brewer, *By Birth or Consent,* 332.

62. See, for example, Gregory Massell's classic study of the unintended consequences of the Bolshevik liberation of women in Central Asia, "Law as an Instrument of Revolutionary Change in a Traditional Milieu: The Case of Soviet Central Asia," *Law and Society Review* 2, no. 2 (1968): 179–228. See also Samuel Moyn, *The Last Utopia: Human Rights in History* (Cambridge, MA: Harvard University Press, 2010).

63. Anne Phillips, "Free to Decide for Oneself," in *Illusion of Consent: Engaging with Carole Pateman,* ed. Daniel I. O'Neill, Mary Lyndon Shanley, and Iris Marion Young (University Park, PA: Penn State University Press, 2008), 99–105. With a different framing of the issue of freedom and constraint, Anthony Giddens argues that the structures of society are "always both enabling and constraining, in virtue of the inherent relationship between structure and agency (and agency and power)"; see Giddens, *Constitution,* 169.

64. Carole Pateman, "Women and Consent," *Political Theory* 8, no. 2 (1980): 19–68; Pateman elaborates these arguments in *The Sexual Contract* (Cambridge, MA: Polity Press, 1988). See also O'Neill, Shanley, and Young, "Introduction," in *Illusion of Consent,* 3–5. For a discussion of the constraints on women as citizens able to participate fully in the workforce, see Anne-Marie Slaughter, "Why Women Still Can't Have It All," *Atlantic,* July–August 2012, 84–102.

65. Carole Pateman and Charles W. Mills, *Contract and Domination* (Cambridge, MA: Polity Press, 2007), 2.

66. See Ruth Gaffney-Rhys, "International Law as an Instrument to Combat Child Marriages," *International Journal of Human Rights* 15, no. 3 (2011): 359–73, for a comprehensive overview of international law regarding child marriages.

67. Annie Bunting, "Stages of Development: Marriage of Girls and Teens as an International Human Rights Issue," *Social and Legal Studies* 14, no. 1 (2005): 18.

68. Ibid., 18–34.

69. Prosecutor v. Taylor, Case No. SCSL-03-01-T, Trial Chamber II, Judgement (May 18, 2012). ¶¶ 119, 1018.

70. Jeffrey R. Boles, "Easing the Tension between Statutes of Limitations and the Continuing Offense Doctrine," *Northwestern Journal of Law & Social Policy* 7 (2012): 227–29. The US Supreme Court, in US v. Midstate Horticultural Co., 306 U.S. 161, 166 (1939), described the term as a continuous, unlawful act or series of acts "set on foot by a single impulse and operated by an unintermittent force, however long a time it may occupy." Also see US v. De La Mata, 266 F.3d 1275, 1288 (11th Cir. 2001) ("A continuing offense is one which is not complete upon the first act, but instead continues to be perpetrated over time"). Continuing offenses are also known as continuous crimes. See, e.g., US v. Mardirosian, 602 F.3d 1, 9 (1st Cir. 2010) ("The possession and concealment of stolen property is a continuous crime").

71. See Greater Manchester Police, "Domestic Abuse: Forced Marriage," http://www.gmp.police.uk/content/section.html?readform&s=19F4925669E7FDF7802579FB004F1C3C, last accessed February 18, 2014.

72. See http://www.state.gov/j/tip/rls/tiprpt/countries/2013/215470.htm.

73. Sandiso Phaliso and Sapa, "Bride Kidnapper Granted Leave to Appeal," Independent Online News, http://www.iol.co.za/news/crime-courts/bride-kidnapper-granted-leave-to-appeal-1.1648213, last accessed February 18, 2014.

74. For an alternative explanation of the relationship between the practice and forced marriage, see Chelete Monyane, "Is Ukuthwala Another Form of 'Forced Marriage'?" *South African Review of Sociology* 44, no. 3 (2013): 64–82.

75. Sally Engle Merry, *Human Rights and Gender Violence: Translating International Law into Local Justice* (Chicago: University of Chicago Press, 2006); Merry and Mark Goodale, eds., *The Practice of Human Rights: Tracking Law between the Global and the Local* (Cambridge: Cambridge University Press, 2007); Fuyuki Kurasawa, *The Work of Global Justice: Human Rights as Practices* (Cambridge: Cambridge University Press, 2007).

76. Tabitha Kanogo, "In Their Own Words: Child-Brides in Kenya," paper presented at the Forced Marriage Symposium, Rochester Institute of Technology, Rochester, NY, April 2013.

77. Alyana Alfara, Sarah Fournier, and Mary Zarikos (Al Jazeera America), "Forced Marriage Victims Coerced into Hard-to-Detect Immigration Fraud," January 23, 2014, http://america.aljazeera.com/articles/2014/1/23/family-saga-revealsforcedmarriageimmigrationfraudandmurder.html, last accessed January 24, 2014.

78. Anna Davis (*Evening Standard,* UK), "Londoners Are 'Morally Ambiguous' about Forced Marriage, Experts Warn," January 16, 2014, http://www.standard.co.uk/news/uk/londoners-are-morally-ambiguous-about-forced-marriage-experts-warn-9063627.html, last accessed January 24, 2014.

79. See, for example, http://www.scotsman.com/news/politics/top-stories/scottish-parliament-backs-forced-marriage-bill-1-3278858.

80. YLA v. PM & MZ [2013], EWHC 3622 (Fam). See also "When Should the Court of Protection Decline to Make a Declaration as to Capacity?" http://www.tsfconsultants.co.uk/blog/2013/12/when-should-the-court-of-protection-decline-to-make-a-declaration-as-to-capacity, last accessed January 24, 2014.

PART ONE

Colonial Struggles

CHAPTER ONE

Constrained Consent

Women, Marriage, and Household Instability in Colonial French West Africa, 1905–60

RICHARD L. ROBERTS

THE 2008 decision of the Appeals Chamber of the Special Court for Sierra Leone in its judgment of the *AFRC* case catapulted issues of forced marriage to the forefront of recent human rights debates. The court ruled that forced marriage involved specific elements of psychological and moral suffering and *not merely* rape, sexual slavery, forced pregnancy, and forced domestic labor. The combined nature of these acts under wartime conditions thus separated them from the crimes of sexual violence and sexual slavery.[1] But debates about forced marriage, arranged marriage, and consent in marriage have a longer history and are related to the complex interactions between African societies and colonial societies in Africa. This chapter explores how the complex and intertwined issues of consent in marriage, patriarchal regimes, property rights in people, and mobilization of domestic labor converged in the socially complex and changing worlds of colonial French West Africa.

African societies and their customary practices were never static. They were dynamic entities that shifted in relationship to broad changes in culture, economy, and polity. Nor was French colonial native policy coherent or stable; it changed over time in response to shifting metropolitan sensibilities about African social practices, periodic colonial crises that shot bolts of reform up and down the administrative hierarchy, and changes that Africans initiated on the ground. Above all, French colonial native policy was shaped by two deep policies: the first involved the legal category of the protectorate, in which the French colonial power agreed to let African societies retain internal sovereignty over their customs; the second was the French commitment to intervene in African practices whenever they contravened or seemed to contravene the French sense of "civilization."[2] These two policies were often in conflict, as French intervention to end practices contrary to civilization often resulted in deep transformations in African societies. The classic example of this is French efforts to abolish African forms of slavery, which entailed many halfhearted attempts before the slaves themselves began to leave their masters and thus forced the French to institute the policy.[3]

African marriage practices also posed considerable challenges to these two sides of French colonial policy. Colonial administrators harbored deeply conflicting opinions regarding African women's consent in marriage. Some likened bridewealth payments to "disguised purchases" of people and thus believed they were contrary to French antislavery policies, whereas others saw bridewealth as the foundation of African family stability and the unquestioned authority of the male household head. This dispute flared brightly for a brief moment in the period immediately following the establishment of newly created native courts in French West Africa in 1905, when waves of disputes regarding marriage, divorce, bridewealth, and child custody filled the courts.[4] These controversies flared again in the mid-1930s following the scandal involving the disguised marriages of girls and women pawned by their impoverished guardians during the Depression.[5] This colonial scandal gained traction precisely because it coincided with the rise of the Popular Front and the Popular Front's willingness to challenge established practices in the colonies. The pawning scandal prompted bursts of activity through the colonial administration and resulted in a surge of new research on African marital customs, especially the place of women's consent in marriage. It also resulted in the Mandel Decree of 1939, which mandated the minimum age of marriage for girls at fourteen and boys at sixteen and required the consent of the parties to be married.[6] The war in Europe stopped further intervention into African marriages and toppled the Popular Front. It was not until the postwar effort at promoting colonial welfare and development that the Jacquinot Decree of 1951 gave women over twenty-one the freedom to marry without parental consent.[7] Of course, by that age most African women were already married.

RICHARD L. ROBERTS

At the intersection of consent in marriage and the often murky separation between arranged and forced marriages lies the problem of bridewealth. Bridewealth, especially in first marriages, significantly constrained girls' and women's capacity to consent to marriage or to imagine alternatives to marriages arranged by their kin.[8] The sections that follow explore colonial perspectives on marriage; child custody disputes brought before the native courts of the French Soudan in the early twentieth century that illuminate the linkage between rights in persons, bridewealth, and marriage; and the linked issues of household instability and women's consent in second and subsequent marriages.

AFRICAN MARRIAGES, BRIDEWEALTH, AND CONSENT

In much of French West Africa (and throughout the patrilineal world of sub-Saharan Africa), marriage involved strategic investments between kinship groups. These investments revolved around building and maintaining webs of kinship and controlling labor and descendants. Camilla Toulmin, an anthropologist who worked among the Bambara, describes marriage primarily in material terms as "a particularly long-term investment." Although the wife provides immediate labor and services to help compensate for the "heavy marriage costs, many of the benefits will accrue over the following 30 years or more." Toulmin further notes that because the consequences of marriage are likely to be with the family for decades, care in making marriage choices is not left to the potential spouses. The preferred spouses come from groups already linked by existing marriage ties. In this way, "the household head hopes to ensure that marriages endure and are free of conflict." "Men and women," Toulmin notes, "may not choose their partners, but love and respect frequently grow between them."[9]

Toulmin's description of Bambara marriage reflects the classical structural-functionalist perspective on African marriages offered by A. R. Radcliffe-Brown in 1950. "The African does not think of marriage as a union based on romantic love although beauty as well as character and health are sought in the choice of a wife," he observed. "The strong affection that normally exists after some years of successful marriage is the product of the marriage itself conceived of as a process, resulting from living together and co-operating in many activities and particularly in the rearing of children." Congruent with the evolutionary thinking then prevalent in anthropology, Radcliffe-Brown likened African marriage to early

English marriage, where the "marriage is an alliance between two bodies of kin based on their common interest in the marriage itself and its continuance, and in the offspring of the union, who will be, of course, kin of both the two kin-groups." Crucial to this alliance "in early England and in a great number of societies in ancient and modern times in all parts of the world" were the marriage payments given by the bridegroom or his kin to the father or guardian of the bride.[10] These payments constituted the making of a "legal" marriage, especially when the state was not (or not yet) an interested party in the marriage and in registering it.

Radcliffe-Brown wanted his reader to understand the difference between bridewealth and purchase. "Some people," he said, "regard payments of this kind as being a 'purchase' of a wife in the sense in which in England to-day a man may purchase a house or a motor-car. . . . The idea that an African buys a wife in the way that an English farmer buys cattle is the result of ignorance, which may once have been excusable, but is so no longer, or of blind prejudice, which is never excusable in those responsible for governing an African people." Instead, Radcliffe-Brown argued, African marriages involved a whole series of "prestations" (payments, gifts, or services). Though most wealth flowed from the husband and his kin to the wife's kin, some flowed in the opposite direction, especially when guardians (and sometimes mothers) provided wedding presents (as a form of token dowry) to their daughters.[11]

According to Radcliffe-Brown, African patrilineal and virilocal marriages consisted of three core characteristics. First was the modification or partial rupture of the relations between the bride and her immediate kin, particularly when she left her family to live with her husband and his family. Second was "legal marriage," by which Radcliffe-Brown meant the transfer of marriage payments that gave the husband and his kin certain rights in relationship to his wife and the children she would bear. This was the crucial part of the marriage transaction: "It is the objective instrument of the 'legal' transaction of the transfer of rights." What was being transacted varied from society to society, but it almost always consisted of rights to the labor of the wife for the well-being of the household, including domestic labor, sexual services, and labor in the household's fields; it also consisted of rights to the children born during the marriage. "Once the payment, or some specific portion of it, has been made the bride's family have no right to fetch their daughter back, and in most tribes, if the union is broken by divorce at the instance of the husband, the payment

RICHARD L. ROBERTS

has to be returned and the woman's family recover the rights they have surrendered." The third characteristic was that the marriage was not simply a union between a man and a woman but also an alliance between two bodies of kin.[12]

To think of marriage as a contract between two bodies of kin and as a transaction involving some rights in the person of the bride helps us understand how little space there was for brides to consent. "In Africa," Radcliffe-Brown wrote, "an unmarried woman is in a position of dependence. She lives under the control and authority of her kin and it is they who afford her protection. . . . At marriage, she passes to a greater or less extent . . . under the control of her husband (and his kin), and it is he (and they) who undertake to afford her protection."[13] Thus, marriage shifted a woman's dependence, but it did not fundamentally alter it.[14]

Bridewealth should also be understood as a bond holding the marriage together. The difficulty of returning the bridewealth should the marriage fail forged the bond. The difficulty stemmed from the uses to which the guardian of the bride put the bridewealth. Only rarely was the bridewealth accumulated and retained by the guardian. Instead, it was more or less immediately redirected and used as bridewealth for the family's sons. As part of his strategy for maintaining the household, the household head was obliged to provide wives for his sons.[15] Thus, the difficulty of returning bridewealth acted as a significant barrier to divorce, although, as we shall examine in the final section, unhappy wives could seek out lovers to help return bridewealth.

WOMEN'S CONDITIONS AND CRISES IN MARRIAGE

Concern about African women's conditions and marriage more generally within French West Africa was rooted in the implementation of the colonial native courts in 1905. Rendering judgments in disputes among Africans at the native courts and in appeals of those judgments revealed wide debates about customs and the value of codification. Those opposed to codification argued persuasively that it would freeze in place previously flexible African customs and rob customs of their ability to adapt to changing conditions. Those in favor of codification wanted an easily accessible guide to facilitate legal judgments rendered in the new native courts and at the level of appeals. The anticodification faction won with the support of Governor-General Ernest Roume.[16]

As the volume of marital disputes increased in the native courts after 1905, pressures to render judgments efficiently persisted and so did calls for codification. In 1912, Maurice Delafosse published his magisterial, three-volume *Haut-Sénégal-Niger,* of which the third volume was his synthesis of the common core of customs for what he considered to be the "Soudanese civilization." In a chapter dedicated to marriage, Delafosse stated that regardless of age differences between the bride and the groom, "there is no question of consent [being needed] by the future bride."[17] Only the consent of the bride's guardian was required.[18]

World War I and postwar reconstruction interrupted further debates on the codification of African customs until 1931 when Governor-General Jules Brevié, a scholar-administrator in his own right, reasserted the usefulness of having a guidebook on customs (*recueils de coutumes*) for use by European administrators overseeing native courts. To that end, Brevié sent out a questionnaire to guide administrators in assembling these reports, which included a question regarding consent in marriage.[19] The responses from the districts varied considerably in quality. The best reports traced changes over time; most were formulaic and consisted of short, descriptive responses to the questionnaire. Bernard Maupoil selected thirty studies from districts in the West African federation organized by colonies for inclusion in the volumes.

The colonial administrators who wrote the reports only rarely probed beneath the surface to explore changes and ambiguities. Many saw bridewealth as a reflection of the transactions in rights in the person of the bride. Captain Courturier of Bilma District in Niger went even further to argue that "the woman is a good that belongs to her relatives and then to her husband. She constitutes a part of the patrimony of her husband and whose relatives include her upon his death into the inheritance and remarry her."[20] Levirate was widely practiced in French West Africa. By its very nature, levirate denied women choice, and it became an element of the French colonial representation of African women as being like livestock.[21] Consent in marriage was the prerogative of the guardians of both the bride and the groom. Gilbert Vieillard captured the constraints on choice when he stated that even the groom "voluntarily accepts the fiancée imposed on him because one does not question the will of the elders."[22] The elders controlled the bridewealth, after all.

Alfred Aubert provided one of the best studies in Maupoil's collection. Aubert's investigation of Bambara custom in the district of Bouguni was attentive to history and to cultural relativism. In his opening sections on marriage, he noted that though the issues of engagement, bridewealth, consent, divorce, and the like "may seem strange to us, the reverse is also true. Our tirailleurs, upon returning from France recount to their comrades who remained at home the amazing stories of the purchase of men by women, about the ceremonies in our churches, the clothes of the bride and groom, all of which have no place here [in Bouguni]."[23] In terms of consent in Bouguni, Aubert agreed that the girl "has no consent to give and she does not know to whom she will be married." But he understood that even under these conditions, girls exerted some agency (even if they did not have power). Even if the betrothal took place while the bride and groom were still young children (perhaps even in utero), the marriage was delayed under the onset of the girl's puberty. Aubert noted that "very often, the girl, who dreads this moment [the onset of menstruation, with impending marriage], hides her condition from her guardian in order to conserve as long as possible her freedom."[24]

Converging with Brevié's practical and scientific interest in African customs was the emerging colonial scandal involving pawning and forced marriages. A series of poor harvests, the long-term deceleration of demand for African commodities in Europe due to the Depression, and the persistent pressure to pay taxes resulted in a resurgence of pawning in French West Africa. In 1931, the League of Nations sent out a questionnaire requesting information about the distribution and practices of pawning, a document that made its way into Brevié's questionnaire on customs. By 1933, however, Monsigneur Joanny Thevenoud, the vicar apostolic of the White Fathers in Ouagadougou, wrote to the governor-general about widespread "sales" of girls in the colony. One year later, drawing on data provided by Thevenoud, Gustave Gautherot, a Catholic senator in Paris, wrote to the minister of colonies about this practice of selling girls in order to pay taxes. The minister put pressure on Governor-General Brevié to explain the sales of girls and women, which seemed to contravene the 1905 decree prohibiting the alienation of another person's liberty. Brevié in turn put pressure on local administrators to inquire about the facts on the ground. The result was a flurry of reports on pawning. Many of the reports explained that pawning had indeed increased but noted that pawning was not a sale and was therefore unlike slavery. Instead, they pointed out, pawning was a long-established credit mechanism that was suited to the rural population due to the lack of private property that could be used as collateral for loans.[25] The most ubiquitous collateral available to a rural household was an individual—usually a girl or a woman—who would work for the creditor until the loan was repaid. The labor of the pawn while in the custody of the creditor served as the interest because it was not compensated. If the loan was not repaid, however, the creditor had the right to dispose of the pawn, most often through marriage either to the creditor himself or to a third party; thus, he recouped through the bridewealth the value of the original loan. The pawn was not consulted on the marriage. Given the depth of poverty during the Depression, repaying a loan was often difficult, and consequently, many creditors married their pawns.

In 1936, the pawning scandal flared anew. In Guinea, poor harvests forced farmers to take their daughters to the central market of Sangalan, where they would be auctioned in order to pay taxes. The Sangalan affair coincided with the rise of the Popular Front in France, which had campaigned for a host of domestic and colonial reforms, including some affecting the condition of African women, and once in power, the front leaders put significant pressure on the colonial administration to address the pawning crisis. Acting aggressively, Brevié and his successor, Marcel Jules de Coppet, annulled the pawning contracts and ordered the girls returned to their homes. Recognizing that these actions would probably not dampen the use of pawns as collateral for loans, Brevié ordered that the pawns receive minimum wages during their tenure as pawns. These decrees did not, however, address the problem of consent, especially as marriage remained a likely outcome for pawns.[26]

Within this context of increasing attention to the status of African women in French West Africa, Soeur Marie-André du Sacré-Coeur published *La femme noire en Afrique Occidentale* in 1939. A member of the White Sisters, she had a law degree, and by 1939, she had served ten years in French West Africa. The White Fathers' efforts to raise attention to the crisis of pawning certainly influenced her thinking. Soeur Marie-André's book was framed as a study of African women's status, and it had all the obvious flaws of generalization. In the book, African women as a group were juxtaposed to Christian converts, for whom consent was an essential part of the sacrament of marriage.[27] Soeur Marie-André's arguments gained attention and contributed to new colonial legislation dealing with marriage.[28] Her starting point was the place of women and marriage within the household order:

RICHARD L. ROBERTS

The head of family has the task of maintaining the prosperity of the family group, which generally involves procuring wives for members of the group. The parties concerned are not necessarily the future spouses; in a number of tribes, the father of the young man or the head of the family begins the necessary steps to procure a first wife for his son. The young girl is never part of the contract; her guardian has the right to decide her future, most often without consulting her. Nevertheless, the question never occurs to her to choose between marriage and celibacy: all African women marry and she will do as her mother and the other women in the family have done, habituated for centuries to servitude and passive submission towards their masters. . . . The young girl can not but ratify the decision taken on her behalf and she must submit. . . . Consent of the future spouses, regardless of their age, is not needed to conclude a marriage.[29]

The last two sentences of this passage are worth examining more fully. If a woman's consent was not needed to conclude a marriage, did she even have the capacity to dissent or "to think otherwise"? If a woman's dependence on a male was the norm, if marriage was an inevitable part of women's position in society, and if a bride's male guardians understood the value in the transactions regarding rights in her person, was consent even a possibility?

In his report on Bambara customs in Bouguni, Aubert underscored the conceptual constraints that limited girls' and women's consent to marriage: "It is necessary to say that there is no immorality in native marriages, and that women are neither unhappy nor mistreated. In any case, the women do not conceive of any other manner of contracting a marriage."[30]

In a subsequent book on African family life, published more than two decades after her 1939 study, Soeur Marie-André elaborated the constrained nature of consent. "The payment of the bride price and its acceptance," she wrote, "confirm the accord between two family heads; they do not signify the consent of the spouses. Where this consent is required, it is given in a symbolic fashion when the bride is led to her husband's home or in a ceremony shortly before the wedding. . . . In the course of the ceremony the bride signifies her consent by tacit acceptance and by going through the prescribed ritual."[31] This notion of tacit consent (or fatalism) stems from both the lack of capacity to dissent and the lack of alternatives to imagine. For further discussions on age and consent in marriage in this volume, see the chapters by Brett Shadle, Bala Saho, Francesca Declich, and Mariane Ferme in particular.

West African bridewealth marriage systems had a number of important consequences. First, there was the constrained consent of the spouses entering into the marriage. Despite Toulmin's assertion that the elders took care to ensure the marriages would persist, they very often did not. Divorce was frequent in almost all groups in French West Africa, and it often entailed disputes over child custody, as we shall see in the next section. Second, precisely because of the practices of bridewealth, girls were valuable and female infanticide was exceedingly rare; this is also linked to child custody. And third, subsequent marriages often involved significantly reduced bridewealth and thus provided far more space for consent in marriage, which we will examine in the final section.

RIGHTS IN PERSONS, BRIDEWEALTH, AND CHILD CUSTODY DISPUTES

In his magisterial *Haut-Sénégal-Niger*, Delafosse attributed the ubiquity of polygyny in the Soudan to the African's primary occupation as an agriculturalist. The African, therefore, "needs many arms, and so it follows that children are for him a source of wealth."[32] Precisely because children were a source of wealth, marital instability translated directly into conflicts over child custody. The Bamako administrator noted in 1909 that "parents, particularly those belonging to the Bambara race, fiercely dispute after divorce or the death of one of the spouses the questions of guardianship and custody."[33] One of the central functions of bridewealth was the transfer of rights in children from the mother's kin to that of the father. Relationships between men and women that resulted in children but were not regularized by bridewealth as well as those where bridewealth was incompletely transferred produced the fierce disputes the Bamako administrator identified.[34]

Delafosse's quote about children being a source of wealth had at least two dimensions, although he only seemed to recognize one. He saw children as sources of extra labor in the fields and in the homes. Children were clearly a source of joy, a means of reproducing the community, and a source of labor to assist both the male household head and the women of the household in their domestic duties. What he did not recognize was

RICHARD L. ROBERTS

that girls were a source of wealth precisely because of their potential to secure goods, cash, and services in the form of bridewealth payments.

In reflecting on the relatively high incidence of civil cases regarding custody of children, the administrator of Sikasso in 1911 argued that the

> disputes surrounding the reclaiming of children have as their source the custom that permits the wife to freely abandon the conjugal dwelling and to take her young children with her. The husband, most of the time, leaves the girls with their mothers until they have reached a certain advanced age and only then does he reclaim them. The mother opposes their departure and in many cases the girls, used as they are to living in the household of their mother, also refuse to leave. This situation gives rise to problems without end.[35]

Nonetheless, because of the nature of the transactions in rights in persons, only rarely did the wishes of the mothers and children influence the decisions taken by the African magistrates of the provincial courts.

In this section, I draw on a body of civil disputes heard in the native courts of the French Soudan from 1905 to 1912. Of the two thousand cases coded in this database, those that are primarily child custody disputes constitute 12 percent.[36] Of these cases, I am particularly interested in those dealing with the claims of husbands/fathers or their kin on their children who had been living with their mothers following divorce.

On July 12, 1907, Faraba Bamakana of Bamako District sued for the recovery of his children. Bamakana's wife had apparently left him, taken her children, and moved back to her father's home. There is a hint in the record that she had left because her husband had been away from the household ("en raison de ses absences") and thus left her without maintenance. The wife subsequently died, although it is not clear how long she had been dead before Bamakana introduced his case. Her children were being raised by their maternal grandfather, the deceased mother's father. But now, Bamakana wanted his children back. The court agreed with his argument and ordered that the children be returned to him.[37] Despite the fact that he had not taken any responsibility in providing for his wife and children, the court ruled in his favor because he had obviously paid bridewealth and the children thus belonged to him.

The disposition of the courts in child custody cases hinged upon evidence of the regularization of marriage through the completion of bridewealth. If bridewealth was transferred, even if only partially, then the courts generally ruled in favor of the male claimant or his kin. If bridewealth was not paid, as in the cases of slave marriages, the courts usually let the mother retain custody. Breast-feeding infants remained with their mothers until they were at least four or five.[38]

Dougou Traore had a daughter with his wife; the couple subsequently divorced, and the wife died. Traore went to court on January 4, 1907, to demand that his former mother-in-law, Cira Koulibali, send his daughter back to him. It is not clear from the record how old Traore's daughter was, but the court did not hesitate to issue its judgment that the custody of the child belonged to the father. Given that the court did not reflect on the issue of bridewealth, it would seem that Traore had fully transferred the bridewealth, rendering the marriage thoroughly legitimate and his claim on custody absolute.[39]

Upon the death of his brother Neguiba Jara, Kanegue Jara, who was also head of the household, was in court seeking custody of his brother's children. His sister-in-law, Koura Traore, had abandoned her husband's home, although the court record did not make clear the circumstances of her departure. The court ruled in favor of Jara's petition and confirmed his custody over his brother's children.[40] As this case underscores, bridewealth transferred rights to the bride's children to her husband's kin regardless of the status of the marriage. The husband's kin, therefore, had the right to claim the children upon the death of their kinsman.

Often, divorced husbands or their kinsmen were not in a rush to regain custody of their children taken by their mothers upon divorce. In one case, the father, Brahima Ture, waited ten years before seeking custody of his child from the mother. The child's mother did not challenge her former husband's claim but asked the court to oblige him to compensate her for the costs of bringing up the child over the past decade. The court ruled in favor of both parties, granting the father custody and the mother an indemnity of one hundred francs in compensation.[41] In an analogous case, either divorce or the death of her husband led Douko Kane to leave the conjugal home. Sometime later (probably a considerable time later), Moussa Bagayogo, brother of the deceased husband, claimed custody of his brother's children. Kane did not dispute the claim, indicating that bridewealth had been transferred, but she asked the court for the costs of maintaining the children. The court gave custody to Bagayogo but required that he compensate Kane for the costs of raising the children.[42]

RICHARD L. ROBERTS

Another case stemmed from Moussa Doumbia's divorce from Sogone Kamara. The court record did not explain when the divorce occurred, but the notes indicated that some significant time had elapsed before Doumbia went to court on August 3, 1909, seeking custody of his daughter. "Since then [the divorce], the girl is now eight and no longer needs her mother's care," the court stated as it granted Doumbia custody.[43]

The timing of many child custody cases may have been innocent, but there seems to have been a strategic quality as to when the claim was brought to court in the case involving Teneba Kouyate. According to the records, "Teneba Kouyate's husband died leaving her with two daughters. She raised her daughters without any assistance from her brother-in-law. The latter now wants custody of the girls and bases his claim on custom. Teneba argues that the only reason her brother-in-law wants custody is to gain the bridewealth." In a rare reversal of custom, the court sided with Kouyate and granted her sole custody of her children.[44]

Sometimes, child custody disputes revealed deep cleavages within extended families, especially when fathers died. The following case appeared to pit the mother of the father against the brother of the father in a dispute over custody of two young girls. Souse Sidibe, the uncle of the girls in question, was in court seeking their custody from Nene Diallo. Nene Diallo was the grandmother of girls, and she had taken custody of them when her son died. At some point, the mother of the girls had "disappeared." Sidibe argued that custom allocated the children to the paternal line and that, as their uncle (the brother of their father), he deserved custody. The court ruled in Sidibe's favor but left custody of the girls with their grandmother until they were thirteen.[45] At that time, the girls would be exactly the age when the guardian would benefit from their bridewealth.

Where bridewealth was not transferred, the children belonged to the mother or the mother's kin. Some cases in this regard dated from the slave era and reflected slave marriages. Few of these marriages were regularized through bridewealth, especially if the master established relations with his female slaves. Such was the situation in May 1908 when Demba Diakite, son of the slave master, went to court to recover custody of the children born to two of his father's former slaves, Mentene Traore and Kaniba Dumbia.[46] Traore and Dumbia argued in court that they were not married to Diakite's father but were merely "his concubines." The court dismissed Diakite's case and left the custody of the children with their mothers. Even though the 1903 legal code establishing these native courts prohibited the mention of the litigants' status, evidence of former enslavement can still be recovered from these records in disguised terms such as *concubines* and *servants*.

Occasionally, mothers went to court seeking to recover their children. Fatima Diabate was in court trying to gain custody of her four children. Apparently, she had fled her conjugal home when her husband, Sory Kouyate, died. Kouyate's sister, Nara Kouyate, had taken custody of her brother's children. Now, eight years later, Diabate was in court asking for custody of her children. Nara Kouyate responded that according to custom the children should remain with their paternal kin and that she had done an excellent job raising these children after their mother departed. The court agreed with Nara Kouyate and dismissed the case.[47]

As these child custody cases suggest, marriages were far from stable, and divorce or marital rupture was quite frequent. More than anything else, the transfer of bridewealth solemnized a marriage. Transfer of bridewealth meant that a mother had little claim on her own children should the marriage fail. One of the great paradoxes of the bridewealth system was that after having been married and divorced, a woman had more choice in her subsequent marriage(s).

MARITAL INSTABILITY AND CONSENT: REMARRIAGES

In a classic life history of a Hausa woman, Baba of Kano described her first marriage in 1904. "When I was about fourteen years old," she related, "it was time for me to be married":

> Dabo, the son of Sarkin Zarewa our town chief, loved me and I wanted him, but my family would not agree to our marrying, they did not like titles and title-holders; they were farmers, they liked their daughters to marry farmers. . . . That was why I could not marry Sarkin Zarew's son. There was also Malam Maigari, who wished to marry me. I promised him I would come to him later.[48]

Instead, Baba married her cousin Duma in a classic cross-cousin marriage between the son of a brother and the daughter of a sister. In the introduction to Baba's life history, anthropologist M. G. Smith wrote that "girls are married between the ages of thirteen and fourteen, and probably remarry two or three times, on average, afterwards. The first marriage is always arranged by the bride's parents, her consent being purely formal.

RICHARD L. ROBERTS

. . . Similarly, divorce, which is frequent among Hausa, is often instigated by one or other of the wife's kinswomen, with a view to arranging a future marriage to somebody preferred by the instigator—often in discharge of some obligation."[49] After three years of marriage to Duma, Baba sued for divorce, which was granted by the local *qadi* (Muslim judge), and subsequently married Malam Maigari, as she had promised to do. Baba's marriage to Malam Maigari lasted fifteen years, but she divorced and remarried twice more during her lifetime.

Marital instability and serial remarriages were quite common in sub-Saharan Africa. Lloyd Fallers argued that, among the Basoga, despite "a belief in the desirability of stable marriages . . . marriage in Busoga is quite unstable." Based on his work with court records, he contended that between one-quarter and one-half of all marriages ended in separation, and 90 percent of those resulted in formal divorce. Without having good data from the precolonial period, Fallers hypothesized that a high divorce rate might have been related to social change and a breakdown in lineage solidarity.[50] What, then, contributed to marital instability in sub-Saharan Africa during the colonial period?

In the early years of the twentieth century, French colonial officials worried that the incidence of divorce both reflected and contributed to "familial anarchy."[51] Already in 1906, the Bamako administrator explained to Lieutenant-Governor William Ponty why so many of the civil disputes brought before the native courts dealt with marriage and divorce. "It is to be remarked," he wrote, "that because the bonds of family are relatively fragile, marriage is easily dissolved."[52] The Gumbu administrator qualified this general assessment when he attributed the incidence of divorce to the "weak bonds attaching the native woman to her new family."[53] Linking women seeking divorce to the organization of the African family and to marriage practices, French district administrators developed components of a discourse about African women and the African family. One of the earliest reports emerging out of the need to explain the high incidence of women seeking divorce was penned by the Bamako administrator following his observations of the new courts' operation: "The young girl is married, or more precisely exchanged for a bridewealth payment, by those who exercise paternal power over her: her father, grandfather, uncle or brother." The Bamako administrator underscored the commodity nature of daughters when he noted that if a household head died leaving a son and a daughter, the son "literally" inherited his sister and the rights to acquire the bridewealth. The administrator's interpretation of inheritance was not quite right in this case, but it led logically to his conclusion: "The social condition of the married woman is very close to that of slavery. She is given the most difficult work and frequently beaten." The administrator contrasted the social condition of the woman married by her male guardians to that of the widow not inherited by her husband's kin. "The widow is then declared free," he observed, "and she can remarry following her own wishes. More independent than the female married as a young girl, she is able to earn her own goods, she is much better treated, and generally does not abandon the home of her [new] husband."[54]

Other administrators began to articulate a causal link between transactions in rights through bridewealth, the bride's lack of choice in partners, and requests for divorce. The Gumbu administrator argued in 1907 that

> the cases heard before the *tribunal de province* concern above all with divorces, which reflect the social development of the native. In effect, the authority of the head of the family permits him to marry his daughters as he wishes. This results in his efforts to squeeze as much as possible from the transactions. The girl is never consulted on the choice of her future husband and she is almost always given to the suitor who furnishes the largest bridewealth.

Faced with the significant outlay of capital to secure his new wife, the husband usually gave this wife the hardest work and mistreated her. Soon, the Gumbu administrator concluded, the husband "tires of his wife's complaints (*doléances*) and in pursuit of peace in the household, divorce is requested."[55] The high incidence of divorce, wrote the Koutiala administrator in 1909, was due to the "conception that the woman is a captive, an instrument of work and of exchange, who can be sold, given away, and repossessed according to the [husband's] whims and means without ever consulting her."[56]

The dissolution of the first marriage always involved the return of the bridewealth. I have already remarked that this was often difficult because the household head did not normally hold on to the wealth thus obtained but used it to secure wives for his sons. Thus, the woman seeking divorce needed to find a lover capable of returning the bridewealth to the husband's kin or else she had to draw from her own wealth.[57] Just as Baba described earlier, the dissolution of the first marriage, in which the bride had little choice, liberated a woman to marry whomever she wanted or whoever had significant resources to return the bridewealth to the first

RICHARD L. ROBERTS

husband. Clearly, then, the need to return the bridewealth imposed its own constraints on the choices of divorced women.

Maupoil's 1939 compilation of *coutumiers* (customary law guides) underscored this fundamental change in women's ability to consent to marriage. F. De Coutouly, in his report on Soninke customs in Nioro, noted simply that a divorced woman could choose "at her discretion a new husband."[58] Administrator Bourouillou of the Bandiagara District juxtaposed the bride's lack of consent in the first marriage to enhanced capacity for agency as soon as that first marriage was consummated. "The lack of consent on the part of the young girl," he noted, "does not break the engagement as long as the kinsmen consent to it. Once the marriage has become definitive, then [the] woman can, if she wants, abandon the conjugal home for another domicile of her choosing."[59] Aubert, of the Bouguni District, emphasized the transformation that followed divorce: "No woman whose marriage has been formally dissolved can be given to a new husband without her consent. This rule is uniformly observed and it explains that the fact of the first marriage produces in the woman the semblance of emancipation."[60]

So how do we explain this transformation in women's consent to marry? It may, as Fallers argued, be related to social change, and indeed the early colonial period witnessed significant change. But it could also be related to the changed nature of rights in persons that lay at the heart of bridewealth, in the changed set of players involved, and in changes to the ideas of personhood discussed in the introduction to this book. The value of girls lay in their linked productive and reproductive capacities. In societies that valued numerous children, a pubescent girl would presumably be fertile for a longer period than a more mature woman. Thus, the length of fertility probably contributed to the value of the rights in persons transacted through bridewealth. A divorced woman had some loss to her fertility simply by having spent a number of years with her former husband. In turn, this diminished fertility meant diminished value. Moreover, for societies that valued female virginity at marriage, a divorced woman was somewhat less valuable.

Although the first divorce involved the reimbursement of the original bridewealth, the second and subsequent divorces may have involved even lower bridewealth. And it is possible that serially divorced women received the bridewealth on their own account, much like the dower in Muslim family law.

As the judge in a recent asylum case argued, the distinction between arranged and forced marriage depends upon "meaningful consent."[61] Meaningful consent assumes a set of conditions that allows girls and women to assess alternatives and gives them the capacity to dissent. The ability to assess alternatives and consequences and the capacity to dissent may be linked to some definition of the "age of reason," but it is also profoundly shaped by cultural constructions of patriarchy, girls' and women's relative autonomy within households, and the degree of their dependence on men. How can we assess meaningful consent if, as Soeur Marie-André remarked in 1939,

> the question never occurs to [a girl or woman] to choose between
> marriage and celibacy: all African women marry and she will
> do as her mother and the other women in the family have done,
> habituated for centuries to servitude and passive submission
> towards their masters. . . . The young girl can not but ratify the
> decision taken on her behalf and she must submit.

The capacity to dissent requires the ability to imagine alternatives and the capacity to implement these alternatives. Girls' and women's acceptance of their futures as wives is deeply ingrained in the culture of patriarchy and the ideology of personhood where women are valued primarily for their labor and reproductive powers. Bridewealth systems of marriage value these rights in women and provide the means to exchange these rights. This helps explain why girls are valuable and why divorced fathers or their kin seek to recover these girls before they reach puberty, when the value of their fertility is at its peak.. As Carole Pateman has argued, when property in persons is at stake, subordination is tightly structured.[62]

The great paradox—and one that needs further conceptualization—is why divorce "emancipates" women from their kin's control over their labor and reproductive capacity. Such emancipation is never complete if women's dependence on men remains unchallenged. A central part of this issue of enhanced consent is whether the capacity to give consent in second and subsequent marriages actually increases the instability of first marriages, when the value of bridewealth is the highest.

In many areas of colonial Africa, girls and women had options other than arranged and forced marriages. Some could seek refuge in Christian missions, in radical Muslim communities that did not recognize bride-wealth in marriage, and in the expanding urban and mining centers. Choosing these options most often ruptured kinship ties, thus exacerbating female vulnerabilities and often replacing the duress of kin with pressures to conform to new communities' rules.[63] These options, however, were not often available to girls and women in many other parts of Africa.

Clearly, the history of girls' and women's constrained abilities to consent is central to the story of the links between patriarchy, the transactions in rights in persons exercised in marriage, and wider regimes of production and property that value unpaid household labor.

NOTES

1. Micaela Frulli, "Advancing International Criminal Law: The Special Court of Sierra Leone Recognizes Forced Marriage as a 'New Crime against Humanity,'" *Journal of International Criminal Justice* 6 (2008): 1033–42.

2. For more explanation, see Shamil Jeppie, Ebarhim Moosa, and Richard L. Roberts, "Introduction: Muslim Family Law in Sub-Saharan Africa," in *Muslim Family Law in Sub-Saharan Africa: Colonial Legacies and Postcolonial Challenges* (Amsterdam: Amsterdam University Press, 2010), 24–37; see also Richard Roberts, "Africa and Empire: The Unintended Consequences," in *Africa, Empire and Globalization: Essays in Honor of A. G. Hopkins,* ed. Toyin Falola and Emily Brownell (Durham, NC: Carolina Academic Press, 2011), 399–415.

3. Martin Klein, *Slavery and French Colonial Rule in West Africa* (New York: Cambridge University Press, 1998).

4. See Richard Roberts, *Litigants and Households: African Disputes and Colonial Courts in the French Soudan, 1895–1912* (Portsmouth, NH: Heinemann, 2005), chap. 5; see also Marie Rodet, "Continuum of Gendered Violence: The Colonial Invention of Female Desertion as a Customary Criminal Offense, French Soudan, 1900–1949," in *Domestic Violence and the Law in Colonial and Postcolonial Africa,* ed. Emily S. Burrill, Richard L. Roberts, and Elizabeth Thornberry (Athens: Ohio University Press, 2010), 74–93.

5. Martin Klein and Richard Roberts, "The Resurgence of Pawning in French West Africa during the Depression of the 1930s," *African Economic History* 16 (1987): 23–37.

6. Marlene Dobkin, "Colonialism and the Legal Status of Women in Francophone Africa," *Cahiers d'Études Africaines* 8, no. 31 (1968): 390–405.

7. Arthur Phillips, "Recent French Legislation Concerning African Marriage," *Africa* 22, no. 1 (1952): 66–69.

8. See the introduction to this volume for a fuller discussion of consent in marriage.

9. Camilla Toulmin, *Cattle, Women, and Wells: Managing Household Survival in the Sahel* (Oxford: Clarendon Press, 1992), 3–4, 237.

10. Elite marriage often involved dowry, whereby brides brought significant resources into the marriages and thus facilitated marriages that were otherwise constrained by primogeniture, which often left second and subsequent sons without significant resources.

11. A. R. Radicliffe-Brown, "Introduction," in *African Systems of Kinship and Marriage,* ed. Radcliffe-Brown and Daryll Forde (London: Oxford University Press, 1962), 46–47. The original edition was published in 1950. On the status of the dower in Muslim marriages, see Elke Stockreiter, *Islamic Law, Gender, and Social Change in Post-abolitionary Zanzibar Town* (New York: Cambridge University Press, 2015).

12. Radcliffe-Brown, "Introduction," 50–51.

13. Ibid., 48–49.

14. Emily Burrill and Richard Roberts, "Domestic Violence, Colonial Courts, and the End of Slavery in French Soudan, 1905–12," in Burrill, Roberts, and Thornberry, *Domestic Violence.* Burrill prefers the concept of "patriarch bargain" to help explain women's position in marriage. See Deniz Kandiyoti, "Bargaining with Patriarchy," *Gender and Society* 2, no. 3 (1988): 274–90, because it provides space for women's negotiations within the confines of patriarchy.

15. See the classic statement by Claude Meillassoux restated in *Maidens, Meal and Money: Capitalism and the Domestic Community* (Cambridge: Cambridge University Press, 1981); Roberts, *Litigants,* chap. 6.

16. Roberts, *Litigants,* 82–90.

17. Maurice Delafosse, *Haut-Sénégal-Niger* (1912; repr., Paris: Maisonneuve and Larose, 1972), 3:64. Delafosse distilled his study of Soudanese customs from the results of a 1909 inquiry into the customs of each district in the colony mandated by Lieutenant Governor Marie François Joseph Clozel. Back in Paris, Delafosse taught courses on African law and customs at the Ecole Colonial as he worked on his three-volume opus.

18. Delafosse, *Haut-Sénégal-Niger,* 3:78.

19. Bernard Maupoil, "L'Etude des coutumes juridiques de l'AOF," in *Coutumiers juridiques de l'Afrique Occidentale Française,* ed. Bernard Maupoil (Paris: Larose for the Comité d'études historiques et scientifiques de l'AOF, 1939), 1:8–15, 17. Jules Brevié had already published *Islamisme contre "naturisme" au Soudan francais: Essai de psychologie politique coloniale* (Paris: E. Laroux, 1923).

20. Capitaine F. Couturier, "Coutumes Toubou et Kanouri," in Maupoil, *Coutumiers,* 3:194.

21. See Roberts, *Litigants,* 126–32.

22. Gilbert Vieillard, "Coutumier du Cercle de Zinder," in Maupoil, *Coutumiers,* 3:123.

23. Alfred Aubert, "Coutume Bambara (Cercle de Bougouni)," in Maupoil, *Coutumiers,* 2:63.

24. Ibid., 2:95, 65. In this world of bridewealth, male household heads' authority, and constraints on female consent in marriage, only female orphans had the freedom to choose their husbands. However, females were rarely independent of males, and thus de Coutouly's remark may have been only rhetorical. F. de Coutouly, "Coutume Marka-Sarakolle," in Maupoil, *Coutumiers,* 2:217.

　　　　　　　　　　　　　　　　　　　　　RICHARD L. ROBERTS

25. Paul Lovejoy and Toyin Falola, eds., *Pawning, Slavery, and Colonialism in Africa* (Trenton, NJ: Africa World Press, 2003).

26. Klein and Roberts, "Resurgence of Pawning."

27. Marie-André du Sacré-Coeur, *La femme noire en Afrique Occidentale* (Paris: Payot, 1939), 221–22, 48–50.

28. Alba I. Zizzamia, "About the Author," in Marie-André du Sacré-Cœur, *The House Stands Firm: Family Life in West Africa,* trans. Alba I. Zizziamia (Milwaukee, MN: Bruce Publishing, 1962), viii.

29. Marie-André du Sacré-Coeur, *La femme noire,* 48–50.

30. Aubert, "Coutume Bambara," 63.

31. Marie-André du Sacré-Cœur, *House Stands Firm,* 81, 88.

32. Delafosse, *Haut-Sénégal-Niger,* 3:62.

33. Rapport sur le fonctionnement des tribunaux indigènes, Bamako, 1st quarter 1909, ANM 2 M 54.

34. For more detail on bridewealth as a "trouble spot" in the native courts of the French Soudan, see Roberts, *Litigants,* chap. 6.

35. Rapport sur le fonctionnement des tribunaux indigènes, 2nd quarter 1911, Sikasso, ANM 2 M 93.

36. Roberts, *Litigants,* 172–78. The ratio is highest in Bouguni District (27 percent) and lowest in Gumbu (4 percent). Child custody cases constituted 8 percent in Bamako district and 10 percent in Segu District.

37. Etat des jugements rendus en matière civile et commerciale par le Tribunal de Province, 3rd quarter 1907, Bamako, ANM 2 M 104.

38. Rapport sur le fonctionnement des tribunaux indigènes, 2nd quarter 1906, Bamako, ANM 2 M 54.

39. Dougou Traore v Cira Koulibali, 4 Jan 1907, Etat jugements rendus en matière civile et commercial par le Tribunal de Province, Bamako, ANM 2 M 104.

40. Kanegue Jara v Koura Traore, 18 Nov 1907, Etat jugements rendus en matière civile et commercial par le Tribunal de Province, 4th quarter, Bamako, ANM 2 M 104.

41. Brahima Ture v Aisatta Jeliba, 3 Jan 1908, Etat jugements rendus en matière civile et commercial par le Tribunal de Province, Bamako, ANM 2 M 104.

42. Moussa Bagayogo v Douko Kane, 25 Sept 1911, Etat jugements rendus en matière civile et commercial par le Tribunal de Province, 4th quarter, Bamako, ANM 2 M 104.

43. Moussa Doumbia v Sogone Kamara, 3 Aug 1909, Etat jugements rendus en matière civile et commercial par le Tribunal de Province, 4th quarter, Bamako, ANM 2 M 104.

44. Teneba Kouyate v Yamadou Kamisako, 11 Oct 1910, Etat jugements rendus en matière civile et commercial par le Tribunal de Province, 4th quarter, Bamako, ANM 2 M 104.

45. Souse Sidibe v Nene Diallo, 23 Jan 1909, Etat jugements rendus en matière civile et commercial par le Tribunal de Province, 4th quarter, Bamako, ANM 2 M 104.

46. Demba Diakite v Mentene Traore and Kaniba Dumbia, 5 May 1908, Etat jugements rendus en matière civile et commercial par le Tribunal de Province, 4th quarter, Bamako, ANM 2 M 104.

47. Fatima Diabate v Nara Kouyate, 19 Jan 1909, Etat jugements rendus en matière civile et commercial par le Tribunal de Province, 4th quarter, Bamako, ANM 2 M 104.

48. Mary F. Smith, *Baba of Karo: A Woman of the Muslim Hausa* (1954; repr., New Haven, CT: Yale University Press, 1981), 102–3.

49. M. G. Smith, "Introduction," in *Baba of Karo*, 25.

50. L. A. Fallers, "Some Determinants of Marriage Stability in Busoga: A Reformulation of Gluckman's Hypothesis," *Africa* 27, no. 2 (1957): 114; Fallers was responding to Max Gluckman's argument linking stable marriages to strong patrilineality in "Kinship and Marriage among the Lozi of Northern Rhodesia and the Zulu of Natal," in Radcliffe-Brown and Forde, *African Systems of Kinship and Marriage*, 166–206.

51. Rapport de l'Administrateur sur le fonctionnement des tribunaux indigènes, 3rd quarter 1910, Bouguni, ANM 2 M 59.

52. Rapport de l'Administrateur sur le fonctionnement des tribunaux indigènes, 2nd quarter 1906, Bamako, ANM 2 M 54.

53. Rapport de l'Administrateur sur le fonctionnement des tribunaux indigènes, 4th quarter 1906, Gumbu, ANM 2 M 65.

54. Rapport de l'Administrateur sur le fonctionnement des tribunaux indigènes, May 1906, Bamako, ANM 2 M 54.

55. Rapport de l'Administrateur sur le fonctionnement des tribunaux indigènes, 4th quarter 1907, Gumbu, ANM 2 M 65.

56. Rapport de l'Administrateur sur le fonctionnement des tribunaux indigènes, 2nd quarter 1909, Koutiala, ANM 2 M 75.

57. See Roberts, *Litigants,* chaps. 7 and 8.

58. De Coutouly, "Coutume Marka-Sarakolle," 216.

59. Bourouillou, "Coutume Kado, cercle de Bandiagara," in Maupoil, *Coutumiers,* 350.

60. Aubert, "Coutume Bambara," 100.

61. An unnamed judge in the *Gao v. Gonzales* case of 2006 quoted in Kim Thuy Seelinger, "Forced Marriage and Asylum: Perceiving the Invisible Harm," *Columbia Human Rights Law Review* 42, no. 1 (Fall 2010): 70.

62. Carole Pateman and Charles W. Mills, *Contract and Domination* (Cambridge, MA: Polity Press, 2007), 2.

63. See, for example, Sean Hanretta, *Islam and Social Change in French West Africa: History of an Emancipatory Community* (New York: Cambridge University Press, 2009), and Derek R. Peterson, *Ethnic Patriotism and the East African Revival: A History of Dissent, c. 1935–1972* (New York: Cambridge University Press, 2013).

RICHARD L. ROBERTS

CHAPTER TWO

Forced Marriage, Gender, and Consent in Igboland, 1900–1936

OLATUNJI OJO

IN 1927, nearly three decades after the British colonial administration officially abolished the slave trade and a decade after the legal cessation of slavery and related practices such as pawnship and panyarring in Nigeria, a woman named Mgbocha, from Kwale in western Igboland, was seized and sold into slavery for the purpose of marriage.[1] In her court testimony, she said that on her way to Port Harcourt around January 1927, she met a man, Oshodimi, who offered to take her by a shorter route. The duo, however, did not travel to Port Harcourt but rather to Azuwama village, where Oshodimi left Mgbocha with a man, Ngashi, who told her he had bought her as a wife. After a number of days, Mgbocha saw some people searching for her, and she reported her story—a story about both slavery and forced marriage. With her sale, she became a slave wife, lacking choice in the selection of a spouse.[2] Forced marriage, age of consent, and women's agitation against forced marriages were recurrent topics of discussion in colonial Nigeria and in other parts of Africa.[3] I draw attention to this discourse because it highlights a central issue whereby, for many women, marriage involved coercion. In western Igboland, forced marriage was not confined to slave wives but extended to other women as well. It victimized many young girls (including infants) whose parents arranged their marriages, often without consulting with them, on the basis that the "parents knew better" and the girls were too young to have an opinion. This chapter explores the sociological and historical context in which forced marriage was common, reflecting the unequal gender relations in early colonial western Igboland. I seek to understand the meaning of forced marriage and marital consent; avenues for forcing women into marriage; and why women, more than men, suffered from forced marriages. Under colonialism, however, the government banned some of the institutional bases of forced marriage—slavery and pawnship—and created opportunities for ending existing coerced marriages.

FORCED MARRIAGE, ARRANGED MARRIAGE, AND CONSENT IN IGBO SOCIETY

Marriage was and remains a highly valued institution in Igbo society. No man or woman is considered complete unless he or she is married. To the degree that marriage was central to societal reproduction as new babies replaced old and dead ancestors, marriage turned children into social adults. Igbo traditions attest to the interest attached to marriage, with girls being given names such as Di wu ugwu (husband is prestigious). Wives, as mothers, produced the next generation of workers and contributed to men's social aggrandizement. The more wives a man had, the higher his social status and potential capacity to acquire economic and noneconomic resources. Across Africa, marriage was not a union of two individuals but the coming together of two communities and a tool for building communal networks and alliances (also see the chapters by Richard Roberts, Francesca Declich, and Bala Saho in this volume). Since marriage was considered mandatory—a rite of passage—it was open to abuse and often used as a means to exploit certain people, especially women when forced to marry or marry particular men against their will. George Basden, an Anglican pastor in eastern Nigeria during the interwar years, wrote that from about age seven, Igbo girls were conscious of their public appearance. So they decked themselves out in ornaments, lotion, and clothes and watched their weight because girls with long, thin legs were considered more attractive to men. The ideal was for a girl to attract a suitor. Yet betrothal often involved coercion, for not every girl had the choice of dressing up to attract men. Often, parents made the decisions, and girls had to comply. Forced marriage foreclosed a girl's right to reject a marriage proposal. Precisely because of the perceived benefit to the communities joined by marriage, many people paid little or no attention to the process that often denied women freedom in the choice of husbands.

To the degree that marriage brought together two or more families or communities, it was also a legal transaction in which all the parties involved had a set of expectations and obligations. Thus, the community at large generally viewed marriage as a "traditional" or "customary" rite or what the early agents of the Church Missionary Society (CMS) in West Africa referred to as "country fashion." This was not necessarily because things remained static but because the origin of these rites lay in the distant past and the pace of change was so slow as to be indiscernible to many. The levers of power were within the socioeconomic and political spheres controlled by senior men and women who were averse to changes that could threaten their upper-class social status. As we will see, young women and young men as well as strangers and those on the periphery of power were the first to embrace changes that would attack "customary" marriage laws and practices.

There were four means of marriage in Igboland during the period under study: child betrothal, pawnship (*igba ibe*), slavery (*ohu*), and *isinmo* (cutting of women's hair). Perhaps the most popular means was child betrothal, whereby shortly after a girl's birth or some years later, a suitor took firewood and palm wine to her mother in order to stake a claim (*igudo-nwanyi*) to the girl.[4] Igbo marriage entailed the exchange of gifts. Bridewealth was for some a token of appreciation paid to parents for caring for a girl; for others, it was compensation given to a family for losing their daughter to the husband. Bridewealth payment (also called bride-price or dowry) and parental consent underpinned marriage. Bride-price can be defined as a gift of money, labor, natural produce, real or personal property, or a combination of any of these, including any waiver in the content or quantum of such a gift, given to the appropriate person in connection with marriage to a woman. The peculiar nature of the bridal payment is that it may be given before or at a marriage under customary law, and no matter how long a couple cohabits or even if they procreate, no valid marriage exists until the payment is made.[5] Among the Igbo, regardless of whether a suitor acted for himself or was represented by others, parents of a young daughter consented to the marriage request by accepting the gift, and the suitor began paying bridal wealth, including periodically working for the girl's father and making gifts of yams, palm oil, and cash to the mother. Ultimately, the bridewealth would give the groom certain rights to the woman: sexual access, power to commandeer her labor, and custody of children even if she had had children by another man. These rights remained in force as long as the bridewealth was not refunded. As I will discuss, women in some areas had no access to divorce.

Bridewealth payments continued for years until the girl reached puberty, marked by the early signs of menstruation; after that point, the suitor made a lump payment, the amount of which varied depending on the age of the girl, her beauty, and the rank of the families involved. A related system involved payment of a fixed amount to the parents of a matured girl by the prospective husband. The final marriage ceremony featured a huge feast, dancing, and more exchanging of gifts, after which the woman went to her husband's compound. The central element of child betrothal was that the girl's parents were the ones who made marital decisions, as they had marital experience and were trusted to make wise choices. This view is captured in an Igbo proverb: *Okenye ada ano nauno, ewu amuo na ogbuli* (No old person leaves a goat in chains when it is under pain of giving birth). It is important to separate arranged marriage from forced marriage.

If child betrothal was coercive, it scarcely matched the violence associated with slave marriages. Suzanne Miers and Igor Kopytoff argue that the demand for wives partly underpinned the development of slavery in Africa.[6] The preference for female slaves may be located in the differential status between free and bonded wives. As seen earlier, a freeborn girl was generally betrothed at an early age, and future spouses confirmed their interest with periodic payments and services to her parents. But a slave wife was cheaper and more controllable than a free woman because marrying a slave had none of the expenses and labor involved in marrying a free woman. Most slave wives were acquired through warfare, as gifts from allies or via purchase.

Igbo men desired slave wives in order to avoid the huge bridal fees required for freeborn girls. The high cost of marriage prolonged slavery, as those who could not afford to marry freeborn girls took to kidnapping or buying female slaves. In 1932, Diribeofor Mgbeke, Jack Ngwu, Okronkwor, and Wokocha appeared before the Okigwi court, accused of stealing and selling a girl, Udorie. Diribeofor had lured the girl away from the police quarters on the excuse that he was sending her to a police officer. Innocently, the girl followed him, and within a few days, she had been sold a couple of times until finally a man named Okpani informed her she was his promised wife.[7] Many female slaves spent time and possibly developed relationships with their captors before becoming slave wives, but girls like Udorie had no such luxury. Many times, their experience of marriage began with rape by the buyer-husband, making marriage a source of victimization because the girls had no voice in their unions and were not in a position to end the alliances. The absence of bridal obligations between consenting families subjugated a slave wife to her master-husband and rendered her malleable. Slave wives had no kin and hence were more dependent on their husbands. And whereas a freeborn woman could call on her blood relations for help if a man mistreated her, a slave wife had no such kinship protection.[8]

Similarly, enslavement tactics such as kidnapping, raids, court judgments, and debt punished more women than men. And girls were at a greater risk of enslavement than female adults. Since Igbo culture permitted early marriage, after 1900 child enslavement was disguised as marriage. Indeed, rather than disappearing under colonialism, the slave trade merely went underground as slavers turned to kidnapping children. The result was a booming trade in child slaves in southern Nigeria until about 1940. These children, some as young as three months, were all stolen and sold as slave wives.[9]

Pawnship—a related institution of credit whereby individuals served as debt collateral and interest on loans—also enabled forced marriages. Although pawnship existed alongside slavery and fed its victims into that system, it lasted longer because it was widely considered benign, since most pawns remained in their own community. The pawn served the creditor until the debt was liquidated. But loans often had no payment deadlines, allowing debtors to spread out repayment; the pawn system also empowered creditors to enforce payment at any time, by seizing debtors, treating pawns like slaves, and using other similar tactics. By the 1920s, girls predominated among pawns and marriage had become a principal means of liquidating debts. The pawning of young girls in Igboland was often disguised as infant marriage. For instance, a man could pawn his young daughter to a creditor with the assumption that she would marry him and that the loans would be converted to prepaid bridal fees. The difference between bridewealth and debt had to be paid to whoever had the balance. Although a creditor could not force a girl to marry him, long-outstanding debts enabled him to take a female pawn as a wife.[10] What qualified such an arrangement as forced marriage was that the female pawn was subjected to the creditor, due to pressure from her family. If she disobeyed, a creditor could enforce credit payment by seizing properties and people owned by the debtor. To avoid untold hardships, debtors pawned their daughters as a sign of their creditworthiness and as a means for liquidating debts, and the girls complied to protect their families from vindictive creditors.[11] The pawning of girls and their ultimate marriage to male creditors or their associates was culturally legitimated much as any form of arranged marriage that involved potential spouses meeting through third-party mediators and parents giving consent and receiving respect.[12]

As early as 1895, Claude MacDonald of the Niger Coast Protectorate said enslavement for debt had historically been the "recognized form of collecting debt and giving trade security."[13] The interface between female pawning and marriage highlights a major source of victimization for girls. Though a female pawn could not be taken as a wife or married to a third party without prior discussion and approval of the debtor, long-overdue debts meant lengthy service in pawnship and made the enslavement of pawns likely.[14] In a 1936 report on forced labor in southern Nigeria, a senior police officer submitted that child marriage was used as a means of paying off debts. Indeed, the first reaction of a man pressed for money was to give his daughter or sister in marriage, no matter her age, and receive bridewealth. Parents had an obligation to protect and support their children, who in turn were culturally bound to serve and assist the former in any way required.

The final system of coerced marriage was isinmo, whereby a man cut a lock of a girl's hair, put an eagle feather on her head, or threw an egg at her and in so doing made her his wife. Historically associated with the creation of a regal mate for the most senior Western Igbo chief (eze), by the 1920s isinmo had become a tactic for forcing woman into marriage and maintaining sexual fidelity even if the husband was not a chief. Men also used the rite to take a woman they could not marry through normal circumstances, for example, when a common or poor man married an upper-class or rich girl or when an old man forced a young and attractive girl to marry him.[15] As with slavery or pawnship, women subjected to isinmo were presented with a fait accompli. A parent could not deny consent, for no other man would marry the girl. Isinmo obviated divorce and adultery, since the woman risked death, exile, enslavement, fine, and/or public ridicule if she took recourse in either of those two acts.[16] By the symbolic or ritual possession of a woman's head, isinmo gave a man full control of his wife. Although isinmo is considered customary, it also carried with it elements of kidnapping and *ukuthwala,* or abduction for the purpose of marriage, as described in Elizabeth Thornberry's chapter on South Africa.[17] But rather than kidnapping a girl and taking her to the husband's house, isinmo involved a temporary confinement of a girl so the abductor(s) could cut her hair.

At the core of forced marriage was the role of the "family" in matters of spousal choice, coercion, consent, bridewealth, and gender. Coercion ignored a girl's interest in marriage. In Igbo society, the community comes before the individual, so a member had to protect societal interests even when this involved coercion. In neighboring Benin, Philip Igbafe notes, the community was deemed greater than the individual, so "a girl could hardly afford the isolation into which a refusal to marry a family-chosen husband would [have] plunged her."[18] The paradox was that in a mostly patriarchal society, adult men dictated the communal interest and the cost of securing it. Communal solidarity gave a girl little freedom in the choice of a husband. She had to accept the man picked by her family, with little or no possibility of divorce. Further, her parents had no desire to terminate a contract they had arranged and had worked on for many years, and they had little incentive to refund bridewealth even if the amount appeared insubstantial. Until the 1960s, researchers focused on supposedly normal marriages, in which parents generally arranged spouses for their children and elders for their juniors in ways that made the marriages alliances between communities rather than unions of consenting adults. In Igbo society, one scholar observes, "when you marry, you marry not only a husband or wife but an entire network of relationships and responsibilities."[19] Well into the colonial period, infant marriage reigned supreme; hence, the consent of a future wife was hardly a crucial factor in marriage relations. Parents claimed to know what was best for their wards, which helps explain Basden's view that "love" did not exist in Igbo marriage and played no part in courtship.[20] As long as parents agreed to a marriage contract, a girl could be forcibly taken to her husband's house and raped for the purpose of impregnating her. According to Flora Kaplan, "Women were given in marriage without consent, and forced to submit if they objected later. If they were ill-treated and unhappy after marriage, they were forcibly restrained from leaving the husband's house, and forcibly returned if they managed to leave."[21] Buchi Emecheta's novel *The Bride Price* makes a literary reference to the linkage between rape and forced marriage in Igbo society. The protagonist, a girl named Aku-nna, was promised to Okoboshi, an arrogant son of a chief, though she loved Chike, a young schoolteacher. She lived in constant fear of Okoboshi marrying her forcefully. Knowing that Aku-nna was not keen on marrying him, Okoboshi and his friends, like their South African counterparts, kidnapped Aku-nna and carried her to his house; the intent was to rape her and make her his wife because no man would marry a defiled woman.[22] In some towns, recalcitrant girls were forced to marry the *obi* (king). If the girl was previously betrothed to another man or if she had another man in mind, that man dared not complain.[23]

A punitive yet common means of enforcing marriage was through seizure—that is, a husband could seize (*fie igwo* in Igbo) his errant wife or her associates. As a form of collective punishment, seizure allowed an aggrieved man, when he found no other way of recovering his wife, to hold an entire community liable for actions such as being rejected by his spouse after he had paid bridal wealth (even when the wife did not want the man and was not party to the original marriage negotiation). At Idumuje, if a girl refused a man and had babies with another man, her father could seize the children and hold them hostage until she agreed to be with the assigned spouse. Under colonialism, bridewealth became an avenue for funding numerous expenses, including tax payments. Therefore, the tendency to force daughters into marriage and compel them to stay married increased. At the same time, however, colonialism led to changes in the institution of marriage.

BRITISH CONQUEST, SOCIAL CHANGE, AND MARITAL CONSENT

From the late nineteenth century onward, a wind of change began to blow across Africa. In Igbo society, this started with conquest and rule by Britain, followed quickly by the expansion of Christian missionaries and changes in economic activities. Britain justified its imperialism in Nigeria on the need to induce socioeconomic reform. In the sphere of marital relations, British colonialism emphasized the personal status of women. In particular, Britain rejected the purchase or pawning of females for the purpose of marriage, child betrothal, widow inheritance,[24] and marriage without spousal consent—practices that directly infringed on the freedom of women. Antislavery laws also addressed forced marriage. The Slave Dealing Ordinance of 1909 and the Slavery Ordinance of 1916 equated child pawning, child betrothal, and panyarring with slavery. In the debate on pawnship, a source of forced marriage, the issue of the age of consent arose. Though the government tacitly conceded child betrothal was customary, it insisted on separating adult and child pawning, with the purpose of ending coerced marriages.[25] Due to British abolitionism, the slave population became composed mostly of females and children, and slavers began to focus more attention on those who could reproduce the next generation of unfree labor, those with more years of exploitable labor, and those who posed minimal opposition to the slave regime. The continued demand for slaves and their short supply led to rising prices. Igbo oral traditions indicate that the average price of a slave in the late precolonial period was only one to two bags of cowries or one to two British pounds in the late nineteenth century. By 1900, however, the price of a female slave had risen to two and a half pounds, jumping to four pounds at Isele Uku and up to eight pounds in nearby Igbuzo on the eve of World War I. The sharp rise in price was due to the scarcity of slaves and the attendant high cost of marriage.[26] Thus, the demand for coercible women and children during the colonial period actually led to the persistence of slavery and the increased victimization of girls.

As early as 1913, investigations highlighted direct relationships between child marriage and the enslavement of young girls. Consequently, the government proposed the registration of new marriages, especially those involving girls.[27] Three years lapsed between the report's submission and its consideration by officials, with Governor Frederick Lugard concluding registration no longer met the practical needs of all segments of the country.[28] Perhaps drawing on his experiences in northern Nigeria, where local cultures permitted early marriage, slavery, and polygyny, Lugard opined that marriage registration could in fact be abused to promote slavery if some people began to perceive marriage certificates as equivalent to property licenses. Through its inaction, the government certainly helped those still involved in the slave trade, since it did not disrupt their operations and might actually have helped them. From the 1920s, reports from Umuahia in Bende Division pointed to the continued sale of young female slaves via child marriages: parents disposed of their children in this way in order to obtain cash and pay for titles.[29] In 1933, T. W. Garden, the police commissioner for Owerri, reported that parents in Bende sometimes failed to consider the fate of their daughters who were purportedly married to third parties.[30]

Colonialism also transformed the economy by introducing new markets and better transportation systems, which meant that women had more trade opportunities. A good road system boosted female mobility and enhanced women's opportunities for making contacts outside of Igboland. Asaba women traded as far as Lagos, Calabar, Aba, Benin City, and beyond, dealing in textiles, palm oil, and foodstuffs. Women's greater access to and control of independent sources of income helped them resist unwanted suitors.

Christian missionaries were closely associated with colonialism on the ground. Although Christianity was introduced into eastern Nigeria in the mid-nineteenth century, it took nearly another three decades before the missions gained a strong footing. In addition to building churches and preaching the Gospels, the missionaries also established schools at Asaba, Igbuzo, and nearby towns. At Asaba, the Catholic Female Institution, founded in the 1890s, trained female teachers, nuns, and nurses. The curricula included topics on domestic science and the virtues of womanhood. As we will see, educated and Christian girls led the protest against forced marriage.

Central to the colonial project, the colonial government established courts headed by British officers. After 1900, the it established native courts that were allowed to administer justice based on indigenous laws or local sensibilities, as long as these conformed to certain British standards. When African laws were incompatible with European concepts of natural justice, equity, and good conscience, the latter were to prevail and the former were to be abolished. The courts thus ruled against child betrothal and forced marriage, which eventually modified Igbo marriage practices.[31]

One method of simplifying marriage procedures and providing avenues for ending unhappy unions was the creation of courts to adjudicate matrimonial disputes and grant divorces under certain criteria, such as the refund of bridal fees, calculated as cash payments to a girl's parents. Bridal payment refund was meant to disentangle young girls from nonconsensual marriages. The courts gave women a way to defy tradition by rejecting marriages imposed by parents.[32] Philip Igbafe and Flora Kaplan note that in Benin Division, north of Igbuzo, with the establishment of marriage courts young girls learned quickly that the colonial government was appalled by the practice of child betrothal, and they began to refuse husbands under such conditions.[33] By attacking certain marriage rites and instituting divorce, colonialism curtailed the power of men who gained most from existing practices and weakened parental control. Christian missionaries, including the priests in charge of the Roman Catholic Mission at Asaba and Igbuzo and Miss Ross of the Anglican Institute at Ogwashi-Uku, also promoted girls' consent in marriage.[34]

Social and economic changes under colonial rule radically altered gender and generational relations. Innovations such as wage labor, Western education, and new laws benefited young men and women more than their parents. Colonialism ended recourse to warfare and slavery as tools of economic activity and as means of conflict resolution. With a diminished capacity to use violence against their subordinates, senior African chiefs lost part of their income and some of the aura surrounding their power. A new elite emerged from among people supportive of British policies. Women reaching maturity under colonialism enjoyed benefits that had been denied to older generations of females.[35]

CONTESTING FORCED MARRIAGE

One of the ways women attacked forced marriage was to challenge marital rites and not marriage per se. Colonial rule also changed bridewealth practices and ultimately the meaning and process of marriage. Brett Shadle discusses the role of bridewealth in Gusii (Kenya) marriage under colonialism, noting how a spike in the value of bridal wealth after 1940 transformed Gusii marriages. With bridal payments priced beyond many young men's reach, more people married late because potential grooms had to work longer to raise the payments; meanwhile young girls waited endlessly for male suitors. Ultimately, exorbitant bridal rites created tension along generational lines, as Gusii youths began to defy old marital forms and wanted to seize from their parents the power to decide who, when, and how to marry. Sometimes, girls promised to men by their parents fled or eloped with other men, prompting contestations on the concepts of consent, bridewealth, and parental control.[36] With girls fleeing from unwanted marriages, the British administration in its various African colonies passed new laws that modified existing marriage practices, especially the value of bridal wealth but also the age of marriage and consent. There are close similarities in the changes introduced in Kenya, as discussed in this volume by Shadle, and in Nigeria.[37] Among the Igbo of southeastern Nigeria, where complaints against exorbitant bridal payments were loudest, colonial policies forced a change in marital processes. In precolonial Igbo society, bridal payments included the transfer of female slaves from the groom to the bride's family. However, the cessation of the slave trade meant bridal fees could no longer be paid in slaves but required cash. The shift increased monetization of the economy in the late nineteenth century and led to a rise in the value of the bride-wealth paid in cash. In the 1890s, cash payments averaged about £2 before rising, on the eve of World War I, to £10–22 at Asaba and £5–10 at Onitsha Olona and nearly £40 pounds in the 1920s.[38] The monetary value of non-cash payments and services increased the total cost of marriage by another 100 to 300 percent. These were huge payments when the average man made no more than £13–40 annually.[39] In fact, marital expenses were so high that Europeans conceived of bridewealth as cash exchanged for girls analogous to the purchase of slaves. There was some rational basis for this opinion. For instance, occasional reports indicated that Igbo parents promised their daughters to multiple suitors, wanted huge bridewealth, and prolonged courtship so they could gain more from marrying off their daughters. In a report compiled around 1910, Northcote Thomas, a colonial anthropol-ogist, claimed an Igbo wife was practically a commodity sold to the hus-band. Her children belonged to him, and "under no circumstances does she pass out of [his] family."[40] In the interwar years, complaints about exor-bitant marriage costs and the high rate of divorce pushed the government to streamline marriage rules by reducing bridal payments to £10, £5, and £2.5, respectively, for pubertal girls, middle-aged women, and women who had been married for some years.[41] The debate over bridewealth changed the meaning and process of marriage in Nigeria.

In attaching a woman's age to the value of bridewealth payable by her spouse, with pubertal girls commanding higher payments than other cate-gories of women, two issues emerged. First, it meant age was a significant factor in marriage considerations. Second, it encouraged the coercion of the most valuable potential brides, young girls, into marriage and denied them the right of consent or marital choice. Because parents frequently anchored their objections to a daughter's choice of spouse on the nonpay-ment of full bridal fees, some girls claimed their spouses had paid in full; technically, this suggested the marriage was proper and had to be allowed. A woman named Mgbolie argued that the £12 her lover paid to her par-ents through the native court was sufficient, but because her parents had promised her to another man, they refused her choice on the basis that the amount the man paid was not enough.[42] Other girls claimed their consent was sufficient for marriage—not their parents' consent, the bridal wealth, sex with their lover, or pregnancy. By rejecting expensive bridal rites or delaying payment, Igbo women sought to avoid complex and inescapable marriage contracts that could subject them to men for whom marriage was a tool of female disempowerment.

New marriage laws enabled Igbo youths who were unafraid of indigenous sanctions to seduce or forge sexual liaisons with the wives of older men. As discussed earlier, in Emecheta's *The Bride Price* Okoboshi, a chief's son, kidnapped Aku-nna, who was promised to him as his wife, only because the girl did not want him. The reason he failed to make the girl his wife was because these events took place during the colonial period. Rather than submit to the rapist, Aku-nna feigned madness; she screamed and lied, claiming that she was not a virgin because she had slept with another man, Chike, whom she wanted to marry. A day after her forcible confinement, Aku-nna and Chike fled to Ugheli, where Chike lived. The two started a happy life together, though Aku-nna felt guilt over her unpaid bridewealth.[43] This story is a literary reference to changing marriage patterns, especially the way in which, under colonialism, young girls used the symbolism of premarital sex to challenge unwanted marriages. Aku-nna's rejection of tradition rested on changes brought about by the imposition of European rule and values such as Western education, wagework, and mobility for educated young men and women.

Since access to colonial courts enabled women to challenge marriage rites, during the interwar years matrimonial cases accounted for about 75 percent of all civil cases in southern Nigeria, and quite often, these cases ended in divorce. The government did not seem to anticipate the dissatisfaction with old marriage rules and the eagerness with which people wanted to end existing contracts. In 1922, the government ordered inquiries into the rise in conjugal disputes following the establishment of native courts in 1900, specifically looking at divorce, return of bridewealth, fugitive wives, seduction, elopement, adultery, and child custody. In his report, the resident for Benin Province, E. B. Dawson, claimed that most civil cases consisted of requests by women seeking "eagerly to end objectionable marriages." The report blamed the marital crisis partly on the court's willingness to grant divorces and on the custom of child betrothal whereby a girl probably did not know the groom until the eve of her wedding. The officer submitted that under existing practices, as long as bridewealth had been paid a woman could not escape from marriage (*inu nwunye*, in Igbo).[44] His counterpart in Warri Province attributed divorce to the victimization of women, insofar as a "high divorce rate was expected as a woman is regarded as a chattel and married against her will to the highest bidder."[45] The investigation emblematized changes in marital practices, specifically regarding spousal consent, in Nigeria from the 1890s to the 1930s.

The popularity of divorce under colonialism prompted a range of reactions from colonial officers, attributing the high divorce rate to moral lapse and not a failure of the existing marriage system. Occasionally, officials accused young women seeking to end their marriages of preferring prostitution to having stable families. In 1922, the resident officer for Owerri Province noted that "native marriage customs are being undermined rapidly and chastity in marriage treated with little regard." He added, "Women were being attracted away by younger men and to an increasing degree by the fine clothes and idle life which they can have in large [urban] centres."[46] Members of the local elite, including some leading scholars, also concluded that colonial marriage practices were detrimental to the morality of marriage and the society. Their argument presumed there had been tranquility under precolonial marriages practices. Igbafe and others blamed colonialism for unstable marriages, as the return of bridewealth associated with divorce became a form of "deposit" that was "refundable whenever the wife decided to leave the husband."[47] Other writers have suggested that the greater amount of divorces during the colonial period indicated troubles with old marriage patterns. They also have debunked the claim that divorce was easy under colonialism, pointing out the obstacles women faced in the courts—courts that were stacked with male judges, some of whom were sitting in cases in which they had interests themselves. Some women could also not afford the high cost of divorce, and many of those who secured divorce lost access to their children and joint properties.[48] In the Gold Coast, Jean Allman writes, Asante chiefs passed a law mandating young women to marry or risk imprisonment.[49] Similar attitudes prevailed in Nigeria. At a meeting of chiefs in northern Nigeria in 1941, certain chiefs conflated unmarried women with prostitutes; hence, they suggested that girls should be forced to marry and that those who failed to comply should be deported.[50] A survey of divorce applications filed by women shows that the courts rarely dissolved a marriage based on a "no default submission" when a woman claimed she no longer loved her husband or when she simply returned the bridewealth. Instead, women generally gave nearly the same excuses, which the court could not overlook: their husbands were persistently cruel and the age difference between the husband and wife was too wide—in other words theirs was a forced marriage.[51]

Women's mounting resolve to contest their marriages in the courtroom corresponded with rising reports of adultery, divorce, and elopement. As noted previously, in adultery allegations Igbo customary laws demanded confession as well as compensation for the legal husband. At Ubuluku, the adultery fine was pegged at £5 for a commoner's wife and death or enslavement for the wife of the *obi*. Under colonialism, the *obi* lost the power to impose capital punishment, so he settled for adultery fees. Comparative rates operated in neighboring towns.[52] In 1922, the district officer for Asaba, W. B. Rumann, produced a new marriage rule to guide the native courts. The guideline divided adultery into two categories based on the rank of the injured husband. Adultery among wives of commoners resulted in fines; adultery among wives of chiefs was a criminal offense, subject to both fines and imprisonment.[53] Most litigants settled for civil charges in order to collect compensation. Yet not every court official supported compensation for adultery. In a society where polygyny was widespread, many secondary wives complained of neglect by their husbands. In Ishan Division, a colonial officer, M. H. F. Marshall, was reluctant to award adultery fees. Though he admitted that adultery violated indigenous traditions, he maintained that not only was adultery a most difficult thing to prove but also that, as often as not, the husband drove the wife into committing adultery in order to reclaim the bridewealth. In his opinion, a woman abandoned by the husband would most likely not remain celibate for long. The man would wait for her to commit adultery so that he could demand refund of his bridal expenses as well as adultery fees.[54]

To reduce the rate of divorce, the government passed a law in 1924 stipulating conditions for granting divorce, setting a marker for other courts in the province in matters of marriage disputes. The law stated that after the consummation of marriage, divorce would only be granted in cases of impotence, cruelty, serious disease, and spousal neglect for at least three years. The law prohibited divorce for pregnant women in order to avoid custody battles over infants borne when the wife was leaving the husband for another man;[55] divorce proceedings could start after the birth of the child. Moreover, the wife was required to refund £10 in bridal payment to the husband. By 1930, due to the economic depression and the fact that people had less disposable income, together with the government's opposition to marriage commercialization, fees refundable upon divorce had fallen to between 15s. and £2.5.[56]

Consent was an ever-present issue in divorce litigations and the central factor in forced marriages. Before 1910, men frequented the courts to demand the return of fugitive wives, adultery fees, and child custody. Later on, women, supported by their lovers, became primary litigants, seeking the dissolution of their marriages to older men. They wanted the court to compel their husbands to refund the bridal wealth. A woman's usual reason, according to Commissioner F. Marshall, was: "I do not want to marry him anymore."[57] Some informants accused girls of faking consent at the time of marriage.[58] Afraid of the backlash from their society, these girls halfheartedly gave consent and then sought a quick end to their marriages. Their strategy was to go along with arranged marriages while hiding their true plans, such as eloping with new lovers and younger men several months or years into their marriages to unwanted suitors. By 1930, fees refundable to jilted husbands had fallen to between 15s. and 50s., based on location, age of the wife, rank of the husband, and whether the wife had children with the husband. Because men got custody of children, women who bore them repaid less bridewealth than young brides who were not yet pregnant.[59] The government agreed that a woman should be able to end an unhappy or unwanted relationship. Marshall distinguished between divorce in forced and consensual marriages, concluding that under no circumstances should a woman marry a husband other than the one she chose herself.[60]

Disputes over consent to marriage flared up in the Asaba area in the 1930s when reports circulated about razor-wielding men cutting off locks of young girls' hair for marriage purposes, regardless of the girls' conjugal tastes.[61] As noted earlier, isinmo, or the cutting of women's hair for the purpose of binding them into marriages, was popular in Asaba District, even when the women were married to abusive men. With the economic depression of 1929 and its aftermath, poor men resorted to isinmo to marry women they could not secure through normal processes. To discourage such unwanted men, as table 2.1 shows, several young girls and women seeking divorce in the Asaba area arranged with their boyfriends and lovers to cut off locks of their hair. The act made the girls unsuitable for other men and gave those seeking divorce the ritual license to achieve their goal because an original husband was ritually prohibited from marrying or keeping as his wife a woman on whom another man had performed isinmo. Although these acts were illegal and officially termed assaults on women, incidents generally did not constitute assault in a legal sense. Most often, women approved of these attacks to express choice and forestall forced marriage.

By the 1930s when this wave of isinmo took place, some young men and women had attended mission schools and been taught to defy old marriage practices. Others had been exposed to new economic opportunities, such as working for wages or being employed in long-distance trade, thereby learning more about Western values in the big cities. Moreover, native courts contributed to the new sense that consent in marriage was normative by granting divorces to women who absolutely refused to remain with their husbands. For example, Mgboani chose as her new lover a man who had not paid bridal wealth. When confronted with the fact that she had an existing marriage, she told the court her marriage lacked merit because she had been forced to marry a man she did not want. Mgboani submitted to isinmo in order to end her unwanted marriage.[62] One could attribute the protests here to the system described earlier whereby family elders negotiated marriage contracts on behalf of their subordinates, creating instances where a girl might not know her real spouse until close to the time of their wedding.

Elopement with a lover, adultery, demand for smaller bridewealth, divorce, and impregnation by a man other than the legal husband were among the various tactics that became widespread under colonialism; all represented women's expression of marital discontent and their withdrawal of consent from marriages that had been arranged by parents. This was evident at the trial of thirty-four men by the Igbuzo court in 1934 on allegations they had either married improperly (having performed isinmo, a rite reserved exclusively for chiefs) or failed to make full bridal payments. But court evidence shows that in most of the cases, the alleged female victims described themselves as the lovers or wives of the young men and testified for the accused against their parents. Twenty-six women consented to the isinmo ritual, and one gave her consent after the rite had been performed on her. Only in six instances did the women deny consent and accuse the men of forced marriage. Women's appropriation of the power to consent was a major step in the reconfiguration of Igbo marriage rites.

TABLE 2.1 *ISINMO* AND MARRIAGE CONSENT

Victim (A)	Accused (B)	Relationship of A to B	With or Without Consent
Susie Okolie	Joseph Nwani Okeze	Wife	With consent
Nwadiafu	Aniemeke	Wife	With consent
Alice	Daniel Okoma	Wife	Late consent
Ukadiga	Okolie	Wife	With consent
Alice Obunuwa	John Uda	Lover	With consent
Otubo Nwote	Idoko	Wife	With consent
Agnes Okonkwo	Okobia	Wife	With consent
Ebonewebka	Okonne	Lover	With consent
Mgbolie	Abubuike	Wife	With consent
Idumaza	Okobi	Wife	With consent
Maggie Osekwe	Mgbodo	Lover	With consent
Maggie Nwabuiwe	Nwalama	Wife	With consent
Mgboani	Mbuzo	Wife	With consent
Matilda Utomi	D. Okonkwo	Wife	With consent
Amulu	Odiogoli Nzekwu	Wife	With consent
Agnes Mgboude	Nwaokolo	Wife	With consent
—	C. Maduagwu	Wife	With consent
Nwakele	Ezolu	Wife	With consent
Nwezebuona	Ofunyeadi	Sister-in-law	With consent
Nwaogwugwu	Mogeme	Wife	With consent
Chionye	James Okobi	Lover	With consent
Jane Moweter	Chibuogwu	Wife	With consent
Nwakele	Utulu	Lover	With consent
Lucy Eke	Francis Ajuku	Wife	Without consent
Nkemuamuna	Onwuezim	Acquaintance	Without consent
Ngbonwale	Okolie II	Acquaintance	Without consent
Mboafo	Amolo	Wife	With consent
Lydia Charles	James Mama	No relation	Without consent
—	Unknown	—	—
Mbuike	Owezim	Wife	With consent
Nwaboshi	Akaluzia	Lover	With consent
Adeze	Mgbolu	Sister-in-law	With consent
Malechi	Akahaiwe	Acquaintance	Without consent
Mgobogo	Okolie Uzu	Acquaintance	Without consent

As Flora Kaplan and Marjorie Mbilinyi reveal for Benin (Nigeria) and Tanzania, respectively, when women could not predict the outcome of a court decision or feared losing their case, they fled.[63] Women also sought to fool the courts. Jean Almann reports that in response to an Asante law forcing young women to marry or risk imprisonment, many women testified in court to nonexistent husbands or arranged with male friends to show up in court as their husbands should they be arrested.[64] In his 1914 report, Thomas noted that Igbo women seeking to end unwanted marriages were escaping to neighboring towns despite the fact that it was risky to do so because powerful chiefs could declare war on the hosts of their runaway wives.[65] If what Thomas saw was a trickle of women fleeing from marriage, it had become a flood by the 1920s. The rate of women becoming fugitive wives was so high that the commissioner for southern Nigeria, William Hunt, was asked to make it illegal for commercial drivers to transport fugitive wives.[66] Hunt did not agree, but his counterpart in Yorubaland supported the expulsion of any man who seduced the wife of a senior chief.

PERSISTENCE OF FORCED MARRIAGE

The world was horrified by reports of the Boko Haram terror organization in Nigeria kidnapping about three hundred teenage girls from a Chibok secondary school in the northeastern part of the country in April 2014. But the greater shock came when the leader of the organization announced he would sell the girls into slavery for the purpose of marriage. Although many of the girls remained in captivity as of late 2015, some have escaped and returned to their parents or relocated in safer communities. Meanwhile, debate continues in Nigeria about the appropriate age of consent. Although the official marriage code has pegged the age of marriage consent for boys and girls at eighteen, some still refer to the old English common law that put the ages at twelve for girls and fourteen for boys. For others, the reference was the Eastern Nigeria Marriage Law of 1956, which stipulated that "marriage . . . between or in respect of persons either of whom is under the age of sixteen years shall be void."[67] The law also criminalized forced marriage, described as aiding, abetting, and promotion of child marriage. Unfortunately, the law is frequently breached, with no fear of retribution. Issues about forced marriage, especially of pubertal girls in Nigeria, and the resistance against it have a longer history and are part of the persistent contestations between adult males seeking "free wives" and their female victims demanding the right to agree to or reject a man. In forced marriage, a girl lacked choice and had no capacity to give consent. In Igbo society, native law did not limit the age at which a girl could be given in marriage, and parents arranged most marriages when a girl was too young to give consent. Children were never part of the negotiation, and in most cases, this meant girls, who generally married early. Their responsibility was to obey their parents and future spouses. Failure to obey their parents could result in flogging or the denial of food and familial support. In the case of pawning, the creditor took the girl home, put her to work, watched her grow, and acquired the bridal fees when the girl reached puberty. With a free girl, a man offered some gifts when the girl was an infant and completed other marital payments and rites several years later.[68] Under colonialism, many repugnant practices facilitating the compulsion of women into marriage were reformed and sometimes abolished. Women did not fail to exploit the opportunities that were provided, and divorce disputes in which women claimed that they did not give consent became rampant. Eventually, Igbo society accepted women's consent in marriage. There is no doubt that the modification occasioned by British rule transformed marriage laws and custom.

NOTES

1. On the abolition of the slave trade and slavery in Nigeria, see Suzanne Miers and Richard Roberts, eds., *The End of Slavery in Africa* (Madison: University of Wisconsin Press, 1988); Miers and Martin Klein, eds., *Slavery and Colonial Rule in Africa* (London: Frank Cass, 1998); Paul Lovejoy and Jan Hogendorn, *Slow Death for Slavery: The Course of Abolition in Northern Nigeria* (Cambridge: Cambridge University Press, 1993); and Adiele Afigbo, *The Abolition of the Slave Trade in Southeastern Nigeria, 1885–1950* (Rochester, NY: University of Rochester Press, 2006).

2. Divisional Officer, Brass District to District Officer Kwale Div., 28 Mar. 1928, Nigerian National Archives Ibadan (hereafter cited as NAI), Kwale Dist 1/162, vol. 1.

3. See the introduction in this volume.

4. George Basden, *Among the Ibos of Nigeria* (London: Seeley, 1921), 69–72, 215, and Victor Uchendu, *The Igbo of Southeast Nigeria* (New York: Holt, Rinehart and Winston, 1965), 49–53.

5. The Eastern Nigeria Limitation of Dowry Law of 1956 regulated the scale of bride-price and set the marriageable age at sixteen years.

6. Igor Kopytoff and Suzanne Miers, "African 'Slavery' as an Institution of Marginality," in *Slavery in Africa: Historical and Anthropological Perspectives,* ed. Miers and Kopytoff (Madison: University of Wisconsin Press, 1977), 67.

7. Afigbo, *Abolition*, 77.

8. Major Garden, "Confidential Report, Feb. 10, 1934," and Memo from Secretary Southern Provinces to Chief Secretary, June 14, 1934, National Archives, Enugu, Riv Prof 2/1/24, C.136, and "Slave Dealing and Child Stealing in Southern Provinces," NAI, Chief Secretary's Office (CSO) 26/1/28994.

9. See "Slave Dealing—Papers Relating to," NAI, Kwale Dist 1/162, vol. 1, 1928–32; "Traffic in Women and Children: Annual Report of," NAI, CSO 26/278387, and "Slave Dealing and Child Stealing in Southern Provinces." Also see Afigbo, *Abolition*, and Olatunji Ojo, "Child Stealing, Slave Dealing, and African Agency in Igboland (Nigeria), c. 1900–1940" (forthcoming).

10. Bernard Bourdillon to W. G. Ormsby-Gore, 7 May 1937, NAI, CSO 26/11799, vol. 4, and Secretary Southern Provinces of Nigeria to Chief Secretary, 8 Oct. 1937, NAI, CSO 26/11799, vol. 5.

11. Gwyn Campbell and Alessando Stanziani, eds., *Debt and Slavery in the Mediterranean and Atlantic Worlds* (London: Pickering and Chatto, 2013).

12. Secretary of State to Governor of Nigeria, Hugh Clifford, 12 Dec. 1922, NAI, CSO 26/06827, vol. 1.

13. Claude MacDonald to Foreign Office, 17 Dec. 1895, National Archives Kew, Foreign Office 2/85.

14. See Campbell and Stanziani, *Debt and Slavery*, and Paul E. Lovejoy and Toyin Falola, eds., *Pawnship, Slavery, and Colonialism in Africa* (Trenton, NJ: Africa World Press, 2003).

15. See Northcote Thomas, *Anthropological Report on Ibo-Speaking Peoples of Nigeria*, pt. 4, *Law and Custom of the Ibo of the Asaba District, S. Nigeria* (New York: Negro Universities Press, 1914), 60–63; J. N. Hill, "Ancient Native Custom of Ibusa People," 1934, NAI, Ben Prof 1/BP 761; and Olatunji Ojo, "Shaving of a Woman's Head: *Isinmo* and Igbo Women's War on Forced Marriages in Southern Nigeria, 1900–1936," *Canadian Journal of African Studies* 47 (2013): 519–36.

16. "Notes of Meeting Held at Ibusa on April 13, 1934," NAI, Ben Prof 1/BP 761, and Intelligence Report on Ogwashiuku Clan of Asaba District, para. 163–64, NAI, Ben Prof 4/3/8.

17. See chapter 5 in this volume.

18. Phillip Igbafe, "Tradition and Change in Benin Marriage System," *Nigerian Journal of Economic and Social Studies* 12 (1970): 73–102, and Igbafe, *Benin under British Administration: The Impact of Colonialism on an African Kingdom, 1897–1938* (London: Longman, 1979), 181–82.

19. Belonwu Okonkwor, "The Role of Matrimonial Consent in Igbo Traditional Marriage, in the Light of the New Canonical Legislations: A Comparative Study" (PhD diss., Pontificia Universitas Urbaniana, 1985), 39.

20. Basden, *Among the Ibos*, 68–77, 214.

21. Flora Kaplan, "Runaway Wives, Native Law and Custom in Benin, and Early Colonial Courts, Nigeria," in *Queens, Queen Mothers, Priestesses, and Power: Case Studies in African Gender*, ed. Kaplan (New York: Academy of Sciences, 1997), 260.

22. Buchi Emecheta, *The Bride Price* (Oxford: Oxford University Press, 1976), 73.

23. Intelligence Report on Ogwashiuku, 152, NAI, Ben Prof 4/3/8.

24. On Igbo widowhood rites, see P. Okoye, *Widowhood: A Natural or Cultural Tragedy* (Enugu, Nigeria: Nucik Publishers, 1995), and Chima Korieh, "Widowhood among the Igbo of Eastern Nigeria" (master's thesis, University of Bergen, 1996).

25. F. D. Lugard to Lt. Governor, Southern Profs, 25 Dec. 1915, NAI, CSO 26/1/03063, vol. 1; *The Slavery Ordinance* (Lagos: Government Printer, 1916); and D. C. Ohadike, "'When the Slaves Left, Owners Wept': Entrepreneurs and Emancipation among the Igbo People," *Slavery and Abolition* 18 (1998): 189–207.

26. Intelligence Report on Ogwashiuku, 170, NAI, Ben Prof 4/3/8, and Thomas, *Anthropological Report,* 112.

27. See Marriage Ordinance, NAI, CSO 26/1/50569, vol. 2, 146–48, and "Marriage Custom: Registration of Native Marriage, Marriages Registration Rules," NAI, Ben Prof 1/1264/II.

28. "Marriage Girls under 16 Years, Proposed Native Court Rule," NAI, Ben Prof 1/68/1927, and Afigbo, *Abolition,* 72–74.

29. See Joseph Harris, "Some Aspects of Slavery in Southeastern Nigeria," *Journal of Negro History* 27 (1942): 41–42, and Kenneth O. Dike and Felicia Ekejiuba, *The Aro of South-Eastern Nigeria, 1650–1980: A Study of Socio-economic Formation and Transformation in Nigeria* (Ibadan, Nigeria: University Press, 1990), 248–49, 262.

30. Acting Secretary of State to Chief Secretary, June 14, 1934, NAI, CSO 26/28994.

31. Lagos Supreme Court Ordinance, sec. 19, 1876, and Omoniyi Adewoye, "Law and Social Change in Nigeria," *Journal of Historical Society of Nigeria* 7, no. 1 (1973): 149–59.

32. Kristin Mann, "Women's Rights in the Law and Practice: Marriage and Dispute Settlement in Colonial Lagos," in *African Women and the Law: Historical Perspectives,* ed. Jean Hay and Maria Wright (Boston: Boston University Press, 1982), 151–71; H. F. Morris, "The Development of Statutory Marriage Law in Twentieth Century British Colonial Africa," *Journal of African Law* 23 (1979): 37–64; Elizabeth Schmidt, *Peasants, Traders, and Wives: Shona Women in the History of Zimbabwe, 1870–1939* (Portsmouth, NH: Heinemann, 1992); and Philomina Okeke-Ihejirika, *Negotiating Power and Privilege: Igbo Career Women in Contemporary Nigeria* (Athens: Ohio University Press, 2004).

33. Igbafe, "Tradition and Change," and Kaplan, "Runaway Wives," 245–313.

34. See Misty Bastian, "Young Converts: Christian Missions, Gender and Youth in Onitsha, Nigeria, 1880–1929," *Anthropological Quarterly* 73, no. 3 (2000): 145–58; Anene Ejikeme, "Mission and Motherhood: Towards a History of Catholic Women and Education in Onitsha, Nigeria, 1885–1964" (PhD diss., Columbia University, 2003); and Victoria O. Ibewuike, *African Women and Religious Change: A Study of the Western Igbo of Nigeria with Special Focus on Asaba Town* (Uppsala: Department of Theology, Uppsala University, 2006).

35. Miers and Roberts, *End of Slavery*; Miers and Klein, *Slavery and Colonial Rule*; Jean Allman, Susan Geiger, and Nakayinke Musisi, eds., *Women and African Colonial History* (Bloomington: Indiana University Press, 2002); and Brett Shadle, *Girl Cases: Marriage and Colonialism in Gusiiland, Kenya, 1890–1970* (Portsmouth, NH: Heinemann, 2006).

36. Shadle, "Bridewealth and Female Consent: Marriage Disputes in African Courts, Gusiiland, Kenya," *Journal of African History* 44 (2003): 241–62.

37. See chapter 3 in this volume.

38. Thomas, *Anthropological Report*, 61–66.

39. See "Dowry Payment," NAI, Warri Prof 2/598; Thomas, *Anthropological Report*, 58–72; and Frederick D. Lugard, *Colonial Annual Report for Nigeria 1914* (London: Barclays and Fry, 1916), 52. In 1956, the Eastern Nigerian Government Legislature passed a law limiting bridewealth payment to £30 sterling. In reality, however, prices varied based on the educational level of the prospective wife. Girls with a primary school education attracted £70 to £80, high school diploma holders fetched £120 to £180, and registered nurses and other female professionals commanded £200 to £300 in bridal fees. See Victor Uchendu, "Concubinage among Ngwa Igbo of Southern Nigeria," *Africa* 35, no. 2 (1965): 187–97.

40. Thomas, *Anthropological Report*, 60.

41. "Intelligence Report on the Irrua Clan," NAI, CSO 26/3/27587/30.

42. Testimony by Mgbolie, NAI, Ben Prof 1/BP761.

43. Emecheta, *Bride Price*, 73.

44. Report from Resident Officer, Benin Province, E. B. Dawson enclosed in Secretary Southern Provinces, Colonel H. C. Moorehouse to Chief Secretary, 3 Feb. 1922, NAI, CSO 26/1/50569, vol. 1.

45. Resident Officers Warri Province in Secretary Southern Provinces to Chief Secretary, Feb. 3, 1922, NAI, CSO 26/1/50569, vol. 1.

46. Secretary Southern Profs to Chief Secretary, Feb. 3, 1922, NAI, CSO 26/50569, vol.1, and Native Children (Custom and Reformation Ordinance), confidential memo from the Secretary, Southern Provinces on Child Prostitution, Feb. 8, 1944, NAI, BP 1/1751.

47. Igbafe, *Benin under British Administration*, 226, 231.

48. See Hay and Wright, *African Women and the Law*; Kristin Mann, *Marrying Well: Marriage Status and Social Change among the Educated Elite in Colonial Lagos* (Cambridge: Cambridge University Press, 1985); Judith Byfield, "Women, Marriage, Divorce and the Emerging Colonial State in Abeokuta (Nigeria), 1892–1904," *Canadian Journal of African Studies* 30 (1996): 32–51; and Kaplan, "Runaway Wives."

49. Jean Allman, "Rounding Up Spinsters: Gender Chaos and Unmarried Women in Colonial Asante," *Journal of African History* 37 (1996): 195–214.

50. Minutes of Chief's Conference, March 22, 1943, National Archives, Kaduna, Secretariat of Northern Province 17/35252.

51. "Native Courts, Marriage and Adultery Rules," NAI, CSO 26/1/1/50569, vol. 2.

52. Thomas, *Anthropological Report*, 74–77.

53. Asaba Marriage Rules, NAI, Ben Prof 1/219/BP199/241, 35.

54. Memo from District Officer, Ishan Div. to Resident Benin Prov., May 23, 1935, NAI, Ben Prof 1/BP1004. See James O. Unumen, "The Impact of Colonialism on Ishan Women with Emphasis on Marriage, Education and Work" (master's thesis, University of Ibadan, 1988).

55. "Marriage Laws, Benin Native Courts 1924," NAI, Ben Prof 1/1004.

56. There were twenty shillings in a pound. Intelligence Report on Ogwashiuku Clan, para. 150, NAI, Ben Prof 4/3/8.

57. "Native Courts, Marriage and Adultery Rules," NAI, CSO 26/1/1/50569, vols. I–III.

58. Victor Chimso, interview, Ose market, Onitsha, May 27, 2009; M. C. Ayeli, interview, Ogboli-Onitsha, May 25, 2009; and Samuel Nkechukwu, interview, about 88 years, Igbuso, May 27, 2012.

59. Benjamin Okpuno, interview, Onicha Olona, July 14, 2009; Alice Obunuwa and Mary Mbuike, interview, Isele-Uku, July 16, 2009; and Matilda Azubuike, interview, Ogwasi-Uku, July 18, 2009.

60. Memorandum from District Officer Ishan Div to Resident Benin Province, May 23, 1935, NAI, Ben Prof 1/BP1004/1.

61. Hill, "Ancient Native Custom," and Captain N. C. Denton, Annual Report on Benin Province, 1936, para. 31, NAI, CSO 26/2/14617, vol. 12.

62. Testimonies by Mgboaniai, Mbuzo, Nkemuamuna, and Onwuesim, April 1934, NAI, Ben Prof 1/BP761.

63. Marjorie Mbilinyi, "Runaway Wives in Colonial Tanganyika: Forced Labor and Forced Marriage in Rungwe District, 1919–1961," *International Journal of the Sociology of Law* 16 (1988): 1–29, and Kaplan, "Runaway Wives." Also see Judith Byfield, "Women, Marriage, Divorce and the Emerging Colonial State in Abeokuta (Nigeria), 1892–1904," *Canadian Journal of African Studies* 30 (1996): 32–51; Jane Parpart, "'Where Is Your Mother?': Gender, Urban Marriage and Colonial Discourse on the Zambian Copperbelt, 1924–1945," *International Journal of African Historical Studies* 27 (1994): 241–71; Sheryl McCurdy, "The 1932 'War' between Rival Ujiji (Tanganyika) Associations: Understanding Women's Motivations for Inciting Political Unrest," *Canadian Journal of African Studies* 30 (1996): 10–31; Schmidt, *Peasants, Traders, and Wives*; and Teresa Barnes, "The Fight for Control of African Women's Mobility in Colonial Zimbabwe, 1900–1939," *Signs* 17 (1992): 586–608.

64. Allman, "Rounding Up Spinsters."

65. Thomas, *Anthropological Report*, 62–63.

66. See Igbafe, *Benin under British Administration*, 229.

67. Age of Marriage Law, chap. 6, sec. 2–4, 1 (Eastern Region 1956).

68. Assistant Commissioner of Police to Inspector General, Lagos, 13 April 1936, NAI, CSO 26/2/11604.

CHAPTER THREE

Debating "Early Marriage" in Colonial Kenya, 1920–50

BRETT L. SHADLE

The Kenya Marriage Act of 2014 set eighteen years as the minimum age of marriage for brides and grooms.[1] This law for the first time established a uniform minimum age, regardless of the type of marriage contracted—Christian, Hindu, Islamic, customary, or civil. It also harmonized the law books, as the Children's Act had already prohibited marriage under eighteen. Now, to enter into a marriage with someone under eighteen or to witness or perform such a marriage constitutes a criminal offense, and the marriage itself would be void. Although the 2014 act will not eliminate the marriage of those legally defined as children, it does create legal clarity over who is marriageable and who is not.

The Marriage Act should be understood as the most recent episode in a long series of debates over the definition of early marriage. The men discussed in this chapter—government officials, missionaries, and elite Africans in colonial Kenya—all concurred that the early marriage of girls was a bad thing. That was simple enough. Beyond this, alas, things became more complex. For there was no clarity on a fundamental point: what, exactly, was early marriage? Despite their shared condemnation of early marriage, these men found it exceedingly difficult to determine what transformed an unmarriageable girl into a woman eligible to be wed. This confusion, combined with administrators' reluctance to meddle in African marital customs, meant that the colonial state remained paralyzed in dealing with early marriage.

In this chapter, I examine three points in time—1926–27, the 1930s, and 1949–50—when colonial officials, missionaries, and elite African men wrestled with the question of early marriage of African females. Virtually all found early marriage deplorable, but it is striking how difficult they found it to decide what made an (unmarriageable) "girl" into a (marriageable) "woman." Most believed the transition was either physical (puberty) or emotional (with girlhood being a period that might extend well into the teen years). Nevertheless, no one ever precisely defined puberty, sexual maturity, "girl," or girlhood. Neither were their reasons for opposing early marriage always consistent. It would seem that if a girl should be considered unmarriageable because she is prepubescent, then her marriage should be equally objectionable regardless of who she marries. Yet many of the men discussed here were more revolted by the marriage of girls to elderly polygamists than by marriages of girls to younger (though still adult) bachelors. Similarly, those who thought emotional development marked the transition from girl to woman expressed special disgust at the marriage of prepubescent girls—meaning that both physical and emotional development retained importance for the making of a woman.

In what follows, I examine how a select group of men tried to decipher the process by which an African girl became marriageable, why marriage before that point was improper, and how early marriage could be stopped. Their discussions produced no legislation; they led to no firm administrative directives.[2] Nor were these the only moments when the question of early marriage provoked protest, confusion, memoranda writing, inaction, and denouement. They are illustrative, however, of elite discussions over early marriage, and they offer a window into the history of contemporary concerns.

THE IMPERIAL CONTEXT

The exchanges over early marriage in Kenya took place within an imperial world caught up in questions over the status of colonized women.[3] From at least the 1890s, the colonized (and later the so-called Third World) woman emerged as an object of European concern. The confluence of several trends after World War I concentrated attention on females in the colonies. British women (over age thirty) gained the vote in 1918, leaving many activists energized and idle.[4] Organizations such as St. Joan's Social and Political Alliance and the British Commonwealth League looked beyond the plight of white women. Eleanor Rathbone, among the first female members of the British Parliament, regularly assailed the Colonial Office with queries and complaints about women's oppression. Her questions in Parliament, mass meetings, and publications galvanized sections of the public; the specter of slavelike Indian and African women refused to be exorcised. The League of Nations similarly offered a public arena in which to raise international issues. Discussions in Geneva and London often turned on the question of the individual liberties to be afforded to colonized women. Too many practices, activists insisted, forced women to do things against their will: to marry, to have sex, to have their bodies mutilated. A nation that prided itself on personal freedom and autonomy; a continent remade out of deference to peoples' rights of self-determination; but colonies in which women were treated as if they were slaves? (Activists expended less energy protesting the fact that colonized peoples as a whole lacked self-determination.)

Within these larger discussions about the colonized female were questions about the nature of girlhood. By the 1880s in Britain, as Sally Mitchell notes, "the concept of girlhood as a separate stage of existence with its own values and interests was only beginning to take shape." With changes in public schooling and labor laws came the emergence of a girl who was "no longer a child, not yet a (sexual) adult."[5] There would be no consensus as to when this girl became a woman. For example, the new Girl Guides movement included females from eleven to sixteen. A magazine entitled *Girls' Own Paper* featured protagonists who ranged from eleven to eighteen, and its readers included females up to twenty-four—which, the magazine suggested, was an opportune age for females to marry.[6]

This new girl—whoever she might be—required protection. Thus, Parliament in 1885 raised the female age of consent for sex from thirteen to sixteen. Yet this law did not treat all "girls" alike. A man who had sex with a female less than twelve years of age was guilty of a felony, but if she was between twelve and sixteen, he had committed only a misdemeanor. Why this distinction? A female under twelve was assumed to be a prepubescent child. Her body was developmentally incapable of safely engaging in intercourse, and she was not yet mentally capable of consenting to such an act. A female over sixteen was presumed to be both physically and emotionally prepared to engage in and freely consent to sex. The years between twelve and sixteen constituted a kind of liminal period. A female might or might not be pubescent; she might or might not have the mental faculties to understand the perils and pleasures of sex.[7] Therefore, those from twelve to sixteen required at least a measure of sexual "protection," in part out of concern for their bodies and in part because they occupied a psychological middle ground between childhood and adulthood, namely, girlhood.

In the colonies, Britons searched in vain for girlhood. Colonial officials seemed blind to any African categories that might approximate British ideas of girlhood. They generally understood females as moving rapidly from children to women, daughters to wives, with no stage in between.[8] In addition, most Europeans believed that females in the tropics reached puberty several years before those in more temperate climes.[9] British girls of twelve to sixteen years might not be physically ready to safely engage in intercourse; they might not be psychologically prepared to consent to intercourse. In contrast, with the early onset of puberty and absent the transitional psychological period of "girlhood," colonized females of twelve years might well be perfectly ready for sex.

The thoughts of Tanganyika's attorney general on the age of consent in regard to sex are instructive. Commenting on a 1926 draft penal code for East Africa, he thought it "unsuitable" to "define the age of consent [to sex] in years."[10] Africans neither measured nor understood time in such a way. Instead, he wrote, a "large body of native opinion" understood puberty "as making a division between permissible and impermissible intercourse." Childhood stopped upon puberty. Using puberty to mark the age of consent appealed to the attorney general because it "expresses the essence of the offense more accurately than an age limit can" and because the "attainment of puberty is a physiological fact." That is, the physical *ability* to have sex was presumed to be accompanied by the psychological or emotional maturity to *consent* to sex. There was no cultural or social category of girlhood as there was in Britain. The line between child and adult was strictly a physiological one. Like many officials elsewhere in the empire, however, the attorney general failed to explain exactly what he meant by puberty. It was a "fact" that could be determined biomedically, although he deferred to Africans as to what that fact was: he suggested vaguely that puberty should be used in "its full meaning, as the natives themselves understand it."

The focus on physiology as opposed to psychology carried over into debates on the minimum age of marriage. In fact, the age of consent in regard to sex and the minimum age of marriage were often intertwined.[11] It was presumed that sex followed immediately upon marriage, and thus, a female could not be ready for marriage unless she was also ready for sex.[12]

BRETT L. SHADLE

For many officials, the reverse was also true: once a female was ready for sexual intercourse, she was ready for marriage.

India saw some of the most intense debates over ages of consent to sex and to marriage. In a ghastly incident in 1890, a thirty-five-year-old man had sex with his eleven-year-old bride, who later died of the resulting injuries. He could not be held criminally responsible for her death because he had engaged in lawful sex with her. She was a year older than the age of consent to sex, and she was his wife—and British law could not conceive of sexual violence within marriage. To remedy the outrage, the imperial government pushed through a law setting the age of marriage at twelve—the presumed age of puberty for Indian girls. That is, marriage at eleven years was wrong because the female was not physically ready for sex, while marriage at twelve years was acceptable because the female was pubescent and thus physically ready for sex. At what age a female became mentally and emotionally prepared for sex and marriage was a question left unasked. Hindu nationalists condemned this interference into the domestic sphere, and for decades, the government shied away from any further legislation on family or gender issues.[13]

Consequently, when missionaries, activists in Britain, colonial officials, and elite African men in Kenya considered early marriage, they took part in empirewide debates over girlhood, maturity, and consent.[14] In Nyanza Province, in Nairobi, and along the coast, they talked about puberty, about emotional maturity, about custom. Officials worried over the true extent of their power to alter African life, missionaries stretched the boundaries of girlhood, and African elites pressed for change. And it seems that no one thought to inquire into the opinions of African females.

NYANZA PROVINCE, 1926–28

In a meeting on September 30, 1926, the Native Catholic Union (NCU) considered the issue of child marriage and the marriage of young girls to elderly men. The history of the NCU has yet to be written, although its origins lay in the Nyanza Province–based Kavirondo Taxpayers' Welfare Association (KTWA), a relatively mild political group. Earlier in 1926, when the KTWA had come too much under the influence of the Protestant missionary W. E. Owen, some members left to create the NCU under the leadership of Father J. A. Wall.[15] The notes of the September meeting of the NCU have not been found, and it is difficult to know if African members or their missionary mentors broached the topic of early marriage. That it came at the height of discussions in India and in the League of Nations is perhaps not coincidental. The NCU members, like Indian reformers, may have been using child marriage as a means of measuring themselves against the tape of international standards.[16]

C. M. Dobbs, the senior commissioner of the province, was receptive to the NCU's concerns. "It is undoubtedly very undesirable," he wrote to the Nyanza district commissioners, "that girls who are still immature should be married, and especially to old men, who may have many wives already." He asked his district commissioners to raise the issue with their local native councils (LNCs)—bodies with a mixture of elected and appointed members, intended to channel political strivings into a controlled arena.[17] Dobbs offered that the LNCs could enact bylaws making it an offense to marry off a girl under the age of fourteen or fifteen years.[18] The Kericho LNC admitted that although "some few girls may be married young," they did not cohabit with their husbands unless they and their mothers gave consent.[19] The Central Kavirondo LNC, however, proposed that to marry a female under fifteen or to allow one's daughter to be married before that age should be an offense punishable by a 150-shilling fine or, in default of payment, a three-month prison sentence.[20] The North Kavirondo LNC passed a similar resolution early in 1927.

LNC resolutions gained the force of law only with the government's assent, which in this case would be denied. The director of medical and sanitation services weighed in, explaining that by age fifteen some African females could not be counted as "immature." If African females were physically "mature," then they were, he implied, fully ready for marriage.[21] J. A. Ross, medical officer for North Kavirondo and Nandi, also dismissed any attempt to establish a minimum age of marriage. Some African females were mature at twelve years or even younger, he asserted. Puberty—and the marriageability of females—could not be predetermined by a calendar. The only means of establishing the "suitability of girls for marriage" was through a visual examination.[22] (What he expected to be revealed by such an exam Ross did not say.) Dobbs countered with a resolution that would omit a minimum age and criminalize only the marriage of "immature" girls.[23] The question was rendered moot by the attorney general, who ruled that LNCs lacked the authority to make resolutions on items "of such gravity as the subject matter in this case."[24]

Nonetheless, the topic of immature marriage lingered along for several more months. In August, the Central Kavirondo LNC resolved that the government should alter section 375 of the penal code, which established twelve as the age of consent for sex in marriage.[25] The LNC recommended the age be increased to fifteen.[26] Thus, a twelve-year-old female could still be betrothed, but the marriage could not be consummated until she reached fifteen. The crown counsel, P. A. McElwane, proved unreceptive. Increasing the age was unnecessary, for (he claimed) even at twelve African females had reached puberty and were ready for sex. Such a change in the law also carried disturbing racial implications. The age of marriage in Britain was still twelve under common law. "If an English girl of twelve can marry in the fullest sense of the word," McElwane wrote, "I see no reason why a girl here should not marry at that age." "If a girl married in England at say the age of fourteen [should] come out here," he asked, "is she not to be allowed to cohabit with her husband in Kenya though she might lawfully do so in England?" Could African definitions of girlhood be more expansive than those of Britons? If anything, he argued, the age of marriage for African females should be lower than that for whites, since the former reached puberty at an earlier age than the latter.[27]

There remained a glimmer of hope for some kind of action. The chief native commissioner wrote the attorney general in October that early marriage was, in fact, a dangerous and growing practice. He claimed it was "against the interests of the tribe from a eugenic point of view, and it appears to be very desirable, in the public interest, to put a stop to the practice."[28] Altering the penal code was a large undertaking and would implicate all residents of the colony. Would other "tribes" be amenable to such a change? the attorney general wondered.[29] Over a year into the discussion, Dobbs turned to white authorities in the province—administrators and missionaries—for feedback.[30] The North Kavirondo acting district commissioner thought that the chronological age of females at marriage was irrelevant, for no "harm is done . . . provided she has attained maturity."[31] Of greater concern to him and his colleague in Nandi was African youths' illicit sexual intercourse with girls as young as ten.[32]

Missionary opinion was mixed. O. C. Keller of the Nyangori Mission thought underage and forced marriages were absent among the Luhyia, although, like the district commissioner, he believed sex between adult men and immature girls was quite common.[33] Eric Beavon of the Seventh-day Adventist (SDA) mission believed that the "evil of immature marriage with consummation is sufficiently widespread" among the Gusii so as to require "special legislation." His colleague, W. W. Armstrong, thought it much less common among the Luo, but H. W. Innis of the Ogada Mission disagreed.[34] Like administrators, Innis opposed setting a minimum age to marry, believing that it was too difficult to reckon an African's age and that girls reached puberty at anywhere from twelve to sixteen years. He instead recommended that marrying off a prepubescent girl should be a serious offense under the penal code and should "be considered such an offence as rape" for all residents of the colony—regardless of race.[35]

At this point, the archival record runs dry. It is unlikely that any revised resolution was ever passed and approved, for nothing was mentioned of it in later correspondence. The discussion reveals, however, competing and contradictory ideas about girlhood and marriage. The primary question quickly shifted from chronological age to physical development as markers of marriageability. All of the men involved seemed to agree with one line of reasoning: marriage meant sex, prepubescent girls should not have sex, and thus prepubescent girls should not be considered marriageable.

Puberty, to Ross, Dobbs, and many others, seemed to be the clearest way to distinguish between a female who could be married and one who could not. Yet many questions were left unanswered or, in fact, were never asked at all. As much as the men in Nyanza wrote about it, they never quite got around to explaining what they meant by "reaching puberty." Was it the onset of outward physical signs of puberty? If so, should the first faint signs of the development of breasts be sufficient? Did first menses mark the onset of puberty—or the culmination of it? That is, did menarche suddenly transform a girl into a woman? And if puberty was intended to mark a female as *sexually* mature and thus ready for marriage, did menarche actually make a girl *physically* prepared to engage—safely—in intercourse?

The focus on puberty and physical development overshadowed any consideration of a female's emotional and mental standing. This latter issue had been part of the Native Catholic Union's original complaint—the marriage of young girls to elderly men. This concern was separate from the physical question: physiologically, it made no difference if a prepubescent girl engaged in intercourse with a man three years her senior, or twice her age, or four times her age.[36] The presumption, however, was that *emotionally*, the girl would be more repulsed by an older man than one closer to her own age. To put it more bluntly: being raped by a young man was not nearly as bad as being raped by an old man. The question of age disparity was soon pushed aside, and thus so too was any consideration of a girl's emotional or mental state in relation to marriageability. Focusing on puberty privileged outward physical signs of adulthood, such that a ten-year-old pubescent girl could be marriageable but not a late-developing seventeen-year-old.

What is perhaps most surprising about these discussions in Nyanza—and indeed all the archival material considered here—is the absolute silence on the matter of female initiation. In many parts of Kenya, including Gusii and some Luhyia areas of Nyanza, females underwent initiation ceremonies that marked their emergence out of childhood. Yet in none of their correspondence or resolutions did these men broach the idea that initiation could be used as a sign of womanhood and maturity. This is in contrast to official discussions surrounding African males. Throughout the colonial period, government officials and members of the judiciary cast about for means of separating men from boys.[37] They resorted to a variety of methods of reckoning a male's age—dental X-rays, the appearance of underarm hair—but evidence of initiation and circumcision were among the commonest.[38] Female excision was, of course, much more controversial than male circumcision, and administrators most often tried to take no official note of it. European men may have thought it more politic to simply ignore female initiation in their consideration of female adulthood.

ARCHDEACON OWEN, FORCED MARRIAGE, AND GIRLHOOD FROM 1930

Archdeacon Walter Owen of the Church Missionary Society began his career in Uganda in 1904, and in 1918, he became archdeacon of Kavirondo (covering much the same area as Nyanza province in western Kenya). He considered himself a defender of African interests against the exploitative practices of state and settler, although he exercised his own forms of paternalistic authority over "his" Africans. By the 1930s, Owen had turned his attention to African women, particularly to (what he believed to be) the large number of forced marriages in his domain and in Africa generally.[39] In August 1935, he published a letter in the *Manchester Guardian* telling of a young woman forced into marriage—and African marriage, he insisted, was little more than "enslavement." Various women's groups quickly called meetings and demanded answers from the Colonial Office, to little effect.

Not to be dissuaded, in June 1936 Owen published a second and more devastating letter. In the pages of the *Guardian,* he related the story of

Kekwe, an eighteen-year-old female living in Tanganyika. Kekwe's parents, as Owen told it, had married her to a man not of her choosing. She left him for another man, and when her (legal) husband came to retrieve her, Kekwe drew a knife. The knife hit its mark, he fell dead, and Kekwe stood trial for manslaughter. A British judge sentenced her to eighteen months imprisonment.[40] A firestorm in Britain ensued. Faced with a small but vocal and politically connected set of critics, the Colonial Office finally succumbed to pressure and ordered an inquiry. Administrators from across Britain's African empire were requested to provide information on the existence (or, as the instructions strongly hinted, nonexistence) of forced marriage.

Owen's letter about Kekwe suggested a different understanding of early marriage. Through much of his crusade against forced marriage, Owen used the terms *girl* and *girlhood*. He described Kekwe as a girl, and he told his readers that "the degradation felt by African girls when dragged off is unspeakable." "We must," Owen continued, "for the sake of African girlhood, teach the tribes that without consent there is no true marriage." He had for many years resisted critiquing African customs, but the "anguish of decent girls" forced him to take action.[41] African societies could never be considered civilized while "such outrages on the personality of girlhood" continued.[42] Although Owen also used the language of girlhood in his personal archive, he certainly understood the rhetorical importance of employing it in his public writings.[43] He was alive to the emotional jolt he made when describing victims of forced marriage as girls. "Although they are 'only Africans,'" he wrote in a letter about Kekwe, "their anguish is no less deep than the anguish of English girlhood."

Owen's definition of *girlhood* differed significantly from those used in 1926 and 1927, when an emphasis on puberty and age precluded discussion of a female's mental or emotional state.[44] The "girl" Kekwe was somewhere between seventeen and twenty years old. Commenting on another case of forced marriage, Owen reported that "many African girls are forced into marriage in their middle 'teens.'"[45] Apparently, it was not a particular age nor physical development that made a girl into a woman. In fact, Owen seems never to have speculated on when a female could be considered marriageable. More important to him was eliminating forced marriage. He did not blanch at a female in her middle teens being married, so long as it was not a forced marriage. (And, after all, Kekwe had killed her legal husband when he came to fetch her from her preferred mate.) Yet Owen also believed it unlikely that a female of thirteen had the psychological fortitude to reject a man to whom she had been betrothed at age nine or ten. The question thus seemed to involve, for Owen, finding a place at which a girl became a woman emotionally—when a child (incapable of refusing or consenting to marriage) became an adult (who could consent and whose ability to refuse marriage had to be protected).

Moreover, Owen and like-minded thinkers in Britain believed that a marriage between a young bride and an elderly, polygynist groom was necessarily a case of forced marriage and an especially vile type at that. For a culture fully immersed in the idea of a companionate marriage, it was highly doubtful to Britons that a young woman would willingly marry a man decades her senior—what interests could they possibly share? What kind of romantic life could they find? A marriage of a young woman to an old man almost certainly had to be forced. Worse still was marriage to an old polygamist. The connection between polygamy and forced marriage seemed patent. It was inconceivable that a young woman would agree to marry an old man with multiple wives—there could be no tenderness there, no bond between two individuals. Christine Spender, commenting on Equatorial Africa, equated polygamy with nonconsensual marriage; Archbishop Alexandre LeRoy, formerly of Gabon, believed it nothing more than slavery.[46] More commonly, the evils of marrying an elderly man or a polygamist appeared so evident as to require no comment.

Owen thus made a special point of noting age disparities when publicizing cases of forced marriage. In his letters to the *Guardian*, he amplified his stories by observing that the groom was "very much older . . . and a polygamist" or by describing "a girl just emerging from childhood" being betrothed to an "old man."[47] On another occasion, he pulled these arguments together as he tried to extract empathy from a district commissioner for African females. He recounted the story of A. ("a girl of 16–17 years") who was caught in a dispute between "an old man" named O. (who had given bridewealth for her) and "an old friend of her father" (who had apparently been promised A. in marriage many years before). "Such unions of old men to young girls," Owen insisted, "must be as repugnant to normal girls as they appear to many of us"—including the district commissioner, presumably. "I would beg yet once again," he continued, "that something be done to save African girls from experiences such as that of 16–17 yrl [*sic*] old A."[48] Later, he told of a "girl" who tried to reject a leviratic union because "she did not want to be married to an elderly man, but wanted a man of her own age."[49]

By the time of Owen's death in 1944, his campaign seems to have borne little fruit. He did gain the release of some females who had managed to reach out to him, and perhaps colonial officials in Nyanza were more sensitive to the plight of pubescent females because of Owen. But there is little evidence that officials took any steps other than dealing with the specific cases he brought to them. Officials believed forced marriage deplorable, as was the marriage of prepubescent girls. The notion that pubescent, teenaged "girls" might not be mature enough to consent to marriage was of less concern.[50]

CHILD MARRIAGE ON THE COAST, 1949–50

The Kenyan colonial administration had its attention drawn to child marriage again in 1949. Seventh-day Adventist missionary W. S. Raitt, stationed in Nairobi, wrote to the district commissioner of Malindi about a "little girl" named Dama. Several months of correspondence fleshed out her tale. Dama's father, Simeon, had once been an SDA adherent but had left the church. Simeon subsequently betrothed Dama and another daughter, and he expended their bridewealth on a wife for his brother and for daily living expenses. Now, according to Raitt, the time had come for Dama to go to her husband, Chief Kalu, but she refused. Raitt feared that the local African court would uphold the marriage contract and force Dama to go to the chief. Raitt relied on language Owen and others had used a decade before. He charged that the buying and selling "of little girls, this forcing them to become the junior wives of old men" was "nothing less than slavery." Quite a scandal would arise, he warned darkly, should the story become public.[51]

The district commissioner, F. R. Wilson, assured Raitt that his facts were incorrect—there was neither scandal nor slavery in the case. After he left the church, Simeon had become a drunkard, and Dama had been more than glad to accept a marriage to Chief Kalu to escape her unhappy home. (Whether he meant that was the case when the marriage was contracted or now that it was time to cohabitate was unclear.) Moreover, basic fairness was in play. "I would not wish you to imagine that I am anything but sympathetic with your view of child marriage," Wilson informed Raitt, but it would be "grossly inequitable" to deny the chief his wife. Kalu had given bridewealth, which an indebted Simeon could not return. Neither was it an issue for intervention: child betrothal was, after all, customary in the region.[52]

Unsatisfied, Raitt took his concerns to Nairobi officials. The native courts officer and the chief native commissioner conferred. As with most social issues, they had little desire to become directly involved. In part, officials shied away from interfering with customs that were critical to African social structures but largely irrelevant to the functioning of the colonial economic order. Female genital cutting was the classic example. When missionaries forced their Gikuyu converts in 1929 to choose either the church or genital operations on their daughters, the pews were left nearly empty. Colonial officials tried as best they could to remain on the sidelines of the resulting furor—no sense in Government getting involved in a matter so central to African culture, as long as taxes were paid and bodies went out to work.

Rather than directly attacking practices they found distasteful, officials preferred to wait for education, social change, and propaganda to slowly alter custom and public opinion. As Africans became more "modern" and Christian, the thinking went, they would naturally come to the conclusion that things such as child marriage and polygamy were backward, harmful, and pagan. The government could push Africans in this direction using propaganda through chiefs and public meetings (*barazas*). Until "public opinion" (a much-used phrase) came round, the government should not otherwise interfere. A law against something such as circumcision would be, in the meantime, widely unpopular—and widely ignored.[53] When its laws were ignored, Government was shown to be impotent, and this would not do. If officials felt that something should be done, they turned to their local native councils. If an LNC bylaw was unpopular, Government could deny responsibility: LNCs represented Africans, African councillors passed their own resolutions, and African-run courts enforced their bylaws. Of course, district commissioners chaired LNC meetings, many bylaws were standardized and written by officials, and the attorney general could veto resolutions. Still, if Africans were going to be upset, better to direct their anger toward their fellow Africans on the LNCs.

Faced with a potential scandal over early marriage, the courts officer, M. N. Evans, thought to turn it over to the local native council. Would it be amenable, he wondered, to passing a resolution "making the contraction of marriages by girls under 16 illegal"?[54] If so, offenders could be prosecuted in African courts. The provincial commissioner hesitated. As they all knew, the LNCs were not always representative, and did not necessarily have that much influence. Thus, a resolution of that kind would be "useless" unless the people were supportive of such a law.[55] Word then reached Nairobi indicating the LNC had, eight years previously, resolved "that it is contrary to Nyika law and custom to give or take in marriage young girls who have not reached maturity and that offenders shall be punished." At that time, government officials (likely through the chief native commissioner or attorney general) expressed their appreciation of the sentiment but rejected the resolution.[56] Evans believed that it had been rejected at that time because it was unenforceable: the people were not behind it. Perhaps now things had changed: perhaps now the majority of Giriama opposed child marriage, in which case a resolution should have government support. The chief native commissioner remained unconvinced that such a resolution would reflect "public opinion" or even a well thought-out debate among LNC members.[57]

Regardless, in April the LNC pushed ahead with Resolution 32/50. Child marriage was a valid custom, it said, but undesirable, since girls were often married off to "much older men." Propaganda and education should be the paths toward eliminating it. In the meantime, fathers and husbands should be prosecuted in African courts if girls were sent to live with their husbands before they reached "fully marriageable age."[58] This resolution apparently passed muster with Nairobi officials, and by November, eight cases had appeared in the native courts involving men marrying or giving in marriage "a girl who has not attained sexual maturity" as an offense against "Native Law and Custom."[59]

As in earlier debates, clarity in definitions of early marriage remained elusive. Raitt wrote of a "little girl," without explaining what he meant: was Dama five? Was she twelve but prepubescent? Was she classed as a teenager still in "girlhood"? Evans first demanded greater precision, proposing sixteen as an age by which all females could be assumed to be marriageable. The word *maturity*, he thought, lacked specificity.[60] The LNC in 1950 spoke of "sexual maturity" but without spelling out what this meant. Evans now began to wonder about emotional or psychological maturity. Thinking of a bride betrothed as a child, he stated, "I should imagine that when the time comes for her to go to her husband, she has little or no hope of being able to resist the pressure from her father and husband, if the transaction is against her will."[61] A child betrothal might therefore still be wrong, even if the female was sixteen and "sexually mature" at the time of cohabitation. Regardless, deferring to the LNC and African court elders satisfied the administrators. The typewriters soon fell silent, the inexactness over "early marriage" unresolved for officials.[62] What became of Dama is unknown.

THE THREE episodes recounted here certainly do not exhaust the archival record, but they were chosen as instructive and provocative points through which to examine the history of early marriage. Many other individuals, across the colonial period and across Kenya, engaged in similar—and equally frustrating—attempts to identify a marriageable female. Early colonial official Charles Dundas in 1915 worried over "the early age at which native girls are married," an "evil which seems to increase year by year."[63] LNCs in Central Province debated the implications of child betrothals for a least two decades from 1929.[64] Other conversations remain to be recovered in the papers of "tribal associations" such as the NCU and Luo Union, in the transcripts of local African courts, and in the reminiscences of the elders. And today, even as the National Assembly takes steps to define *child* and *adult, marriageable* and *unmarriageable,* Kenyans of all stripes—parents, educators, children, government officials—along with nongovernmental organizations (NGOs) continue to negotiate the definitions and meanings of *childhood, girlhood* (the *"girl child"*), and *adulthood.*[65]

These discussions were not limited to colonial Kenya but ranged across the British Empire and beyond. As the other chapters in this volume demonstrate, there were ongoing discussions among Africans and Europeans over all manner of issues involving women and marriage. Was bridewealth a means to bind two families—or the enslavement of a woman? Was child betrothal an innocuous custom—or child slavery? To what extent should missionaries and government officials intervene in marital practices? At what point did parental rights shade into exploitation? Did the protection of women's liberty come at the cost of women's licentiousness? And again, as authors in this volume show, many of these debates continue today. Even as numerous groups and individuals fight to end forced marriage, we continue to find ourselves faced with the questions posed long ago by African councillors, Owen the missionary, and Evans the official. How does one define *force*? How does one measure consent? Who is a girl and who is a woman? What social, legal, biological, and/or emotional factors are critical to making a female marriageable? Legislation such as the Kenya Marriage Act of 2014 may help clarify the legal aspects of these issues, but they will not put all the questions to rest.

NOTES

1. The text of the law can be found at http://kenyalaw.org/kl/fileadmin /pdfdownloads/Acts/TheMarriage_Act2014.pdf, accessed Nov. 30, 2015.

2. In fact, colonial officials never fully worked out definitions of *childhood* and *adulthood* in regard to criminal responsibility, the legal capability to move to a mission station, marry without parental consent, and so on. See, for example, Tabitha Kanogo, *African Womanhood in Colonial Kenya, 1900–1950* (Oxford: James Currey, 2005), chap. 1; *Report of the Committee on Young Persons and Children* (Nairobi: Colony and Protectorate of Kenya, 1953), 2–3; "Rights of Missions to Keep Minors, 1914," Kenya National Archive (hereafter cited as KNA): PC/COAST/1/10/181. (Thanks to Paul Ocobock for allowing me to see his notes on this file.)

3. The following paragraph draws on Leila Rupp, *Worlds of Women: The Making of an International Women's Movement* (Princeton, NJ: Princeton University Press, 1997); Susan Pederson, *Eleanor Rathbone and the Politics of Conscience* (New Haven, CT: Yale University Press, 2004); Pedersen, "Metaphors of the Schoolroom: Women Working the Mandates System of the League of Nations," *History Workshop Journal* 66 (2008): 188–207; Brett L. Shadle, *"Girl Cases": Marriage and Colonialism in Gusiiland, Kenya, 1890–1970* (Portsmouth, NH: Heinemann, 2006), 56–71.

4. Suffrage was extended to all adult women a decade later.

5. Sally Mitchell, *The New Girl: Girls' Culture in England, 1880–1915* (New York: Columbia University Press, 1995), 1, 3.

6. Michelle J. Smith, *Empire in British Girls' Literature and Culture: Imperial Girls, 1880–1915* (New York: Palgrave Macmillan, 2011), 7.

7. The International Convention for the Suppression of the White Slave Traffic of 1910 identified another liminal period for female maturation. It recommended that *woman* be defined as a female over twenty, such that movement of a female below that age could be considered trafficking. That is, a female of sixteen was mature enough to consent to sex but not mature enough to consent to entering into the sex trade.

8. Some of the better administrators-ethnographers had a stronger grasp of life stages in certain African communities, but this knowledge seems not to have influenced policy.See, for instance, K. R. Dundas, "Kikuyu Rika," *Man* 8 (1908): 180–82.

9. In 1914, for example, the Kenya government introduced a bill to bring the law into conformity with the White Slave Traffic Agreement of 1904 and the International Convention for the Suppression of the White Slave Traffic of 1910. The wording of the bill, the attorney general explained, was taken almost verbatim from British laws, but the age of consent for white women (sixteen) and nonwhite women (twelve) differed "on the ground that a native woman as a rule arrived at maturity at an earlier age than a white woman." With no Africans in the Legislative Council until the 1940s, such racial understanding of girlhood passed without comment. Legislative Council debates, Aug. 4, 1914; Criminal Law Amendment Ordinance, Ordinance 18 of 1914, section 7, Gazette of the East African Protectorate XVI, 380, Aug. 19, 1914.

10. Note on Sections 111 and 126 Draft Penal Code, enclosure in Governor Cameron to Secretary of State, June 12, 1926, British National Archive (hereafter cited as NA), CO 533/631. Cameron noted that he agreed with the attorney general's opinion.

11. The League of Nations Advisory Committee on the Traffic in Women and Protection of Children in 1925 undertook an inquiry into "the age of marriage and the age of consent," and in 1932, Eleanor Rathbone petitioned the Colonial Office to collect information on both topics.

12. Child betrothal was a different question, so long as cohabitation was delayed until puberty.

13. The issue emerged again in the late 1920s, this time raised by Indian politicians eager to prove themselves civilized according to Western standards. See Ashwini Tambe, "The State as Surrogate Parent: Legislating Nonmarital Sex in Colonial India, 1911–1929," *Journal of the History of Childhood and Youth* 2 (2009): 393–427, at 406. On this era, see also Ishita Pande, "Sorting Boys and Men: Unlawful Intercourse, Boy-Protection, and the Child Marriage Restraint Act in Colonial India," *Journal of the History of Childhood and Youth* 6 (2013): 332–58; Mrinalini Sinha, *Specters of Mother India: The Global Restructuring of an Empire* (Durham, NC: Duke University Press, 2006).

14. And these debates were ongoing. In 1951, Arthur Philips was in the midst of his *Survey of African Marriage*. At his request, the Colonial Office issued a circular on legislation regarding the minimum age of marriage. The responses revealed that it was an area virtually unregulated by the law and clouded by confusion over what made a female marriageable. See NA: CO 323/1929/14.

15. Bethwell A. Ogot, "British Administration in the Central Nyanza District of Kenya, 1900–60," *Journal of African History* 4 (1963): 249–73, at 264–65; Gilbert E. M. Ogutu, *An Outline History of the Catholic Church in Western Kenya to 1952* (Nairobi: Palwa Research Services, 1989), 61–62; Carl Rosberg and John Nottingham, *Myth of Mau Mau: Nationalism in Kenya* (New York: Praeger, 1966), 91.

16. Members of the KTWA likewise pledged "not to aid or abet the marriage of girls under 16 years of age." Quoted in Rosberg and Nottingham, *Myth of Mau Mau*, 91.

17. Some LNCs included representatives of the NCU. George Bennett, "The Development of Political Organizations in Kenya," *Political Studies* 5 (1957): 113–30, at 120.

18. SC Nyanza to DCs, Oct. 2, 1926, KNA: PC/NZA 3/28/4/1.

19. DC Kericho to SC Nyanza, Oct. 11, 1926, KNA: PC/NZA 3/28/4/1.

20. The resolution, proposed by Chief Ojungo, stated that early marriage was a recent development and "contrary to old custom." It is conceivable that the district commissioner proposed such language: LNCs' resolutions were more likely to gain government approval if they dealt strictly with "native law and custom." Ag. DC Central Kavirondo to SC Nyanza, Dec. 4, 1926, KNA: PC/NZA 3/28/4/1; CNC to AG, May 12, 1927, KNA: AG 23/293.

21. SC Nyanza to DC North Kavirondo, Apr. 20, 1927, KNA: PC/NZA 3/28/4/1.

22. J. A. Ross, Medical Officer, North Kavirondo and Nandi, to DC North Kavirondo, May 5, 1927, KNA: PC/NZA 3/28/4/1.

23. SC Nyanza to DC North Kavirondo, Apr. 20, 1927.

24. AG to CNC, June 10, 1927, KNA: PC/NZA 3/28/4/1.

25. Until the early 1930s, Kenya operated under the Indian Penal Code, and thus had inherited the 1891 legislation on child marriage.

26. DC Central Kavirondo to SC Nyanza, Aug. 5, 1927, KNA: PC/NZA 3/28/4/1.

27. P. A. McElwane, Senior Crown Counsel, to CNC, Sept. 14, 1927, KNA: AG 23/293.

28. CNC to AG, Oct. 14, 1927, KNA: AG 23/293. This is the only reference to eugenics in any of the archival material discussed here.

29. AG, to CNC, Oct. 25, 1927, KNA: AG 23/293.

30. SC Nyanza to DCs, Nov. 11, 1927, KNA: PC/NZA 3/28/4/1.

31. DC NK to SC Nyanza, Nov. 14, 1927, KNA: PC/NZA 3/28/4/1.

32. DC Nandi to SC Nyanza, Nov. 18, 1927, KNA: PC/NZA 3/28/4/1.

33. O.C. Keller, Nyangori Mission, Kisumu, to SC Nyanza, Jan. 3, 1928, KNA: PC/NZA 3/28/4/1

34. Beavon quoted in W. W. Armstrong to SC Nyanza, Nov. 24, 1927; and H. W. Innis, Ogada Mission Station, Nyahera, to SC Nyanza, Dec. 27, 1927, both in KNA: PC/NZA 3/28/4/1. The district commissioner from this area, however, thought such legislation was "unnecessary," as people understood the "evils of the practice and are bringing public opinion to bear to such an extent that the practice is said to be dying out." S. O. V. Hodge, DC SK, to SC Nyanza, Dec. 8, 1927, KNA: PC/NZA 3/28/4/1.

35. Innis, Ogada Mission, to SC Nyanza, 27 Dec. 1927.

36. This may be the context for the CNC's raising of the eugenics issue. In India, some proponents of a higher age of marriage worried about the effect on the nation or race of unions between young females and older men.

37. This primarily had to do with whether an offender should be confined to prison, caned, or sent to juvenile rehabilitation.

38. My thanks to Paul Ocobock for information on this point. See also his "Spare the Rod, Spoil the Colony: Corporal Punishment, Colonial Violence, and Generational Authority in Kenya, 1897–1952," *International Journal of African Historical Studies* 45 (2012): 29–56.

39. On Owen, see Cynthia Hoehler-Fatton, *Women of Fire and Spirit: History, Faith, and Gender in Roho Religion in Western Kenya* (New York: Oxford University Press, 1996); Opolot Okia, *Communal Labor in Colonial Kenya: The Legitimization of Coercion* (New York: Palgrave Macmillan, 2012); Shadle, *"Girl Cases,"* 62–63.

40. The judgment and Owen's letter are both reprinted in the 1938 white paper, *Correspondence Relating to the Welfare of Women in Tropical Africa, 1935–37* (Cmd. 5784, 1938).

41. Archdeacon Owen to *Manchester Guardian,* June 29, 1936, clipping in NA: CO 847/6/11.

42. Owen to *East African Standard,* June 18, 1936, clipping in Archives of the Church Missionary Society (hereafter cited as CMS) ACC 83 O 16.

43. See, for example, Notes on the Case of [A], Jan. 3, 1940, CMS ACC 83 O 16.

44. Owen appears not to have been involved in these discussions; the only explanation I can imagine for this is that he was absent from Kenya at the time.

BRETT L. SHADLE

45. Archdeacon Owen, letter to *Manchester Guardian,* Oct. 9, 1936, p. 291.

46. Christine Spender, "Polygamous Marriages in Equatorial Africa," *Catholic Citizen,* June 15, 1933; Arch. LeRoy to *Catholic Citizen,* Oct. 15, 1933.

47. Owen, in *Manchester Guardian,* Aug. 30, 1935, p. 177; Owen in *Manchester Guardian,* Aug. 21, 1936, p. 151. Or, in the picture Soeur Marie-André drew, "an intelligent civilized girl" married to "an old man or a leper." Soeur Marie-André, "The Legal Position of Women," *Catholic Citizen,* Apr. 15, 1938. For a more detailed description of her ideas on African marriage, see the chapter by Roberts in this volume.

48. "The Case of [A] d/o [O] w/o [O], March 1, 1940," in Owen to DC CK, Mar. 1, 1940, CMS ACC 83 O 16.

49. "Notes on the Case of [T] d/o [A] w/o [O]," Nov. 6, 1940, CMS ACC 83 O 16. Colonial officials were of many opinions on the nature of young women marrying elderly polygamists. Few officials criticized polygamy—it was among the customs they dared not touch, for fear of provoking deep hostility or, worse, of being ignored. A dramatic difference of ages made some uncomfortable. One official in South Kavirondo in 1930 believed marriage before maturity to be harmful, his only explanation being that such girls would be likely to be married to older men. W. A. Perreau, district commissioner in Central Kavirondo, reassured Owen that one particular case of forced marriage was not so bad as it first appeared: the woman was perhaps twenty-four and the husband thirty-two, and thus, the age difference was relatively insignificant. Had it been greater, it was implied, Perreau may have sided with Owen on the case. Other officials suggested that a wide difference in ages was not strictly an African phenomenon and therefore was unworthy of concern. In 1930, Katharine Stewart-Murray, Duchess of Atholl, informed the secretary of state that in Kenya, high bridewealth could mean women ended up with wealthy old men. In the margin of her letter, a member of the Colonial Office penciled, "This is not peculiar to Africa!" Philip Mitchell in Tanganyika, always among the most perturbed by the metropolitan lobbies, suggested that such marriages marked an advance over European practice. There, older men took mistresses or turned to prostitutes. In Africa, they married more wives. Questionnaire on marriage, 1930, KNA: PC/NZA 19/27; DC Central Kavirondo to Owen, Apr. 11, 1939, CMS 83 O 16; Atholl to Secretary of State, Aug. 6, 1931, NA: CO 822/38/9; Mitchell, "Female Circumcision and the Status of Women in Tanganyika Territory," Apr. 26, 1930, NA: CO 323/1067/2.

50. Some officials in Kenya admitted that females might lack the will to withstand parental "moral coercion" to marry, but they did not consider this *real* coercion. See Shadle, *"Girl Cases,"* 66.

51. W.S. Raitt, Karuru SDA Mission, Nairobi, to DC Malindi, Nov. 3, 1949, KNA: MAA 7/700.

52. DC Malindi to Raitt, Nov. 1, 1949, and Nov. 14, 1949, both in KNA: MAA 7/700.

53. The provincial commissioner of Central Province in 1957 remarked, in regard to excision in Meru, "The solution to this problem lies in the progressive education of public opinion over a considerable time rather than in attempting to overcome any prejudice by sudden action." Quoted in Lynn Thomas, *Politics of the Womb: Women, Reproduction, and the State in Kenya* (Berkeley: University of California Press, 2003), 88.

54. NCO to General Secretary, Christian Council of Kenya, Jan. 7, 1950, KNA: MAA 7/700.

55. PC Coast to NCO, Jan. 12, 1950, KNA: MAA 7/700.

56. DC Kilifi to PC Coast, Feb. 15, 1950, KNA: MAA 7/700. Some cases may have been taken to the native tribunals anyway. See Arthur Phillips, *Report on Native Tribunals* (Nairobi: Colony and Protectorate of Kenya, 1945), 127.

57. CNC, handwritten note, Mar. 2, 1950, KNA: MAA 7/700.

58. J. D. Stringer, DC Kilifi, to Chief Secretary, Apr. 13, 1950, KNA: MAA 7/700.

59. Stringer to Chief Secretary, Nov. 30, 1950, KNA: MAA 7/700.

60. M. N. Evans, handwritten note, c. Mar. 1, 1950, KNA: MAA 7/700.

61. NCO to CNC, Apr. 24, 1950, KNA: MAA 7/700.

62. NCO to CNC, Jan. 27, 1950; CNC to NCO, Jan. 30, 1950; NCO to CNC, Apr. 24, 1950, all in KNA: MAA 7/700.

63. Charles Dundas, "The Organization and Laws of Some Bantu Tribes in East Africa," *Journal of the Royal Anthropological Institute of Great Britain and Ireland* 45 (1915): 234–306, quote from 284.

64. Kanogo, *African Womanhood in Colonial Kenya*, 149.

65. For a study of recent discourses around girlhood, see Heather Switzer, "Disruptive Discourses: Kenyan Maasai Schoolgirls Make Themselves," *Girlhood Studies* 3 (2010): 137–55.

CHAPTER FOUR

Italian Weddings and Memory of Trauma

Colonial Domestic Policy in Southern Somalia, 1910–41

FRANCESCA DECLICH

MARRIAGE ARRANGEMENTS in African societies have been widely debated by anthropologists and government officers since the colonial period. In the Horn of Africa, as well as elsewhere, colonial officers and anthropologists saw marriage transactions as forms of buying and selling insofar as women were exchanged among families and/or men.[1] The Italian colonial officer Alberto Pollera described the ways consent was solicited from all actors, including the bride, and demonstrated how complex marriage negotiations focused on goods and chattels. Despite his own insights, he concluded that marriage was often little more than an economic transaction.[2]

In the contemporary era, "arranged marriages" are often considered abusive and equated with "forced marriages." In isolated cases, asylum seekers have invoked fleeing an unwanted arranged marriage as the ground for a "well founded fear of persecution" and have thus been granted refugee protection status in Europe and elsewhere.[3] In order to understand contemporary arranged marriages, it is crucial to situate them in an ethnographic, socioeconomic, historical context and to recognize the importance of the social networks into which the new spouses enter by wedding. Similarly, the notion of forced marriage is also historically constructed and, as such, needs to be contextualized in the historically determined sociocultural environments from which it stems.

In this chapter, I demonstrate that forcing people into monogamous marriages was an integral part of Italian colonial policy, as implemented in Gosha, in the Middle and Lower Juba of Somalia, during the last fifteen years of the Fascist period before the British Military Administration (BMA) took over the area in 1941. As an explicit colonial policy, however, forced marriage was completely different from the indigenous institution of arranged marriage. The prevailing indigenous practice of arranged marriages ensured that young men, women, and children in vulnerable stages of their lives were embedded in a web of controlled social relations. The Italian forced marriage policy was implemented as a mechanism of labor control over men and women, and it operated uncomfortably alongside a traditional practice of arranged marriage. Forced marriages generally took the form of wedding contracts imposed by colonial officers on couples, who were then forced to work on the colonizers' farms. But in Gosha, a Maay Maay– and Bantu-speaking area of the Italian Somali colony, forced marriages were imposed on girls only. The Italian practice in Gosha demonstrates that regardless of the purported values asserted by the colonial state, real practices subjugated women and tied them to a European patriarchal norm of family structure. Colonial forced marriages effectively conveyed power to each man and enabled unrestricted access to a girl's body, thereby permitting physical and emotional abuse of married women. By contrast, the historical practice of arranged marriages frequently ensured a web of social relations that supported the new couple emotionally and materially.

Paola Tabet has demonstrated how much of the colonial moralizing discourses about the sexuality of women, "on the legitimate or illegitimate use of the women's body," are discourses about "form of property in women."[4] Tabet's comparative analysis of marriages highlights the very diversified practices of offering sexual services in Africa and elsewhere.[5] My research builds on these observations and demonstrates how moralizing attitudes toward "polyandric" forms of marriage in southern Somalia were nothing if not a reflection of the desire to channel and control African labor.

ARRANGED MARRIAGE AND SOCIAL NETWORKS

In a subsistence farming economy, such as that in colonial southern Somalia, webs of social relations among women are essential to ensure the provision of food and availability of child care. Kinship and neighborhood

networks support women who work on farms while simultaneously raising children. Individual women, moreover, need people they can trust to
offer protection or assistance in times of need. In the absence of state-
based and religious welfare, people invest in other forms of social protection throughout their life cycle. Such protection limits choices individuals
may exercise during the course of their lives in contexts where capabilities
and aspirations are constrained both by the environment and by poverty.

In this light, it is useful to reflect on the distinction some feminist
scholars draw between negative and positive freedoms.[6] Saba Mahmood
notes that the former refers to "the absence of external obstacles to self-
guided choice and action, whether imposed by the state, corporations,
or private individuals," and the latter concerns the "capacity to realize an
autonomous will, one generally fashioned in accord with the dictates of
'universal reason' or 'self-interest,' hence unencumbered by the weight of
custom, transcendental will, and tradition."[7] Both concepts of freedom
embed the idea of individual autonomy, whereby choices and actions are
a consequence of one's "'own will' rather than custom, tradition, or direct
coercion."[8] In material contexts wherein everyone experiences resource
scarcity, webs of kinship relations and neighborhood ties provide the ideal
of freedom from relations of domination. Freedom does not exist in a
vacuum but ought to be analyzed against the context of various degrees of
dependence. It may thus be more appropriate to describe arranged marriage agreements in terms of contracts among families in which individual spouses may play more or less autonomous roles, depending on their
character and personal options. Spouses, however, ensured a web of relationships that, particularly in poverty, were crucially important.

SOMALI LINEAGES AND SOMALIA

At the turn of the nineteenth century, the country that is now split into
Somaliland, Somalia, and Puntland was inhabited by a minority of Oromo
and Bantu speakers and a majority of people who spoke Somali language;
the latter were organized in groups of patrilineages also aggregated in
larger patrilineal clans. Some practiced pastoral nomadism; some were
farm owners and farmed mainly through slave labor in riverine and interriverine areas; others were urban dwellers and traders.

Somali lineages living in urban dwellings were genealogically interrelated with the pastoral nomads and/or the farm owners, and weddings

as well as trade reinforced such ties. Several coastal groups were descendents of migrants from countries of the Indian Ocean (Hadramaut and Gujarat, for instance) and had connections with their previous countries. The population—especially in the central and southern territories of Somalia, in the urban settlements along the Shebelle and Jubba Rivers—was socially stratified: it was divided into those who had control over the territory and were considered "noble" and those considered commoners who "belonged" to lineages. Commoners might or might not have different statuses in the elders councils, subordinated to the nobles of the prominent lineages from whom they had sought protection.[9] It was not uncommon for a group initially in the position of being protected to increase in number with the arrival of members of the same clan from other areas and then override the previous "owners" of the land.[10] In addition, there was a category of people considered outcasts, composed of hunter and gatherers, ironsmiths, and other kinds of artisans; the latter lived within the other groups but were bound by rules of endogamy. Moreover, there were slaves who were bought or acquired through raids, as well as escaped or freed slaves. Finally, groups of free ex-Bantu language speakers were likely to live in the northern areas of the Shebelle River. Aggregates of lineages exerting control over a certain territory are addressed in the south as *reer*.[11] To complicate our understanding of the social organization, smaller lineages could be adopted by larger ones following different patterns, thus yielding even finer gradations among these broad categories, especially among so-called nobles. These were fluid categories, making it very difficult to map lineages and their locations in space.[12]

FORMS OF MARRIAGES AND MARRIAGE TRANSACTIONS

Within this fluid social landscape, family and lineage interactions were continuously reinforced through intermarriages. Among pastoral nomads, exogamic marriages were usually arranged to maintain alliances between patrilineages as well.[13] Unlike the situation among the northern Somali clans, marriage among the Rahanweyn interriverine groups could serve as a first step to actually changing one's clan.[14] During the first decades of the twentieth century, weddings and marriages in Somalia were held according to several modalities.[15] The marriage practices of slaves, nobles, and commoners had some variations in terms of the transactions of wealth and in the actors involved. The latter reflected the set of social relations that were activated or reinforced as a result of the wedding.

The most common was the arranged marriage, in which the families of spouses undertook most of the agreements prior to the wedding. The future spouses had some degree of consent about the choice of partner, depending primarily on the relations they had with their parents. Variations of custom, however, were recorded in different groups of patrilineages. Two ways of marrying, for instance, were reported in the 1920s among the Somali Hawyie Abgal: in the first, a boy and girl would meet and agree to elope together; in the second, the potential groom negotiated with the brother or father of the bride.[16] Among the Somali Habar Hintiro, future spouses might make an informal agreement with their respective family members before eloping: the groom might leave a cloth and some money for the mother of the bride, and she might, in turn, later hand that money to the daughter (now wed) to buy domestic tools.[17]

Within the context of arranged marriages, a bride or groom could often suggest the choice of a specific partner. But such subtle suggestions were not always involved, and adolescents often submitted to the will of their parents. Some marriages were prearranged before puberty, mostly for daughters of very old fathers or for orphans. The principle expressed in this practice was that of securing the future of the female child through an early agreement with a trustworthy man.

Because weddings were celebrated at or within one year of puberty, close relatives usually made the decision about a child's marriage. In the event that the two potential spouses were not in agreement with their families' decision, if they felt their voices went unheard, and/or if the groom was ill prepared to pay the bridewealth requested, the couple could opt for marriage by elopement.[18] This option—wherein the couple decided to escape somewhere else and thereby refuse to engage with the families' and lineages' requests in wealth—was also apparently quite common in Somaliland in the 1950s, and it still exists today.[19] After several months, the eloped couple returned to their respective families. At that point, the husband agreed to make some kind of payment reflecting the marriage transactions in order to formally establish relations between the families; otherwise, the families would not recognize the couple and would not want to meet them and their children. By seeking such reconciliation, the eloped couple hoped to reestablish webs of relations and thus guarantee future protection and support in a variety of ways.

Marriage by abduction was also possible. This kind of union was common in areas of Somalia where raids by nomads were daily occurrences, such as in frontier areas between the Oromo and Somali speakers in southern Somalia.[20] In such cases, customary law differentiated the children of the couple according to the lineage membership of the spouses. Such norms were fragmented and varied according to area. For instance, when a Somali Marrehan man abducted an Oromo Borana woman, she became a slave, but both she and her children would be considered free individuals as soon as she bore a child.[21] Alternatively, in Migiurtinia it was considered dishonorable for men to have sexual relations with slaves, apparently because most slave women were of Swahili origin.[22] A number of variations pertaining to the treatment of kidnapped women and children existed throughout Somali territory.[23]

Massimo Colucci, who compiled a consuetudinary of rights and practices in southern Somalia, demonstrated that the forms of marriages varied widely among the different lineages and groups in large territories.[24] In light of such diversity, he suggested that some forms, such as a Gherra reer case he described, were survivals of primitive stages of social organization. Among the Gherra, three forms of marriage existed: the first was by elopement (bòb) and involved a consenting woman acting without the approval of or against the will of those who had parental authority over her; the second was an irregular union, or dur-kuburs, that was engaged when a man did not have the means to respond to the requests of the family of a particular woman; and the third was the nicàh, which Colucci defined as "derived from an original buying and selling of a woman with elements of some Islamic precepts." Most interestingly, among the Gherra was a practice that he considered a remnant of "a form of collective marriage" within the reer.[25] He described this in detail:

> When all the practices that compose the nicàh . . . are completed, at the very moment in which the bride should enter the conjugal house, she rather escapes. She goes to a Gherra rer [sic] which is not her rer nor the one of her husband; there she lives bestowing herself to all those men of the rer who desire it. After a while, sometimes several months later, when the woman's pregnancy is already visible, the bride is dressed of a futa [rectangular cloth] given to her as a present, and the entire rer who hosted her—men and women, pubescents and fit— go with her to the rer to which the groom belongs.[26]

Slavery was widespread in Somalia until 1904. The actors involved in slave marriages were different than among free people, as the network of social responsibilities in the former case involved the masters. Many masters arranged their slaves' weddings. Masters of women slaves received the bridewealth for giving their slaves in marriage, and they retained ownership of the offspring of the marriage.[27] Presumably, the masters also paid for the genital labia cutting and infibulations of the women slaves.[28]

After emancipation in the early twentieth century, some former slaves maintained relations of dependence and protection with their masters. Wedding practices were recorded among freed slaves of the Somali Abgal in 1919: the groom first entered the house of the woman he liked; served the parents of the girl; built a hut; prepared the beds and the domestic tools; and thereafter forced himself, often violently, into the house of the woman he wanted. The man symbolically beat his bride with a stick while she was in the hut.[29]

Great diversity also existed in the female initiation practices of slaves as well as ex-slaves in southern Somalia. Slaves and ex-slaves who had been integrated into the main Somali clans over many generations adopted the clans' customs, including the ritual female genital cutting of girls before puberty; some escaped slaves did not adhere to this practice. Many ex-slaves who were more recently enslaved kept their own traditions as opposed to those of their masters. The Zigula and the Makua, for instance, lived in Gosha and did not infibulate women but instead cut a piece off the top of their clitorises.[30] The Njanja, many of whom lived in Gosha villages during the early twentieth century, practiced a completely different form of initiation in which a *namkungwe* (ritual teacher) taught gender habits, discipline, and sexual practices.[31] To this day, the Njanja of Mozambique and Malawi impose labia minora stretching on adolescent women, ostensibly in preparation for erotic practices.[32] The denial of feminine sexual pleasure, therefore, was not as common among slave women as it was among free Somali women who were infibulated. Both the Yao and the Njanja were matrilineal, and husbands did not control wives in a manner commonly associated with patrilineal groups. Among matrilineal people, such as the the Makua of Mozambique, slavery and marriage of women by abduction was quite common and gave rise to a peculiar, if inferior, status within the lineage of the master to the children of the slave woman. But within some generations, the entire lineage, stemming from the woman kidnapped and enslaved as a concubine/wife, might reverse its status.[33]

At the turn of the twentieth century, the area of Gosha in the Lower Jubba was inhabited mainly by descendants of escaped or freed slaves of a wide variety of origins. Customs involving initiations and marriages were therefore quite diverse and varied according to the degree of dependence such groups and single people had maintained with their masters after emancipation. Freed slaves, for instance, who belonged to slave lineages and who were integrated into the main clans, often lost their original languages and assimilated many Somali customs. In contrast, slaves who had emancipated themselves and rejected their former masters were more likely to transmit to their descendants the customs of their groups of origin, such as the Yao, Njanja (there referred to as Niassa), Zigula, and Makua.[34] The Zigula and the Makua, who in the 1980s spoke Kizigula, initiated their girls with *mphambula* and/or *gango*, which were different stages of *buinda* (female initiation) celebrations. These initiatory celebrations involved divinatory dances, attended exclusively by women in the case of the *mphambula*, which followed a period of seclusion at home of the pubescent girl.[35] The Yao, who at the time spoke the Maay Maay version of Somali, held some puberty initiation rituals in which masks of lions would appear in the village during the period of seclusion following a girl's first menstruation. Some villages held schools of initiation in which age sets of adolescent girls and boys were assembled, divided by gender, and taught under the leadership of the *namkungwe* (ritual leader).[36]

In the 1930s, weddings in the largely ex-slave villages of Gosha involved considerable diversity among those of different ethnic origins. The groom's family had to collect goods and wealth to convey to the family of the bride. Then and now, the exchange of goods that sanctioned those wedding was an occasion for exchanging prestige goods among the women's network of the mother of the bride.[37]

Earlier Italian observers of the Gosha seemed to have imposed stereotypical Western notions on the matrimonial and sexual habits of the people they encountered. They seemed rather unaware of the criteria underlying the marriage transactions. In the next section, I highlight how their arguments were mainly driven by the need to devise possible ways to control the labor force and channel it into industrial and agricultural development.

THE SOUTHERN SOMALI COLONY LABOR FORCE AND SEXUAL HABITS

Two large rivers, the Shebelle and the Jubba, cross the southern area of the Somalia colony, formerly known as Benadir, and provide fertile ground for agricultural production. Gosha is the southernmost territory of the region then called Benadir. Until 1905, the administration of the Benadir region, which comprised the port of Uarsheikh and the three coastal towns of Mogadiscio, Merca, and Brava, was an Italian protectorate. Colonial government operated by concession and was, in contemporary parlance, outsourced to private companies—first the Società Filonardi and later, from 1898, the Società Anonima Commerciale del Benadir.[38]

One of the more problematic aspects of this "privatized" colonial administration model emerged via a scandal about the persistence of slavery in the colony.[39] Slaves cultivated productive areas, and domestic slavery was widespread and not truly prohibited during the rule of the private companies. In a narrative that mirrored that of the contemporaneous Congo Free State, the two companies were accused of having ignored the international resolutions mandating the abolition of slavery in all African territories. Specifically, the companies did not impede the inland trade of slaves from the western hinterland—and actually colluded with slave traders—by collecting taxes on the trade in slaves, as demonstrated by transactions recorded in the *qadi*'s register, containing the records of the civil cases dealt with by Muslim judges.[40] International pressure, a public scandal in Italy, and subsequently a parliamentary inquiry ultimately ended private contracts and thrust the territory under formal colonial control. Investigations into these abuses provide important information about the conditions of slaves and the role of African labor in the agricultural development of the colony.

The productive farming areas along the Shebelle River were cultivated with the labor of slaves until the turn of the nineteenth century. Two large communities of freed or escaped slaves existed, Hawai and Gosha. Escaped slaves and slaves who were freed by the colonizers either went there on their own initiative or were sent there by the Italian officers. The officers regarded the farms surrounding these communities as not fully exploited and asserted that only a new reorganization of the labor force could allow a productive agricultural policy. Reporters envisioned a labor force drained from Gosha, along the Jubba River, and ushered toward the farms of the Shebelle.[41]

The Italians conducted two investigations about the presence of slavery in the colony: the first by members of Parliament republican Gustavo Chiesi and Ernesto Travelli on behalf of the Società del Benadir, and a second by Luigi Robecchi Bricchetti for the Società Antischiavistica. In spite of their differing political and economic agendas, both investigations recommended that slavery not be abolished by decree. The reports observed that southern Somali society was so deeply based on slave labor that freeing all slaves at once would create uncontrollable disorder among former slaves and the current Somali employers/masters. Indeed, the 1904 Somali Bimaal revolt was at least partly prompted by rumors that the Italians wanted to abolish slavery immediately.[42] The southern Somali of Benadir depended on the labor of slaves' lineages, and a flourishing slave trade originated not only from seaports but also from the hinterland. Slaves were seized from among the Oromo. Somali farm owners had vested interests in keeping their slaves, and tribal and clan leaders insisted that they had only tolerated the Italian presence in their country because they were promised they would not be deprived of their slaves.[43] Many Somali leaders maintained that they would not be able to survive without slaves: they feared that their farms would be abandoned and that nobody would shepherd their herds.[44] To be sure, both private companies accepted these general principles on their arrival in the region.

LAND AND FORCED LABOR

Chiesi's study recommended to the Italian Parliament that three factors had to be taken into account if adequate modalities were to be created to make the region agriculturally productive—namely, land, capital investment for infrastructure, and labor. With respect to land, Chiesi suggested that for specific experimental purposes, such as cotton production, some land concessions should be acquired from the natives who held nominal tenure.[45] Later, however, he asserted that all land of the colony was to be declared state owned (*demaniale*); thereby, some of it could be distributed to customary owners so that the greater part could be allocated by the state to investor concessions.[46] In Eritrea, the Italian defeat at Adwa, Ethiopia, pointed to the riskiness of large dispossessions of land, but in Somalia, this policy was proposed for the most fertile areas of Somali Benadir.[47]

Advocates of colonial development encouraged private investment. Capital investments were to be solicited from private investors for the purpose of building infrastructure. The final and crucial aspect of colonial development rested on the control and management of African labor. Chiesi argued that development depended upon the capacity "to regulate and discipline the habits" of the people to the point that they became adequate to the tasks involved in the future agricultural development of those areas. He expressed concern that certain habits might "render sterile and parch the biological sources of the race," and he suggested controls on "the immoral behavior," including the "promiscuity of the polygamic customs."[48] Polygyny was thus identified as "the big, the true plague of Gosha."[49]

The republican argued that freed slaves or escaped slaves performed little in the way of work. He also exaggerated their sexual habits, which he saw as characterized by a sort of polyandry. Such behaviors, he believed, hampered the reproductive capacity of that population and spoiled the "race." Chiesi thought that some marriages were not properly institutionalized; for instance, he asserted that "no special commitment rules the weddings of the Wa-Goscia—a man takes a fancy of a woman—it does not matter if she was or still is of somebody else—he attracts her to him, she is his wife for as long as his crush lasts."[50] No agency whatsoever was accorded to the woman in the choice of husband. His description assumed that men managed the interchangeability of couples.

Chiesi drew on useful information regarding this type of marriage from officers' reports on a nearby Hawai community. He wrote, "In Hawai's population there is a scarcity of women [and] with the exception of a few chiefs who take advantage of their own authority and also have two wives, only half of the men [are] married and, therefore, it is rather hard to pursue the objective of increasing the population number."[51] The scarcity of women among the emancipated communities of Hawai was thus a common lament.[52] Supposedly, female scarcity was a problem in Gosha too, in spite of it being a much older settlement.[53] To be sure, the scarcity of women, together with the matrilineal habits of many of the ex-slaves, may have been among many factors that fostered women's opportunity to choose their husbands and to change husbands relatively easily, despite the lack of agency accorded them in Chiesi's description.

Why were there more men than women in these communities? One reason might have been an increased number of male slaves in those communities. It is likely that most slaves who were freed or who were declared free by the government after presenting themselves to the Italian authorities were males. They were usually sent to either the Hawai or the Gosha communities.[54] Chiesi counted approximately twenty-five hundred individuals who had arrived in Hawai in the last decades of the nineteenth century.[55] However, reading between the lines of the report, it may well be that women freed by the Italians were not sent to the communities in equally large numbers. Some Somalis Chiesi interviewed were convinced, rightly or otherwise, that emancipated women were bought by Italian officers as concubines and not actually freed,[56] and it was indeed a habit of some officers to organize orgiastic events with them.[57] Moreover, women with dependent children would have little reason to move to a freed slave area, especially if they had to leave their children with their former masters. They would likely have employed different strategies after emancipation.

The experience of domestic slavery was deeply gendered.[58] As I have argued elsewhere, in southern Somalia slave women and men had differing chances for social mobility.[59] A *suria* (concubine) who gave birth to a master's child could raise her status and gain access to a relatively better standard of living. And even if she did not bear her master a child, escaping may well have meant abandoning her own children, since most women became pregnant shortly after menarche (which was also the age of their marriage). As such, women above sixteen or seventeen years of age may have preferred not to flee from slavery or their masters. It was quite different for male slaves, who had little claim on their own children and left them behind with their mothers. Some slave women actually might have had vested interests in remaining slaves if only to have their children supported by their masters. Some former slave women migrated to urban areas where their lives may have been somewhat easier than for women who remained with their former slave husbands on remote farms. Other former female slaves chose to live as *masuria* (pl. of *suria*) on farms of wealthier lovers where their living standards might be significantly improved.[60]

It has been asserted that in certain Swahili contexts and in the Mauritanian context described by Ann McDougall in this volume, the word *suria* may not be translated directly as "concubine," for once the owner had entered into such a relationship with his woman slave, he could no longer sell her as a slave and upon his death she became free.[61] Masuria had different prerogatives depending on the juridical school respected in a specific area. However, entering into an intimate web of dependence with a master could afford a woman more security than marrying an emancipated slave, with whom she would have to flee and farm in a remote area; living on a farm in an area of inconsistent precipitation; or working as a prostitute. For example, the records of the qadi of Brava report a slave woman at the turn of the twentieth century who, having been kidnapped and sold as a slave among the Mobileen, escaped and returned to her owner in Brava rather than emancipating herself in one of the communities of freed slaves or requesting a

FRANCESCA DECLICH

manumission certificate, for which she would have felt in debit toward those who awarded it.[62] In other words, women had different sorts of roles than slave men, and they were likely to return to the domestic slavery circuit. Hard manual labor on a master's farm was more easily expected from men than from women, and hence, the men had a stronger incentive to escape.

Slave women were often more fully integrated into their masters' households. Farther south in Mombasa, slave women participated in their masters' weddings.[63] We do not know enough about such practices in the Benadir coast, but as late as 1988 in Mogadishu and along the coast, women of ex-slave lineages performed erotic dances at weddings of their Somali former masters, while "noble" Somali women did not dare to dance themselves, as it was considered shameful to mimic coitus. In the Benadir, however, former female slaves who maintained close relationships with women of their masters' families did not diminish class distance as happened in Mombasa.[64]

At the same time, Italian authorities were deeply concerned about freed slave women. The government tried to restrain the movement of women without husbands, especially when this could lead such women to work on their own rather than for somebody else or even for the government. On December 2, 1903, around twenty women, some of whom were slaves asking for manumission certificates, went to the government offices to request permission to accompany the caravan of the explorer Ugo Ferrandi from Brava as far as Bardera.[65] The officials denied them the certificates on the grounds that caravans were forbidden to travel with women and that such women could only have one intention—to practice prostitution. The women wanted to travel closer to their own original homelands in the Boran, where they had been caught as slaves. The Italian officials rejected their petition. The officials held that that Oromo-speaking Boran area was continuously raided by slave traders active in the Mobileen and the Audegle markets and, therefore, unsafe. In short, leaving aside the scorn with which these women were treated, they were denied the right to travel to Bardera.[66]

The report justified the denial in this way: "None of those domestic slaves had reasons to complain about the respective masters, because they earn enough, by carrying water and construction material for the Government, and they could earn much more if, rather willingly, [they] would not abandon their work to dedicate themselves to gluttony and guzzling."[67] The argument demonstrates that granting manumission papers had very little to do with offering individual "freedom" to these women; rather, it was a matter of controlling their movements, labor, and bodies. That these women wanted to set themselves free and to return to their own country, even if it meant exchanging sexual services for protection in the caravan, was not seen as a legitimate concern.

At the heart of this incident was the female slaves' desire to control their own sexuality. As slaves, the women could be forcibly taken as concubines by their masters, who could obtain their sexual favors without payment. But the possibility of offering sexual services for payment, rather than being obliged to have sex without earning money, may have been an attractive option.[68] In Zanzibar and Pemba islands in 1902, many freed women slaves dedicated themselves, sometimes temporarily, to prostitution.[69] And when prostitution provided a good income and autonomy, it might also give rise to envy and revenge on the part of men and previous owners.[70] In Brava, an appeal was made to the court to regulate the extent of ownership of a woman slave who also sold her body occasionally.[71] This activity was certainly more remunerative in urban or densely populated areas than in remote farming ones. But prostitution could also be engaged in occasionally on an ad hoc basis to earn money, which the Italian resident in 1903 did not allow.

In short, the Italians sought to organize the transition from slavery to "freedom" as a way of transferring the labor force from one owner to another, whereby the latter was in fact the colonial state. Women's bodies were also considered property whose ownership was to be regulated by the state regardless of the women's own wishes. The law proposed by Gustavo Chiesi and Ernesto Travelli to favor a transition from slavery to paid work underscores this. It explained that freed slaves, once they received their manumission certificate, would be required to live for five years in the place assigned by the governor (or on his behalf by the resident of the station); further, they would be obliged to supply work under the conditions and compensation established in predetermined contractual forms. Article 22 called for the habitual vagrancy of freed men and the prostitution of women to be punished with imprisonment for two months, with an extra month for each recidivist action.[72]

PROMISCUITY AND LABOR

Chiesi recommended that most of the workers should be chosen from the Gosha area, which was more densely populated than Hawai, in part to impose some order on that community, given its lack of work discipline.[73] The republican argued that once freed—or left to their own devices—the Gosha did not work as before. If they obtained a good harvest, they refused to work for others and only engaged in libertine pursuits and sexual promiscuity.[74] In the economic interests of the colony, which needed "a numerous and healthy population of workers," attention was to be placed on "disciplining the present infinitely free marriage consuetude."[75] Despite this alleged sexual freedom in Gosha, there was no scarcity of women.[76] In contrast, in Hawai, which was ruled by a strict work regimen, men outnumbered women.[77]

Chiesi thus linked his labor policy to a moral reorganization in this part of the colony, designed to prevent a degradation of the race and thus improve the labor force. A new law was to be immediately promulgated, in line with Muslim precepts, obligating men to work in order to prepare a dower for their bride or brides; it would remain with the woman in case of repudiation without fault. Chiesi believed that such a law would prompt men to work in order to accumulate the necessary wealth for this dower and would serve as a deterrent to the circulation of wives from one husband to another, a practice that constituted "a degrading polyandry, i.e. one of the main causes of sterility in the women."[78] Marriages had to be registered with the qadi with payment of a nominal tax.[79]

In other words, polyandry was considered dangerous to the genetic reproduction of the group. Therefore, it was thought that polygyny should be fostered because it was more in line with the free Somalis' traditional habits and served as a first step toward the longer-term objective of abolishing polygamy in all its iterations and establishing monogamy. For this purpose also, "moral propaganda through example and facts" and practical persuasion about "the advantages of constituting regular families" would have to be enacted.[80] This was a prelude to the later policy in Gosha, between 1935 and 1937, whereby forced labor recruitment included the enforcement of monogamous unions, known as *nikaax talyiani*.[81] This entire agricultural development effort was designed so that it could only be implemented by monogamous worker couples. Ironically, the best study analyzing the indigenous cultivation practices, conducted years earlier, had depicted the ideal farm labor force as being composed of a man, his wife, and their children.[82] Even with no direct intention of imposing such a monogamous family structure, the agronomist study implied it was the best model.

Among the many who advocated for planned farming in Somalia, it was agronomist Romolo Onor, who traveled in the region's farms and moved along the rivers to verify the feasibility of such plans, talking with local farmers, studying indigenous farming methods, and assessing the successes and failures of other farming experiments. Based on the data collected, he recommended a system of "colonia parziaria" or more precisely co-investment.[83] Italian investors would share the risks of farming with their Somali laborers, variously investing in and working the land and together progressively improving indigenous methods. According to Onor's assessment, the local conditions did not lend themselves to industrial farming; animals could not be used to plow because of tsetse flies, infrastructure was nonexistent, and last but not least the available labor force was inadequate due to the abundance of land devoted to subsistence cultivation. When the need arose for intensive field labor on their own farms, workers would abandon salaried work to dedicate themselves to the family subsistence farms. And yet, even if people could be coerced to work on Italian farms (a policy already in place to a certain extent), their labor would be inadequate for the purposes of increasing the agricultural production.[84] Onor was, however, concerned that the state would supply labor for a handful of private Italian investors. Giacomo De Martino, governor of the Somalia Italiana between 1910 and 1916, as well as Governor Carlo Ricci disregarded Onor's concerns, as did the Fascist senator and governor between 1926 and 1928, Cesare Maria De Vecchi. He decided to support the opposite policy, in which Italian investors were trusted to comprise the only real engine to enhance productivity on Somali farms. Land was to be given in concessions to Italians, who were to find agricultural manpower among the local population of farmers, thereby endorsing a policy of coerced labor.

In southern Somalia, local farmers preferred working on their small subsistence farms rather than working as paid laborers on Italian estates. Subsistence labor ensured food security even during slavery, when slaves were allowed to work in their fields daily or at least once a week.[85] The only way to channel manpower to the Italian farms was to coerce the population with forced labor mandates.[86] Forced labor was accomplished through the farming contract, or *Bertello,* which compelled workers to labor for ten hours a day.[87] Forced labor was to be provided by the villages closest to the Italian farms and assembled with the help of local recruiters paid by the government. Local leadership was co-opted into the system with salaries and through the benefit of being allowed to decide, to a certain extent, who could skip such forced labor.[88]

To be able to supply sufficient labor for the Italian farms, the resident of Margherita (today's Jamaame) applied new marriage regulations that were considered useful for improving worker output. Adolescent and adult males and females from Gosha were forced to work all week on Italian estates. Following Chiesi's ideals, the resident of Margherita believed that monogamous weddings would discipline and increase the productivity of both men and women, and they both would work on the Italians' farms. The men would be more productive if they all had a wife in close proximity. Indeed, the colonial government assumed the presence of women would improve a number of aspects of male productivity: a man with a wife would not seek sex with local prostitutes, he would not need money to pay for prostitutes, and he would have a wife to cook for him. All of this would contribute to the "reproduction" of the labor force. Women, for their part, would be obliged to follow the men they married and work in the farms rather than in the villages. These new regulations, known locally as *nikaax talyiani,* allowed a man to choose a wife without obtaining either her own or her relatives' consent.[89] As stated by many who were interviewed in Gosha, a man could just go to the Italian district authorities and make his own choice of only one woman to be his wife. A man from the village of Mugambo in 1988 explained, "You could only request one woman and you were not allowed to divorce her. You were both slaves of the estates."[90] Yet even though consent was not requested from the bride and her family, the new regulation endowed individual men with a power they had never enjoyed before.

Giving a man the authority to choose a wife without her consent (even if he was only allowed one wife) was definitely an incentive in a society in which the traditional procedure required a host of social relations: an agreement between families, a marriage contract, and a number of marriage transactions whereby the man demonstrated his high esteem for his future bride. Arrangements for traditional marriages required time and determination on the part of the groom and his family, who also had to assemble the goods for the ceremony. The new decree swept all that away. Any man could walk into the Italian resident's office and indicate the girl he wanted; she then became his wife. Although identifying himself to the resident meant that the man could no longer avoid forced recruitment into labor, which was not easy anyway, this strategy certainly drew to the estates men who otherwise might have resisted or revolted. Unrestricted access to one woman was the reward for compliance.

Nonetheless, this strategy gave rise to a number of conflicts within the Zigula, dividing the group from the inside. Some men embraced this type of marriage to exact revenge against families who had previously denied them a wife. Sometimes, a man utilized this decree to marry a girl who had been refused to him and promised to another, just to spite the girl's relatives and the promised husband.[91] Nikaax talyiani allowed men to skip the preparation of bridewealth for their spouses, as well avoid other responsibilities to the bride's family. But women were left at the mercy of abusive relations, and many were deprived of the social guarantees previously offered by the arrangement of the marriage transactions through kin. In fact, in this context many girls were married before puberty. An elderly Zigula man remembered that some girls were taken in marriage when they were just six or seven years old.

Not only were many of the girls selected as wives under this system extremely young, they were also taken from the ritual seclusion of their initiation into adulthood on the occasion of their menarche, before the initiatory *buinda* ritual dance. Mame Nthukano Mnongerwa recalled how she and two other teenage girls were taken from the seclusion of the buinda ritual:[92]

> I was taken to the town of Margherita (Jamaame) to be handed over to the man who had requested me in marriage. As I was a *mwali*—in the process of being initiated—my head and body was covered with a white *kaniki*, that is, white cotton cloth. In Margherita, I was told that five men had chosen me as their wife and it was only when I was in the Resident's presence that he discovered that I was already married to Mze Mnongerwa. The Resident recommended that my husband come to reclaim me as a matter of urgency, otherwise he would give me to another man on the spot.[93]

Mnongerwa arrived, and the resident released Mame Nthukano. She also recalled, "Myself and other girls who had not yet passed our menarche were taken from home under the pretext of working on the estates. Instead, we came back home with the *ndanga* on our head."[94] (The *danga madow* is a black scarf used by married women.) In other words, some of the girls were taken away from their ritual space with the excuse that they

FRANCESCA DECLICH

were to go to work but instead were forced to marry an unwanted man on the estate.

Women who married this way did not receive any of the goods and commodities new wives usually acquired as a result of gift exchanges through the marriage transactions. Such goods not only were for domestic purposes but also constituted a small sum of capital in the form of exchangeable commodities that new wives could sell or barter in order to gain prestige within the neighborhood and/or to purchase other kinds of commodities they wanted.[95] The regulations thus fostered a gendered interaction characterized by abusive male domination, and they also created chaos in local social organization, a fact remembered by both male and female oral informants.

In contrast, nikaax talyiani enforced by colonial decree caused great social confusion and profound internal divisions. Male oral sources mentioned these results, but only women recounted the mistreatment and damage they suffered as a result of this decree. I collected oral histories of these experiences through female biographies. Although both genders recalled the chaos created by "the Italian wedding" as negative, men's and women's oral and written testimonies of the period produced very different results. For instance, an anonymous report mentioned by K. C. Dower in 1944 asserted that during the Italian colonial period, "bachelors were forced to marry women who had been born and bred on the estate."[96] Men of the Jubba River area remembered not the imposition of marriage but rather the liberty of being able to choose a wife without the traditional political or familial constraints. Male informants also recalled that men would not have stayed on the estates the whole week if they did not have women to sleep with. Women remembered being married without their or their parents' consent, before their menarche, and before they could be initiated; further, they did not receive any of the usual gifts presented to a bride by her mother's friends and relatives.

Taking both female and male oral sources into account produces a more complete picture of the cultural and institutional chaos created by the Italian regulations. Male sources tended to view continuities between kin-based arranged marriages and nikaax talyiani.[97] If one listens as well to female voices, one has the impression that it was the brides who were hurt most by the Italian wedding law. Brides were forced to marry men who were willing to harass them as well as harm their relatives and ancestors. Moreover, the brides were obliged to establish permanent relationships with men and thus give up the social guarantees usually supplied by the network of relatives assembled through the very process set up by the exchange of marriage transactions. And as a further offence to the brides' families, mothers lost their daughters' support in the domestic domain without having any voice in the matter. By putting into practice a policy of forced marriages, the Italians promoted a situation that led to abusive behavior, even encouraging and legitimating it in the eyes of local men. The policy certainly negatively empowered individual men over women as never before in their social group.

SLAVERY, FREEDOM, AND OPTIONS IN MARRIAGE

In this chapter, I have explored the differences between arranged marriages and forced marriages in "Italian Somaliland." Arranged marriages before the era of forced labor in Gosha offered the new spouses and their children entry into webs of social relations and familial protections. These marriages also clarified specific rights of heritage and an individual's position within one or more lineages. By contrast, the colonial era's nikaax talyiani was a method to ensure labor for private Italian farms by forcing marriages on women and in the process opening new chances for men to exploit the privileges accompanying their gender. More specifically, men were able to disentangle themselves from the ties of dependence within their respective social networks, ties they would otherwise have acquired by performing a traditional marriage. The Italian marriage arrangements eliminated the need to establish new connections and responsibilities toward the family of the spouse, to exhibit respect for their own relatives, to assume responsibilities toward the offspring, and so on. In this way, men were offered a sort of "positive" freedom that allowed them to break the constraints and norms of responsibility within kinship relations.

By intertwining sexual policies and forced labor in order to foster industrial agricultural production, the forced marriages of the colonial era empowered men to abuse their wives without social repercussions. Even in situations where men were obliged to marry women born on the estate, they still had the ability to choose which women they preferred. Brides had no ability to consent to or decline these arrangements. Colonial forced marriages thus constituted a total subjugation of women. But in either case, individual "positive" freedom of choice in this context may not be the only criterion for describing choices in marriages because, as one informant said, both husbands and wives were slaves in the farms. Colonial era forced marriage fostered a new idea of masculinity. And yet, old women in 1988 were still traumatized by the unexpected abuse they suffered as adolescent brides on the colonial estates.

The nikaax talyiani of the colonial era demonstrates the significant differences between customary arranged marriages and forced marriages. As outlined by Mariane Ferme in this volume, the Western legal emphasis on the rights of the individual misconstrues the choices individuals make within social environments shaped by scarcity. In such contexts, men and women often choose to invest in social networks that provide subsistence security and protections against abuse, even if it means they have less "choice" in marriage partners. Moreover, as discussed in the introduction to this volume, the concept of personhood underscores the embedded nature of individuals within social webs, rather than as autonomous rights-bearing individuals detached from kin and communities. The individualization of the self as a basic aspect of personhood is a specific cultural construction that is historically determined and located in certain contexts of Western society.[98] Although the evolution of the self as progressively more individualized is generally considered a crucial aspect of modernity, culturally constructed views of less individualized personhoods that entail cooperation among members of groups may be more adaptive in circumstances dominated by specific constraints inherent in material poverty.

We also need to be mindful about claims on tradition, as Bala Saho discusses in this volume. Claims on tradition are most often political claims for maintaining hierarchies and privileges. However, moral claims to subsistence security and protections from domestic abuse also flow from invoking tradition. The Italian policy of forced marriage fostered the individualization and emancipation of the male subject from his community as opposed to the acquiescence and submission of women, establishing a new male-centered hierarchy of nonindividualized and dependent women in marriages that, at the time, was presented as promoting the health and moral improvement of colonial subjects.

NOTES

I wish to thank the three editors of this book for their incredible patience in going over the chapters and fruitfully discussing with me the best shape mine could take in interaction with the other contributors in this volume.

1. Carlo Conti Rossini, *Principi di diritto consuetudinario dell'Eritrea* (Rome: Tip. dell' Unione editrice, 1916), 755–59; Werner Munzinger, *Studi sull'Africa orientale* (Rome: Voghera Carlo, 1890), 402–3; A. Pollera, *I Baria e i Cunama* (Rome: Reale società geografica, 1913), 162–73; Massimo Colucci, *Principi di diritto consuetudinario nella Somalia italiana meridionale: I gruppi sociali—La proprietà* (Florence: La Voce, 1924), 37.

2. Pollera, *Baria e i Cunama*.

3. E.g., the Somali Dutch ex-member of Parliament Ayaan Hirsi Ali. See Ali, *Infidel: My Life* (New York: Simon and Schuster, 2007).

4. Paola Tabet, *La grande beffa: Sessualità delle donne e scambio sessuo-economico* (Soveria Mannelli: Rubbettino, 2004), 34.

5. Paola Tabet, "Du Don au Tarif: Les Relations Sexuelles Impliquant une Compensation," *Les Tempes Modernes* 490 (May 1987): 1–53; Tabet, "'I'm the Meat, I'm the Knife': Sexual Services, Migration and Repression in Some African Societies," in *A Vindication of the Rights of Whores,* ed. Gail Pheterson (Seattle, WA: Seal Press, 1989), 204–26; Tabet, *La grande beffa*.

6. Saba Mahmood, "Feminist Theory, Embodiment, and the Docile Agent: Some Reflections on the Egyptian Islamic Revival," *Cultural Anthropology* 16, no. 2 (May 2001): 207.

7. Ibid.

8. Ibid.

9. For the institution of lineage adoptions in Somali called *arifa* and *sheegad,* look also at Francesca Declich, "Fostering Ethnic Reinvention: Gender Impact of Forced Migration on   Bantu Somali Refugees in Kenya," *Cahiers d'Études Africaines,* no. 157 (2000): 25–53; Enrico Cerulli, *Somalia,* 3 vols. (Rome: Amministrazione Fiduciaria Italiana della Somalia, 1957–64); Corrado Zoli, *Oltre Giuba* (Rome, 1925), 139–40; and B. Helander, "Clanship, Kinship and Community among the Rahanweyn: A Model for Other Somalis?" in *Mending Rips in the Sky: Options for Somali Communities in the 21st Century,* ed. Hussein M. Adam and Richard Ford (Lawrenceville, NJ: Red Sea Press, 1999), chap. 4, 134–35. See also Helander, *The Slaughtered Camel: Coping with Fictitious Descent among the Hubeer of Southern Somalia* (Uppsala: Uppsala University, 2003); Virginia Luling, *Somali Sultanate: The Geledi City-State over 150 Years* (Piscataway, NJ: Transaction, 2002); Francesca Declich, *I Bantu della Somalia: Etnogenesi e rituali mviko* (Milan: Franco Angelli, 2002).

10. Enrico Cerulli, *Somalia,* vol. 2, 83. See also Cerulli, *Somalia,* vol. 1, 67; Zoli, *Oltre Giuba,* 141–44.

11. Colucci, *Principi di diritto consuetudinario,* 34–36. The modern correct Somali spelling is *reer,* although Italian sources report it as *rer*.

12. Helander, "Clanship, Kinship and Community." Older maps of Somalia usually depicted lineages living in certain areas, but these maps do not reflect with precision the distribution of the territories by the controlling clans or reer. Hence, ethnic group names such as Migurteen, Habar Hintiro, Abgal Hawyie, Rahanweyn, Tunni, Gherra, Zigula, Macua, and Gosha in this text refer to either lineages, clans, or reer as from the sources. The majority of the people spoke Somali and Somali

dialects, some spoke Oromo and Bantu languages, and customary habits were not at all the same.

13. Mohamed Abdi Mohamed, "Somalia: Kinship and Relationships Derived from It," in Adam and Ford, *Mending Rips*, chap. 10, 151–53. We know very little about marriages between rural- and urban-dwelling lineages. Virginia Luling made a study of the prevalent marriage patterns in Afgoi in the sixties, but her material is as yet unpublished.

14. Helander, "Clanship, Kinship and Community," 137.

15. Cerulli, *Somalia*, vol. 1, 305–10; I. M. Lewis, *Marriage and the Family in Northern Somaliland* (Kampala: East African Institute of Social Research, 1962); S. Musse Ahmed, "Traditions of Marriage and Household," in *Somalia—The Untold Story: The War through the Eyes of Somali Women*, ed. Judith Gardner and Judy El-Bushra (London: CIIR, 2004), 51–68; Colucci, *Principi di diritto consuetudinario*, 35–37.

16. Cerulli, *Somalia*, vol. 2, 303.

17. Ibid., 404.

18. Colucci, *Principi di diritto consuetudinario*, 37.

19. Lewis, *Marriage and the Family*, 12.

20. Cerulli, *Somalia*, vol. 1, 57, 67–69.

21. Ibid., 83.

22. Ibid., 84.

23. Ibid., 83–84; Cerulli examines the great diverstiy of such practices based on extensive interviews during the early twentieth century.

24. Colucci, *Principi di diritto consuetudinario*, 35; Cerulli, *Somalia*.

25. Colucci, *Principi di diritto consuetudinario*, 36, 37.

26. Ibid.

41. The futa is a piece of cloth worn in the fashion of a local dress. This old text used the Italian spelling *rer* for the modern Somali spelling *reer*.

27. Francesca Declich, "Dynamics of Intermingling Gender and Slavery in Somalia at the Turn of the Twentieth Century," *Northeast African Studies* 10, no. 3 (2003): 58; Luigi Robecchi Bricchetti, *Dal Benadir: Lettere illustrate alla Società Antischiavistica* (Milan: Soc. editrice La Poligrafica, 1904), 29.

28. The practice that persisted among ethnic Somalis involved female labia cutting followed by the sewing of the wound to leave only a small hole for urination; tradition states the hole should be no larger than a grain of corn. I will call this practice infibulation to distinguish it from other forms of less dramatic female genital mutilation.

29. Cerulli, *Somalia*, vol. 2, 305–6.

30. Declich, *I Bantu della Somalia*, 156.

31. Ibid., 216–17.

32. During fieldwork in 2007, I had confirmation that this practice is still common in Ulongwe in Mozambique at the boundary with Malawi.

33. C. Geffray, "La condition servile en pays Makhuwa," *Cahier d'Études Africaines*, no. 100 (1985): 505–35.

34. In 1986, the girls' puberty initiation practices were differentiated by lineages and groups.

35. Declich, *I Bantu della Somalia*, 207–12.

36. Ibid., 202–6.

37. See how marriage transactions were exchanged at weddings in 1986 in Francesca Declich, "The Significance of Marital Gift Exchange among Women in Southern Somali Riverine Communities on the Juba River" (Msc diss., London School of Economics, 1990). The institution of the *fidis*, the event of publicly showing the presents for the bride during the wedding celebrations, was an important occasion for women's social circles.

38. See http://archivio.camera.it/patrimonio/archivio_della_camera_regia_1848 _1943/areo10/documento/CD1100056725, accessed November 3, 2013.

39. Robecchi Bricchetti, *Dal Benadir*, 9; Istituto Coloniale Italiano, "Gustavo Chiesi," *Revista Coloniale* (1909): 3–15, 7.

40. Gustavo Chiesi and Ernesto Travelli, *Le questioni del Benadir: Atti e relazioni dei commissari della Società* (Milan: Società commerciale italiana del Benadir, 1904); Alessandra Vianello and Mohamed M. Kassim, *Servants of the Sharia: The Civil Register of the Qadis' Court of Brava, 1893–1900* (Leiden: Brill, 2006); Robecchi Brichetti, *Dal Benadir*, 33.

41. Gustavo Chiesi, *Note per lo sfruttamento agricolo, commerciale, industriale del Benadir* (Milan: Tip. La Stampa Commerciale, 1905), 20.

42. Chiesi and Travelli, *Questioni del Benadir*, 275–76.

43. Gustavo Chiesi, *La colonizzazione europea nell'Est Africa* (Turin: UTET, 1909), 292–94, 297.

44. Chiesi and Travelli, *Questioni del Benadir*, 266.

45. Chiesi, *Note per lo sfruttamento agricolo*, 20.

46. Gustavo Chiesi, "Per la messa in valore della Somalia meridionale Italiana e Benadir: Studi e proposte relativi alle colonie di Dominio Diretto," in *Congresso degli Italiani all'Estero*, ed. Istituto Coloniale Italiano (Rome, 1908), 21–23.

47. Giulia Barrera, "The Construction of Racial Hierarchies in Colonial Eritrea: The Liberal and Early Fascist Period (1897–1934)," in *A Place in the Sun: Africa in Italian Colonial Culture from Post-unification to the Present*, ed. Patrizia Palumbo (Berkeley: University of California Press, 2003), 84; Tekeste Negash, *Italian Colonialism in Eritrea, 1882–1941: Policies, Praxis and Impact* (Uppsala: Uppsala University, 1987), 126.

48. Chiesi, *Colonizzazione europea nell'Est Africa*, 638.

49. Ibid., 639.

50. Ibid., 638.

51. Reported in Chiesi and Travelli, *Questioni del Benadir*, 300; see also Robecchi Brichetti, *Dal Benadir*.

52. Robecchi Bricchetti, *Dal Benadir*, 147.

53. Gosha had been reported as already settled by escaped slaves seventy years prior to Klaus Von der Decken's travels of 1865. Otto Kersten, *Baron Klaus von der Decken's Reisen in Ost-Africa in den Jahren 1862 bis 1865* (Leipzig, 1871), 303.

54. Chiesi and Travelli, *Questioni del Benadir*, 238.

55. Ibid., 299.

56. Ibid., 270. Chiesi, *Colonizzazione europea nell'Est Africa*, 285–86. This situation highlights the mutual misunderstandings entailed in the encounter between, on the one hand, the status given to concubines and slave women according to customary law or local shari'a interpretations and, on the other hand, the ideas the colonizers had about lovers or prostitutes.

57. Ibid., 270.

58. For a discussion, see especially Margaret Strobel, *Muslim Women in Mombasa, 1890–1975* (New Haven, CT: Yale University Press, 1979).

59. Declich, "Dynamics of Intermingling Gender," 45–69, 62.

60. Ibid., 55–56, 62–65.

61. Katrin Bromber, "*Mjakazi, Mpambe, Mjoli, Suria*: Female Slaves in Swahili Sources," in *Women and Slavery: Africa, the Indian Ocean World, and the Medieval North Atlantic,* ed. Gwyn Campbell, Suzanne Miers, and Joseph C. Miller (Athens: Ohio University Press, 2007), 116–17.

62. Declich, "Dynamics of Intermingling Gender," 64; Vianello and Kassim, *Servants of the Sharia.*

63. Strobel, *Muslim Women in Mombasa,* 8–21.

64. Ibid., 21.

65. Chiesi and Travelli, *Questioni del Benadir,* 121.

66. Ibid. In British East Africa also, apparently, slave concubines became entitled to manumission some years later than other slaves, as reported by Brett Shadle in this book.

67. "Gluttony and guzzling" is the translation for the Italian *crapula.* Chiesi and Travelli, *Questioni del Benadir,* 121.

68. Robecchi Bricchetti, *Dal Benadir,* 27–28.

69. According to a 1902 report cited in Chiesi and Travelli, in an agglomerate of barracks on Zanzibar where prostitutes were working, 75 percent were freed slave women; see a report concerning slavery abolition written by the British consul and diplomatic agent, Mr. Cave, to the Ministry of Foreign Affairs in London, Marquess of Landsdowne, dated February 21, 1902, and translated into Italian by Chiesi, in Chiesi and Travelli, *Questioni del Benadir,* 285.

70. See, for instance, the case of the woman slave Auvai reported in Robecchi Bricchetti, as described in Declich, "Dynamics of Intermingling Gender," 58–59.

71. Robecchi Bricchetti, *Dal Benadir,* 27–28.

72. Chiesi and Travelli, *Questioni del Benadir,* 292.

73. Chiesi, *Colonizzazione europea nell'Est Africa,* 635–38; 646–47; Chiesi and Travelli, *Questioni del Benadir,* 307.

74. Chiesi, *Colonizzazione europea nell'Est Africa,* 647.

75. Chiesi and Travelli, *Questioni del Benadir;* Chiesi, *Colonizzazione europea nell'Est Africa.*

76. E. Perducchi, *Statistica della Goscia, fatta sul luogo paese per paese* (Rome, 1901), Archivio Storico del Ministero dell'Africa Italiana (ASMAI) Pos. 68/2. These statistics show an approximately equal number of men and women. Gosha was much farther from Mogadishu (approximately 380 kilometers) than Hawai (approximately 40 kilometers).

77. Chiesi and Travelli, *Questioni del Benadir,* 300; Robecchi Bricchetti, *Dal Benadir,* 147.

78. Chiesi, *Colonizzazione europea nell'Est Africa,* 638.

79. Ibid., 638–39.

80. Ibid., 639.

81. *Nikaax talyiani,* here quoted in Somali language writing, literally means "matrimonio all'italiana."

82. Romolo Onor, *La Somalia italiana: Esame critico dei problemi di economia rurale e di politica economica della colonia* (Turin: Bocca, 1925), 86.

83. Ibid., xxiv, xxix, 78–79.

84. Ibid., 78.

85. Colucci, *Principi di diritto consuetudinario,* 74–75; Gherardo Pantano, *Nel Benadir* (Livorno: Belforte, 1910), 96; Onor, *Somalia italiana,* 80.

86. Angelo Del Boca, *Gli italiani in Africa orientale,* vol. 2, *La conquista dell'impero* (Bari: Laterza, 1986), 83, 203–7.

87. Angelo Del Boca, *Italiani, brava gente?* (Vicenza: N. Pozza, 2009), 163–65.

88. Field notes (1988), o/sto. For more information on the classification system used for my field notes, see Francesca Declich, "Gendered Narratives, History, and Identity: Two Centuries along the Juba River among the Zigula and Shanbara," *History in Africa* 22 (1995): 117. See also Francesca Declich, "Unfree Labour and Resistence along the Juba," in *Resisting Bondage in Indian Ocean Africa and Asia,* ed. Edward A. Alpers, Gwyn Campbell, and Michael Salman (London: Routledge, 2007), 24–39.

89. Field notes (1988), o/sto: 120; field notes (1988), p/sto: 49; Kenneth Menkhaus, "Rural Transformation and the Root of Underdevelopment in Somalia's Lower Jubba Valley" (PhD diss., University of Southern California, 1989), 259.

90. Field notes (1988), p/sto: 65.

91. Field notes (1988), o/sto: 65.

92. For a description of the ritual, see Declich, *I Bantu della Somalia,* 207–12.

93. Field notes (1988), o/sto: 65.

94. Field notes (1988), cr2: 49.

95. Declich, *Significance of Marital Gift Exchange among Women.*

96. K. C. Dower, *The First to Be Freed. The Record of British Military Administration in Eritrea and Somalia, 1941–1943* (London, 1944), 60.

97. Menkhaus, *Rural Transformation,* 259. For a study of marriage transactions along the Jubba River, see Declich, "Significance of Marital Gift Exchange among Women."

98. Anthropological and psychological literature on this issue is flourishing. See, for instance, Hazel Rose Markus and Shinobu Kitayama, "Cultures and Selves: A Cycle of Mutual Constitution," in *Perspectives on Psychological Science* 5, no. 4 (2010): 420–30; Richard A. Shweder and Edmund J. Bourne, "Does the Concept of the Person Vary Cross-culturally?" in *Cultural Conceptions of Mental Health and Therapy,* ed. Anthony J. Marsella and Geoffrey M. White (Dordrecht: D. Reidel, 1982), 97–137.

PART TWO

Postindependence Transformation

Ukuthwala, Forced Marriage, and the Idea of Custom in South Africa's Eastern Cape

ELIZABETH THORNBERRY

SINCE 2008, a series of cases in which young girls had been abducted and forcibly married to much older men have come to the attention of South Africa's national media. In some instances, the girls' parents or family members were implicated in the forced marriages; in others, girls were abducted without the knowledge of their families. Participants and investigators in these cases, which have occurred primarily in the Eastern Cape and KwaZulu-Natal Provinces, grouped them together under the heading of "*ukuthwala* cases" (where *ukuthwala* refers to a form of irregular marriage that can involve the abduction of women for the purpose of marriage). Police statistics show that 255 cases of ukuthwala were reported nationally in 2012–13.[1] This number represents a small fraction of all such cases, since many young women face social and familial pressure not to report their experiences and indeed to stay in these unwanted marriages. Even when complaints are made, however, they do not often result in prosecution. The 255 reported cases led to only 21 arrests.

Public discussion of these abductions has revolved around the question of custom. Should ukuthwala be understood as a legitimate custom? And if so, do these particular cases meet the customary requirements of ukuthwala? More fundamentally, to what extent do the ethical claims of custom override those of human rights? For women's rights activists, ukuthwala is a form of forced marriage and a "harmful traditional practice," a label that simultaneously accepts the customary status of the practice and rejects its claim to legitimacy.[2] For many of the parents and would-be husbands involved in these abductions, however, custom serves as a defense of ukuthwala. Police often share this belief, which contributes to the low rate of prosecution.[3]

However, representatives from the Congress of Traditional Leaders of South Africa have asserted that such marriages are contrary to the actual custom, a claim that is also backed by several scholars of customary law. Here, I will argue that the stakes in calling ukuthwala a custom or, conversely, insisting that such forced marriages are not properly customary are grounded in an ongoing struggle in contemporary South Africa over the locus of the right to determine the nature and content of recognized custom. At the same time, however, these debates are constrained by a shared commitment to a historical understanding of custom. Then I will explore what nineteenth-century (precolonial and colonial) understandings of custom, marriage, and ukuthwala might reveal about these contemporary debates. I will contend that the practice of ukuthwala shifted over the course of the nineteenth century, both taking on a much more coercive form and becoming "customary" in a way that it had not been previously.

CUSTOM AND THE IDEA OF HISTORY

In contemporary South Africa, the English phrase "it is our culture" is used by black South Africans to explain a variety of practices unfamiliar—and occasionally distasteful—to their white, "colored," and Indian fellow citizens, as well as to foreign researchers.[4] The South African constitution provides that "persons belonging to a cultural . . . community may not be denied the right, with other members of that community, to enjoy their culture."[5] The claim that a practice is traditional or customary carries an ethical weight in less technical usages too, in English as well as in Xhosa and its close relative Zulu—the most commonly spoken African language in South Africa and the lingua franca of the African population of the country's largest urban center. In contemporary Xhosa and Zulu, the word *isiko* is typically used to render "culture," "custom," and "tradition."[6] In twenty-first-century South Africa, claims about custom have become central to a set of debates over the rights of women to access property and participate in politics within rural areas.[7]

At least three sources of authority for the appeals to custom are at work in current discussions. First is the body of officially recognized custom that

ELIZABETH THORNBERRY

was encoded in various ways during the colonial and apartheid periods and that continues to function as law in many areas despite its dubious legal status. This conception of custom has the vigorous support of some traditional leaders, who wish to ground their authority in a discrete set of customary powers rather than in the consent of those whom they govern. Second is the "living custom" that has been recognized as the appropriate source of legal authority in South African jurisprudence. Living custom is defined by the current practices and accepted standards of local communities, and as such, it is much more heterogeneous and flexible than the versions of customary law that received official sanction in the past. Politically, it is invoked by people seeking to reject the blanket authority claims of traditional leaders, as well as by activists and academics seeking to reconcile the idea of custom with the rights guaranteed by South Africa's constitution. Finally, people also use the term *custom* to refer to historical and particularly precolonial norms and practices. In Xhosa, the word *isiko* has the connotation of historical continuity. Although not necessarily a reference to precolonial practice, the term often carries an ethical claim based on the rejection of the right of a government formed through colonial conquest to demand changes in the culture of the colonized. This last sense of *custom* appears in the invocation of African custom as a justification for acts that defy the norms of urban South African political discourse—including, most sensationally, during the rape trial of President Jacob Zuma shortly before his election; it is also used as a bulwark against demands that custom be "developed" to comply with the constitution.[8] Depending on the context, references to customary law—that is, the subset of custom that is enforced in legal venues, whether traditional courts or those run by the South African state—may invoke any of these three conceptions of custom.

These three definitions of custom are irrevocably intertwined. Living customary law has been indelibly shaped by the official versions enforced over the past century and a half. At the same time, for many people the moral authority of even living custom rests on its claim to a strong continuity with historical practice. And of course, precolonial practice—itself unstable, flexible, and varied—contributed strongly to both the forms of custom that were enforced by colonial and apartheid governments and to the living customary law now practiced. Nonetheless, recognizing the different valences that an appeal to custom can take on is helpful in identifying the stakes of the invocation of custom in the current debates over ukuthwala marriages.

From a strictly legal perspective, ukuthwala's customary status is not relevant. The 1998 Recognition of Customary Marriages Act specifically requires the consent of both parties in order to validate a customary marriage, and it sets the minimum age of marriage at eighteen.[9] More recently, the 2013 Prevention and Combating of Trafficking in Persons Act explicitly criminalized forced marriage. Nonconsensual ukuthwala "marriages," then, should receive no legal recognition, and the men involved are open to prosecution.[10] Indeed, depending on the specifics of the case, men participating in ukuthwala marriages can be charged with abduction, kidnapping, assault, or rape; where women's families participate in ukuthwala, they can be charged as accessories to the last three of these crimes.[11] The ability of the state to modify or withhold recognition of custom is the subject of legal debate, given the constitutional protection of both customary law and the more general right to cultural practice.[12] However, the constitution subordinates both of these rights to the individual rights protected by the bill of rights, so a claim that the state must recognize ukuthwala marriages would be unlikely to prevail. The customary status of ukuthwala does, though, carry significant discursive weight in both local and national discussions of the practice. And even as the various voices in these discussions invoke different sources of authority for custom, they share a propensity to invoke past practice in their arguments.

The attacks on the customary nature of ukuthwala as currently practiced prompt a number of specific critiques. Academics sympathetic to African customary law, including T. W. Bennett, have described the normative practice of ukuthwala as a "mock abduction" in which a young woman "would be expected to put up a show of resistance."[13] Although Bennett acknowledges that the ukuthwala custom carries the "potential for . . . violence and [rape] to force women into submission," he considers that those who engage in such violent acts are "exploiting culture for their own ends" rather than engaging in a legitimate customary practice.[14] In this view, the problem with current ukuthwala practices is that these are forced marriages, taking place against the will of the young women concerned. By contrast, in the "correct" form of ukuthwala, young women would merely feign their unwillingness to go along with the marriage. Rhetorically, this critique has the advantage of eliding any potential conflict between the rights of the young woman and the right to culture, since culture properly understood already accommodated the wishes of young women in marriage.[15] The "true custom" as practiced in the past is carefully distinguished from the current, exploitative practices.

ELIZABETH THORNBERRY

Major representatives of traditional leadership in the Eastern Cape have offered their own critiques of recent cases of ukuthwala. Xhanti Sigcawu, a member of the Xhosa royal family and a representative of CONTRALESA (Congress of Traditional Leaders of South Africa), differentiated between ukuthwala properly practiced, "[when] the families of the young man and the girl would meet and negotiate . . . [and] reach an arrangement," and kidnapping, "when a husband takes a woman without interaction with her parents."[16] Nangomhlaba Matanzima, chairperson of the Eastern Cape House of Traditional Leaders, drew a slightly different distinction, telling the South African Press Association that "they are taking children from 13, 14. . . . That is not ukuthwala, that is not a custom. You can't go for the little ones."[17] In these critiques, the problem with ukuthwala is not the young woman's or girl's lack of consent but rather the failure to gain the consent of the family or the breaching of the culturally appropriate lower boundary on the age of marriage. The advantage of this line of argument lies precisely in its avoidance of the issue of women's consent to marriage. Traditional leaders can condemn a practice that garners negative publicity and threatens to taint the entire realm of custom without undermining a broader claim to the authority of household heads over their dependents. These claims must also be understood as, at least in part, an assertion of the authority of traditional leaders to make decisions over what counts as proper custom and what does not. And again, current practices are condemned by reference to their departure from the correct customs of the past.

Yet members of families implicated in ukuthwala cases, as well as some (certainly not all) other residents of Eastern Cape communities where the practice is prevalent, claim that ukuthwala as currently practiced is indeed customary. According to Ncedisa Paul, who works for a local health nongovernmental organization (NGO), "People say that's just the way it is—it is part of their culture, they say."[18] Similar turns of phrase recur in research on the issue. Kate Rice's ethnographic research has likewise found that people in the Eastern Cape view ukuthwala as "an older, more 'traditional' practice"—even, in the words of one man, as an example of "walking exactly on the culture."[19] And though many prominent traditional leaders condemn nonconsensual forms of ukuthwala, others defend it as customary. In 2012, Mandla Mandela, Thembu chief and grandson of Nelson Mandela, called ukuthwala "a pure custom, which has not been diluted by European sensibilities," implying that consent itself is a European concept.[20]

All sides of this debate implicitly invoke history to assert the rightness of their own position. Those who claim that current forms of ukuthwala are customary—and conversely, those who assert that they violate customary norms—turn repeatedly to the past to provide evidence for their assertions. A history of ukuthwala cannot directly adjudicate between these competing claims, yet it can show how certain forms of the practice came to be broadly accepted as customary, whereas others are contested. What, then, is the history of ukuthwala in the Eastern Cape? Do current forms of the practice have deep historical roots, or are they perversions of a more benign practice? Certainly, British perceptions of forced marriage as a problem predated the colonial conquest, when treaties between the Cape Colony and independent Xhosa polities included provisions for the protection of Christians who "refus[ed] to comply . . . with the Kafir customs of forcible abduction or violation of females." And an 1870 set of regulations in what would become Nqamakwe warned the area's residents against "the forcible abduction and marriage of young women."[21] Early descriptions of Xhosa marriage "customs" (such as those found in John Maclean's *Compendium of Kaffir Law and Custom*) do not reference the term *ukuthwala* or describe similar practices, but disputes over "irregular forms" of marriage that took place without the consent of a woman's parents appear in the earliest extant colonial court records, beginning in the 1860s.[22]

The term *ukuthwala* itself began to appear in public discussions of marriage, as well as in both civil and criminal court cases, during the 1880s.[23] People used the word to refer to a variety of irregular forms of marriage that took place without the prior consent of a woman, of her father, or of both. In its early usages, then, ukuthwala included both the types of consensual mock abductions that contemporary commentators seek to assert as the "proper" form of the custom and also more violent abductions. The Tembu chief Matwa described it as follows: "The custom of 'twala' is after a girl is carried off by her sweetheart, the girl is followed up by her brothers, and then a marriage is arranged."[24] The reference to a girl's sweetheart implies an ongoing, consensual relationship. However, the term was also applied to cases in which, for example, a father told the court that his daughter "was forced against her will to go to" the man who had taken her away and that "the messengers did not ask my consent to let them have the girl."[25]

The customary status of ukuthwala was also the subject of debate. Men accused of abduction sought to defend themselves by referencing the "custom of ukuthwala," but one father retorted, "I call it stealing a man's child."[26]

ELIZABETH THORNBERRY

In 1883, William Sigenu thought that the "modern custom" of ukuthwala was "becoming very general," and the magistrate A. H. Stanford complained that "of late years a custom known as ukuthwala has come much into vogue."[27] These descriptions contain something of a contradiction when read alongside contemporaneous definitions of isiko (custom) itself as "our fathers and progenitors did thus, and ruled thus, and handed down their manners and customs to us. These ancient customs are virtually unalterable, but . . . [may] imperceptibly become modified, or slightly altered by mutual consent."[28] In what sense, then, could one refer to ukuthwala (or anything else) as a "modern custom"? This uneasy language choice points to a deep tension in understandings of ukuthwala in the nineteenth century as well. Indeed, as I will argue, much of the current debate over the supposedly "customary" status of ukuthwala marriages—and over the proper form of this custom—can be traced to shifts in the economic and social context of marriage that took place in the late colonial period.

MARRIAGE AND CONSENT IN NINETEENTH-CENTURY XHOSALAND

In order to understand these debates, we must situate ukuthwala within the larger context of the use of a discourse of custom to regulate sexuality and marriage. In the precolonial and colonial periods, Xhosa household heads used the language of custom to assert control over the sexuality of their female family members. This control was a broadly accepted social norm, if far from universally adhered to. Families monitored the sexual lives of unmarried daughters through regular physical examinations in order to ensure that premarital sexual experimentation stopped short of penetrative intercourse. Young men and women were permitted to engage in *ukumetsha*, meaning, in the words of one woman, "that men and women get together and go through all the performances of married people save and except actual sexual intercourse and copulation."[29] Although European commentators considered ukumetsha an "unnatural connection," it set strict limits on the forms of sexual play that unmarried young women engaged in. Customary fines for the seduction of unmarried girls enforced these limits. John Knox Bokwe reported, "Seduction of virgins according to the customs of the Amaxosa ancients, generally got one of the heaviest fines inflicted over all the other crimes."[30]

The precolonial and early colonial discourse of custom extended familial control to the choice of marriage partner. The family of either the woman or the man could initially broach the subject of marriage, and negotiations took place between representatives of the families, not between the prospective spouses themselves.[31] A young woman was expected to assent to her father's or guardian's decision. Ludwig Alberti reported in 1807 that "a matrimonial alliance is agreed upon and concluded, without the consent of the girl being required, who in this matter is simply dependent upon the wish of her parents."[32] Women were not expected to approach marriage joyfully or with overt enthusiasm; rather, they were to exhibit a degree of grief over the transition from childhood home to marital family. Even a much-desired marriage was a solemn affair for the bride, who was "lectured on her future conduct" by the groom's family while "standing before them in perfect silence."[33] This discourse shaped the evidence of many of the African witnesses who testified before the 1883 Commission on Native Law and Custom, which canvassed "experts" on Xhosa custom across the Eastern Cape—including William Sigenu and A. H. Stanford, quoted earlier—in order to decide whether and how customary law should be accommodated by the colonial state. Several witnesses who appeared before the commission affirmed that a woman

> is not consulted; she is called to the kraal where the men are assembled, and they say to her, "You must smear yourself with red clay today, we are going to send you to so-and-so," meaning her intended husband. She then gets herself ready, and the bridal party leaves accordingly. Even if the girl says she does not wish to go with the man mentioned, she will be compelled to do so. If she goes to the chief, she would be ordered to obey her parents.[34]

The affective performance that weddings required of young women acknowledged the subordination of personal desires to familial obligations.

These ceremonies thus placed familial control over marriage within a broader framework of respect, obedience, and deference to custom. In the words of Thuka, an elderly Ngqika Xhosa man, "We train up our children to obedience in order that when they marry they are good and obedient wives. If we allowed them their own wills at the kraals where they were brought up, they might want to use their own wills at their husband's kraal."[35] Even Xhosa men who opposed "forced marriage" agreed that "according to the old custom, if a girl refused to go where her father wished her, she was beaten."[36] These senior men were speaking to a commission charged with deciding the future of customary law in the Cape Colony, and they had every interest in staking the largest possible claim to authority over their children. As I have argued elsewhere, the discourse of custom that men presented in such circumstances conceals the practical limits of these claims. Yet the claims did have moral authority, as missionaries residing in the Eastern Cape found out when they attempted to intervene in disputes between young female converts and their fathers over the fathers' desire to arrange marriages to non-Christian men. In one case, the chief Gwashu "sent one of his daughters to be married to a man who had already one wife. The young woman was very unwilling to go in consequence of an impression which she had that by so doing she should sin against God," but go she did.[37] These cases contributed to the missionary estimation that "a father has absolute authority over his daughter, and can dispose of her in marriage as he pleases. Sometimes a degree of attention is paid to the inclinations of the child but in general the predominant principle with the father is to make the best bargain for himself that he can."[38] When one Wesleyan convert rejected her family's choice, missionary Samuel Young recorded her family's response: "She was then addressed by her uncle (a Chief of considerable influence) upon the evils of disobedience to her father . . . and also upon the impropriety of a girl's refusing to conform to a custom which had been handed down to them by their fathers."[39] The discourse of custom (*amasiko*) insisted that a young woman submit to her family's choice of a marital partner.

COLONIALISM AND THE CONFLICT OVER CUSTOM

If the discourse of custom assigned control over women's sexuality to their fathers and husbands, it also set the stage for disputes between men over sex and marriage. As Brett Shadle's work in colonial Kenya reminds us, the interests of men themselves were not uniform, even within one generation.[40] As the interests of fathers were sometimes pitted against those of husbands or suitors, men also invoked *amasiko* (customs) to claim exceptions to the broad principle of familial control of women's sexual and reproductive labor. These conflicts created opportunities for women to exert power over their own lives, but they did not disrupt the generalized claim that female sexuality should remain under the control of their families.

Such conflicts of interest were perhaps most evident in marriage negotiations. Parental permission was an essential part of a valid marriage in nineteenth-century Xhosaland; it was the passage of bridewealth that made a marriage. The immediate payment of bridewealth, followed by a ceremony held at the homestead of the husband's family, seems to have been widely recognized as a normative ideal. This form appears in most accounts by European observers, as well as in later works such as J. H. Soga's *The Ama-Xosa*, that self-consciously narrate marriage "customs."[41] In many—perhaps most—marriages, however, the passage of bridewealth was processual, more closely matching the transactions described by John Comaroff in Tswana communities.[42] Marriages might have begun with the payment of a few cattle, with the expectation that subsequent payments would bring the bridewealth up to the normative level of eight to twelve cattle, at which point a ceremony would ideally be held to mark the marriage. Such accommodations were particularly important in times of economic stress, as experienced in western Xhosaland during the late 1850s and 1860s—the period following the twin disasters of "lung sickness" (bovine pleuropneumonia) and a millenarian movement that called for the mass killing of cattle, both of which devastated cattle herds.[43] The status of such marriages, however, was open to dispute if conflict arose between father and husband. In one 1861 case, for example, Jikelana told a colonial court that "plaintiff co-habited with my daughter from about the commencement of the lungsickness (1855) until last winter . . . they never had a dance [ceremony] . . . I allowed her to live with him until he could afford a proper dowry which I think would have been about ten head of cattle." Ntsabo, by contrast, considered that he had already completed his marriage to Jikelana's daughter and owed no further bridewealth.[44]

To come to a satisfactory arrangement, men who wished to marry—or to find wives for their sons—needed to persuade the women's families to accept the bridewealth they could offer. Ukuthwala, whether it took place with or without the consent of the women involved, was one way for would-be husbands to exert pressure on women's parents. The implicit threat that a couple might live together—or at least sleep together—without benefit of marriage provided an incentive to negotiate. Ukuthwala was effective in placing pressure on women's families in part because of the tight conceptual link that existed between sex and marriage. Evidence from rape cases shows the degree to which having sex with a woman was seen as synonymous with marriage. In cases from the early colonial period, men invoked marriage both as a justification for nonconsensual sex—as when Mpaubani asked the father of the girl who accused him of rape, "How did I rape her when she is my wife?"—and as a reason to commit rape—as

ELIZABETH THORNBERRY

when Kupiso confessed to the court in 1880 that "I wanted to steal Nonto-zonke and make her my wife . . . I woke her up for the purpose of asking her to be my wife." When she refused and began to call for her father, Kupiso "threw her down and ravished her."[45] This link between sex and marriage remained an important part of understandings of rape into the late nineteenth century. In 1893, a woman's assailant claimed, "I proposed to Mary and she accepted me" (which Mary denied), seeking to explain his presence in her family's home as a part of courtship behavior.[46] A woman assaulted on a footpath the same year recounted to the magistrate how she "asked [her assailant] if I was his wife."[47] The conceptual link between sex and marriage meant that marriage excused sexual coercion, and sex could—some men hoped—make a marriage.[48] Ukuthwala marriages, whether coercive or consensual, traded on this same link.

The claim that ukuthwala marriages had the sanction of custom, then, allowed young men to claim social legitimacy for their actions and to gain leverage within marriage negotiations that they did not otherwise have. The stakes of this claim were magnified by the recognition of customary law within the colonial legal system—a recognition that was formalized in the legislation annexing the "Native Territories" of the Transkei and that was applied on an informal basis in the Ciskei.[49] Colonial courts applied customary law in civil cases between African litigants. Colonial recognition raised the stakes by advancing the claim that ukuthwala was not simply a practice but also a legitimate custom that the courts should recognize. By the 1880s, the practice of "abducting" one's desired bride in an effort to force her father's consent to the match was recognized in colonial courts as having the status of custom. As Justice of the Peace John Verity explained in a letter to the solicitor general, "It is a [Xhosa] custom to abduct (*twala*) a girl as a preliminary step to marriage."[50] This recognition in turn magnified disputes over what actions, precisely, this supposed custom legitimated.

During the colonial period, the word *ukuthwala* was variously translated—and litigated—as "abduction" and "elopement," the latter potentially forming the basis of a civil claim of seduction. As an alternative route to marriage, the term encompassed a number of different departures from normative marriage practices. European witnesses assumed that these so-called abductions happened with the cooperation of the women involved, and this was often substantiated by evidence. As one woman told the magistrate, "He is my man, I term him my husband. I went away with him. I never received my father's consent. I went with him of my own free will."[51] One headman explained to the Nqamakwe magistrate's court in 1891 that ukuthwala cases were frequent and that the woman was "generally a consenting party."[52] And ukuthwala did work in many cases to persuade reluctant guardians to permit a marriage. In one bridewealth dispute, a woman's brother told the court that "the plaintiff at first carried off my sister under the custom of '*ukutwala*' but subsequently paid four head cattle dowry and I consented to his marriage on condition that he should pay out 10 head in all. To these terms I still adhere."[53] Although the men argued over the appropriate amount of bridewealth, the woman's brother was willing in principle to assent to a marriage that had begun through ukuthwala. Some men also used ukuthwala to pressure their own fathers to provide support for marriage; after Tshemerse "carried off one of Dilika's girls," his father agreed to pay the bridewealth necessary to convert this action into a marriage.[54] By committing ukuthwala, a son could drag his father into negotiations over compensation payments, hoping that the father would see the wisdom of negotiating a marriage in the process. The contentious dynamics at work are evident in the way that the details of Tshemerse's marriage entered the archival record: he was accused of assaulting his father, with whom he had not been on good terms since the ukuthwala.

Despite its increasing recognition as a "custom," however, ukuthwala remained controversial. Some fathers objected strenuously to young men's efforts to bypass normative procedures and payments in forging a marriage; as one told the court, "I call it stealing a man's child."[55] The defendant in an 1889 Nqamakwe civil case admitted to the court that he "know[s] it is wrong to 'twala' a girl. [Although] it is a crime among us in Tembuland to 'twala' a girl it is commonly done." He justified his actions, however, by stating that "the woman was not a virgin when I 'thwala'd' her she had already had a child."[56] The recognition of ukuthwala as "custom" happened over the objections of men who tried to insist on its status as a wrongful, if common, act. These objections foundered, however, on the colonial state's sharp delineation between enforceable custom and unenforceable practice; in the eyes of the state, ukuthwala either qualified as custom or did not, and its frequency in practice made its recognition as custom the path of lesser resistance for colonial magistrates. This elevation of practice to custom offers one way in which to understand the description of ukuthwala as a "modern custom."

ELIZABETH THORNBERRY

Yet while inscribing ukuthwala as enforceable custom, colonial administrators were at pains to distinguish between "correct" and "incorrect" versions of the practice. In the former, which they insisted was normative, men staged mock abductions of young women who usually knew in advance and consented. In any case, the couple would not have sex before marriage negotiations had been concluded or, as A. H. Stanford put it, the woman "in the meantime not having been treated as a wife."[57] Certainly, many cases of ukuthwala did follow this description—and the court records that contain the most detailed evidence on the practice necessarily oversample the more contentious cases. However, it is clear that throughout the colonial period Xhosa men and women used the term *ukuthwala* to refer to a broader array of practices, including instances in which young women were subject to significant violence and raped. Even in the earliest extant cases, some men did push the limits of what was acceptable as part of an ukuthwala marriage. In one early colonial case, four men were accused of abducting a nineteen-year-old girl for one of them to marry; although they claimed that she was a willing participant, she told the court otherwise, and a witness observed them beating her to force her to cooperate.[58] The insistence that such cases were not correct forms of ukuthwala did not eliminate them. If anything, the reconceptualizing of ukuthwala as *lawful* because *customary* provided increased rhetorical justification for men to engage in actions that increasingly departed from the normative form of ukuthwala.

In a dramatic case that reached the Eastern Districts Court, Buti Swartbooi attempted to ukuthwala Martha after she objected to their engagement and asked her father to return the bridewealth cattle that Buti had paid.[59] According to Buti's family, her father proposed that Buti thwala Martha, since he could not return all of the bridewealth. Martha's father strenuously denied this suggestion, although Martha herself told the court that she had left her father's homestead and was "running away from the marriage. My guardian was annoyed & fetched me back." In any case, Martha was vehemently opposed to the union, and her abduction was a violent affair during which Buti's friends beat her with a *sjambok* (a rhinosaurus hide whip) to force her to accompany them. In handing down his conviction, the resident magistrate wrote,

> To "twala" or carry off a girl is a custom of the natives though it is
> not usual where the marriage is to be by Christian rites. It is done
> secretly by the lover assisted perhaps by one or two friends carrying

off the girl when found alone, the girl offering little or no resistance. A "twala-ing" in the manner it was conducted in the present case, even accepting the defence account, would certainly not be considered regular. If [the father] had consented it would have been the easiest thing possible to have arranged to carry off the girl secretly.

The case was appealed to the Eastern District Court, where the solicitor general asserted that "this Court will not recognize the barbarous custom of 'twalaing' as a defence to a charge of assault which will be committed on a girl." Buti Swartbooi pushed the bounds of what could be condoned as ukuthwala beyond the willingness of either Martha's family or the colonial state. In East London, however, Pieter Soldaat was more successful in justifying abduction and rape through an appeal to custom. Nomini told the court that she "had known Pieter for three years and we have been sweethearts all the time." She would have married Pieter "if my guardian is willing," but she "was not willing that Pieter should have sexual intercourse with me" without marriage. Her brother and guardian had already arranged her marriage to another man, and he told the court that "it is a native custom for a man to take a girl away. Pieter was wrong in taking my sister away as she was about to be married to Notoyi." The complexities of this situation apparently overwhelmed the solicitor general, who declined to prosecute Pieter for either abduction or rape, writing: "It is difficult to apply the technicalities of our law of abduction to people whose custom it is to carry away girls from their home, and to give them moderate and acceptable compensation of a beast for such a wrongful act."[60] The colonial approach to custom could not comprehend that an act might be customary, in the sense of existing as an acknowledged practice in Xhosa communities, without being considered acceptable. Because colonial officials did not think of custom as a subject of contestation but rather assumed that an entire community had to accept a custom for it to be valid, they could not reconcile an acknowledgment that ukuthwala was customary with a complaint against it. Men who committed ukuthwala without the consent of the women involved used the vagueness surrounding the act's relationship to custom to legitimate sexual assault.

IRREGULAR MARRIAGE AND FAMILIAL CONSENT

As Buti Swartbooi's case suggests, by the late nineteenth century the term *ukuthwala* was being used to describe instances of what would by the twenty-first century be described as forced marriage. Rather than young men or women attempting to increase their influence over their marriages, household heads had begun to use ukuthwala as a tactic to (re)assert control over women's marriages. This shift had its roots in a broader set of changes in negotiations over marriage in the last decades of the century, as young men and women gained more power to choose their own marriage partners.

As long as the norm of familial control over marriage remained broadly accepted within Xhosa communities, the necessity of eventually winning fathers' consent placed limits on the forms of ukuthwala that might end in accepted marriages. Although the threat of premarital sex played a role in convincing women's families to recognize these unions, the need for recognition persuaded most men to remain within socially acceptable boundaries. It also meant that most (though not all) ukuthwala unions did involve the consent of the woman, since her implicit threat to remain with her would-be husband regardless of parental consent significantly increased the pressure on families to assent to the union.

Over the second half of the nineteenth century, however, interventions by the colonial state threatened the hegemony of familial control over female sexuality. Christian missionaries and colonial officials alike decried "forced marriage" and advocated for a mechanism to ensure female consent to marriage. Although proposals to resolve the issue by enforcing marriage registration on the model of Natal were never implemented, magistrates did order the dissolution of marriages when they decided that women had been coerced. As Robert Dick, special magistrate at Tamacha in King Williams Town, explained, there were still "a large number" of cases of forced marriage in his area. Women, he claimed, were aware that they could "appeal to the magistrate for protection," but they "never avail themselves of the privilege." Instead, a man and woman "live together for a short time, and then she comes up to complain of his harsh conduct."[61] The presence of magistrates' courts thus changed the balance of power in the negotiation of marriages, reducing fathers' abilities to control their daughters' marriages. Nathaniel Umhala agreed that forced marriage was becoming "very seldom" because people "begin now to see that it is unnatural and unkind, and the law stops them also."[62]

As revealed in the variety of testimony given on the subject of forced marriage to the 1883 commission, colonial influence on this matter was not uniform across the landscape of the Eastern Cape. Christians, who inherited the missionary concern for forced marriage as part of their general concern for Xhosa sexual depravity, were more likely to actively espouse new models of female choice in marriage. Tshuka, an Ngqika man living near the Presbyterian school at Lovedale, attributed the greater immorality that he perceived on mission stations to the fact that "their parents can no longer endisa (marry) them, and the girls themselves wish to exercise their own will with reference to marriage."[63] Opposition to forced marriage also was one way by which Fingo men distinguished themselves from Xhosa. Mendela, a Fingo headman in Engcobo district, maintained that "according to our old customs, a girl was not forced to marry a man but we got this custom among the [Xhosa]. Now, since we have come under Government, we have reverted to our old custom, and do not force a girl to marry against her wishes."[64] David Matomela, a Fingo headman in Peddie, related the rejection of forced marriage to the founding myth of Fingo origins in a different way, telling the commission it was true that "in Natal . . . a father [could] force a girl to marry without consulting her wishes" and that "it was the same in Hintza's." According to Matomela, Fingos began "to consult the girl's wishes" only "since we came amongst the white men."[65] Revealingly, George Mabandla, who testified along with Mendela, claimed that "among the Fingoes both systems are practised. The better class of men will not force their girls to marry, but the other class will force them against their will."[66] As Poppy Frye has argued, Fingo identity came into being alongside a new status hierarchy;[67] to say that only the "better class" of Fingos rejected forced marriage suggests that such rejection was—along with agricultural innovation and Christian conversion—a distinctive part of Fingo identity. Finally, the effect of colonial interventions on marriage negotiations also varied from west to east in the Eastern Cape. In the west, where colonial intervention had a longer history, even non-Christian headmen testified that parental control was on the decline. Pombani noted that "in former days we used to compel our daughters to marry the man we selected for them. Now we have learned this is not right and the girls wishes are consulted."[68] Further east in the Transkei, by contrast, significant areas were still independent in 1883, and the colonial legal system was not yet a force in the social landscape.

Across the region, however, there was a consensus that men's ability to control their daughters' marriages had declined over the last few decades of the century. In addition to the influence of Christian doctrine, social and economic forces were eroding familial control over marriage. The rise of

ELIZABETH THORNBERRY

labor migration provided young men with independent access to the cattle necessary to pay bridewealth and increased their leverage in marriage negotiations; for some couples, this development also gave young women greater voice in the choice of their marriage partners. The livestock epidemics of the 1880s and 1890s only accelerated this process, as homestead heads depended on the cash earned through migrant labor to replenish their herds. Perhaps most important, in the areas under colonial rule the possibility of civil marriage at the magistrate's office provided a means for couples to avoid the need for parental consent entirely—and by the 1890s, young Xhosa men and women were taking up this option in significant numbers.

This decline of familial control sparked a shift in ukuthwala marriages. The term began to be applied to marriages in which a woman's husband and her family had colluded to thwala her in order to force her into a marriage against her wishes. As long as the norm of familial control remained broadly accepted, this form of ukuthwala was unnecessary; a broad set of social and cultural pressures assured that most women would accept their family's choice of husband. But as this norm shifted, fathers and male guardians turned to ukuthwala in an attempt to reassert their authority over the marriages of their female family members.

Msitshana Mhaka sued for the return of his bridewealth after his wife—married through ukuthwala—left him and returned to live with her natal family. Her father admitted during the trial that she had never desired the marriage but "was forced against her will to go to Pl[ainti]ff" In an attempt to convince the court to let him retain the cattle, he added that "the messengers did not ask my consent to let them have the woman . . . there was no marriage." However, her aunt admitted that "we did not give any alarm."[69] When another man, Mnxeba, sued for the return of his bridewealth cattle after his wife left him, a witness told the court that "the girl refused to go to her husband at first but she was forced to go but she ran away subsequently. . . . Mnxeba eloped with the girl after the cattle had been paid." Her own father admitted that she had tried to commit suicide during the marriage, for which he had accepted nine head of cattle as bridewealth.[70] These ukuthwala marriages would not have made much sense in an era of undisputed familial control over marriage, when broader social norms would have supported a father's right to dictate his daughter's marriage partner without the need to resort to irregular marriage forms such as ukuthwala. As that right came into dispute, however, fathers as well as would-be husbands found in ukuthwala marriages a means of (re)asserting their power over marriage. As a result, the term expanded to include this new form of forced marriage, a development that further complicates the question of what forms of ukuthwala, if any, should be considered customary in the present day.

BY THE late nineteenth century, then, ukuthwala had transformed from an irregular if not uncommon practice to a more firmly accepted "custom." The extent of the actions that could be justified under the framework of custom, however, remained subject to debate. The legitimacy that the custom label afforded enticed some men to try to push the boundaries of acceptability. Others insisted that customary forms of ukuthwala should remain more narrowly circumscribed. Thus, when modern interest groups appeal to custom to defend their own preferred versions of ukuthwala, they all have some claim to accuracy. More important, however, the history of these debates suggests that ukuthwala itself became more common as other forms of familial control over marriage—including many situations that might merit the label of "forced marriage" in contemporary discussions—diminished. To insist that nonconsensual forms of ukuthwala are not "customary" is to ignore the broader customary validation of familial control over women's marriage, in both the past and the present.

In current debates over ukuthwala, therefore, the question should not be whether coercive forms of the practice are properly customary. (According to at least some definitions of *custom*, they are.) Rather, researchers and activists should focus on the underlying tensions and transformations that have shaped the practice of ukuthwala. Coercive forms of the practice appeared as a backlash against an increase in young women's power to choose their own marriage partners.

Interventions against forced marriage must work to support young women's autonomy in marriage. In some communities, doing so may require a further redefining of *custom* to explicitly exclude coercion in marriage. Coercive forms of ukuthwala may have been customary in the past, but as the changes in the pracice through history demonstrate, they need not remain so in the future.

NOTES

1. Rebecca Davis, "When Culture and Policing Collide: Circumcision Deaths and Ukuthwala—Unpunished Crimes," *Daily Maverick*, October 11, 2013, available at http://

ELIZABETH THORNBERRY

www.dailymaverick.co.za/article/2013-10-11-when-culture-and-policing-collide
-circumcision-deaths-and-ukuthwala-unpunished-crimes, accessed November 11,
2013. The statistics referenced here were presented by the South African Police Service
at a parliamentary briefing, and they represent cases of abduction in which ukuthwala
was a factor.

2. See, for example, Commission for Gender Equality, "Ukuthwala in Kwazulu-
Natal: An Investigation into State Prevention and Response," 2012: 7, available at pmg
.org.za/files/130320ukuthwala.pdf, accessed December 27, 2015.

3. Melanie Hamman-Doucakis, quoted in Davis, "When Culture and Policing
Collide."

4. See, for example, the repetition of this phrase in an Associated Press write-up
on the occasion of Jacob Zuma's marriage to Tobeka Madiba, his third concur-
rent wife: "Zulu Wedding for President," *Samoa Observer*, n.d., available at http://
www.samoaobserver.ws/index.php?view=article&id=17379%3Azulu-wedding
&option=com_content&Itemid=87, accessed November 11, 2013. The ubiquity of
this phrase is signaled in Nicola Ansell's choice of title: see Ansell, "'Because It's Our
Culture!' (Re)Negotiating the Meaning of Lobola in Southern African Secondary
Schools," *Journal of Southern African Studies* 27, no. 4 (2001): 697–716.

5. Constitution of the Republic of South Africa, 1996, chap. 2, sec. 31. This section
of the constitution does stipulate that such cultural rights "may not be exercised in a
manner inconsistent with any provision of the Bill of Rights."

6. *Umkwa* was also sometimes used in the nineteenth century to translate "custom"
into Xhosa. J. W. Appleyard, *The Kafir Language: Comprising a Sketch of Its History,
Which Includes a General Classification of South African Dialects—Ethnographical
and Geographical Remarks upon Its Nature; and a Grammar* (King Williams Town,
South Africa: Wesleyan Missionary Society, 1850), 129.

7. In addition to Barbara Oomen, *Chiefs in South Africa: Law, Culture, and Power
in the Post-apartheid Era* (London: Palgrave Macmillan, 2005), and Lungisile Ntsebeza, *Democracy Compromised: Chiefs and the Politics of the Land in South Africa*
(Leiden: Brill, 2005), see Cheryl Walker, *Women and Gender in South Africa to 1845*
(Bloomington: Indiana University Press, 1991), and Aninka Claassens and Ben Cous-
ins, eds., *Land, Power and Custom: Controversies Generated by South Africa's Communal Land Rights Act* (Cape Town: University of Cape Town Press, 2008).

8. For discussions of the politics of custom and culture in the contemporary
period, see Oomen, *Chiefs in South Africa*, and Ntsebeza, *Democracy Compromised*.
This discussion is particularly influenced by Jean Comaroff and John L. Comaroff,
Ethnicity, Inc. (Chicago: University of Chicago Press, 2009), although I do not follow
their analysis entirely.

9. Act 120 of 1998, 3(1)(a)(ii).

10. Act 7 of 2013, 4(2)(b).

11. See T. W. Bennett, "The Cultural Defense and the Custom of *Thwala* in
South Africa," *University of Botswana Law Journal* 10 (June 2010): 7, who explic-
itly rejects a cultural defense for assault and rape, and Lea Mwambene and Julia
Sloth-Nielsen, "Benign Accommodation? *Ukuthwala*, 'Forced Marriage,' and the

South African Children's Act," *African Human Rights Law Journal* 11, no. 1 (Spring 2011): 21.

12. See, for example, Sindiso Mnisi, "Reconciling Customary Law and Democratic Decentralisation to Ensure Women's Land Rights Security," Institute for Poverty, Land, and Agrarian Studies Policy Brief 32, 2010.

13. Bennett, "Cultural Defense," 7. See also D. S. Koyana and J. C. Becker, "The Indomitable Ukuthwala Custom," *De Jure* 40, no. 1 (2007): 139–44.

14. Bennett, "Cultural Defense," 25.

15. Indeed, Bennett, in ibid., 9, claims explicitly that "it was unusual in African custom for young people to be forced to marry, because everyone was well aware that unhappy matches resulted in discord, with unhappy implications for the whole family."

16. Center for the Study of Violence and Reconciliation, "An Inconvenient Truth . . . Is There a Link between Harmful Traditional Practices and Sexual Violence in South Africa?" report on a roundtable held on August 27, 2009, available at http://www.womensnet.org.za/resource/there-link-between-harmful-traditional-practices-and-sexual-violence-south-africa, accessed on November 11, 2013.

17. Jenni O'Grady, "Justice Dept Concerned about Ukuthwala," *Citizen*, 7 December 2010, available at http://www.citizen.co.za/citizen/content/en/citizen/local-news?oid=157048&sn=Detail&pid=334&Justice-dept-concerned-about-ukuthwala, accessed on November 11, 2013.

18. Mia Malan, "Abduction a Perversion of the Past," *Mail and Guardian*, December 15, 2011, available at http://mg.co.za/article/2011-12-15-abduction-a-perversion-of-the-past, accessed on December 27, 2015.

19. Kate Rice, "Ukuthwala in Rural South Africa," *Journal of Southern African Studies* 40, no. 2 (May 2014): 381–99.

20. Nomboniso Gasa, "We Need to Shine the Light in the Dark Corners of Our Cultures," *Rural Women's Movement*, August 11, 2010, available at http://rwmsa.org/2010/08/11/nomboniso-gasa/ Mandela spoke in Xhosa; his words were translated by Gasa, accessed November 11, 2013.

21. Western Cape Provincial Records and Archives Service (hereafter CA), Records of the Fingo Agent (hereafter cited as FA) 2/1/1 Colonial Secretary to Superintendent of Natives, Transkeian Territory, November 5, 1870.

22. The first reference to an ukuthwala case that I have found is CA, Special Magistrate's Office, Middledrift (hereafter cited as MDS) 7, Daniso v. Pelele, 1866. See also FA 4/1/3, cases no. 509 and 550 of 1871, which are complaints of "taking forcible possession of his daughter" and "forcibly carrying away his daughter," respectively.

23. It seems likely that the term's emergence within public debates lagged its usage in less formal contexts. Nonetheless, the absence of the term from earlier accounts of "custom" is striking, as is the fact that none of the early Xhosa dictionaries relate the term *ukuthwala* (which has the literal meaning "to carry away") to marriage.

24. Nqobele v. Sihele, Report of the Eastern Districts Court (hereafter EDC), December 6, 1893.

25. CA, Magistrate's Office, Nqamakwe (hereafter cited as 1/NKE), 2/1/1/44, Msitshana Mhaka v. Gqibinyanga Julela, March 14, 1912.

26. CA, NKE 2/1/1/1, Xabeleni v. Qashiwu, December 11, 1891.

27. Testimony of William Sigenu in Cape of Good Hope, Commission on Native Laws and Customs, *Report of the Commission on Native Laws and Custom* (Cape Town: W. A. Richards and Sons, 1883), Minutes of Evidence, 401, 283.

28. Testimony of J. Liefeldt in Cape of Good Hope, Commission on Native Laws and Customs, *Report of the Commission*, Minutes of Evidence, 124.

29. CA, 1/NKE 2/1/1/9, Gangata Maxegwana v. Thomas Maxegwana, September 30, 1890.

30. John Knox Bokwe, "Remarks on the Summary of Kaffir Laws and Customs," in Cape of Good Hope, *Report of the Commission*, 39.

31. H. H. Dugmore, "The Rev. H. H. Dugmore's Papers," in John Maclean, *Compendium of Kafir Laws and Customs* (Grahamston, South Africa: J. Slater, 1906 [1858]), 48–49.

32. Ludwig Alberti, *Account of the Tribal Life and Customs of the Xhosa in 1807*, trans. W Fehr (Cape Town: A. A. Balkema, 1968), 3. See also John Barrow, *An Account of Travels into the Interior of Southern Africa in the Years 1797 and 1798* (New York: Cadell and Davies, 1802), 195.

33. Dugmore, "Rev. H. H. Dugmore's Papers," 53.

34. Testimony of Ngqaba, in Cape of Good Hope, Commission on Native Laws and Customs, *Report of the Commission*, 94.

35. Ibid., 99.

36. Testimony of William Shaw Kama in ibid., 240.

37. Archives of the Wesleyan Methodist Missionary Society, Incoming Correspondence—Southern Africa, Albany District (hereafter cited as WMMS Albany), Samuel Young, Wesleyville, July 22, 1832.

38. Archives of the Wesleyan Methodist Missionary Society, Incoming Correspondence—Southern Africa, Cape Town District (hereafter cited as WMMS Cape), William Shaw, Wesleyville, South Africa, October 21, 1824.

39. WMMS Albany, Samuel Young, ibid.

40. Brett Shadle, *"Girl Cases": Marriage and Colonialism in Gusiiland, Kenya, 1890–1970* (Portsmouth, NH: Heinemann, 2006).

41. J. H. Soga, *The Ama-Xosa: Life and Customs* (Lovedale, South Africa: Lovedale Press, 1931), 25–35.

42. John L. Comaroff, "Goodly Beasts, Beastly Goods: Cattle and Commodities in a South African Context," *American Ethnologist* 17, no. 2 (1990): 195–216.

43. Jeff Peires, *The Dead Will Arise: Nongqawuse and the Great Xhosa Cattle-Killing Movement of 1856-7* (Bloomington: Indiana University Press, 1989).

44. CA, MDS 7, Ntsabo v. Jikelana, April 24, 1861.

45. CA, 1/NKE 1/1/1/4, R. v. Mpaubani, August 16, 1887; CA, Solicitor General (hereafter SGG) 1/1/62, R. v. Kupiso, March 7, 1870.

46. CA, SGG 1/1/442, R. v. Bota Soduwa, April 4, 1893.

47. CA, SGG 1/1/425, R. v. Dyassop, March 24, 1893.

48. Brett Shadle has found a similarly complex interplay between consent, sex, and marriage in colonial Kenya. See Shadle, "Bridewealth and Female Consent: Marriage

Disputes in African Courts, Gusiiland, Kenya," *Journal of African History* 44, no. 2 (2003): 241–62; Shadle, *"Girl Cases"*; Shadle, "Rape in the Courts of Gusiiland, Kenya, 1940s–1960s," *African Studies Review* 51, no. 2 (September 2008): 27–50.

49. This process is too complicated to fully explain here; see Elizabeth Thornberry, "Colonization and Consent: Historicizing Sexual Violence in South Africa's Eastern Cape, 1947–1902" (PhD diss., Stanford University, 2011), chap. 3.

50. CA, SGG 1/1/354, R. v. Bukwana, March 22, 1890.

51. CA, SGG 1/1/425, R. v. Damoyi, June 29, 1892.

52. CA, 1/NKE 2/1/1/11, Xabenlini v. Qashiew, December 11, 1891.

53. CA, 1/NKE 2/1/1/7 Sobuza v. Vice, November 21, 1889.

54. CA, 1/NKE 1/1/1/10, R. v. Tshemerse, March 16, 1891.

55. CA, 1/NKE 2/1/1/11, Xabenlini v. Qashiew, December 11, 1891.

56. CA, 1/NKE 2/1/1/7, Somunyo of Tembuland v. Jack Ngqwala of Matolwene, December 5, 1889.

57. Testimony of A. H. Stanford in Cape of Good Hope, Commission on Native Laws and Customs, *Report of the Commission*, Minutes of Evidence, 283.

58. CA, SGG 1/1/118, R. v. Mhaya Kopisini, Wright, Montintili, and Manayo, January 18, 1876.

59. CA, 1/NKE 1/1/1/39, R. v. Booi Swartbooi and others, May 17, 1916. All of the following information comes from this record.

60. CA, SGG 1/1/706, R. v. Pieter Soldaat and Ntlangeni, December 15, 1903.

61. Testimony of Robert Dick in Cape of Good Hope, Commission on Native Laws and Customs, *Report of the Commission*, Minutes of Evidence, 182.

62. Testimony of Nathanial Umhala in Cape of Good Hope, Commission on Native Laws and Customs, *Report of the Commission*, Minutes of Evidence, 258.

63. Testimony of Tshuka in Cape of Good Hope, Commission on Native Laws and Customs, *Report of the Commission*, Minutes of Evidence, 119.

64. Testimony of Mendela in Cape of Good Hope, Commission on Native Laws and Customs, *Report of the Commission*, Minutes of Evidence, 394.

65. Testimony of David Matomela in Cape of Good Hope, Commission on Native Laws and Customs, *Report of the Commission*, Minutes of Evidence, 168.

66. Testimony of George Mabandla in Cape of Good Hope, Commission on Native Laws and Customs, *Report of the Commission*, Minutes of Evidence, 394.

67. Poppy Fry, "Allies and Liabilities: Fingo Identity and British Imperialism in South Africa's Eastern Cape, 1800–1935" (PhD diss., Harvard University, 2007).

68. Testimony of Pombani in Cape of Good Hope, Commission on Native Laws and Customs, *Report of the Commission*, Minutes of Evidence, 303.

69. CA, 1/NKE 1/1/44, Msitshana Mhaka v. Gqibinyanga Julela, March 14, 1912.

70. CA, 1/Magistrate's Office, King Williams Town H2/1/1/, Mnxeba v. Tshaya Nqezito, April 28, 1884.

CHAPTER SIX

Concubinage as Forced Marriage?

Colonial *Jawari,* Contemporary *Hartaniyya,* and Marriage in Mauritania

E. ANN MCDOUGALL

"To MARRY one's slave is as easy as eating a meal," an elder named Al-Hadrami explained to me in the central Mauritanian town of Atar in 1983: "[Masters] marrying female slaves happens frequently. Islam only permits four wives. But to marry one's slave is easy; it is like eating a meal. On this, the Qur'an is clear." He went on to say that slave wives who married their masters were called *jawari* (sing. *jariya*); children borne by them were especially valuable, for their *metissage* (mixed blood—in this case with blacks from the Sudan) was honorable, and they were treated just like their father's other children.[1]

Only in retrospect did I reflect upon the phrases "to marry one's slave" and "on this the Qur'an is clear." Al-Hadrami understood jawari, or slave wives, in juxtaposition to wives. According to Islamic law (shari'a), the number of wives was limited (to four), but there was no limit set for the number of slave wives—shari'a specifically allowed for an unlimited number of concubines. For him, the association of slave wives with concubines was natural. The problem is that this part of his explanation was not consistent with the Qur'an: shari'a stipulates that a free man cannot marry his own slave, and because a jariya was by legal definition a slave, it follows that her master could not legally marry her. Concubines (slaves) could not be wives any more than wives (free women) could be concubines.[2] The metaphor of "eating a meal" was meant to emphasize the difference between the easy relationship concubinage allowed and the not so easy relationship formal shari'a marriage demanded.

Al-Hadrami's brief but revealing comments underscore two additional points. First, the reference to metissage implies a racial aspect associated with slavery in Mauritania—slaves are black (*sudan*), masters are white (*bizan*).[3] Although this metissage, if really as common over time as he suggested, would have physically diminished actual racial differences by the 1980s, its ideological and cultural importance was firmly embedded in his vision of society. Second, *jariya* in Arabic simply means "female slave," but in Mauritania, it specifically refers to "concubine." Black, female slaves, property of their masters, had no voice of their own in the matter of this "meal," easy or otherwise. In contemporary terms, one would surely argue that Mauritanian concubinage as practiced in the early 1980s was a form of forced marriage, one overlaid with both class and race.

I see this interview as marking a kind of historical watershed. In this chapter, I first try to explain how and why we could have been having the conversation we were about slaves, concubines, and slave marriage in 1983, a reality not unrelated to the fact that slavery itself had only been officially abolished in Mauritania in 1980–81. Then I explore the evolution we see in those concepts over the next generation, essentially from the 1990s through to today. This is a discussion that draws us into intersecting discourses of Islamic law, colonial narrative, and modern-day slavery, understood against the backdrop of a modern democratizing, poverty-stricken Mauritania. What emerges is a picture of a Muslim society in which the institution of slavery as mediated by Islamic law had a long history among Mauritania's bizan and in which a particular form of that slavery, concubinage, emerged alongside marriage as an accepted social norm. Historical evidence that might explain when, why, and how this occurred is rather thin, but at least one fatwa, or religious opinion, from the southwest region of Trarza attests to its presence in the early nineteenth century, and colonial observations from the early twentieth century offer interpretations as to why it persisted.[4] Interviews from several fieldwork trips in many regions of Mauritania, carried out between the mid-1980s and the first decade of the 2000s, confirm that concubinage was widespread and entrenched until very recent times, just as Al-Hadrami claimed.[5]

Elsewhere, I have argued that the taking of slave wives is related to the Saharan practice of fattening (Fr. *gavage*, H. *leblouh*), the custom by which a bizan girl of marriageable age was force-fed until reaching extreme obesity.[6] This physical representation of the family's wealth and status not only rendered a woman almost immobile but also reduced her fertility and interfered with her ability to carry a pregnancy to term. Slaves, by contrast, matured naturally, were generally active (they worked), and by all accounts were physically able to bear children normally.[7]

A second explanation reflects another Mauritanian particularity, namely, serial monogamy. Islam's permitting of four wives notwithstanding, bizan women have traditionally required a contractual commitment to monogamy from future husbands; taking a second wife could thereby trigger divorce by the first.[8] In this social and religious context, concubines arguably became substitutes for additional wives, as they required the formality of neither divorce nor marriage—"as easy as eating a meal." Although the tradition of monogamy persists today, legal slavery does not. What this means for marriage practice has yet to be fully explored. I will suggest that various concubine-like relationships, including something called secret marriage, have gained considerable currency as a consequence.

Much of this story belongs to and is about bizan men and women, yet it must inevitably revolve around the experience of the slave wife, or jariya, herself. This is a more difficult voice to recover, but I draw upon interviews with former slaves (pl. *haratine*; m. *hartani*, f. *hartaniyya*) in an attempt to do exactly this. This effort found slave wives who were technically not concubines but remained the property of their masters while being married (with his permission) to other slaves. These women delivered slave children to their masters' families.[9] But the relationship that emerged as central to the dynamic of concubinage as forced marriage was the one that allowed for a slave concubine to give birth to free children, simultaneously acquiring a special kind of freedom for herself. Shari'a stipulates that the progeny of concubines are born as free children of the master and that jawari acquire the status of *umm al-walad* (mother-of-the-child); they were not to be sold and were to be freed upon the death of the master, if not sooner. But this required that the master acknowledge paternity; if he did not, technically both mother and child remained slaves unless a legal challenge could be made on behalf of the child's legitimacy.[10] We will see that even umm al-walad status did not always bring the promised social elevation or freedom. Though I am discussing women of slave status in the past tense here, in the final section of the chapter I also argue that persistent and pervasive poverty among haratine today renders many hartaniyya no less vulnerable to entering into such ambiguous relationships

with wealthier, well-placed bizan than their jawari mothers and grandmothers had been.

Concubinage in the Qur'an

Al-Hadrami was not wrong about the Qur'an or about its clarity on the
question of marriage. The *Surat al-nisa* ("The Women," 4:3) permits a man
to take up to four wives, with the important stipulation that they be treated
equally: "Marry such women as seem good to you, two, three, four; but if
you fear you will not be equitable [just], only one, or what [those] your
right hands possess."[11] "What your right hands possess" is a euphemism for
female slaves; the option of "marrying" one or more female slaves rather
than second, third, or fourth wives is clearly authorized here. Although
the stated reason for this derives from the difficulty of ensuring equity between wives, the option equally lends itself to the situation of Mauritanian
husbands restricted to monogamy.

But the equity requirement was not the only issue that differentiated
"concubine wives" from legal wives. All four major schools of Islamic law
stipulate the need for marriage contracts between the bride's and groom's
families; these include negotiations of bride-price, or *mahr*.[12] Marrying a
slave involved neither a marriage contract nor mahr; the master's rights
over the slave, including sexual rights, were considered to be purchased
along with her person.[13] The term *marry*, however, did have a recognized
legal meaning: it was the exclusive right to sexual relations with the woman
and to any progeny issuing from her. Thus, this marriage right was also acquired through concubinage. These were the only legitimate ways a man
could expand his lineage.[14] The *Surat al-mun'inum* ("The Believers," 23:5,
6) states that believers are those "who abstain from sex ('guard their private parts') . . . except with those joined to them in the marriage bond, or
those whom their right hands possess."[15] As noted, children born of "those
whom their right hands possess," like those born "in the marriage bond,"
were, in principle, free.[16] As we can see from the wording of these *surat*
(chapters of the Qu'ran), the association of jariya with wife (slave wife)
and concubinage with marriage ("to marry one's slave") was not a difficult
one to make in spite of the actual prohibition against such a relationship
in Islam. It is in this context that Al-Hadrami understood what he said
to me in our interview; for him, there was nothing contradictory about

his words or his memorable metaphor. Nevertheless, this explanation begs the more obvious question of why slavery, jawari, and the umm al-walad status were still social realities in 1983.

Concubinage and Colonialism

When the French conquered the territory that would become Mauritania, between 1905 and 1912, they promised to respect the "customs, values, property and religion [Islam]" of the indigenous bizan.[17] In 1918, the local administrator in Shinqiti wrote:

> We have therefore recognized a situation of fact: the slaves stay in the family of their owner for whom they constitute the labor force . . . [as for slave trading] it can happen that in certain contracts between Moors, for the constitution of a bride-price for example, it is specified that a slave be given by the spouse. This is not, in my opinion, an act of slave trading—a slave whose condition we have already recognized, remains in the family. . . . This is not a loss for the masters. These are the only transactions [to] which we can close our eyes.[18]

Domestic slavery was to remain virtually untouched. And as male slaves were increasingly freed to become haratine and provide wage labor to the colonial economy, those left in domestic slavery were almost exclusively women and children. Masters attached special importance to controlling them because in 1929, the French affirmed their right to include slaves in customary inheritance settlements. Two years later, local administrators objected that most of these settlements allocated fractions of slaves, "above all women," to different owners. Although they urged that these practices be modified, masters successfully resisted by arguing that "to receive even one-quarter of a female slave gives a possible profit of one or several children," referring to children born of servile marriages. Shinqiti elder Mohamed Lemine ould Habbot explained the principle to me in terms of a female slave's "valuable fertility," insofar as "her children augmented your slaves if you were her master and if your female slave was married to someone else's male slave, the children also belonged to you."[19] Together, colonial officials and local masters ensured that domestic slavery, especially the role of female slaves in its reproduction, remained firmly embedded in Mauritanian society.[20]

Masters were also giving female slaves as wives to haratine working in adwaba (adabaye sing.—agricultural villages) that were often far away;

haratine from these regions recounted to a researcher in the late 1980s that these women did not always accept their situation and occasionally fomented resistance against the masters.[21] But in Al-Hadrami's town of Atar, a well-known hratani who had successfully exploited the colonial economy and become a slave owner himself, Hamody ould Mahmoud, practiced both gender-specific manumission and arranged marriages. It is said that Hamody bought "[male] slaves of quality" in order to free them but that he rarely freed his female slaves. He frequently arranged marriages between his haratine and slave women, descendants of whom were among my 2004–5 informants. They proudly claimed association with Hamody.[22]

What neither published colonial documents nor my field interviews addressed openly was a role for jawari in reproducing bizan society itself. However, a few comments unearthed in unpublished archives draw attention to this intriguing suggestion. In 1931, a pamphlet accusing French administrators of allowing for and participating in the exploitation of female slaves provoked the following response: "Black *servantes* [are actually the] base of the Moorish family" and contribute in large part to its reproduction.[23] "Women of the Moorish race are often sterile [and were in any case], insufficient in number."[24]

In 1946–47, an observant French traveler linked concubinage to the same bizan marriage practices and the health issues I noted earlier:

> Moors are monogamous and their women are not very fertile, much less than the *negresses* among the slaves. The acceptable usage of black concubines chosen from among the slaves—happy to find themselves thusly liberated [a reference to the umm al-walad]—assured a minimal level of birthing, at the same time bringing "more vigorous blood" to a white people weakened by undernourishment and the Saharan climate [anticipating Al-Hadrami's appreciation of metissage].[25]

This discussion provides important glimpses into the continuing role of concubinage in colonial Mauritania.

Concubinage was well masked by the French rhetoric of "domestic slavery," which remained in place as late as 1948–50. At that time, local reports referred to *servants* (f. *servantes*) born in the household "as their slave parents had been before them" and also to masters who provided for them. And as had been the case since early in the century, domestic slavery was articulated in terms of religion: the Qur'an permits slavery, and to oppose it is to oppose the "*Musulmane* religion" itself.[26] French respect for the slavery inherent in Mauritania's "customs, values, property and religion" remained intact throughout the colonial era.[27] When combined with the changes brought about by the new colonial political economy and its policies opposing slave trading, this respect actually reinforced domestic concubinage; it assured bizan reproduction and the use of slave wives to sustain servile (slave and hratani) communities. If we were to look at this evidence through a contemporary prism, we would have to say that what had emerged were various iterations of forced marriage, significant for the social and demographic structures of both free and freed populations.

THE ISLAMIC REPUBLIC OF MAURITANIA
Life Histories of Haratine

The first president of the postcolonial state of the Islamic Republic of Mauritania, Mokhtar ould Daddah, oversaw his nation's ratification of the United Nations Declaration of Human Rights in 1961. But he had no intention of letting it affect domestic slavery, concubinage included. The life histories of contemporary haratine that I collected between 2009 and 2011 confirm that the early decades of independent Mauritania knew little change in this respect.[28] A fifty-something informant from the eastern Hodh (born around 1960) said his mother was jariya; another from the southern Brakna claimed the emir took jawari from his community as recently as the 1970s.[29] The latter was from an elite group of military haratine who were given their own slaves in reward for service. When asked if these masters ever took their slaves as jawari, he replied, "No never—but we took our own slaves in this way."[30] A third informant from the same region said his mother had been jariya in her master's family for a long time and had had several children. He noted that "although she continued to work in the household pounding grain, making meals and cleaning—each time she had a child, it was born free." She was freed when she could no longer bear children; one of her former master's sons provided her with a sort of pension as acknowledgment of her position in his father's household.[31]

The complicated kin relationships that concubinage could sometimes create between masters' families were illustrated in a life history from Trarza. Our informant's grandmother, who was of one clan, had been taken as jariya by a master from a different clan; the informant identified primarily with that former master's family, rather than with his grandmother's. Asked why, he explained that his grandmother's master had "adopted" his father, and his family remained "very appreciative"; it had gradually been absorbed.[32] Though his grandmother had been umm al-walad to her master and bore him free children, our informant's father was apparently not among those children, hence his hratani status. Like the Brakna jariya mentioned earlier, she must have been freed before her master's death, subsequently giving birth to the hratani son who fathered our informant. It is notable that the sense of kinship deriving from his grandmother's umm al-walad status carries sufficient weight, even to this day, to keep his family tied to the former master's clan.

I conclude this section with reference to a very well known family whose history straddles both the Sahara and the colonial and postcolonial eras. M'barek ould Beyruk of the famous Beyruk commercial dynasty of southern Morocco was born and raised in Atar. His merchant grandfather arrived in Atar in 1913, shortly after the installation of the French; he took one of his slaves as jariya.[33] He also had several wives from his own clan over the years.[34] M'barek was descended from his grandfather's jariya. Although he clearly distinguished between his grandfather's wives and his concubine, he explained the importance of becoming jariya by conflating marriage and slavery: "A young female slave when she is married as concubine changes statute [status?] completely—it is said that her stomach becomes 'free,' therefore all her progeny thenceforth are free." Like Al-Hadrami, whose words began this chapter, M'barek used the term *married* deliberately to suggest that a jariya anticipated becoming umm al-walad and, like a legal wife, giving birth to free children.

M'barek went on to say that there was nothing unusual in his grandfather's "marrying his slave." However, it was also common in his family for a master who wished to terminate the relationship with his umm al-walad to "marry her off" to a hratani:

> [In this way] children of the master become the maternal brothers of
> *haratine*. . . . I know people who have half-brothers who are *haratine*
> and they are very attached to their brothers and half-brothers. This
> creates a lot of psychological pressure because they always regard
> their brothers as free. . . . They say: you cannot take my brothers as
> slaves; you must respect my brothers. This is a daily battle. [But] at
> the same time, it is a means of assuring attachment between *haratine*
> and their masters. This creates strong ties.[35]

E. ANN MCDOUGALL

It is evident that a marriage to a jariya was forced, but the precise nature of a marriage with a hratani is not entirely clear. Technically, once freed and thanks to her service as umm al-walad, she should have had a choice in the matter. But M'barek's characterization of masters habitually "marrying off" such women suggests something more in line with Hamody's arranged marriages than the freedom anticipated with hartaniyya status.

Although M'barek's story looks back to the colonial past, it also abruptly brings us into the twenty-first century with its references to contemporary daily battles to negotiate respect for haratine brothers whom others would treat as slaves. Even though slavery was abolished a generation ago first by proclamation, then by 'law' in 1980-81, the fact that many bizan families are in part shaped by relations established through concubinage and many hratani families owe their social position to such relations means that slavery cannot be easily forgotten. There has been much discussion in the media and among human rights activists about the failure of abolition to change conditions for those living in slave-like circumstances, including women said to be subject to sexual exploitation by masters. But such cases are not addressed with any consideration for the history of taking slave wives or becoming jawari. How have people adjusted actual marriage and reproductive practices to respond to the legal prohibition of concubinage engendered by the ending of slavery? How have their own perceptions and representations of the institution changed given its deep roots in both their social and personal experience?

Concubinage in "Postslave" Mauritania: A Contradiction in Terms

M'Barek's interview conflates the discourse of past and present but offers little insight into the legacies traditional concubinage has bequeathed to this ostensibly postslave society. A recent publication by anthropologist Corinne Fortier on secret marriage may help in this respect.[36] She argues that Mauritania is an unusually "aware" society in terms of shari'a law, especially as it concerns the family; even illiterate women learn orally from mothers and grandmothers about the religious rights they can exercise within the marriage contract. Because the ultraconservative Maliki law was enshrined in the country's 2001 Personal Status Code, arranged marriages for minors—families betrothing children while they are still infants or toddlers—remain legal.[37] However, the code stipulates eighteen as the age of majority; past this age, paternal authority weakens in the face of the negotiated marriage contract in which the bride's family usually insists on monogamy as a marriage condition.[38]

But as Fortier notes, this is also a society in which men, historically, were absent for long periods of time, as nomads following camel herds or as merchants in the trans-Saharan trade. In this context, men took advantage of Islamic laws that permitted forms of nonpermanent marriage, *as-sirriyya* or secret (*sir*) marriage being one. This type of marriage has no built-in expiration date, making it legal under Maliki law.[39] The religious ceremony is the same as for an official marriage, although the contract is oral, not written; neither requires a *qadi* (judge), and both need witnesses. Fortier compares as-sirriyya to temporary marriage in places such as Egypt, but the better comparison is to *misyar* marriage, which literally translates as "traveling or ambulant marriage," currently growing in popularity (and controversy) in and around the Gulf States.[40]

Secret marriage (like misyar) is nevertheless contentious. Many Maliki jurists argue that to be legal, marriage requires public rituals such as an engagement celebration—in other words, the antithesis of secret marriage. But recently, others have asserted with accepted authority that the required presence of two witnesses at the ceremony means the marriage is not really secret and therefore is legitimate.[41]

Legality aside, other differences between the two types of marriage are important. Shari'a marriage requires negotiations between two families; as-sirriyya is strictly between the two individuals concerned. The former involves providing gifts to and economic security for the wife; the latter entails neither. Lastly and significantly, children born within a shari'a marriage are assumed to be progeny of that relationship and are automatically legitimate; those born of a secret marriage must prove their paternity. As Fortier puts it, their legitimacy depends "entirely on the goodwill of the father."[42]

From our perspective, the most significant questions Fortier discusses are why these marriages occur and with whom. The very success Mauritanian women have had in writing monogamy into marriage contracts means that men who wish for sexual relationships with women other than their wives and who could, as Muslims, take second or third wives actually risk divorce if they do so. Secret marriage provides them with licit access to such relationships. Historically, according to Fortier, the secret was "generally well-guarded" and was only revealed if the husband had a child with his "secret wife." Yet such a child was sometimes the reason the man contracted as-sirriyya:

> In Mauritania, generally when a man cannot have children with his
> wife, he will choose to contract a secret marriage with a woman of his

E. ANN MCDOUGALL

choice, usually of inferior social status such as a descendant of a slave *(hartaniyya)*, rather than repudiating his wife and remarrying. . . .

Because the secret marriage is considered by the Moorish jurists to be legal, a child born from this union is legally recognized as legitimate.[43]

What is so striking about as-sirriyya is its similarity to jariya marriage: both involve licit sexual relations outside the permitted four wives, the production of legitimate children for the master, the requirement that such children be acknowledged by the father, and the lack of formalities such as written contracts and public announcements.

There is one key difference, however. Fortier argues that a man will seek out this secret relationship in order to have legitimate children, just as one might argue men took slave wives historically. But a jariya had no rights to her children, for she was reproducing the master's family and not her own, whereas a secret wife—a free woman—should have the same claim to children as a shari'a wife would. In other words, in order for the man to claim these children as his legitimate progeny, would he not have to officially marry their mother? Fortier indirectly addresses that question when she notes that wives who have been unsuccessful in giving birth sometimes recognize the legitimacy of their husbands' other children rather than risk divorce, or they may choose to live in formal polygyny.[44]

We also need to take into account why women enter into as-sirriyya. Though love may lead some women to accept being secret wives, Fortier argues that economic reasons are more compelling. Secret marriage still requires the payment of mahr, so there is a financial gain involved. "Secret marriages, therefore, involve primarily women of inferior social status." Such women are often hartaniyya. When the woman is under eighteen and therefore still subject to her father's authority (as per the Personal Status Code), "it is often her family that forces her to contract a secret marriage with a wealthy man for economic reasons."[45] In such circumstances, both the woman's social status and her economic situation would mitigate against her successfully launching a legal challenge for rights to her children. In any case, if Fortier's analysis is correct, the woman's motivation for entering into this relationship is quite different from the man's—hers being one of socioeconomic betterment, not progeny.

Considering this situation in the context of Mauritania's extreme poverty, Fortier's conclusion that the institution is declining is surprising. Elsewhere, the opposite has been asserted: "Clandestine Marriages on the

Rise in Mauritania" was a lead article in *al-Arabiya* on June 24, 2010.[46] Like Fortier, the author of the article notes that men are avoiding restrictions on polygamy written into contracts as well as circumventing unhappy arranged marriages. And the author also underscores the role of economic hardship: "In order to lure the bride's parents into accepting the marriage, the husband pledges to support them financially throughout the duration of the contract. Peasants in the countryside, recent immigrants to the city, or girls from nomadic tribes are the main target of the suitors, who take advantage of their dire conditions." But young girls sometimes voluntarily enter these relationships to help support their families. A woman who claims to have been in two such marriages is quoted as explaining that "the girl agrees to live in the shadow because of the money the groom pays not realizing that [she] is falling victim to her family's ignorance and her husband's selfishness."[47]

For all the understanding of the economic context expressed in this article, there is little appreciation of Mauritania's social structure or its historical development, and the wives in these marriages are characterized exclusively in terms of their "poverty and ignorance." Fortier, by contrast, is fully cognizant of the fact that most of these poor, ignorant women are hartaniyya from hratani families. Though it may be unclear as to whether we are seeing an increase or decrease in as-sirriyya, which by nature of its secrecy is difficult to document, it must surely be significant that, like traditional relations of concubinage, such marriages are largely defined by bizan men looking to satisfy their sexual and reproductive desires with descendants of former slaves. In fact, information about contemporary marriages from my interviews with haratine conducted at about the same time these publications appeared suggests that what we may be seeing is the morphing of the traditional master-jariya relationship into a form or forms of modern as-sirriyya.

Earlier, I referred to a hratani from Brakna who spoke of the emir taking jawari from his community as recently as the 1970s. Equally revealing was the continuation of this person's response, the story of a local hartaniyya who had given birth to the emir's daughter but remained with her child in the hratani community. The informant referred to this situation as a marriage, but its inclusion in his discussion of jawari, as well as the fact that neither the daughter nor the mother was taken into the emir's camp, is suggestive of something "other." Moreover, he had responded positively to the question, "Was there concubinage between the emir and your *hartaniyya*?" in spite of the inherent contradiction (that is, that since a hartaniyya is not a slave, she cannot be a concubine). A neighboring Trarza informant suggested that it is still normal for male children to go with the father, whereas girls remain with their hartaniyya mothers in the village because "sometimes the father wishes to hide his marriage."[48] Are these two strikingly similar situations a form of as-sirriyya in which we are also seeing gender preference—a willingness to reveal the relationship when its outcome is a son who contributes to the family lineage but not when that progeny is a daughter? Is this perhaps a reflection of how concubinage operated in practice as distinct from principle—were boys normally the ones acknowledged as free, rendering the women umm al-walad, whereas girls remained enslaved along with their mothers?[49] Building on this, was our Brakna informant's response to the concubine/hartaniyya question a reflection of how he and his community understood what was happening, irrespective of its illegality, precisely because of its continuity with past reality?

These are tenuous speculations, but they tend to be supported by informants from Gorgol and Guidimaka, two heavily populated southern agricultural regions where close relations exist between bizan clerics and their haratine. In each region, we were told that the clerics did not marry their slaves—they "married *hartaniyya*"; in Gorgol, it was claimed that "all *bizan* clerics had *hartaniyya* mothers," and in Guidimaka, "most" did. In Gorgol, mothers and children of these marriages continued to live in the hratani community, as we saw in Brakna (though our informant implied both male and female children remained). But both responses raise the issue of what exactly marriage means in these communities.[50] Even taking into account the likelihood that the percentage of bizan clerics with hartaniyya mothers was exaggerated by the informants, the larger picture here seems to show that the concubinage we know historically has persisted well into recent times. Only by being sons of jawari could these men technically be born bizan.[51] Our fifty-something informant from the Hodh, who was dark-skinned and had grown up in a hratani adabaye, brought this point home vividly. He immediately asserted that he was the son of a jariya as a way of telling us we were mistaken in thinking him to be hratani.[52]

Between 2009 and 2011 (unlike in 1983), the term *jariya* appeared to belong to the past; contemporary discourse spoke of hartaniyya and marriage. Informants knew the difference in reality, however. In Guidimaka, for example, the informant specified that bizan married their daughters:

"Yes, that happens here. One of our *marabouts* [a French colonial term for cleric] claimed that the wife was his slave; although he did not say this, it was clear. A second marriage took place for which we celebrated the engagement but this is a natural marriage."[53] In the first instance, the terminology of marriage was used, including *wife,* but based on how the so-called marriage took place ("it was clear"), the informant knew that the bizan regarded this as concubinage and his wife as jariya. The point was underscored by contrasting this with a second marriage involving a public engagement, a requirement of shari'a marriage (which he called "natural"), distinguishing it from concubinage, as-sirriyya, or some conflation of the two. What is notable is that the informant spoke of these two types of marriage as occurring in the present tense.

To be sure that this was not an anomaly, we can return to the Trarza informant who earlier spoke of a father wishing "to hide his marriage." He was the only one to address a contemporary change in marriage practice and the critical aspect of choice. In this, he was perhaps the most important commentator on the issues raised by our earlier discussion of secret marriage. "In the past," he recounted, "*hratani* marriage had to be guaranteed by the Moorish master who had to accept it [it was not legitimate unless approved by the master], but the situation has changed now":

> Now, marriage does not depend upon tribal belonging [a reference
> to the master's authorization], you find marriages mixed between
> tribes. You can also find Moors who marry *hartaniyya* wives,
> sometimes because they consider them like their slaves—*Abid,*
> which is comparable to concubinage, commonly called *Tjowri*
> [*jawari*] and sometimes as a natural marriage.[54]

Like our Guidimaka informant, he clearly differentiated between the two types of marriage, interestingly also using the term *natural* to mean "shari'a," or "legal." But he went on to describe the "marrying" of hartaniyya as often being "comparable to concubinage," even going so far as to use the local term *jawari.* And he went one important step further: he gratuitously observed that "*hartaniyya* appreciate very much being married by a Moor. On the whole, marriage here is a question of agreement."[55]

These last comments bring us back to the issue of forced marriage and our discussion of as-sirriyya—but this time from the perspective of a hratani patriarch. It is difficult to say to what degree the daughters in his community truly appreciate marriage to bizan and to what degree this is the perspective of the community's male family members. Historically, these hartaniyya's mothers, aunts, and grandmothers—often jawari and umm al-walad in these same bizan families—might indeed have enjoyed the elevated status and appreciation promised by Islam and implied in some life histories. But the contemporary overlay of poverty seems to have blurred some of those kinship linkages and religious concerns. More local fieldwork that probes individual family histories while bringing to bear awareness of the socioreligious customs that may have structured relations within those families is necessary to further understand such developments, including secret marriage.

LEGACIES OF SLAVERY: THE HIDDEN DYNAMICS OF CONTEMPORARY FORCED MARRIAGE

Contemporary human rights and gender equity reports looking at forced marriage and child marriage reflect many of these realities, even if they are not explicitly analyzed as such. Fortier draws a comparison between as-sirriyya and neighboring Morocco's *fatiha* ("The Opening") marriage, for example.[56] In early 2011, fatiha marriages were described as "under-age marriages" of girls of twelve and thirteen years, with payment being made up front for betrothals to even younger girls who might not be marriageable for several years. Although contracted in the name of tradition (the part of formal marriage wherein the contract is signed and the man recites the Sura al-Fatiha—hence the name; it can precede the public wedding party by some time and for numerous reasons), the report concluded, these marriages were clearly attempts to escape poverty.[57] The 2012 Gender Index on Mauritania documented instances of "early marriage" and "minors being forced into marriage," echoing the Moroccan report.[58] And information on forced marriage among Mauritanian women published by the Immigration and Refugee Board of Canada in 2012, generally for the purpose of determining refugee status, identified three "prevalent types." The first, "cousin marriage," involved ensuring that women were well supported. Although not clarified in the document, this referred in particular to bizan; cousin marriages would account for many of the unhappy arranged marriages the *al-Arabiya* article (discussed in some detail previously) held responsible for what it argued was a rise in "clandestine marriage." The second type involved girls from poor families being forced to marry rich men "who they do not love." Again, though not identified in Mauritanian social terms, most of these girls were almost certainly hartaniyya marrying rich bizan. Leaving aside the questionable relevance of marrying for love, this would seem to be the most likely scenario to generate as-sirriyya or forms thereof. And the third type referred again to poor girls, in this case being forced into polygamous marriages with wealthy and influential men. The direct opposite of secret marriage, this also would appear to be the least likely type to become more prevalent, given the contract stipulations on monogamy among wealthy and influential bizan families.[59]

What is notably common across these three types of forced marriages and instances of underage betrothal/marriage is the economic hardship faced by the bride and her family. It would be easy to conclude then, as the media generally does, that forced marriage relations in hartani communities today are being driven almost exclusively by poverty. Without denying the importance of that factor, it must be remembered that this conclusion obscures the long history of concubinage and slave marriage that lies at the heart of and still unites many Mauritanian bizan and hratani families. I would argue that adding these historical, social, and religious perspectives to how we think about and shape our research on forced marriage will produce a significantly deeper understanding of the realities influencing marriage in general in Mauritania today.

NOTES

1. Al-Hadrami, interview, Atar, August 7, 1983.

2. A free man could marry a slave as long as she was not his own or owned by his close kin; with marriage, she became his wife but remained her master's slave. Islamic law regulated a wide range of issues generated by slavery and marriage. See Kecia Ali, *Marriage and Slavery in Early Islam* (Cambridge, MA: Harvard University Press, 2010), 67–72, 164–86.

3. Bizan (also spelled bidan or beidan) are elite Saharans of Arab origin (also called Moors) who control Mauritania's economy and government.

4. Abdel Wedoud ould Cheikh (personal translation), from Yahya ould al-Barra, *Al-Mi'yâr al-Muhît fî fatâwâ wa nawâzil wa ahkâm bilâd Shinqît*, vols. 1–12 (Rabat: 2010), 1:n.p. The fatwa addressed a situation unfolding from around 1820 to 1840 and concerned a contentious paternity case. Mukhtar, born of a slave, claimed he was free because his father had been his mother's master. The claim was challenged on behalf of the deceased master's grandchildren, who were said to have inherited him from their late mother. The case hinged on whether the master had ever acknowledged paternity.

E. ANN MCDOUGALL

5. Colonial sources are discussed in the following pages. Fieldwork was funded by the Killam Post-doctoral Fellowship Programme (1983–84); Killam and University of Alberta Research Grants (2000, 2004–5); and Social Sciences and Humanities Research Council of Canada (SSHRC) Research Grants (1993–96; 2008–12).

6. "H." stands for Hassaniyya, Mauritania's Arabic/Berber dialect.

7. E. Ann McDougall, "'To Marry One's Slave Is as Easy as Eating a Meal': The Dynamics of Carnal Relations within Saharan Slavery," in *Sex, Power, and Slavery*, ed. Gwyn Campbell and Elizabeth Elbourne (Athens: Ohio University Press, 2014), 140–66. Reports as recent as July 2013 insist the practice continues: see http://www.dailymail.co.uk/femail/article-2364060/Force-fed-husband-How-Mauretanian-women-fattened-like-foie-gras-geese-dangerous-animal-growth-hormones-satisfy-mens-love-larger-lady.html, accessed February 29, 2016.

8. Corinne Fortier, "Women and Men Put Islamic Law to Their Own Use: Monogamy versus Secret Marriage in Mauritania," in *Gender and Islam in Africa: Rights, Sexuality and Law*, ed. Margot Badran (Washington, DC: Woodrow Wilson Center Press, 2011), 213–32.

9. Ali, *Marriage and Slavery*, 67–72. Whose power (master's or husband's) took priority was a matter of contention; ownership of the children was not.

10. As in the story of Mukhtar in note 4.

11. Translation varies; this is from http://quran.com/, accessed February 29, 2016.

12. The four major schools of Islamic law are Hanafi; Hanibali; Shafi'i; and, in Mauritania, Maliki.

13. This practice was attributed to the prophet Muhammad: when asked what bride-price he gave to marry captive Safiya bint Huyai, he reportedly said, "Her manumission is her *mahr*." Translation from Sahih Bukhari, *Hadiths*, vol. 1, bk. 8, no. 367, available at http://www.quranwebsite.com/hadith/bukhari_volume_1.html, accessed February 29, 2016. Also see Ali, *Marriage and Slavery*, 29–64.

14. Ali, *Marriage and Slavery*, 38, 39.

15. "Marriage and slavery intersected at the institution of concubinage. . . . To discuss marriage in the pre-modern period without discussing slavery would fundamentally distort the jurists' way of thinking," in ibid., 8.

16. Paternity was rarely an issue within "the marriage bond," but in concubinage, where exclusivity of sexual access was more difficult to ascertain, it was; personal communication with Abdel Wedoud ould Cheikh.

17. E. Ann McDougall, "A Topsy-Turvy World: Slaves and Freed Slaves in Colonial Mauritania," in *The End of Slavery*, ed. Suzanne Miers and Richard Roberts (Madison: University of Wisconsin Press, 1988; reissue 2005), 366.

18. E1 28 Archives Nationales de la République Islamique de Mauritanie, Nouakchott (hereafter cited as ANRIM), Shinqit Resident to Commander of Adrar Region, October–November 1918,

19. Mohamed Lemine, interview, Shinqit, August 22, 1984.

20. McDougall, "Topsy-Turvy World," 376; McDougall, "'To Marry One's Slave,'" argument developed throughout.

21. McDougall, "'To Marry One's Slave,'" 168n68, citing Meskerem B'hrane, "Narratives of the Past, Politics of the Present" (PhD diss., University of Chicago, 1997).

22. Isselmou ould Hamody, Bilal ould M'Barak, Mohamed Mahmoud ould Barak, and Abeidya ould Matallah, interviews, Atar, 2004; Harra mint Mahmoud, interview, Atar, 2005; and Mohamed Mahmoud ould Hamody and Swaifya mint Hamody (children of Hamody), interviews, Nouakchott, 2004.

23. Discussed in E. Ann McDougall, "Setting the Story Straight: Louis Hunkanrin and *Un forfait colonial,*" *History in Africa* 16 (1989): 285–310.

24. E1 18, Esclavage, 15 avril 1933, ANRIM; Chazelas, "Haratines et serviteurs dans l'Assaba," 1933, 9G7, Archives Nationales de Sénégal.

25. E2 223, Odette du Puigaudeau, "L'évolution d'esclave noir en Mauritanie," c. 1946–47, ANRIM. She implies there have been changes since a voyage in 1936.

26. G. Poulet, "Aperçu sommaire sur la question des serviteurs en Mauritanie," 2K15 174 MAURITANIE, 17 mai 1949, Archives Nationales de Sénégal.

27. Paul Lovejoy, in "Concubinage and the Status of Women Slaves in Early Colonial Northern Nigeria," *Journal of African History* 29, no. 2 (1988): 266, suggests the British began from a similar platform: "British views of slave women attempted to blur the distinction between concubinage and marriage, thereby reaffirming patriarchal Islamic attitudes."

28. SSHRC project, "The Sahara's Invisible People: *Haratine,* History and Social Identity in Mauritania and Morocco," 2008–12. According to Ethics Review instructions, the interviews are cited anonymously. The format is: ### (interview number assigned by the project); X. o/ Y. (initials of informant's name—Mohamed ould Ahmed becomes M. o/ A.); and (m., 75, Assaba) (gender, age, and region). When the informant is a public figure (e.g., #187), the full name is used.

29. #187, Barka ould Saleh, Imam, Nouakchott (m., 50+, Hodh).

30. #127, E. o/ Md. V. (m., 64, Brakna).

31. #211, B. o/ B. (m., ?, near Aleg).

32. #109, B. o/ B. (m., 80, Trarza).

33. M'barek ould Beyruk, interview, Nouakchott, November 4, 2009. He is a writer and published a novel about slavery and concubinage.

34. This is consistent with the discussion of marriage, concubinage, and the Tekna (the Beyruk clan) in Pierre Bonte, "Fortunes commerciales à Shingîti (Adrar Mauritanien) au dix-neuvième siècle," *Journal of African History* 39, no. 1 (1998): 10; Ghislaine Lydon, *On Trans-Saharan Trails: Islamic Law, Trade Networks and Cross-cultural Exchange in Nineteenth-Century Western Africa* (New York: Cambridge University Press, 2009), 348. On p. 181, Lydon notes that the patriarch of this family also practiced the equivalent of serial monogamy.

35. M'barek ould Beyruk, interview. He added that these "masters" were often the eldest sons.

36. Fortier, "Women and Men."

37. Ibid., 214; texts taught in Mauritania, note 2, pp. 227–28. This *Code de statut personnel* (sometimes referred to as the Family Code in English) regulated everything related to marriage, divorce, family, and inheritance issues.

38. "'Africa for Women's Rights Ratify and Respect,' Dossier of Claims (Mauritania)" availabe at http://www.africa4womensrights.org/public/Dossier_of_Claims

/Mauritania-UK.pdf, and "Islamic Family Law" (Guide), Harvard University Law School, available at http://guides.library.harvard.edu/content.php?pid=120215&sid =1035282, both accessed February 29, 2016.

39. Maliki law defines marriage in perpetuity, making an end date to the contract incompatible with the essence of the institution.

40. Fortier, "Women and Men," 215–18; 221–22; Tofol Jassim Al-Nasr, "Gulf Cooperation Council (GCC) Women and Misyar Marriage: Evolution and Progress in the Arabian Gulf," *Journal of International Women's Studies* 12, no. 3 (2011): 49, 50.

41. Fortier, "Women and Men," 215; 222–23. The other objectors are Womens' Rights Activists; see Al-Nasr, "Women and Misyar Marriage."

42. Fortier, "Women and Men," 221.

43. Ibid., 223, 224.

44. Ibid. 224.

45. Ibid.

46. See http://www.alarabiya.net/articles/2010/06/24/112179.html, accessed November 29, 2013; no longer accessible as of January 10, 2014. Author retains copy.

47. See http://www.alarabiya.net/articles/2010/06/24/112179.html, accessed November 29, 2013; no longer accessible as of January 10, 2014. Author retains copy.

48. #109, B. o/ B. (m., 80, Trarza).

49. We might reconsider M'Barek Beyruk's account: perhaps his references to bizan having maternal hartine "brothers" and preventing his "brothers" from being seen as slaves had significance not evident in the interview.

50. #125, Md. V. o/ S. o/ E. (m., 75, Gorgol).

51. Everything here (and see later discussion) mitigates against the likelihood that so many "noble" clerics entered into shari'a marriage with hartaniyya, the only other situation that could have produced a reality in which "most clerics had *hartaniayya* mothers."

52. #187, Barka ould Saleh.

53. #123, M. o/ M. (m., 78, Guidimaka).

54. #109, B. o/ B.

55. Ibid.

56. Fortier, "Women and Men," 222.

57. "Morocco: Underage Marriages Increase," CRIN (Child Rights Information Network), 2011, available at http://www.crin.org/resources/infodetail.asp?ID=23980, accessed February 29, 2016.

58. "Mauritania," available at http://genderindex.org/country/mauritania, accessed February 29, 2016.

59. "Mauritania: Prevalence of Forced Marriage," Immigration and Refugee Board of Canada (IRB), posted on UNCHR-REFWORLD website, http://www.refworld .org/docid/5035f2ea2.html, accessed February 29, 2016.

CHAPTER SEVEN

Challenges and Constraints

Forced Marriage as a Form of "Traditional" Practice in the Gambia

BALA SAHO

Nbaa niŋnfaa	Mummy and Daddy,
Niŋ a ye a tara, ali be nii la,	If you wish to give me away in marriage,
Ali si nkili, ali ye n ñininka.	Call me and seek my opinion.
Saayiŋ tiloo,	Nowadays,
Moo te nte nii noo la,	No one can force me to marry,
Fo ali maŋ a je,	Don't you see,
Buŋ jaŋo loota n ñe.	I am on top of a skyscraper?

Teenage Mandinka girls usually sing this song while they play in village squares under moonlit skies, contemplating their lives and relationships. In the song, the girls are pleading with their parents not to forcefully give them away in marriage without their consent because they have their own dreams and expectations about life. The girls are cognizant of the fact that these days, they cannot be married without their consent, and they are calling on their mothers and fathers to be attentive to their wishes. The metaphor of a tall building symbolizes an expectation of a life far beyond village squares and huts to high rises and sprawling urban centers, representing the changes taking place as a result of rural-to-urban drift since the establishment of colonial rule. As populations move from rural areas to urban centers, many customary practices are transplanted, but they are simultaneously being questioned and challenged by the younger generations. Importantly, the song reveals that forced marriage is a common occurrence in these communities and that the young girls are condemning the practice.[1]

In a recent assessment of the legal status of women and children in the Gambia conducted by the Female Lawyers Association–Gambia (FLAG), one is struck not only by the incidence of forced marriages but also by the impact and influence of tradition and custom in the consummation of marriages in this former British colony.[2] The concepts of tradition and custom are complicated because of their endless journey in time and because they are endlessly debated. Some of the debates involve ways in which colonial administrators in Africa went about reconfiguring African traditional practices for the functioning of colonial enterprise and how African leaders used it to their own advantage. For example, for Terence Ranger, the British colonial administrators invented African traditions for Africans through codification, thereby transforming flexible custom into hard prescription. Martin Chanock sees tradition as devices employed by rural elites to enforce the claim on labor of elders over the young, of husbands over wives, and of property owners over domestic slaves.[3]

Thomas Spear also argues that tradition remains critical in understanding historical processes of social change and representation.[4] In this way, linking to certain traditions can validate groups and individuals who maintained such traditions. When individuals, families, communities, or nations act in a "traditional way," we need to ask, as Elizabeth Thornberry does in chapter 5, in whose interests it is to act this way. Also, because human societies are dynamic, so too are their traditions. This raises the question of why the customs and traditions about forced marriage and the related practices of early marriage persist to this day. Is it possible that some of the young girls act in their own interest by accepting early marriages for prestige and for social and economic reasons—to increase their chances of getting support from their husbands due to the prevailing disadvantageous position of women in this particular society? For example, in the Gambia, 65.8 percent of adult women are illiterate compared to 51.4 percent of men, and the lives of over 90 percent of Gambian women are subject to the shari'a and/or customary law, which could infringe on the development of women.[5] In short, it is difficult to determine where traditions begin or end. Nonetheless, for the purpose of this chapter, I use the term *tradition* to refer to practices passed down from earlier generations to the present generation and specifically the traditions and customs of arranged and early forced marriage practices.

A recent case involving a girl named Mariama illuminates the problems of the persistence of the traditions regarding arranged marriages in the Gambia. In 2009, at age fourteen, Mariama was forced to marry a man older than her father. She became the third and youngest wife of the husband, as under Islamic law, a man may marry up to four women. No matter how much Mariama protested, the marriage proceeded. Then, her husband mysteriously died. The man's elderly wife was arrested and detained at a police station on suspicion of having poisoned him, charges she denied. After three days of reflection, Mariama walked to the police station and revealed that it was she who poisoned the husband because she had been forced to marry him.[6]

Mariama's story corresponds with a case investigated by FLAG. The police had arrested Kura, then a fourteen-year-old girl, because they suspected that she had poisoned her husband. The police alleged that the man died after drinking green tea that she prepared. However, several others also drank the tea and did not die. Kura was initially detained by the police and then put in prison, where she remained for nearly three years without charge. After FLAG's intervention, the court declared her detention unlawful, and she was released.[7]

These cases reflect how some girls and young women respond to traditional marriages that involve coercion and force. Driven into untenable relations because of various social, cultural, and economic issues, some will resort to murder to escape them.

In this chapter, I investigate two types of traditional or customary marriage practices and their implications for forced marriage, bearing in mind, as Brett Shadle does in chapter 3, that in the Gambia, forced marriage almost always involved a young girl below the age of consent. According to the Convention on the Rights of the Child, the term *early marriage* refers to any marriage of a child younger than eighteen years old; it is recognized as a violation of a child's rights.[8] A *forced marriage* is defined as a marriage that is conducted without the valid consent of one or both parties and that involves duress, whether physical or emotional.[9] Like forced marriage, an *arranged marriage* is conducted by parents and family members without necessarily obtaining the consent of the bride and groom: it is the family members who make the important choices. As Richard Roberts argues in chapter 1, an arranged marriage is essentially a forced marriage because the bride and groom cannot say no to their relatives' choice. This practice questions the age of consent or the age at which a girl should be married. In the Gambia, this is usually after first menses, which can be at thirteen or fourteen for some girls.

I examine the cultural and traditional meanings of marriage practices and trace difficulties surrounding the interpretation of forced marriage, especially with regard to the tradition of arranged marriages. I argue that in order to understand the complexities of forced marriage—in which parents determine whom their children should marry, an arrangement that is sometimes made when the children are infants—the sociocultural, economic, and traditional norms and values as well as the livelihood practices of the people concerned should be understood. In other words, there is a need to investigate more thoroughly how forced marriage may be seen as an institution essential for preserving the economics of a way of life. For this chapter, I have used archival and secondary sources as well as oral interviews I conducted between 2010 and 2013. In particular, I asked elderly men and women of the central and south bank regions in urban and rural areas of the Gambia about cultural norms and values, about marriage practices, and about the question of forced marriage.

DISCRIMINATION AGAINST WOMEN

The song quoted at the outset of this chapter and examples from FLAG and several nongovernmental organizations attest to the fact that early and forced marriages have deep roots in Gambian society, and these marriages persist despite the harm they do. In fact, the song is particularly revealing because it is a form of protest against the persistence of forced marriage at the village level. The village squares provide platforms for girls to express their desperation about such practices. In the same vein, Mariama's readiness to face punishment by openly admitting to poisoning her husband illustrates that young girls are indeed challenging the institution of arranged and forced marriages and not merely by song. In extreme cases, girls forced into marriages refuse to have babies to protest against the union. Caroline H. Bledsoe and her colleagues suggest that young women in forced marriages use contraceptive injections to prevent pregnancy in the hope that their husbands, discouraged by their failure to conceive, will decide they are sterile and free them to marry men of their own choosing.[10]

Numerous scholars have studied the subject of forced and arranged marriages in Africa.[11] Mariam Ouattara and others have demonstrated that in some West African states, such as Benin, Ivory Coast, and Burkina Faso, early marriage is a common practice, whereby girls as young as ten to thirteen are kidnapped from their families and taken to their husbands. These authors have also shown that girls are betrothed at or before birth by their parents, based on friendships or on a system of exchanging women between ethnic groups within the community. The husband-to-be and his family may have given presents (*dadaho*) or provided services (*glodian*) to their future in-laws according to custom. Parents feel a strong obligation to respect the pledge, forcing the girl to marry the man they have chosen for her. It is not unknown for a desperate girl, unwilling to marry a man she does not know or love, to commit suicide.[12] My findings in the Gambia are consistent with these conclusions.

The effort to reform marriage dates to the early colonial period. Colonial officials were also concerned about violence against girls and made attempts to stop the practice of forced marriage. Most of the colonial era debates centered on what officials saw as early forced marriage in the Gambia colony and protectorate and what measures should be taken to redefine marriage practices, especially the age at which a girl should marry (the age of consent). Toward those ends, the officials promulgated a series of marriage laws. In 1862, one of the first of such laws, the Marriage Ordinance, was enacted. The ordinance provided that in the case of a person who was under twenty-one and wished to contract a marriage, the consent of the parents or guardians or a judge of the Supreme Court was necessary. This law was supposedly meant to curtail child marriages.[13] Unfortunately, the legislation did not have much impact on the status of women, as it was impossible to implement due to opposition from the Muslim community. Nowadays, the nongovernmental organizations, in particular women's rights organizations, are working to raise awareness and to encourage the government of the Gambia to enact and implement laws prohibiting the discrimination against girls and women.[14] The Gambia is a signatory to various international instruments on human rights, which form the basis for the protection of human rights, especially the rights of women and children (the International Bill of Human Rights, the African Charter on Human and People's Rights, the Commission on the Status of Women [CSW], the Convention on the Elimination of Discrimination against Women [CEDAW], and the Convention on the Rights of the Child [CRC]).[15]

The government of the Gambia has taken some positive steps since the 1970s to ratify these instruments, to address issues of discrimination against women, and to promote women's access to education. For example, section 27 of the 1997 Constitution provides that marriage shall be based on the full consent of both parties and "complete and equal respect" between men and women, and it should be entered into voluntarily by men and women of "the requisite age and capacity." Section 28 underscores the rights of women, providing that "women shall be accorded full and equal dignity of the person with men."[16] However, enacting and implementing effective laws in the interest of women and young girls has been problematic for many reasons.

Although the 1997 Constitution prohibits any discrimination based on gender, it also explicitly proclaims the need to preserve traditions and customs. For instance, the authorities have on several occasions since 1997 taken a stand against female genital cutting (FGC), but they have often argued that this practice is part of Gambian culture and that the government cannot prohibit it. As a result, the Gambia has shown reservations regarding most of the international and regional conventions that it has ratified.[17] By invoking tradition, officials prefer not to offend those who are interested in maintaining customary practices of the population, rather than implementing the law. Sally E. Merry argues that governments invoke culture in international forums as an excuse for their failure to act energetically to promote gender equality and the values of autonomy and choice that are at the heart of the human rights system. Transnational women's human rights activists maintain that governments' claims to respect the particularities of local cultures, traditions, or religious practices are forms of resistance to their efforts to promote women's equality.[18] The CEDAW report of 2003 states that the Gambia has not integrated the legislative and legal provisions contained in the conventions it has ratified into its legislation. Its internal law is therefore in complete contradiction to the Convention on the Elimination of All Forms of Discrimination against Women, especially those articles concerning marriage and divorce.[19] The president of the Gambia Bar Association, Justice Loubna Farage, recently reminded participants at a workshop on gender-based violence that two bills—on sexual offense as well as domestic violence—have not yet been ratified despite being in the pipeline for a long time.[20]

Another factor that hinders progress to enforce legislation prohibiting discrimination against women is the traditional preference for boys.

Although boys are generally encouraged to be high achievers, girls are mentored to become housewives and to be obedient to their husbands. When a family is presented with a choice to send one of their children to school, it is the girl who most often remains at home. Early school leaving has significant repercussions for the future success of these children. Whereas a boy can remain unmarried for many years, an unmarried girl is soon labeled as "too old to marry." What is striking about these kinds of attitudes is that they are anchored in everyday speech and proverbs. One of the popular sayings is "*Niŋ I ye miraŋo koyoo je suntukunŋoto, I si a loŋ ko feŋ ne keta a la*" (If you see a clean calabash at a cesspool, know that the bottom has a hole). This supposedly means that if a girl has remained unmarried for many years, something must be wrong with her. It is important to grasp the social consequences of these traditional practices and explain why they persist in the Gambia.

DIMENSIONS OF FORCED AND ARRANGED MARRIAGES

In the Gambia, tradition and custom play a vital role in the arrangement of a marriage between a man and a woman. Many of these traditional practices involve elements of force and coercion, since the marriage is arranged without the consent of the young people and especially without the consent of the young girl. Claude Meillassoux reminds us that in domestic communities, control of marriage is linked to control of political power as a mean to control the mechanisms of social reproduction: access to wives, land, and personhood.[21] In the Gambia, parental obligations and controls are strictly adhered to, especially in matters pertaining to marriage. Parents usually make a final decision on a traditional marriage arrangement. On many occasions, the bride and groom may never have met; no courtship would have taken place between the two members of a future couple. These preconjugal arrangements often involve immediate parents and distant kin groups. One reason that these arranged marriages persist is economic. Under custom, the groom has to either perform several years of labor for the prospective bride's father (helping him on the farm and performing tasks such as mending fences) or pay bridewealth. Bridewealth can be money or services transferred to the girl's parents by the parents of the husband-to-be, in kind or cash, before a marriage can take place. Bridewealth compensates the bride's kin for the resources that the girl's parents spent in her upbringing and for the loss of her future labor and children, which will be lost when the girl leaves the household. Among some groups, such as the Fulani, Wolof, and Mandinka, arrangements take place several years before the intended girl reaches the age of marriage.

One of these traditional arrangements is known as *londiroo* (to make it stand; wait; betrothal) or *bulu mutoo* (to hold hands), whereby the girl is tied to, allocated to, or arranged to marry a cousin or any other person. Among the Mandinka, this practice is essentially regarded as an arranged marriage. It is a situation in which little girls are betrothed at tender ages.[22] In this arrangement, when both sets of parents agree a piece of cloth is symbolically tied to the little girl's arms—hence, the terms *londiroo* or *bulu mutoo*. This practice has long-lasting implications for the girl and the boy's parents. When seen as an investment, the husband-to-be and his parents assume the costs of raising the child and helping her parents. The traditional bond of londiroo guarantees that when the girl reaches the age of thirteen or fourteen, she will become the bride of the groom. In such cases, the girl has very few choices, since she has been betrothed for many years.

Abduction (*musu suñaa*) is another form of marriage common in the Gambia as well as many other parts of Africa.[23] Musu suñaa is a traditional practice that empowers husbands to abduct their new wives, with or without advising the wife first and usually against her will. In some cases, this is done with the knowledge of the parents of the husband or of the girl. Musu suñaa is carried out mainly in two ways. In a situation where the marriage is consummated between a boy and a girl and the boy has failed to pay or has taken too much time to complete the payment of the bridewealth, the girl's parents also drag their feet in letting the girl transfer to her husband's home. In such cases, the husband may, with the approval of his parents, organize his friends in an expedition to snatch the girl. Once abducted, the girl finds it hard to go back to her parents, and the husband can dictate the mode of payment of the bridewealth.[24] A girl named Ramatoulie expressed the tradition well when she recollected how she was kidnapped by a group of young men from her village in the Upper River Region of the Gambia:

> In the evening, my husband and some of his friends, four of them came to visit me and my parents. After hours of conversation, my mother asked me to see them off. The village was quiet by then. As soon we were out of earshot, I was seized. My mouth was covered with cloth so I could not cry for help. They carried me off and I am still here. Now it is too late to try to return because of my children.[25]

All the elderly women at my interview with Ramatoulie corroborated her story. They were in the village when it happened.

The women added that even if the girl tries to return, it comes to no avail because the husband uses spiritual means to force the woman to stay.[26] I asked the interviewees to explain further.

> Q: What kinds of spiritual means do men use to force girls to stay in such marriages?
>
> A: (laughter) Oh! They have means. Go talk to those men sitting over there. One of the ways is to use an amulet. When the husband comes into the compound and finds you sitting, he would call your name and press the amulet. He would call your name aloud; "Ramatoulie, you are sitting?" Once you answer to him in the affirmative, he would press the amulet and you would never think of running away.
>
> Q: Do you know anyone who has been forced to stay in her marriage?
>
> A: Yes, some years ago, one lady committed suicide by jumping into a well. It was sad because we knew that she never wanted to stay with her husband.
>
> Q: Why do you think men kidnap their wives?
>
> A: You know, usually, people who do that are not wealthy and we tend to spend wealth in marriage. It is cheaper to carry your wife in this way than paying for bridewealth at once and spending lots of money for the marriage ceremony.

Other interviews provided further insights into the practices of forced marriage in the Gambia.

In an interview with two elderly women in the village of Fula Bantang in the Upper River Region, Awa Baldeh and Konkon Baldeh revealed that when men marry girls, women have no say in it.

> As a mother, you cannot decide who should marry your daughter. Men make the decision and the girl cannot refuse. You cannot reject men's decisions; you will be flogged out of your sense. There have been occasions here where girls were unwillingly taken to their husbands and this has resulted in bad consequences for the girl.[27]

Nfamara Jatta, an elderly man of Janjanbureh, told me that he had some of his daughters married without their consent, and he explained that economic reasons were the motives for doing so. "In marrying your daughter, you need to be sure whether the husband to be can afford the basic needs for your daughter and her children." He continued to say that his kin group attempted to give away one of his daughters in marriage without her consent, a move he did not support. His refusal was based not on the legality of the act but on the fact that the kin group wanted her to marry a man who was poor or, as he puts it, "*a buloo maŋ a koo beŋ*" (a man who cannot make ends meet).[28]

Scholars who study marriage in northern Nigeria, such as Barbara Gallaway, underscore Jatta's economic concerns about the subsistence obligations in marriage: "A man has not only moral but legal responsibility for the support of his family. The remedy for non-support for a woman is divorce, which is granted by an Islamic court and generally is not difficult to get."[29]

Another way in which the practice of musu suñaa is executed is by forcefully carrying a girl to a man with whom no particular kind of arrangement has been made. In this case, the girl does not know the husband to be. Thus, both parents make the arrangement without the knowledge of the girl or the boy. Dado's story is an example:

> In 1993, in the town of Jarra Soma, Gambia, Dado, a young girl at the age of 13 was kidnapped by three youths on the orders of her parents. She was bundled in a vehicle bound for Guinea Conakry. Dado was being forced to marry her cousin. After two years in Guinea, Dado came back to Soma with a baby girl, apparently having eloped with her boy-friend. The parents made no further effort to return her to her husband.[30]

Early and forced marriage further speaks to the economic situation of parents. Jatta insists that poor parents are likely to marry their girls early to ameliorate their economic conditions. As a result of high bridewealth in some parts of the country, fathers demand significant resources for their daughters.[31] Early marriage is also a means to prevent girls from getting pregnant out of wedlock—a matter related to the issue of saving face.[32]

MAINTENANCE OF "TRADITIONAL" MARRIAGE

In placing emphasis on the maintenance of tradition in marriage, we must again ask, in whose interest are certain traditions being upheld and preferred over others? Scholars have already examined the subject of tradition, and it is clear that traditions can be selective. For instance, in Africa some Muslims invoke a lineage to the prophet Muhammad and Arabs to legitimate themselves and their positions among fellow Muslims. Also, many Africans are quick to reference relations to past legendary figures as efforts to communicate and validate themselves and their ethnicity. In the process, control of certain traditions, including marriage, becomes the monopoly of elderly men.

According to Meillassoux, two basic ways to control social power are by controlling women and controling tradition.[33] In a discussion with Kantong Suwareh of Ndanka village, North Bank Region, I asked him why many young boys and girls are being married. He responded with a question. "Why do you think these young boys prefer to stay in this remote village, far from the main road, no electricity, no running water and with farm labor? It is because of these young girls and without controlling the girls, I doubt if we can control these boys."[34] For Kantong, having control of the young boys and girls is important because he will have access to their labor while they study the Qur'an. In the Gambia, with the advent of peanut production in the mid-nineteenth century, child labor was renewed because more land was required than ever before for the cultivation of the crop. In this way, young boys and girls are encouraged to marry early, which, as Meillassoux reasons, is to the benefit of elders implicitly for labor expectations.[35]

The interest in the perpetuation of traditional marriage goes beyond labor requirements to the circulation of goods and the solidarity it creates. According to Meillassoux, the control, subordination, and direction of pubescent women into alliances are defined by their community's obligations, so that procreation takes place in the context of male relations of descent.[36] In such traditions, elderly men maintain their authority in the family and community. Also, maintenance of tradition can represent efforts by elders to keep the norms and values of society together, so that each person acts in the common interest of the group, and that, of course, benefits the elderly men in authority.

Here, it is essential to underline the "traditional thinking" that constitutes norms of practice and fundamental principles and guidelines for members of society to continue to live together—a pattern of thinking that holds in reverence certain kinds of hierarchical systems to protect a way of life. In most African societies, adhering to the voices and judgments of elders is the societal norm, even if their words or rulings are disadvantageous to some individuals in the society. In words and practice, the ethic is: "This is how our forebears did it, and this is how we will do it. This is how we lived, and we are going to continue to live this way." This ethic is commonly expressed by the Mandinka as *foroya mu kaŋo le ti* (honoring one's word is noble), which is deduced from a generic principle of adherence to society. In such a society, those who obey orders, abide by the penalties, and honor authority are regarded as having been brought up in a cultured family. They have honor.[37]

Consequently, if a father agrees to marry his daughter to someone, it must be done even if the girl does not consent because it is better to save face than to be ashamed in society. In other words, if an individual is to live with honor, it is the society that bestows that honor—but the individual must first claim it.[38] Alhagi Sunkare Marakong of Wassu in Central River Region showed happiness and pride that he was able to decide whom his two daughters were to marry. He emphasized his role as the family head and stressed that all the children were abiding by his rules. For Sunkare, obedience was what would bless the marriage of his children because it was by obeying his parents that his own marriage was blessed.[39] Such resolve cannot be divorced from the cultural context and livelihood practices of people such as Sunkare, whose life revolves around community, farmwork, and religion. The key issue for the persistence of tradition can vary. Thus, obedience is pivotal for Sunkare, but for Jatta and Suwareh, the economic value of bridewealth and access to labor, respectively, are key. These stories illustrate the complications of forced marriage, especially when marriage is seen as a cultural practice with important and direct impacts on the livelihood of the families involved. In addition, these examples show the continuation of the tradition of forced marriage not only because of an unthinking pride or resistance to change but also because it is seen as a most effective way of dealing with specific aspects of fast-paced economic and social upheaval.

CONSENT AND FALSE CONSCIOUSNESS: ARE ARRANGED MARRIAGES THE SAME AS FORCED MARRIAGES?

Gender equity advocates, such as Isatou Touray, insist that forced marriages almost always involve young girls who have not reached the age of consent. Touray's view is that when a girl is forced to marry at a young age, her mother lives in continuous fear because the girl is too young to endure the trials of marriage. In Touray's work with numerous women around the Gambia, she has found that mothers whose daughters marry early in life live with stress and anxiety.[40]

"*Luŋ-wo-luŋ, nbuloo be n kuŋoto. I ye a futundi le, a koo kiloo maŋ meŋ*" (Every day, I cry 'my hands are on my head.' They married her but her backbones are not yet strong). How can a girl be married at the age of thirteen or fourteen? Touray asks.[41] By chance, a few days before my interview with Touray I met a fourteen-year-old girl who was already married and was on her way from a village in the Central River Region to join her husband in the city. She expressed happiness and a willingness to join him. Every time I asked whether she was happy with the choice she made, she would nod her head and smile.

Touray's concerns and the fourteen-year-old girl's eagerness to get married raise a number of central questions. What is the age of consent in the Gambian cultural context? At what age is marriage appropriate and acceptable to society? What other factors necessitate early or forced marriage in a patriarchal society such as the Gambia's? Here, it is important to underscore not only why these marriage practices have continued over time but also the broader effects of the practices on young girls, their parents, and the society at large. It is necessary to discuss ways in which some of these marriages are arranged—ways that may amount to compulsion. At what point do arranged marriages become forced marriages? Or can all arranged marriages be classified as forced marriages, since it is almost always young girls who are put through the trials of these marriages? For instance, in discussing the complications surrounding issues of early forced marriage, Sundari Anitha and Aisha Gill note that consent and coercion in relation to marriage can be better understood as two ends of a continuum, between which lie degrees of sociocultural expectation, control, persuasion, pressure, threat, and force.[42] To understand the practice of forced marriage, it is therefore vital to look at the multiple meanings and implications of marriage as an institution sanctioned both by tradition and by religion.

First, in the Gambia, when viewed through a cultural lens, marriage is not about the girl and her husband as described earlier but about society. The act of marriage can improve social networks, reinforce kinship ties, and also affirm group identity.

Second, we need to examine the impact of Islam, the religion of the majority of Gambians, on the country's cultural traditions. Since the arrival of

Islam centuries ago, most Gambians have adopted both Islam and Islamic culture. In many instances, customary laws and Islamic laws coexist. This means that Gambians subject themselves to Islamic law, or shari'a, and Islamic traditions (*hadith* and *sunnah*), especially when it comes to marriage. The Gambia legally recognizes four types of marriage—Christian, Muslim, customary, and civil. Civil marriage is not compulsory, nor is there a minimum legal age for marriage, which means that the law does not explicitly prohibit the marriage of children.[43] Therefore, age of consent is not a matter critical to the arrangement of marriage.

Although Islamic commentators and various legal schools differ on the age at which a girl should be married, there is a general consensus that they should marry at the age of puberty.[44] Essentially, marriage can only take place when the girl has had her first menstrual cycle, but of course, the problem is that girls first menstruate at different ages. Moreover, because the girl's father has the right to marry her to whomever he chooses without consulting her, he can betroth his daughter at birth, as in the case of londiroo described previously. Londiroo is clearly against the spirit of Islamic law, which favors the idea that girls should make their own decisions when it comes to marriage. This notion of choice is enshrined in one of the most popular hadith, which tells that a girl went to the Messenger of Allah and reported that her father had forced her to marry without her consent. The Messenger of God gave her the choice between accepting the marriage or invalidating it.[45] Qadi Alhagie Masamba Jagne of the Banjul Muslim court reasoned that whenever the girl child does not consent to a marriage, that marriage should be abandoned. In his view, both members of a couple must be prepared to undergo the trials of marriage because it makes no sense to create a union that will not last.[46]

However, in societies such as the Gambia's where bridewealth is an important economic exchange, divorce can be difficult and problematic, especially if a woman initiates it. When the woman seeks the divorce, she has to return the bridewealth that the husband paid at the time of marriage, and this is usually wealth already spent or consumed. In other words, when a woman wants a divorce, she and her parents must find ways to refund the money. Jane Guyer notes that in most places, both British and French colonial legal practice increasingly favored marriage by bridewealth, which combined the features of marital stability, limiting women's ability to be "capricious" with male authority, and clear public markings of the interfamily contract.[47] Hence, the economic challenges of returning bridewealth oblige women to bear the ordeals of forced marriages. Women also find that tradition and culture can be barriers to leaving unhappy marriages.

EFFORTS AT DISCOURAGING FORCED MARRIAGE

Some women's groups in the Gambia maintain that early and forced marriage is tantamount to controlling women's sexual and reproductive rights, a view that has been gaining the attention of the Gambian government. Since the turn of the twenty-first century, the government has increased its efforts with regard to girls' education. It has created "girl-friendly schools" that encourage the education of females and a "girls' education desk" in the Ministry of National Education. It has also established free, state-run primary schools, which has encouraged poor families to educate their daughters. Meanwhile, local women's organizations are making strenuous efforts to translate international instruments to the national level.

Women's rights activists insist that forcing girls to marry against their will undercuts their ability to reach their full potential as women. They argue that these girls will not be able to have a proper education once they become child mothers. And their physical and mental growth will be stunted. Most important, a forced marriage conditions the girl to be dependent on her husband and the husband's kin group for financial and economic support.[48] Added to these are issues of male patriarchy, whereby the girl's father can decide when she is to get married and to whom without her consent. Traditionally, women have been supposed to be subservient, obedient, and faithful to men.[49]

Tradition empowers the elderly to feel they can size up the younger generations and determine the path their lives should take without realizing that cultures are changing and shaping people in new ways. Generational changes in economic and social differentiations result in new forms of relationships, which can influence young people to make their own decisions, including what kinds of marriage arrangements they want. Social mobility can open up ways in which people with different cultural and social backgrounds can meet, making issues of marriage more complicated in a society where marriage is regulated by tradition and religion.

Amira Mashhour, in her work on parts of northern Africa, observes:

> Although women's rights in non-Muslim societies are not totally
> fulfilled, oppression of women's rights in Muslim societies is unique

in that it is primarily done in the name of Islam. These communities claim that certain discriminatory practices are congruent with *shari'a* law and that their personal status laws, for instance, are based on Sharia law. By doing so, Muslim societies create a sacred justification for any discrimination or inequality already in existence or that could be stipulated in the future.[50]

The disadvantaged social position of women in a patriarchal society such as the Gambia's can make young women vulnerable to being forced to marry early and/or without their consent. Culturally, marriage is viewed as primary and sacred, the institution on which the family is constructed. It is a moral duty for Muslim men and women to enter into and honor the marriage contract. As Touray observes, to Gambian mothers customary marriage and forced marriage revolve around what is regarded as honor and shame: "How would society judge me and my unmarried daughter?"[51] For many parents, compulsion is preferable to living in disgrace and with the fear of facing a single life. Many parents fear that their daughters, if left to their own devices, will have children out of wedlock, become prostitutes, or decide not to have children in their lives. Also, as demonstrated in the introduction to this volume and in the chapter by Mariane Ferme, the arranged marriage often tends to have parental consent (even if out of a social or cultural pressure) with all its cultural fanfare. It is imperative to view forced and arranged marriages against the backdrop of the livelihood practices of the communities involved if we are to attempt an understanding of all its implications.

There are, however, encouraging signs that the tradition of forced and early marriage is changing. In 2011, a human rights campaign group noted a decrease in the abuse of young women in the Gambia. While delivering his speech on behalf of the Sare Ngai Steering Committee on Female Genital Mutilation (FGM) during the minideclaration of another twenty-five communities within the Wuli West, Wuli East, and Sandu districts at Sare Ngai village in Upper River Region, Mr. Jawneh noted their data have shown that forced marriage has dropped from 82 percent to 12 percent and that early marriage has also declined, from 66 percent to 8 percent, between 2007 and 2010.[52] In fact, Gambian lawmakers recently passed with a unanimous vote the Domestic Violence Bill 2013 during the fourth meeting of the National Assembly in the 2013 legislative year, as a measure to address both gender and domestic violence.[53] Yet even though progress has been made in some areas, more actions need to be taken to end discrimination against girls and women. In the same vein, more work is needed to investigate how Gambians understand these changes and how they reconcile tradition and change.

NOTES

1. For recent comments on forced marriage and other abuses against women, see the *Banjul (Gambia) Point,* September 13, 2013, and April 18, 2012, and the *Banjul (Gambia) Daily Observer,* October 22, 2012.

2. Female Lawyers Association–Gambia, Case Report, 2007–2011, May 2012.

3. Terence Ranger, "The Invention of Tradition in Colonial Africa," in *Perspectives on Africa: A Reader in Culture, History and Representation,* ed. Roy Richard Grinker, Stephen C. Lubkemann, and Christopher B. Steiner (Malden, MA: Wiley-Blackwell, 2010); Martin Chanock, *Law, Custom and Social Order: The Colonial Experience in Malawi and Zambia* (Cambridge: Cambridge University Press, 1985).

4. Thomas Spear, "Neo-traditionalism and the Limits of Invention in British Colonial Africa," *Journal of African History* 44, no. 1 (2003): 3–27. See also Jan Vansina, for whom traditions embody continuity and shape the future for those who hold them and as such can be continually renewed; Vansina, *Paths in the Rainforest: Toward a History of Political Tradition in Equatorial Africa* (Madison: University of Wisconsin Press 1990), 257–58.

5. International Federation of Human Rights (IFHR), Note on the Situation of Women in Gambia 33rd Session, July 5–22, 2005, New York. This note is the result of an international investigation mission, led by Sophie Bessis, deputy secretary-general of the FIDH, in the Gambia from April 24–29, 2005. It is an attempt to examine the situation of Gambian women in order to bring to light the discrimination against them.

6. Mr. and Mrs. Foday Manka, interview, Janjanbureh, MacCarthy, Central River Region, July 10, 2013, with Hassoum Ceesay and Alieu Jawara.

7. Female Lawyers Association, 2007–11, 7.

8. See http://www.unfpa.org/swp/2005/presskit/factsheets/facts_child_marriage .htm#ftn2#ftn2, accessed September 16, 2014.

9. See http://www.unicef.org/publications/index_26024.html, accessed September 16, 2014.

10. Caroline H. Bledsoe, Allan G. Hill, Umberto D'Alessandro, and Patricia Langerock, "Constructing Natural Fertility: The Use of Western Contraceptive Technologies in Rural Gambia," *Population and Development Review* 20, no. 1 (1994): 81–113.

11. For information on marriage practices, see Luigi M. Solivetti, "Family, Marriage and Divorce in a Hausa Community: A Sociological Model, Africa," *Journal of the International African Institute* 64, no. 2 (1994): 252–71; Alma Gottlieb, "Cousin Marriage, Birth Order and Gender: Alliance Models among the Beng of Ivory Coast," *Man,* n.s, 21, no. 4 (December 1986): 697–722. Also see Augustine S. J. Park, "'Other

Inhumane Acts': Forced Marriage, Girl Soldiers and the Special Court for Sierra Leone," *Social and Legal Studies* 15, no. 3 (2006): 315—37; Carol E. Kaufman and Stavros E. Stavrou, "'Bus fare please': The Economics of Sex and Gifts among Young People in Urban South Africa," *Culture, Health and Sexuality: An International Journal for Research, Intervention and Care* 6, no. 5 (2004): 377–91.

12. Mariam Ouattara, Purna Sen, and Marilyn Thomson, "Forced Sex: The Perils of Childhood for Girls," *Gender and Development* 6, no. 3 (1998): 27–33; Annabel Erulkar, "Early Marriage, Marital Relations and Intimate Partner Violence in Ethiopia," *International Perspectives on Sexual and Reproductive Health* 39, no. 1 (2013): 6–13.

13. In the Gambia as in most colonial states, colonial officials were concerned about regulating marriage. See Minimum Age of Marriage of Consent (Inside Outside Marriage in the Gambia—Memorandum), Colonial Secretary's Office (hereafter cited as CSO) 2/1395 and 3/304, Forced Marriage of African Girls, National Records Service, Banjul, the Gambia; Brett L. Shadle, "Bridewealth and Female Consent: Marriage Disputes in African Courts, Gusiiland, Kenya," *Journal of African History* 44, no. 2 (2003): 241–62.

14. Spearheading the awareness campaign in Gambia are the Committee on Traditional Practices (GAMCOTRAP), the Association for the Promotion of Women & Girls Advancement (APWGA), and FLAG.

15. International Federation of Human Rights, Note on the Situation of Women.

16. FIDH—Gambia note/CEDAW, 6. See also United Nations Convention on the Elimination of All Forms of Discrimination against Women (CEDAW/C/GMB/1–3), Concluding Comments on Gambia, July 22, 2005.

17. FIDH—Gambia note, 3.

18. Sally Engle Merry, "Human Rights and Transnational Culture: Regulating Gender Violence through Global Law," 2006, New York University, prepared for presentation at the Harry W. Arthus Symposium, Toronto, Canada, May 5, 2005, p. 75. See also Merry, *Human Rights and Gender Violence: Translating International Law into Local Justice* (Chicago: University of Chicago Press, 2006).

19. FIDH—Gambia note, 7.

20. *Banjul (Gambia) Daily Observer,* November 25, 2013; *Banjul (Gambia) Point,* November 29, 2013. See Saida Hodzic, "The Logics of Controversy: Gender Violence as a Site of Frictions in Ghanaian Society," in *Domestic Violence and the Law in Colonial and Postcolonial Africa,* ed. Emily S. Burrill, Richard L. Roberts, and Elizabeth Thornberry (Athens: Ohio University Press, 2010), 220–38.

21. Claude Meillassoux, *Maidens, Meal and Money: Capitalism and the Domestic Community* (Cambridge: Cambridge University Press, 1975), 12.

22. This practice can be compared to what is known as *Jaba jibɳo* (to garden or to water), a practice whereby men choose young girls to become their future wives by giving them gifts. This practice, however, is not binding by custom or tradition.

23. For more on this type of forced marriages, see Brett Shadle, *"Girl Cases": Marriage and Colonialism in Gusiiland, Kenya, 1890–1970* (Portsmouth, NH: Heinemann, 2006); Caroline Sweetman, ed., *Gender, Development and Marriage* (Oxford:

Oxfam GB, 2003); Lea Mwambene and Julia Sloth-Nielsen, "Benign Accommodation? *Ukuthwala,* 'Forced Marriage' and the South African Children's Act," *Journal of Family Law and Practice* 2, no. 1 (2011): 5–16; and Thornberry's chapter in this volume.

24. Wife stealing is a common traditional practice in some African societies. For example, in South Africa *ukuthwala* is a form of abduction that involves the kidnapping of a girl or a young woman by a man and his friends or peers with the intention of compelling her family to endorse marriage negotiations. Sometimes, it is undertaken with the consent of the girl, parents, or guardians. See Chelete Monyane, "Is Ukuthwala Another Form of 'Forced Marriage'?" *South Review of Sociology* 44, no. 3 (2013): 64–82; M. J. Maluleke, "Culture, Tradition, Custom, Law and Gender Equality," *Potchefstroom Electronic Law Journal* 15, no. 1 (2012): 2–22.

25. Ramatoulie Bah, interview, Sarengai, Central River Division, the Gambia, July 5, 2013.

26. Ramatoulie Bah, Aja Baldeh, Mariama Baldeh, and Oumie Baldeh, group interview, Sarengai, Central River Division, July 5, 2013.

27. Awa Baldeh and Konkon Baldeh, interview, Fulabantang, Central River Division, the Gambia, July 5, 2013, with Hassoum Ceesay and Alieu Jawara.

28. Nfamara Jatta, interview, Georgetown, Janjanbureh, the Gambia, July 6, 2013. *A buloo maŋ a koo beŋ* (he cannot make ends meet, in Mandinka).

29. Barbara Gallaway, *Muslim Hausa Women in Nigeria: Tradition and Change* (Syracuse, NY: Syracuse University Press, 1987), 39.

30. Other forms of forced marriage continue to be practiced in parts of the country. For example, in *bundaa soroŋo* (door locking), on her first visit to the husband, a wife would be detained (locked inside the house) against her will by her spouse. The girl would stay in the husband's home and transition to married life. This kind of action contradicts the practice wherein a girl waits in her mother's house so that formal marriage procedures can take place, including a formal ceremony.

31. In her book about her work in Afghanistan, Deborah Ellis examines how poverty or the lack of economic opportunities forces families not to keep their girls at home but instead send them to marry early, especially in a situation where there are few educational and economic options. See Ellis, *Women of the Afghan War* (Westport, CT: Praeger, 2000).

32. Nowadays, baby dumping, an activity associated with having children out of wedlock, is common in the Gambia. Recently, a court ordered a woman to be hanged for infanticide. In her testimony, she stated that she dumped her baby into a well because she was afraid her father would kill her if he learned that she was pregnant out of wedlock. For this story, see the *Banjun (Gambia) Daily Observer,* October 25, 2011.

33. Meillassoux, *Maidens, Meal and Money,* 78.

34. Alhagi Kantong Suwareh, discussions, Ndanka village, North Bank Division, the Gambia, August 3, 2013. Kantong runs a clerical school and has a number of students.

35. Meillassoux reasons that in agricultural communities, men depend on their wives for food—and because of this dependence, which arises from the cultural division of labor, a young man cannot fulfill himself socially unless he has a wife.

But this cultural choice works to the elder's benefit. Meillassoux, *Maidens, Meal and Money*, 78.

36. Ibid., 76.

37. For issues of forced and honor marriages, see Marie Macey, *Multiculturalism, Religion, and Women: Doing Harm by Doing Good?* (New York: Palgrave Macmillan, 2009). See also William I. Zartman, ed., *Preventive Negotiation: Avoiding Conflict Escalation* (Lanham, MD: Rowman and Littlefield, 2001).

38. Augsburger describes this honoring of "face" as the public self-image that each person wants to claim for herself or himself. He says that "face is a psychological image that can be granted and lost and fought for and presented as a gift. It is a projected image of one's self in a relational context. Face is an identity defined conjointly by the participants in a setting"; David Augsburger, *Conflict Mediation across Cultures: Pathways and Patterns* (Louisville, KY: Westminster John Knox, 1992), 85.

39. Alh. Sunkare Marakong, interview, Central River Division, Wassu, the Gambia, July 5, 2013.

40. Dr. Isatou Touray is the director of GAMCOTRAP.

41. Dr. Isatou Touray, interview, Kanifing, the Gambia. July 25, 2013.

42. Anitha Sundari and Aisha Gill, "Coercion, Consent, and Forced Marriage Debate in the UK," *Feminist Legal Studies* 17, no. 2 (2009): 165–84. See also Aisha K. Gill and Sundari Anitha, eds., *Forced Marriage: Introducing a Social Justice and Human Rights Perspective* (London: Zed Books, 2011); Anne Phillips and Moira Dustin, "UK Initiatives on Forced Marriage: Regulation, Dialogue and Exit," *Political Studies* 52, no. 3 (2004): 531–51.

43. FIDH—Gambia note, 6–7.

44. Principal Qadi Alhagi Masamba Jagne, interview, Banjul Qadi Court, Banjul, the Gambia, July 23, 2013. A qadi is a Muslim judge.OK?

45. Ajaratou Maimouna Savage, interview, Kanifing, the Gambia, July 25, 2013.

46. Jagne, interview; Ajratou Savage Maimouna, interview, Kanifing, July 23, 2013.

47. Jane Guyer, W*omen and the State in Africa: Marriage Law, Inheritance, and Resettlement* (Boston, African Studies Center, Boston University, 1987), 4–5; Thomas Håkansson, *Bridewealth, Women, and Land: Social Change among the Gusii of Kenya* (Uppsala, Sweden: Almqvist and Wiksell International, 1988).

48. Human Rights Watch indicates that in places such as the Sudan, as a result of failures and inadequacies in legal structures, traditional practices, and economic systems, many women and girls continue to struggle with the often devastating and long-lasting consequences of child marriage. In addition to posing health risks, early marriage also limits women's access to education, knowledge, and skills, as well as their autonomy to think and act for themselves.

49. Among many of the communities in the Gambia, legendary epics and songs popularize and valorize women who are obedient to their husbands. For example, one of the Gambia's late Kora maestros, Lalo Kebba Drammeh, has a powerful song in Mandinka that urges women to be obedient to their husbands: "*Musu soŋ bali te kanda wuluu la*" (A disobedient woman will not give birth to a prosperous child). Likewise, the Wolof have similar adages that admonish women to be hardworking

and faithful to their husbands: "*Ligaay yaay, agni doom*" (Mother's hard work benefits the child—in the physical and spiritual sense).

50. Amira Mashhour, "Islamic Law and Gender Equality—Could There Be a Common Ground? A Study of Divorce and Polygamy in Sharia Law and Contemporary Legislation in Tunisia and Egypt," *Human Rights Quarterly* 27, no. 2 (2005): 563–64.

51. Touray, interview. Dr. Touray believes education and awareness will help young girls and mothers to make informed choices.

52. *Banjul (Gambia) Point,* February 4, 2011.

53. *Banjul (Gambia) Daily Observer,* December 18, 2013.

CHAPTER EIGHT

Resisting Patriarchy, Contesting Homophobia

Expert Testimony and the Construction of Forced Marriage in African Asylum Claims

BENJAMIN N. LAWRANCE AND CHARLOTTE WALKER-SAID

ALLEGATIONS OF forced marriages and attempted forced marriages cited by African refugees as grounds for asylum in the United Kingdom and the United States highlight a central contradiction in postcolonial Africa. In some respects, many postcolonial African states continue to make strides toward clearly proclaiming gender and sexual rights by providing greater civil and social protections. But in other regards, the ideological underpinnings in many postcolonial African democracies—notably, religious views and a reified understanding of "innate" or "natural" African cultural practices—have led to the persecution of particular communities. Some targets, such as women exercising their rights to higher education, family planning, or political expression, may be viewed as part of a rich historical pattern of gender oppression and intolerance for female autonomy. Other targets, such as gay men, lesbians, bisexuals, transgender and intersex people, and other sexual minorities represent, in many ways, a new dimension of another historical tradition vilifying difference, "alterity," and perceived deviance.[1]

Refugee claims constitute a unique and discrete entry point into the lived experiences of contemporary African women, men, and children. The narratives supplied by refugees provide firsthand oral accounts of exploitation, abuse, persecution, and social and private life. Like many forms of legal petition, they are deeply structured by their context. Notwithstanding these considerations, however, they offer an unusually vivid and personalized vantage point from which to examine the changing structure of African family life in the context of the transformative forces of globalization; such forces include information technology, international travel and migration, internationalized rights discourse, and gender and sexuality equity practices and resistances.[2] In this manner, they may be viewed as a contemporary parallel to the rich tradition of African historical research in the precolonial and colonial past, anchored by personal oral testimony.[3]

As the introduction to this volume argues, forced marriages may be regarded as part of a larger intellectual apparatus investigating gender subordination, sociolegal regulation, resistance, and liberation in Africa. But forced marriage refugee claims are both similar to and qualitatively different from other descriptions of persecution and gender-based violence, for several reasons. On the one hand, as many scholars and activists have observed, both the 1951 Convention Relating to the Status of Refugees and the 1967 Protocol Relating to the Status of Refugees entirely omit gender as a category of persecution, and decision makers fail to account for the gendering of politics and the relationship between gender and state practice.[4] On the other hand—unlike with rape, forced impregnation or sterilization, sexual slavery, domestic violence, or female genital mutilation (FGM)—there continues to be, as Kim Thuy Seelinger observed in 2010, "no precedent establishing forced marriage *per se* as a form of persecution" consistent with the definitions emerging from the convention and from the protocol or its domestic iterations throughout North America, Europe, and Australasia.[5]

Likewise, attention has only recently been paid to examining forced marriage's viability as a distinct crime of international law.[6] As a result, individuals alleging forced marriage or attempted forced marriage are compelled to dismantle their claims and reassemble them into what Seelinger calls "more concrete" or "component" harms, using terms with which adjudicators have some familiarity, such as trafficking, rape and sexual assault, physical beating, domestic violence, and FGM.[7] The rearticulation of forced marriage narratives can further occlude the sociocultural contours of forced marriage practices.[8] Refugees fleeing forced marriages inhabit a "forced marriage paradox" insofar as they remain deprived of a consistent set of definitions yet struggle to describe their often violent experiences and constraints without employing terminology that seemingly validates illegitimate actions and further erases their agency.[9]

Because experts assist in rendering refugee narratives comprehensible to adjudicators, their experience provides an avenue for exploring the impact of the dismantling and reassembling of narratives and for observing both how a claim centered on forced marriage originated and how it was rearranged for presentation before an adjudicator. Although many forced marriages and attempted forced marriages may include extreme violence, our experience serving as expert witnesses for dozens of women and men supports Seelinger's contention that many, if not most, are "quieter, subtler affairs."[10] Recognizing various forms of harm to bodily integrity and limits to individual agency is thus a sensitive task and requires a disentangling of self-identity and actual harm from social or cultural influences concealing forced marriage components.

This chapter examines the dynamic nature of forced marriage asylum claims from the perspective of the expert witness. We argue that one consequence of the omission of forced marriage, *qua* gender, from the international language of refugee protection is that asylum advocates are ultimately compelled to reformulate or "squeeze" forced marriage narratives into recognizable concepts and established frameworks. In our experience as experts, we have found that legal counselors are cognizant that judges and adjudicators may more easily understand or appreciate familiar concepts such as patriarchy, patrimonialism, sexism, and homophobia but shy away from complex terms or multivalent concepts that span a number of interrelated practices.[11] As witnesses to the conditions and lifestyles lived by claimants, experts have the capacity to establish new paradigms for recognizing the persecutory harm, such as forced marriage, based on broader principles of human dignity, autonomy, and consent.[12] But our experience suggests that lawyers, many of whom are outcome driven, routinely adopt a more conservative approach and prefer to articulate a need for protection based on existing precedents of gender-based violence.

We have served as expert witnesses in more than two dozen refugee claims from women and men from West Africa alleging various forms of forced marriage. Based on our experience, we contend that two distinct trends have emerged with respect to the framing of the claims vis-à-vis the description of the practices and the identity description of the survivors' persecutory harm. In cases where women flee coerced unions or attempted forced marriages and describe bride-price, contracts, dowries, slavery/indenture, and gender expectations, asylum claims are framed as flight, whereby women *defensively resist* patriarchy and "traditional" expectations for marriage and family life. In the three specific instances from more than twenty lesbian, gay, and bisexual (LGB) claims we examine here—wherein lesbian, gay, and bisexual individuals are escaping heteronormative marital regimes (we have not personally encountered transgender or intersex cases to date)—asylum claims are framed as *affirmatively contesting* homophobia.

As a form of legal mediation, whereby the vernacular content and idiomatic nature of the refugee narrative is translated into a context governed by precedent and jurisprudence, the experience of expert witnessing offers an important new, albeit narrow, window into the lives of Africa's most vulnerable individuals. When forced marriages are dismantled and reassembled as either resisting patriarchy or contesting homophobia, opposite-sex and same-sex practices embedded within forced marriage narratives are inaccurately situated as oppositional. The conservative, outcome-driven representation of claims erases the "newness" and capacity for legal innovation, with the unfortunate consequence of reifying African cultures as primitive, primordial, backward, and rights-violating. In our conclusion, we suggest that individuals involved in African forced marriage practices should more accurately be represented as sexual minorities and their identities understood as part of a gender-sexuality continuum.

Although many asylum cases include a forced marriage claim embedded within a larger set of rights violations, it rarely features as a "central criterion for any refugee claim."[13] Whereas James Hathaway argued cogently in 1990 that forced marriage should be understood as persecutory harm, the difficulties outlined by Seelinger with respect to establishing the context of persecution remain.[14] Asylum narratives, an underutilized vantage point for evaluating what has heretofore been shrouded in legal and humanitarian analyses, are "rich documentary archives tethered to discrete legal contexts" that speak to "analytical categories, constructed identities, and personal narratives of fear, trauma and violence."[15] This chapter thus presents the voices of asylum seekers in order to better understand the basis for this legal claim of persecution and the history of forced marriage as persecution in various countries; it also provides a hypothesis for estimating the likelihood of future jeopardy. In what follows, we draw on our experience serving as experts in forced marriage cases from Cameroon, Togo, Sierra Leone, Benin, and Ghana.

Resisting Patriarchy

The most common form of asylum claim we have reviewed alleging forced marriage or attempted forced marriage is rearticulated as defensively resisting patriarchal authority and perceived or imagined ideals and norms of traditional marriages. In such cases, attorneys adapt language used routinely to describe arranged marriage and domestic violence—including defenselessness, vulnerability, victim, and survivor—to particularize as well as develop conventional understandings of gendered violence.[16] This language establishes the exceptionality of the victim's experience compared to that of his or her peers, and it reveals the crucial dimensions in order that the persecutory harm of so-called forced marriage becomes clearer. Fleeing a forced marriage is thus reassembled as a defensive action of self-preservation. The concepts of patriarchy, misogyny, gerontocracy, polygamy/polygyny, and bridal contracts constitute the foundational architecture of these claims. Such concepts are instantly recognizable to many adjudicators and immigration officials, not that this necessarily guarantees claims will be accepted and asylum granted—far from it. But such terms resonate with adjudicators' knowledge of and imaginings about life in contemporary Africa.

Many countries have civil codes and marriage laws requiring that both parties enter marriage of their own free will. Yet country of origin information research demonstrates that forced conjugal association appears to know no geographic or political boundaries.[17] Two examples are illustrative. Although illegal in Cameroon and criminalized under section 356(1) of the Cameroon Penal Code, "compelling another person to marry" remains a prevalent matrimonial practice.[18] In a report from the United Nations High Commissioner for Refugees (UNHCR), an official from the Ministry of Women's Empowerment and the Family indicated that forced marriage is a "common form of violence against women and girls both in the northern and southern regions of Cameroon."[19]

Similarly, in Togo a legal marriage requires the consent of both parties, a minimum age, and the registration of the marriage at the *État-Civil* (civil tribunal). Law No. 2007–005 of 2007 specifically prohibits forced marriage. Title 2, chapter 2 specifically bans a narrowly defined form of forced marriage. Article 11 accords all Togolese "the right to freedom and security of the individual," including the right to sexual reproduction, health, and legal protections. Women are specifically protected against "*mariages forcés, et/ou précoces*" (forced and/or prepubescent marriage). Article 16 states that every individual, at legal maturity, has the "right to chose freely . . . to marry or not to marry." But in reality, gender discrimination exists in the 1980 Family Code (*Le code des personnes et de la famille*), which creates the context for forced marriage. The code recognizes, among other things, *polygamie* (polygyny), difference in ages for marriage for men and women, and the supremacy of the father or husband in all matters. Parental authority (*l'autorité parentale*) is the subject of article 101, wherein *le mari est le chef de famille* (the husband is the head of the family)." Levirate (widow inheritance) also exists, subject to article 54, which states that in the event of the death of the husband, levirate is only prohibited if the marriage had been "dissolved by divorce."[20] Since the passage of the law, there have been no prosecutions or convictions of individuals attempting to force others into marriages. Furthermore, there is no evidence of government implementation of the 2007 law.

As Bala Saho's and Francesca Declich's chapters in this volume demonstrate, claims about tradition are often really political claims embedded within language seeking to maintain existing hierarchies and established privileges. To be sure, the long history of the ways in which women's bodies are connected to nation-state formation is situated firmly at the site of marriage and reproduction as moral and material struggles.[21] What is often missing from these accounts, however, is the degree to which larger patriarchal and customary struggles take place at the local, familial level. Women in forced marriages or attempted forced marriages constitute part of a politically polarized arena: the local community. Individuals coerced into marriages are routinely compelled to uphold family confederations that are presumed to be critical to the functioning of their society, however small or "local" it may be.

The cases we will describe all concern adult women who have been coerced into unions but whose cases were reassembled by attorneys in a manner considered optimal. Each case highlights the workings of a particular social system in which forced marriage fulfills a specific function. Importantly, each of the cases demonstrates the salience of long-standing cultural practices as well as the adaptability of local values to economic and religious changes, proving that cultural specificities are mutable and respond to new incentives. Forced marriages serve as a lens through which to view the convergence of religion, moral standards, and socioeconomic

BENJAMIN N. LAWRANCE AND CHARLOTTE WALKER-SAID

attitudes in the realm of gender, family, and marriage. Based on demographic surveys and human rights reports, as well as our anecdotal survey of asylum claims, forced marriage appears widespread throughout West Africa and all ethnosocial communities.[22] The most prevalent forms of forced marriage we have encountered include early betrothal, arranged marriage, and the practices of levirate and sororate (by which a woman marries her sister's husband, in case of childlessness or death of the sister). Acting as the keystones of multiple and overlapping alliances, the following examples of women from Cameroon, Togo, and Benin demonstrate how attorneys reassemble women's actions within the frame of defense against the gendered and political relations of community and society, such as lineage-based alliances, polygamy, and inheritance in the context of traditional religion.

In 2010, Aissatou, a Cameroonian woman with a degree in typing and accounting, was compelled to divorce her Chadian husband and remarry a Fulani man from the northern Cameroonian region surrounding Adamawa in order to fulfill her family's political pledge to their local Fulani community.[23] Aissatou was educated and considered herself free to marry the Chadian she met while working in an office in a city far from her hometown. Her first marriage to a social and political "outsider" threatened her family's political and economic status, since her father and his relatives were tied by blood and marriage, as well as by a loyalty pledge, to their local Fulani lineage in Adamawa. As such, they were compelled to make visible and profound gestures that demonstrated such loyalty through intracommunity marriage alliances of their daughters and sons. Although Aissatou's first husband shared her religion—Islam—as well as ethnoregional commonalities (he also spoke Fula), he was not a member of the socioeconomic cohort of her extended family in the Adamawa region of Cameroon, and the marriage could not seal the bonds on which her kin depended. In order to stabilize relations between her father, uncles, and other relatives and the Fulani leadership, Aissatou was forced to separate and remarry a "local."

Aissatou's local community considered marriage an unambiguous political and economic commitment. Descent and family and ethnosocial group membership remained inextricably tied to relations of power and economy, which made marriage a strictly guarded ritual and form of association. Though intercommunity marriage had become a "tradition," Aissatou could not place its origins in long-established historical practice but rather in precedents that were roughly two generations old. "My uncles kidnapped me and held me until I agreed to marry the man to whom they had promised me," she recounted. She continued, "They believed my marriage was null because it had never been sanctioned by them and they had agreed to no wedding contract and had received no gifts. I did not even get a legal divorce. I simply never returned to Chad, separated from my husband, married my new husband in a new town, and began a new life."[24] There were no accounts of "traditional" ceremonies or long-venerated religious rituals or customs enacted as part of her new marriage. Rather, Aissatou's marriage, though ostensibly enforced as part of an enduring code, was intended to fulfill very recent provisions.

Critically, Aissatou attested that based on the way inheritance laws were conceived and enforced in her Fulani community in the Adamawa region, her father and uncles could be disinherited by their extended kin and economically excluded from their society if Aissatou did not fulfill the expectations of matrimony that cemented the alliances within the lower-level lineage. As she articulated, "Our shops, mosques, businesses, and farms operate through the families and everyone must assist in doing the work. There is no sharing with outsiders. Those who do not contribute are cut off from the surplus." Those on the lowest rungs of the lineage—the unmarried or childless daughters, sons, and grandchildren of the higher orders—were expected to fulfill their elders' pledges to maintain the bonds of the Fulani social unit, where economic networking and mutual assistance defined collective identity.

In this particular social system, forced marriage imposed commitments upon kin and community using the rhetoric of tradition, but it fortified exclusionary boundaries defining the distribution of resources in a time and place of scarcity, thereby fulfilling a very contemporary function. Thus, in their successful representation of their client, Aissatou's advocates strategically reframed her flight from Cameroon to the United States as withdrawal from a form of indenture to her family and to the connective structure of the lineage with which it was related and associated. Rather than simply refusing an "arranged marriage"—which could be construed as an everyday practice of all citizens and thus a benign cultural norm—Aissatou's resistance was reassembled as escape from networked dependencies that demanded allegiance and effected serious vulnerabilities. In Cameroon, divorce from the man whom she was coerced to marry was not only socially proscribed, it was also an economic liability for her entire immediate and extended family. The moral burden of responsibility—not to mention the threat of death or bodily harm should she disavow her responsibility—required a dramatic act of emancipation, that is, escape from Cameroon and the filing of an asylum claim.

The case of a Togolese woman who fled an attempted forced marriage and sought refuge in the United Kingdom demonstrates how attorneys dismantled and reassembled her claim to foreground the polygyny component of her persecution, effectively downplaying other grounds for asylum. Konda had fled Togo, and with her initial application for asylum, focused on her political involvement with an opposition party, she was granted temporary protection because she was a minor. After attaining maturity, she again petitioned for asylum but included developments predating and postdating her flight, notably, her parents' attempt to lure her back to Togo and marry her off. Whereas the political grounds for the first ruling still held true, Konda's second attempt to remain permanently in the United Kingdom was reframed by the forced marriage dimension. The concept of polygamy is familiar to adjudicators, and Western audiences generally view the practice with revulsion, although attitudes are changing.[25] It is also important that in the United Kingdom, forced marriage receives considerable public policy attention in part because of the belief that UK families duplicitously "arrange" marriages between UK residents and foreigners, against the will of one or both parties, in order to evade migration controls; in fact, the UK Home Office has a division entirely focused on exposing "fake" marriages.[26] Konda's lawyer, however, made a calculated decision to prioritize polygamy because of the nature of the evidence in her case.

Konda's risk of forced marriage was certainly an original basis for her flight to the United Kingdom. In her first interview, she explained, "I fled Togo owing to a number of political problems and also because I was pressured to marry a man who was already married with four wives." But in her initial account of her claim, presented when she was a minor, the man's three existing unions were viewed by immigration officials as an indication that he was a morally and legally upstanding citizen, thus diminishing Konda's credibility. The alleged perpetrator was assumed to be a law-abiding and upright man; more important, because Konda was a minor the adjudicators did not need to decide the case on its merits. After she reached legal maturity and her case was again reviewed, her lawyers considered her political activities important but possibly insufficient for asylum status. Consequently, her claim was expanded and reframed: her parents' attempt to coerce her into a union was presented as a mechanism with which to ameliorate the damage her political actions had allegedly caused her family.

In their attempt to coerce Konda into marriage, her parents arranged for a story to be published in a Togolese biweekly newspaper that gave the impression she was "lost" (*perdu*) and needed "help" (*assistance*). Their narrative portrayed her as a misguided girl who had fallen in with bad company and needed rescuing. The story was carefully and intentionally designed as a means of entrapment, whereby an unwitting bystander or resident seeing Konda could possibly take pity on her plight and bring her whereabouts to the attention of the authorities and her estranged family. The article featured an image of Konda in full *hijab* (headscarf), in the manner of a betrothal photograph—the type of image produced by parents to facilitate the arrangement of a marriage. The photograph was genuine: Konda explained that her parents had required her to sit for it some time before she fled Togo, although she had not, at the age of fifteen, understood that the photograph was a mechanism for eliciting marriage proposals. Together, the newspaper article and the photograph conveyed an unmistakable message to an urban Muslim readership, namely, that Konda was a runaway bride. Whereas her political grounds for asylum had been questioned by the UK Border Agency, the potential persecution awaiting her upon her return in the form of a coerced polygynous marriage was undeniably embedded in the betrothal photograph and accompanying text, and this assured the success of her claim.

A final example, from Benin, illustrates how attorneys highlighted the means whereby affiliates of a traditional religious network mobilized inheritance practices to influence vulnerability in order to constrain or enforce participation, adherence, and compliance. Dopé, originally from the village of Cové, was an educated, married woman living in the country's economic capital, Cotonou, who fled to the United States after a harrowing experience. She claimed she was kidnapped as an adult by the adherents of a vodou priest (*bokono*) and taken to his *atikevodou* (healing vodou) shrine of Sakpata (*Xapata*), where she was imprisoned and repeatedly raped.[27] Dopé believed her experiences *as an adult* were the result of her betrothal as a child to a vodou as a form of indebted inherited slavery (*trokosi*)—a punishment exacted on her mother for her alleged infidelity. Dopé's lawyers made the strategic decision to reframe her claim by documenting broadly misogynistic forced marriage practices and child abuse, including vodou, child slavery, and the widespread belief in wife inheritance or levirate.

Dopé's narrative was extremely difficult for the lawyers to grasp, and they feared no judge would consider it plausible or credible. Dopé explained that her predicament was the result of her public disavowal of the *trokosi* (ritual enslavement for punishment) obligations when she reached maturity. She had been raped and abused by her kidnapper's brother multiple times as a child. But when she reached maturity, she simply walked out of the compound and moved to Cotonou and began a new life. The individual to whom she was betrothed had made no attempt to entice her to the shrine, but after his death, the brother of the deceased dispatched men to kidnap her in accordance with his understanding of levirate practice. The primarily Yoruba settlement of Cové, in the Zou *department,* is the location of a powerful religious community called Egungun. The many religious communities in the area are all tied to the Yoruba religion, and they share many values, preeminent among them being the honoring of spirits (*vodoun*). Cové is the site of multiple sects, most famously the Gelede secret society. Ritual enslavement for punishment, a form of female religious bondage necessitated by debt obligations, is of decreasing prevalence in parts of Ghana, Benin, Togo, and Nigeria, particularly among the Ewe-speaking communities. Trokosi, literally meaning "wives of the spirit Kosi," is one form of *vodounsi,* or bondage to a *vodoun*. Although the origins of the institution are somewhat unclear, purportedly egregious cases of exploitation in the 1990s highlighted by local and international human rights organizations brought renewed attention to this form of slavery and sexual abuse.[28]

Ritual enslavement and vodou may have puzzled an adjudicator, but defensively resisting slavery, kidnapping, rape, and imprisonment—in a country where vodou is publically sanctioned and where the state has designated National Voodoo Day—enters established grounds for social group persecution.[29] The constitution and the statutes of Benin prohibit many practices attendant to slavery, but importantly, they make no mention of trokosi and vodounsi, sexual slavery, forced marriage (*mariage forcé*), and sexual assault in the context of marriage. Revisions to the Family Code in 2004 repealed many discriminatory aspects of the 1931 *Coutumier du Dahomey* (Benin Customary Code). But even though customary law is no longer recognized by the courts, many women "continue[d] to be subject to the 'Coutumier du Dahomey' which treat[ed] them as legal minors and accord[ed] them limited rights in marriage and inheritance."[30]

At the time of Dopé's hearing, the practice of levirate was documented in Benin.[31] Aspects of her forced marriage narrative may have been illegal under the 2004 revision of the Family Code, but the practice of levirate remained quasi-legal insofar as it was not specifically prohibited.[32] The 2004 Family Code explicitly prohibited forced marriage, but there was no evidence of enforcement.[33] And though the governments of Ghana and Togo, from the mid-1990s, made concerted efforts to stamp out the remaining vodounsi, including trokosi, and mediate the relocation and retraining of individuals, Benin passed no similar law.[34] Dopé's legal team thus successfully reassembled her narrative as that of a woman fleeing multiple backward, traditional, and misogynistic practices, at the center of which was a very violent form of forced marriage for which there was no plausible expectation of state protection.

Contesting Homophobia

A second group of three separate claims from the more than twenty we have evaluated—of forced marriages, attempted forced marriages, and assertions citing a fear of forced marriage—are routinely dismantled and reassembled by attorneys as affirmatively contesting homophobia. Although many of the specific forced marriage acts evidenced in the first category are also present here (such as bride-price, contracts, rape, and threats of ostracism), lawyers reframe the narratives of LGB refugees as part of a larger (*qua* global) struggle against homophobia and homophobic violence. African LGB refugees, part of a rapidly expanding refugee class, are represented as resisting homophobia, and the rights violations they experience are described in language that resonates with minority rights discourse.[35] In these cases, sub-Saharan African nations are represented as rights violators and "behind the curve" in terms of the global evolution of human rights as experienced by and embodied in LGB individuals. From our experience, we discern a crucial but subtle distinction in the affirmative framing: though some adjudicators may not necessarily embrace sexuality as a human right and others may struggle with the concept of heteronormativity, in denying such an asylum claim a judge risks being marked by the discourse of explicit sexual discrimination and suspicion.

Attorneys representing men and women alleging forced marriages and attempted forced marriages increasingly categorize their clients as victims of homophobia—not (or not only) because they face an "exceptional level of violence" based on their nonnormative sexual or conjugal status but rather (or also) because they are political and economic agents as a result of their sexual and conjugal roles; further, their agency is uniquely vulnerable to cultural, social, and religious criticism and retribution based on their sexual, conjugal, or familial behaviors, over which the forcibly married have little control. On the personal level, LGB forced marriages are no less onerous and stigmatizing than the first category discussed earlier. But LGB refugees face the added dimension that the home communities from which they have fled embody the hegemony of a version of gender normalcy. In this way, society-wide persecution and prosecution contextualize LGB asylum claimants and ground them as members of a social group in order to meet the Refugee Convention's definition of *refugee*. LGB individuals implicated in forced marriages are subjected to the stigmatizing and constraining practices of a heterosexual marriage that commits them to a life of double accommodation. These individuals must gratify social and communitarian demands to serve the collective interests in the marriage and conform to expectations of heteronormative conjugality. Three cases illustrate how dismantling a claim and reassembling it as affirmatively contesting homophobia can be based on real experiences, hypothetical or imagined risks, or generational and historical practices.

Christelle, a lesbian from Douala, was hastily forced to marry a family friend following her arrest for "homosexual activities." She worked as a hairdresser and salon owner and interacted with gay and lesbian Cameroonians in the professional spheres of fashion, styling, and art. Christelle met and fell in love with a woman, and thereafter, they spent the majority of their time together, broadened their network of homosexual friends, and began to appear in public together more often. After a raid on a "homosexual party" in which police observed Christelle kissing a woman, she was arrested, tortured, and imprisoned until her father came to retrieve her from New Bell Prison.[36] Although she was never charged or tried for a crime, her family believed she was at severe risk of police surveillance and possible rearrest, torture, and imprisonment. The marriage to a family friend was ostensibly arranged to protect her.

Christelle never consented to the marriage, but she knew that her life was in danger because of the threat of having a public identity associated with homosexuality. Cameroon is one of the world's most homophobic countries; there, intolerance of same-sex conduct is widespread, and murders of and threats against sexual minorities are met with official inaction.[37] The police had her status on record, but more importantly, because Cameroonian society widely rejects homosexual acts and identities, she would be at risk for social and political retribution by everyday citizens.[38] Facing the possibility of a long sentence should she be arrested again or mob violence, social ostracism, and community exclusion, Christelle conceded that her security was worth a sham marriage.[39]

The Cameroonian citizenry's severe antipathy toward homosexual individuals and homosexual acts (and nonnormative sexual acts and identities in general) is well established. But LGB individuals in Cameroon are afforded a modicum of leeway in certain circumstances—specifically, if the persons in question hide behaviors, relationships, and identities that are offensive to the law and citizenry from full public view or if the homosexual community discreetly operates on the margins of society. This kind of leeway is conditional, however, on general social peace. The moment that political sentiments are stirred and scapegoats are needed or if social or economic tensions arise and there are pressures to isolate or avenge or placate leaders and demagogues, sexual minorities become a focus of violence. During the 1990s, demands for democratization and economic change caused Cameroon's authoritarian regime, under President Paul Biya, to allow a certain level of public political discourse.[40] Conservative Christian leaders in Cameroon's political sphere rose to prominence by speaking out against moral crimes, ostensibly attacking the government for immorality but also criticizing the wider populace. Allegations of homosexuality became a means of attacking the elite while working within acceptable modes of discourse.[41]

The specter of homosexuality looms large in public discourse because it is framed as "foreign," "corrupt," and "elite"—the embodiment of all the malaise in Cameroon.[42] Thus, antihomosexual sentiment in the country is largely the result of relatively recent political participation and the public expression of resentment for those perceived to be at fault for Cameroon's poverty and corruption, notably, the wealthy, decadent, degenerate, and effete.[43] Christelle's forced marriage to a man contravened her sexual orientation and obligated her to assume a position and status that offered her the only pathway to personal security in Cameroon. But her attorneys privileged the broad social ostracism and political scapegoating of homosexuals—potentially resulting in bodily harm or death—as the root cause of Christelle's persecutory harm. Coercion took place at the level of the nation-state and public citizenry, rather than at the family and community level. Expectations to uphold a normative order can be localized, but they can also be broadened to include an entire citizenry, as in the case of antihomosexual sentiment in Cameroon. Although the national threat was prioritized in legal proceedings and was indeed a legitimate basis of fear of persecution, it overshadowed the parallel and coordinated threat of the immediate family who would not join her in countering the public menace but rather sought to suppress her individual will as a coextensive reaction to her homosexuality.

In contrast to Christelle's legal team, lawyers representing Taziff from Sierra Leone reassembled his case as affirmatively resisted hypothetical exposure to homophobia by reference to analogy and hearsay. Taziff first fled Freetown after being forcibly conscripted into a militia and then escaping, but he subsequently sought asylum in the United Kingdom because he began to self-identify as gay once he was residing in London. Taziff's fears were not misplaced. Like Cameroon, Sierra Leone is a deeply homophobic country, and antigay violence there is widespread and endemic and family members coerce LGB individuals into marriages.[44] The United Nations Human Rights Committee observed that Sierra Leone lacks any constitutional or statutory provision expressly prohibiting discrimination on grounds of sexual orientation or gender identity, and it criticized the widespread prevalence of stereotypes, prejudices, and reported acts of violence against LGBTI persons.[45] The US State Department noted that homophobia is rooted in an 1861 statute prohibiting male-to-male sexual acts ("buggery" and "crimes against nature"), which carries a penalty of life imprisonment for "indecent assault" upon a man or ten years for attempted assault. Lesbians were victims of "planned rapes" initiated by family members seeking to "change" their sexual orientation.[46]

Taziff feared homophobia based on what he heard from other Sierra Leoneans while residing in Freetown and what he has learned from exiles living in Europe. He explained: "If I were in Sierra Leone and am asked out by a man some part of me would always be afraid that when I were to say yes, I would be putting myself at possible risk. I would still take this risk despite my fears because I cannot lie about who I am." Taziff's narrative almost appears to be influenced by recent European Union and British jurisprudence underscoring that for adjudicators to expect that gay men or lesbians ought to remain in the closet to safeguard their personal well-being constitutes a human rights violation.[47] Taziff stated, "If I were to hide who I was I would feel angry, frustrated and upset. I just cannot even begin to imagine not telling the truth, even though my life would be in danger." His hypothetical risk was initially at least firmly and proudly grounded in a new awareness that it was his human right to be out.

For Taziff, as news of his petition for asylum spread, the threat of return to Sierra Leone was increasingly encumbered by the expectation that he had to marry and have children. In this regard, his refugee claim was hypothetical and contingent; although he was never openly gay in Sierra Leone, his expectations for how he would be received were he forced to return were tied to the experience of others. He "remember[ed] seeing a man being attacked for being a gay" when he was ten. Rather than imagining his own forced marriage, however, he should, his legal counsel advised, narrate an experience he witnessed as a child. Taziff explained:

> I was living in the town because I was attending school there. I was at home when I heard a lot of noise and so I came outside to see what was going on. Everyone in the area appeared to have left their house to see what was happening. I saw a man being attacked by a group of people. I knew what was happening because I heard people talking. They were saying he was "homo." I later learned that this was a serious allegation to make as people do not believe that you can be gay. I think that the man was almost killed, as he was bleeding from head to toe when an ambulance came and took him away. The police stations and hospitals were not very active during the war, so I do not know if he survived. At the time I was frightened to see what had happened to him. He was in a terrible state, bleeding and so on. I had seen rebels attack people and at first I thought that a rebel had been captured. It was only when I went to see what was going on that I found out it was a man accused of being "gay." This was the only time I had seen something like this.

Taziff's witnessing of homophobic violence became the center of his refugee claim, but the attack was presented as an echo of earlier political violence. This intentional slippage frames how the Sierra Leonean state not only provides no protection against homophobia but also is often complicit in homophobic persecution, much as state actors were implicated in crimes against humanity during the civil wars.

Rather than speculating about the prospect of a forced marriage, Taziff anchored his reassembled narrative with concrete incidents he had witnessed firsthand. His ostensible jeopardy was contingent on a forcible return and buttressed by an account of a beating he saw as a child. Building on this deep-seated homophobic foundation, Taziff added vague and overlapping claims about possible abuse. He described social attitudes that he heard expressed "on a number of occasions," including how men would "talk about gay men in a negative and insulting way." He narrated a climate of homophobia employing Krio colloquialisms, such as "batty men." And then he turned to what would become of him if he were forced to return, recounting the mixture of pressures and threats family and friends had made via text message, e-mail, and standard mail. Instead of concrete rights violations per se, his stories of how his brother had "found a wife for him" and how his "mother wants grandchildren" became proxies for backward and regressive social values. The final part of Taziff's narrative turned to the intense psychological damage done to LGB individuals forced to conform to familial expectation. Taziff noted that once he "knew" he was gay, he "felt bad inside" when he overheard friends or family members plot a solution, that is, a forced marriage. His emotional spectrum included shame, revulsion, anger, and guilt. In this way, Taziff's forced marriage narrative resonated with adjudicators because it was reassembled as a narrative of "surviving" homophobic violence; the speculation of future persecution in the form of forced marriage was merely a coda. Taziff had no personal experience of beating or rape, and his claim was represented as an opportunity for an immigration official to ensure that he never would.

A final example, from Ghana, demonstrates how a forced marriage claim may be dismantled and reassembled as a historical and generational struggle affirmatively contesting homophobia. Ali is a young man from a chiefly lineage near Bolgatanga in the Upper East Region of northern Ghana, and until recently, he was a practicing Muslim. As a child, he witnessed his parents fighting, and his father beat his mother in regular acts of extreme violence. Then suddenly, while he was still a child, his father disappeared from the village. Several months later, he learned that his father had fled Ghana to go to the United Kingdom with a British man and now lived with him. From that day onward, Ali was subject to abuse from his extended patriclan. He was kicked and beaten, and although he lived with his paternal aunt's family, he was denied food, forced to sleep in the streets, and routinely subjected to verbal abuse. His father's family ostracized him, calling him sick, weak, and mentally ill. People flung excrement at him in the streets. Even though he himself had never expressed any same-sex attraction or emotion, he was treated as if he were gay and sent to a "healing camp" and subjected to traditional cures.

Later in his teenage years, Ali returned to his village from the so-called healing camp and tried to catch up with all the schooling he had missed. He exceeded all expectations and was sponsored by one uncle to attend a private college. He graduated first in his class and moved on to a university in Accra. There, he met a man named Usama, and they fell in love. Ali began to recognize his feelings and identity, and he started to identify as a gay man. But he felt he could never be happy. He could never tell his family. And he had no knowledge of his father's whereabouts. Ali went to the United Kingdom to attend a professional conference and stayed with an uncle in London. He met a woman at a party, and they married hastily in 2012. But after some time, she discovered his private journal and read it. She confronted him about his sexuality, "outed" him to his family in Ghana, and then sought the dissolution of the marriage.

Ali's claim for asylum was centered on evidence that he would be subject to horrific violence, forced imprisonment, and widespread societal homophobia if forced to return to Ghana; the persecutory harm of the threat of forced remarriage to his former wife was sidelined entirely, and indeed his lawyers felt his previous marriage weakened his claim.[48] LGBTI individuals suffer intense personal and group discrimination in Ghana, including violence perpetrated by both private individuals and agents of the state. Homosexuality is criminalized under Ghanaian law via the Criminal Code of 1960, chapter 6 (Sexual Offences), article 105. Ghanaian statutes are not relics of colonial law but rather are actively enforced and publicly supported.[49] The head of Ghana's Commission for Human Rights and Administrative Justice, Emile Short, ruled out any idea of the commission advocating for gay rights, since homosexuality is frowned upon. Short claimed that in countries where there was an antidiscrimination section in the law, gay rights could be described as human rights, but this did not apply in Ghana.[50] Ali's lawyers also presented evidence to demonstrate how the majority of Ghanaians considered mentally ill are subject to extreme human rights abuses, including chaining and beating.[51]

Ali's case is instructive because it speaks to how lawyers prefer to elevate homophobia above forced marriage in LGB asylum claims even when there is rich evidence of a familial legacy and multigenerational practice of forced marriage. Once Ali's secret identity emerged, details of his father's experience percolated once again among the community, and Ali's narrative resonated with his chiefly lineage as an echo of his father's experience of being forced to remain with Ali's mother in the semblance of a union, no matter the physical or emotion cost. Ali's lineage was described as cursed. In his first asylum narrative, he explained that whereas he had indeed married a woman to hide his sexuality, the marriage and subsequent divorce were his own choices. But if forced to return to Ghana, he asserted, he would be pressured to remarry the woman or marry anew, ultimately to produce a chiefly heir, in much the same way as his father had been forced to marry and sire a male heir several decades earlier. But in the lawyers' representation to the court, evidence of widespread public persecution and private prosecution of LGBTI individuals marginalized multigenerational forced marriage practice.

FORCED MARRIAGE SURVIVORS AS SEXUAL MINORITIES?

Forced marriage is a complex site for refugee adjudicators who must determine claims based on conventions and protocols that make no mention of gender. So it is hardly surprising that patterns have emerged in the manner in which attorneys frame the narratives of their clients. In our experience, narratives that are clearly forced marriage claims at their core are routinely separated into two groups—defensively resisting patriarchy and affirmatively contesting homophobia—that gesture toward the violence of particular "component" claims, including rape, kidnapping, polygyny, torture, or sexual enslavement, rather than addressing forced marriage as a distinct and primary condition. Although it should be appreciated that an outcome-driven rationale inherently lends itself to conservative argumentation, as experts we are uncomfortable with the flattening and erasing that take hold when narratives are forced into tropes that reinscribe prejudices about Africa.

Throughout the regions of Africa in which we work and from which forced marriage testimonies have emerged, forced marriage is prevalent in both rural and urban areas. In cases alleging forced marriage in-country or by those who have already fled, the marriage in question was often principally a means of cementing intragenerational ties and preserving continuities that link the past with the current era. Of course, there are often secondary justifications at work, including wealth transfer, political and social stabilization, cultural punishment, or even procuring justice or vindication, yet it is the obligations that frame the bonds or linkages that shape a marriage "tradition." And together, these factors threaten the bodily integrity and personal autonomy of the individual in the forced marriage. As is evident in all the cases described in this chapter, family heads and other lineage leaders, as well as local elders and officials, negotiate the terms for young brides and grooms, widows and widowers, and other family members who have little say in the beginnings or endings of their marriages.

In the cases we have described here—and in our wider experience working with persons coerced to marry—forced marriage does not principally create a servile position within the household; rather, it renders a spouse or spouses captive to an interlacing web of codependent members. The forced marriage refugees whose cases we have evaluated may indeed have benefited from having their narratives reassembled according to "components" with jurisprudential traction, but we will never know how their claims of forced marriage would have been adjudicated had they been left intact. Evidence of the continuum of gender and sexuality in Africa was erased when their claims were dismantled to meet the exigencies of convention and precedent.

But what if refugee claims pertaining to forced marriage were adjudicated on their merits alone, wherein the majoritarian violence of coercion was front and center? What patterns might we discern if men and women seeking refuge from forced marriages were viewed as a distinct social category worthy of protection because of their subordination to majoritarian sexual and marital frameworks and norms? Perhaps it would be worthwhile to view forced marriage refugees as a distinct group of "sexual minorities," namely, individuals whose sexual and social lives are subjected to a dominant "sexual majority" with decision-making powers that implements a normative conjugal order.

Scholars and lawyers often view men and women in forced marriages as distinct from LGB individuals because those in forced heterosexual marriages appear to conform to heteronormative gender and conjugal configurations that would ostensibly entitle them to social inclusion and political acceptance. However, this is not necessarily—and in fact rarely is—the case. Those in forced marriages nearly always carry political and economic obligations that limit their power over their own bodies and

BENJAMIN N. LAWRANCE AND CHARLOTTE WALKER-SAID

reproductive capacities and their authority over their progeny. They are also subordinated to dominant marital and sexual prescriptions and privileges, which make them sexual minorities as they represent an "orientation" as a dimension of social inequality with implications for bodily integrity, social and political outcomes, and personal vulnerability. The recognition of both heterosexuals and LGB individuals in coerced unions as sexual minorities acknowledges the minority status of the social vulnerability of those who are subject to the tyranny of majoritarian coalitions that seek to preserve continuities via heteronormative marriage and sexual life. Denial of a marriage of choice, gay or straight, is still ultimately subjection to a majoritarian sexuality.

Those in forced marriages become sexual minorities because in the forced marriage process, they transform from autonomous individuals (or equal members of a single community with coherent expectations) into subordinate members of multiple communities to whom they must fulfill reciprocal and competing duties, particularly when their home community changes their expectations in light of the altered marital status of its member. Furthermore, communities in Africa often resist acceptance of LGB identities and lifestyles among their members for the same reason that they reject actions against forced marriage: they are seen as threats to the community's sense of social stability, moral integrity, and financial prosperity. Where social and familial ties are bound—and economic and political responsibilities and obligations contracted—little individual autonomy is possible. This orientation toward networked obligations, which require sexual and conjugal duty as well as financial and political responsibility, demands recognition as a particular legal status as well as a status that must be identified within a broadened category of "sexual minorities."

NOTES

1. Gayatri Chakravorty Spivak, "Who Claims Alterity," in *Remaking History*, ed. Barbara Kruger and Phil Mariani (New York: New Press, 1989), 269–93.

2. The foundational work for understanding the formulaic nature of petitions remains Natalie Zemon Davis, *Fiction in the Archives: Pardon Tales and Their Tellers in Sixteenth-Century France* (Stanford, CA: Stanford University Press, 1987).

3. Benjamin N. Lawrance and Galya Ruffer, "Witness to the Persecution? Expertise, Testimony, and Consistency in Asylum Adjudication," in *Adjudicating Refugee and Asylum Status: The Role of Witness, Expertise, and Testimony*, ed. Lawrance and Ruffer (Cambridge: Cambridge University Press, 2015), 1–24.

4. UN Secretary General, Convention Relating to the Status of Refugees, July 28, 1951, 189 UNTS 137/ [1954] ATS 5, 1951; UN General Assembly, Protocol Relating to the Status of Refugees, January 31, 1967, United Nations, Treaty Series, vol. 606, p. 267, available at http://www.refworld.org/docid/3ae6b3ae4.html, accessed January 19, 2015; Heaven Crawley, "Gender, Persecution and the Concept of Politics in the Asylum Determination Process," *Forced Migration Review* 9 (December 2009): 17–20. See http://www.fmreview.org/sites/fmr/files/FMRdownloads/en/FMRpdfs/FMR09/fmr9 .6.pdf, accessed December 26, 2015.

5. Kim Thuy Seelinger, "Forced Marriage and Asylum: Perceiving the Invisible Harm," *Columbia Human Rights Law Review* 42, no.1 (2010): 57. Rape, forced impregnation, and sexual slavery, among other sexual crimes, are recognized as crimes against international law before tribunals and are discussed, for example, in Catherine A. Mackinnon, "Defining Rape Internationally: A Comment on Akayesu," *Columbia Journal of International Law* 44 (2006): 940–58, and Kristen Boon, "Rape and Forced Pregnancy under the ICC Statute: Human Dignity, Autonomy, and Consent," *Columbia Human Rights Review* 32 (2001): 625–76.

6. Neha Jain, "Forced Marriage as a Crime against Humanity," *Journal of International Criminal Justice* 6, no. 5 (2008): 1013–32.

7. Seelinger, "Forced Marriage," 57.

8. Connie G. Oxford, "Protectors and Victims in the Gender Regime of Asylum," *NWSA Journal* 17, no. 3 (Fall 2005): 18–38.

9. Benjamin N. Lawrance, "Asylum and the 'Forced Marriage' Paradox: Petitions, Translation, and Courts as Institutional Perpetrators of Gender Violence," in *The Invention of Contemporary Slavery,* ed. Annie Bunting and Joel Quirk (University of British Columbia Press, 2016), forthcoming.

10. Seelinger, "Forced Marriage," 59.

11. A UK Department of International Development and UKAID study about violence against women in Sierra Leone notes that "violence . . . is shaped by a number of factors, related to cultural attitudes, the history of conflict, the political environment and donor interventions." See Lisa Denney and Aisha Fofana Ibrahim (Overseas Development Institute), "Violence against Women in Sierra Leone: How Women Seek Redress" (London: December 2012). Available at http://www.odi.org.uk/sites/odi.org .uk/files/odi-assets/publications-opinion-files/8175.pdf, accessed December 26, 2015.

12. Boon, "Rape and Forced Pregnancy," 625; Benjamin N. Lawrance et al., "Law, Expertise, and Protean Ideas about African Migrants," in *African Asylum at a Crossroads: Activism, Expert Testimony, and Refugee Rights,* ed. Iris Berger, Tricia Redeker Hepner, Benjamin N. Lawrance, Joanna T. Tague, and Meredith Terretta (Athens: Ohio University Press, 2015), 1–7; Lawrance and Ruffer, "Witness to the Persecution."

13. Jenni Millbank and Catherine Dauverge, "Forced Marriage and the Exoticization of Gendered Harms in United States Asylum Law," *Columbia Journal of Gender and Law* 19, no. 3 (2011): 57.

14. James Hathaway, *The Law of Refugee Status* (Toronto: Butterworths, 1991), 112; Seelinger, "Forced Marriage," 57.

15. Lawrance et al., "Law, Expertise, and Protean Ideas," 2.

16. Warren Richey, "Does the Prospect of Arranged Marriage and Abuse Warrant Asylum in the US?" *Christian Science Monitor,* March 23, 2007.

17. On Guinea, see, for example, Immigration and Refugee Board (IRB) of Canada, "Guinea: Prevalence of Forced Marriage—Legislation Affecting Forced Marriages" (2009–September 2012), October 9, 2012, GIN104197.FE, available at http://www .refworld.org/docid/50aa23a52.html, accessed October 25, 2014; for Mauritania, see IRB Canada, "Mauritania: Prevalence of Forced Marriage," June 27, 2012, MRT104131.E, available at http://www.refworld.org/docid/5035f2ea2.html, accessed October 25, 2014; for Nigeria, see IRB Canada, "Nigeria: Forced Marriage under Islamic Law— Whether an Islamic Marriage Requires the Final 'Fatiha' Ceremony," March 17, 2006, NGA100418.E, available at http://www.refworld.org/docid/45f1478428.html, accessed October 25, 2014; for Togo, see IRB Canada, "Togo: Forced Marriage, Particularly in Lomé," (2010–February 2013), April 2, 2013, TGO104316.FE, available at http://www .refworld.org/docid/53392eda4.html, accessed October 25, 2014.

18. Carlson Anyangwe, *Criminal Law in Cameroon: Specific Offences* (Oxford: African Books Collective, 2011), 566–68.

19. IRB Canada, "Cameroon: Prevalence of Forced Marriage in Southern Cameroon," April 10, 2013, CMR104378.E, available at http://www.refworld.org/docid /5193855a2bdb.html, accessed October 25, 2014.

20. A 2006 report by Alexandra Kossin, Cécile Trochu, and Patrick Mutzenberg of the Organisation Mondiale Contre la Torture reported that the majority of these practices take place in contexts of poverty, and many marital arrangements are made without the consent of one or both parties as a result of financial necessity, debts, and related matters. See http://www.omct.org/files/2005/09/3070/togo_cat_0406 _violences_etatiques_fr.pdf, accessed December 26, 2015.

21. E.g., Lynn M. Thomas, *Politics of the Womb: Women, Reproduction, and the State in Kenya* (Berkeley: University of California Press, 2003); Mary Louise Roberts, *Civilization without Sexes: Reconstructing Gender in Postwar France, 1917–1927* (Chicago: University of Chicago Press, 1994); Carina Ray, "Decrying White Peril: Interracial Sex and the Rise of Anticolonial Nationalism in the Gold Coast," *American Historical Review* 119, no. 1 (2014): 78–110.

22. UN General Assembly, "Preventing and Eliminating Child, Early and Forced Marriage: report of the Office of the United Nations High Commissioner for Human Rights," A/HRC/26/22 (April 2, 2014), available from www.undocs .org/A/HRC/26/22; UN Children's Fund, *Ending Child Marriage: Progress and Prospects* (New York: UNICEF, 2014); Claudia Zu Bentheim, *Forced Marriage in Africa: Examining the Disturbing Reality* (London: Consultancy Africa Intelligence, 2013); "Ethiopia: Surviving Forced Marriage," IRINnews, February 23, 2007, available at http://www.irinnews.org/report/69993/ethiopia-surviving-forced-marriage, accessed January 19, 2015; "Child & Forced Marriage Fact Sheet," Forward: Safeguarding Rights & Dignity, available at http://www.forwarduk.org.uk/key-issues /child-marriage, accessed January 19, 2015.

23. This is a pseudonym. All names have been changed to protect the identity of refugees.

24. Testimony of Aissatou Beko in Matter of Aissatou Beko in Removal Proceedings, January 18, 2013, interview by Charlotte Walker-Said.

25. Prakash A Shah, "Attitudes to Polygamy in English Law," *International and Comparative Law Quarterly* 52, no. 2 (2003): 369–400; Thomas Phillip Madison, "Polygamy Is Creepy, Wrong, and Sick! (However, I Find It Fascinating): Parasocial Comparison, Parasocial Processing, Parasocial Contact Hypothesis, and Polygamy" (PhD diss., Louisiana State University, 2013).

26. See https://www.gov.uk/forced-marriage#forced-marriage-unit, accessed January 21, 2015.

27. Sakpata is an extremely powerful vodou and feared generally. His influence waned among vodou communities in the 1970s and 1980s with the eradication of smallpox, but more recently, with the emergence of HIV/AIDS, new strains of tuberculosis, and Ebola, he has regained prominence. See Pierre Fátúmbí Verger, *Dieux d'Afrique: Culte des Orishas et Vodouns à l'ancienne Côte des Esclaves en Afrique et à Bahia, la Baie de Tous les Saints au Brésil* (Paris: Paul Hartmann, 1995); P.-Y. Le Meur, "State Making and the Politics of the Frontier in Central Benin," *Development and Change* 37 (2006): 871–900.

28. Yakin Erturk, "Report of the Special Rapporteur on Violence against Women, Mission to Ghana," Human Rights Council, Promotion and Protection of All Human Rights, Civil, Political, Economic, Social and Cultural, Including the Rights to Development, Its Causes and Consequences, A/HRC/7/6/Add.3, February 21, 2008; Robert K. Ameh, "Trokosi (Child Slavery) in Ghana: A Policy Approach," *Ghana Studies* 1 (1998): 35–62; Elom Dovlo and A. K. Adzoyi, *Report on the Trokosi Institution* (Legon, Ghana: Department of Religious Studies, University of Ghana, 1995); Judy Rosenthal, *Possession, Ecstasy, and Law in Ewe Voodoo* (Charlottesville: University of Virginia Press, 1998).

29. National Voodoo Day (*La fête nationale du Vaudou*) has been celebrated on January 10 since 1994. See BBC News, January 10, 2006, available at http://news.bbc.co.uk/2/hi/africa/4599392.stm, accessed December 26, 2015.

30. Social Institutions and Gender Index (SIGI), available at: http://genderindex.org/country/benin, citing a 2002 CEDAW report, accessed December 26, 2015.

31. See USAID document available at http://www.usaid.gov/our_work/cross-cutting_programs/wid/pubs/WLR_Y3_BestPractices_JUNE_06.pdf, accessed December 26, 2015, and interviews by Anna Rotman for research on the Benin constitutional court system, available at http://www.law.harvard.edu/students/orgs/hrj/iss17/rotman.pdf, accessed December 26, 2015. Sources in French also indicate aspects of its prevalence; see, e.g., Christian Dieudonné Houegbe, "Le calvaire psychologique du lévirat," *Amazone: Journal Mensuel Béninois*, no. 006 DE 08/99 (1999), 14, and also http://psycause.pagesperso-orange.fr/020_21/le_levirat.htm, accessed December 26, 2015.

32. See http://www.ric.bj/documents/code_pf.pdf.

33. A Canadian IRB report noted that forced marriage is still "practiced in certain rural zones." See http://www.unhcr.org/refworld/country,,IRBC,,BEN,,45f146f220,0.html, accessed December 26, 2015.

34. See Aziza Naa-Kaa Botchway, "Abolished by Law—Maintained in Practice: The *Trokosi* as Practiced in Parts of the Republic of Ghana," *Florida International University*

Law Review 3, no. 2 (2008): 369–93; D. Soyini Madison, *Acts of Activism: Human Rights as Radical Performance* (Cambridge: Cambridge University Press, 2010).

35. For homophobia as a basis for refugee claims generally, see Thomas Spjikerboer, ed., *Fleeing Homophobia: Sexual Orientation, Gender Identity and Asylum* (London: Routledge, 2013).

36. New Bell Prison, outside Douala, has a reputation for squalid and dehumanizing conditions and torture. See "Cameroon: Dire Prison Conditions Threaten Writer's Health," *Amnesty International News,* April 12, 2011, available at http://www .amnesty.org/en/news-and-updates/cameroon-dire-prison-conditions-threaten -writer%E2%80%99s-health-2011-04-12, accessed October 24, 2014; US Department of State, *2011 Country Reports on Human Rights Practices—Cameroon,* May 24, 2012, available at http://www.refworld.org/docid/4fc75ab1c.html, accessed October 24, 2014.

37. "Cameroon: No Action on Homophobic Violence in Cameroon," *IRIN Humanitarian News and Analysis,* September 16, 2013, available at http://allafrica.com /stories/201309171051.html, accessed November 2, 2013.

38. Article 347 of the Penal Code criminalizes sexual contact between members of the same sex, with a penalty of six months to five years in prison and a fine of 20,000 to 200,000 CFA francs, and homosexual acts both between men and between women are illegal in Cameroon. See UNHCR and the US Bureau of Citizenship and Immigration Services, *Cameroon: Information on Treatment of Homosexuals,* November 21, 2002, CMR03001.ZAR, available at http://www.refworld.org/docid/3f51e8734 .html, accessed January 12, 2014.

39. Note 12, testimony of Christelle Nanfack in Matter of Christelle Nanfack in Removal Proceedings, October 9, 2012, interview with Charlotte Walker-Said.

40. Kathleen M. Fallon, "Transforming Women's Citizenship Rights within an Emerging Democratic State: The Case of Ghana," *Gender and Society* 17, no. 4 (2003): 525–43.

41. Charlotte Walker-Said, "Sexual Minorities among African Asylum Claimants: Human Rights Regimes, Bureaucratic Knowledge, and the Era of Sexual Rights Diplomacy," in Berger et al., *African Asylum at a Crossroads.*

42. Andrew Meldrum, "Fifty Public Figures Named in Gay Witchhunt by Cameroon's Papers," *The Guardian,* February 5, 2006; Charles Gueboguo, *La question homosexuelle en Afrique: Le cas du Cameroun* (Paris: Harmattan, 2006).

43. "Joseph: A Courageous Cameroonian Lesbian," *AGW: A Globe of Witnesses Online Journal,* May 2002, available at http://thewitness.org/agw/nyeck.050302.html, accessed January 11, 2014.

44. Global Rights: Partners for Justice, "Discrimination on the Basis of Sexual Orientation and Gender Identity in Access to Health Care and Violence/Bias: A Sierra Leone Case Study," May 2012, p. 21, case 4 from Bo, available at http://www .globalrights.org/sites/default/files/docs/2013_LGBTI_Report_Sierra_Leone.pdf, accessed December 26, 2015.

45. UN Human Rights Committee, "Concluding Observations on the Initial Report of Sierra Leone," March 25, 2014, CCPR/C/SLE/CO/1, available at http://www .refworld.org/docid/533562eb4.html, accessed November 6, 2014.

46. US Department of State, "2013 Country Reports on Human Rights Practices—Sierra Leone," February 27, 2014, available at: http://www.refworld.org/docid/53284a741b.html, accessed November 6, 2014.

47. HJ (Iran) v. Sec'y of State for the Home Dep't (HJ and HT), [2010] UKSC 31 [2011] 1 A.C. 596 (appeal taken from Eng. & Wales C.A.), which echoed an earlier Australian Appellant S395/2002 v Minister for Immigration & Multicultural Affairs (S395) (2003) 216 CLR 473. For a discussion of HJ and HT, see Ryan Goodman, "Asylum and the Concealment of Sexual Orientation: Where Not to Draw the Line," *NYU Journal of International Law & Policy* 44, no. 2 (2012): 407–46; James Hathaway and Jason Pobjoy, "Queer Cases Make Bad Law," *NYU Journal of International Law & Policy* 44, no. 2 (2012): 315–89; Janna Weßels, "HJ (Iran) and Another: Reflections on a New Test for Sexuality Based Claims in Britain," *International Journal of Refugee Law* 24, no. 4 (2012): 815–39; Jenni Millbank, "The Right of Lesbians and Gay Men to Live Freely, Openly, and on Equal Terms Is Not Bad Law: A Reply to Hathaway and Pobjoy," *NYU Journal of International Law & Policy* 44, no. 2 (2012): 497–527.

48. International Gay and Lesbian Human Rights Commission, "Nowhere to Turn: Blackmail and Extortion of LGBT People in sub-Saharan Africa," 2011, available at http://www.iglhrc.org/binary-data/ATTACHMENT/file/000/000/484–1.pdf, accessed December 16, 2012.

49. The 2014 Pew Global Attitude Survey on morality demonstrates the deterioration in attitudes in Ghana and the rapid increase in homophobia. The 2007 Pew Global Attitudes Survey identified Ghana as one of the least tolerant nations with regard to homosexuality. Eleven percent of Ghanaians expressed the view that homosexuality should be tolerated. The 2014 survey, however, noted a 98 percent "unacceptable" rating for homosexuality; see http://www.pewglobal.org/2014/04/15/global-morality/country/ghana/, accessed January 28, 2015.

50. See http://www.asylumlaw.org/docs/sexualminorities/GhanaCUSO.pdf. The director of public prosecutions, Gertrude Aikins, "has indicated that persons caught engaging in homosexual activities could be liable for prosecution" in Ghana under current law, in June 2011; see http://www.ghanaweb.com/GhanaHomePage/NewsArchive/artikel.php?ID=210533, accessed December 26, 2015.

51. The majority of mental health patients receive no medical care but rather are untreated or treated informally or "traditionally" in so-called prayer camps. See Human Rights Watch, "'Like a Death Sentence': Abuses against Persons with Mental Disabilities in Ghana," 2012, available at http://www.hrw.org/reports/2012/10/02/death-sentence-0, accessed December 26, 2015. The head of mental health care in Ghana, Dr. Kwesi Osei, stated that mental illness is often viewed in supernatural terms "even among professionals"; see http://www.irinnews.org/report/93563/ghana-mental-health-bill-to-address-stigma, accessed December 26, 2015. Also see Ursula M. Read, Edward Adiibokah, and Solomon Nyame, "Local Suffering and the Global Discourse of Mental Health and Human Rights: An Ethnographic Study of Responses to Mental Illness in Rural Ghana," *Global Health* 5, no. 13 (2009): 13.

PART THREE

Contemporary Perspectives

Consent, Custom, and the Law in Debates around Forced Marriage at the Special Court for Sierra Leone

MARIANE C. FERME

This chapter analyzes concepts and evidence brought to bear on the criminalization of forced marriage at the Special Court for Sierra Leone (SCSL)
in the aftermath of the 1991–2002 civil war, against the backdrop of marriage practices and attitudes toward sex crimes outside the conflict setting.
Differences between forced and customary marriages were critical to court
arguments about the former's criminalization. My analysis highlights tensions between notions of individual and collective consent, which in some
instances mimic gender biases in customary law. I argue that the criminalization of forced marriage at the SCSL had paradoxical consequences
for women's rights at the time because it appeared to be predicated on establishing some forced relations as crimes against humanity while accepting others as "customary." Witness testimony and ethnographic evidence
examined in this chapter offer a more complex understanding of women's
experiences of marriage in Sierra Leone.

My goal is in part to explore the messy terrain between notions of
agency and consent in marriage emerging in international humanitarian jurisprudence and among ordinary Sierra Leoneans.[1] I do not seek
to resolve the tension that inevitably exists between these different and
to some extent incommensurable arenas; rather, I want to examine the

configurations of power/knowledge it produces, particularly around the figure of the "bush wife."

Forced marriage was added to the roster of crimes against humanity at the Special Court for Sierra Leone—which was established to try war crimes and crimes against humanity committed during the 1991–2002 civil war—first as precedent in the appeals phase of the Armed Forces Revolutionary Council (AFRC) trial and then as a successful article of indictment in the Revolutionary United Front (RUF) consolidated trial. Scholars writing or testifying in court in favor of establishing this new crime drew on anthropological scholarship on normative forms of customary marriage, as well as on wartime ethnographic evidence, to highlight the *sui generis* and harmful nature of forced marriage in war.[2] The juxtaposition was prompted by the apparent mimicry between the crime of forced marriage and arranged marriages in peacetime because in the latter, too, a woman's consent was absent. Additional evidence offered here, particularly on Sierra Leonean marriage practices and on the treatment of marital and sexual breaches in customary courts, provides a richer context for debates surrounding forced marriage in Sierra Leone and elsewhere.

In what follows, I argue that the focus at the SCSL on a more robust prosecution of sexual crimes in war was predicated on varying degrees of erasure of peacetime violations of women's human rights in marriage, since these risked undermining the case in favor of criminalizing forced marriage. Furthermore, the "forced marriage" terminology euphemistically aligned a sexual crime with ordinary conjugality, which did not have the stigmatizing resonance of "sexual enslavement," particularly in the collective imagination of an older generation in postconflict Sierra Leone that experienced the social humiliation of domestic slavery within recent historical memory. Ambivalent attitudes toward the forced marriage terminology even at the court gained the upper hand during the Charles Taylor trial—the final case heard at the SCSL—in which, despite the absence of indictments on this count, the judges held that forced marriage should "be considered a conjugal form of enslavement."[3]

ADVANCING JURISPRUDENCE AND
UNDERSTANDING VICTIMS' EXPERIENCES

Debates around the criminalization of forced marriage illustrate the process of "enriching the jurisprudence" in international humanitarian law, which is among the key goals of war crimes courts, and an aspect of their knowledge-production work.[4] According to the court's first chief prosecutor, the American David Crane, the SCSL's notable achievement was making "gender crimes the cornerstone" of its indictments and contributing to the criminalization of forced marriage in particular.[5] Both women in the three-judge chamber at the AFRC trial discussed at length instances of sexual enslavement and rape prosecuted in the International Criminal Tribunal for Rwanda (ICTR) and the International Criminal Tribunal for the Former Yugoslavia (ICTY), together with the applicability of those precedents to the Sierra Leonean case. In part through their efforts, sufficient novel thinking was introduced in the AFRC trial to set precedents and secure convictions for the new crime of forced marriage against the Revolutionary United Front.[6]

Court arguments about forced marriage at the SCSL also suggest, however, that the process of enriching the jurisprudence does not follow a linear progression; it is characterized instead by sometimes discordant developments. For instance, only in the RUF trial was evidence of sexual violence perpetrated against men and boys discussed at any length, even though, conceptually, the move to put "gender crimes" at the center of the court's agenda—Prosecutor David Crane's opening manifesto—would have called for including from the beginning a critical stance toward the automatic "feminization" of their victims.[7] This move also made visible the ways in which the complementary masculinization of aggressors had masked abuses committed by female combatants.[8]

Feminist legal activists and scholars greeted with enthusiasm Crane's plans to vigorously prosecute crimes against women at the SCSL.[9] But in practice, the court got off to a rocky start in the area of gender crimes: during the first consolidated trial, involving three leaders of the Civil Defense Militia (CDF), evidence about sexual violence was excluded from the trial on procedural grounds.[10] In this placement of "expediency and efficiency before the prosecution of crimes of sexual violence," critics saw an instance of the court's excessive emphasis on the rights of the accused at the expense of those of the victim-witness—a problem also noted in the war crimes tribunals of the 1990s, particularly the ICTR.[11]

Aware of the fact that the trials were unfolding in a country where ordinarily customary marriages took place without the consent of the bride-to-be, SCSL staff sought to highlight differences between the practices they aimed to criminalize and those accepted as normal by the surrounding population. In one instance, the office of the prosecutor instructed an expert preparing a briefing paper "to create a clear distinction between the custom of arranged marriage and the crime of forced marriage. Without this distinction, the court might also declare arranged marriage a war crime, and that is something the prosecutor did not want."[12] Though forced marriage encompassed rape and sexual enslavement, debates at the SCSL about its specificity as a crime tried to capture, too, a broader range of harms, including the "distinctive status" conferred by being considered a "rebel" or "bush" wife. Attention was also given to the lasting stigma deriving from having borne "rebel babies," who would live on as reminders of the violence in which they were conceived.

A key expert witness for the prosecution in the Armed Forces Revolutionary Council trial, Zainab Bangura, testified in 2005 about her encounters with bush, or "junta," wives who had been abducted and forced into marriages that, though *mimicking* (in the words of a judge summarizing her testimony) "peacetime situations in which forced marriage and expectation of free female labour are common practice," carried with them a stigma that permanently ostracized the women from their communities, along with any offspring conceived during the relationship.[13] In various ways, therefore, the court came to accept "common practices," even when harmful to particular individuals, because of the legitimating and supportive roles played by collectivities—in this case, the extended families contracting a marriage.[14] Thus, perhaps to further the goals of advancing the rights of individuals and protecting them from harm, the SCSL in this instance chose the legal strategy to privilege the rights of collectivities over the interests of individuals—particularly women. This position appeared to contradict arguments for the criminalization of forced marriage, in which the absence of an individual's consent was of central importance. Elsewhere, I have argued that this naturalization of what is, in effect, a logical contradiction has to do in part with implicit assumptions in some transitional justice thinking about the benign nature of familial, residential, and other "communities" that were problematic in the context of a civil war that highlighted deep divisions precisely within such collectivities.[15]

During the AFRC consolidated trial, the prosecution's indictment initially called for forced marriage to be considered under the rubric of "sexual slavery," established as a crime against humanity at the International Court for Crimes (ICC), with the first, precedent-setting prosecutions taking place at the ICTY in the *Kunarac* case.[16] But as the cases unfolded, arguments were advanced for making forced marriage a distinct crime

MARIANE C. FERME

under "other inhumane acts," to shift the focus from sexual elements to the totality of the violent experience. The prosecution was unsuccessful in making this argument and failed to secure convictions in the AFRC trial.

The presiding judge, Julia Sebutinde, reprised Zainab Bangura's observation of the similarities between the violation of women's rights in arranged marriages in peacetime and forced marriage in wartime. In her opinion, she wrote that though the former were surely violations "under international human rights instruments," such as the 1979 UN Convention on the Elimination of All Forms of Discrimination against Women (CEDAW), they were not recognized as crimes in international humanitarian law. By contrast, she wrote, forced marriage in wartime "is clearly criminal in nature and is liable to attract prosecution"—even as she found that the prosecution had been unsuccessful in proving its case in this particular trial.[17] Judge Sebutinde favored classifying forced marriage as a form of sexual slavery, but in her partly dissenting opinion, Judge Teresa Doherty argued for distinguishing them because the former posed greater obstacles to the ability of victims "to reintegrate to society . . . thereby prolonging their mental trauma."[18] In the end, her argument won the day: the appeals chamber found that the trial judges had "erred in law" and that forced marriage should be considered "not predominantly sexual," "distinct from the crime of sexual slavery . . . [and] amount[ing] to other inhumane acts under Article 2(1) of the Statute."[19]

Thus, from the beginning there were concerns about the mimicry between forced marriages in wartime and in peacetime. Yet arguments proposing criminalization of forced marriage insisted on its value as an umbrella term that encompassed multiple harms. One article of legal scholarship that circulated widely among the lawyers working at the SCSL in 2008 and whose language echoed in arguments at the court asserted:

> None of the other crimes against humanity that comprise forced
> marriage describe the *totality* of the perpetrator's conduct or the
> victim's experience. Enslavement describes the loss of personal
> freedom, but obscures the sexual violence inherent in the crime.
> Sexual slavery describes the loss of personal freedom and the
> sexual violence, but does not speak to the forced domestic labor,
> childbearing, childrearing, and degradation of the institution of
> marriage. Torture, rape, and forced pregnancy do not address the
> victim's loss of personal liberty and individually may not be present
> in all cases of forced marriage.[20]

The authors went on to argue that forced marriage was "a profound deprivation of individual autonomy" and "the denigration of an important and protected social and spiritual institution." But the very fact that forced marriage could capture the totality of a complex experience for some was seen by others as a troubling lack of specificity and redundant in the face of prior charges of sexual slavery—an already established crime against humanity.[21]

Judge Doherty added the element of time in her arguments in favor of using a distinct indictment for the crime of forced marriage. The conferral of this status on a captive, she argued, resulted in trauma well into the future of a victim's life, in part because "the label 'wife' may stigmatize the victims and lead to their rejection by their families and community, negatively impacting their ability to reintegrate into society and thereby prolonging their mental trauma." This was due partially to the lasting and equally stigmatizing legacy represented by any children conceived in violence.[22] Here and in earlier arguments, the ICTY and ICTR precedents informed the concern for future harms. Furthermore, the marriagelike practice, it was argued, also enabled a perpetrator to continue abusing his victim over time. In other words, temporality—in the form of duration (of violent abuses) and of a future orientation in considering social stigma and traumatic consequences—was another key element in the conceptual apparatus supporting the criminalization of forced marriage.

Although the SCSL "entered the first-ever international criminal convictions for the crime against humanity of sexual slavery" in the RUF trial and "solidified" its definition in international humanitarian law, the jurisprudence on forced marriage, in the end, had more ambivalent outcomes.[23] On the one hand, the precedent established in the appeals phase of the AFRC trial set the stage for its criminalization and led to calls for prosecuting instances of sexual enslavement and forced marriage elsewhere. On the other hand, some legal practitioners and scholars argued that the conceptual foundations for establishing forced marriage as a crime were shaky at best, given that nothing resembling a "marriage" could be said to have taken place in cases examined at the SCSL Thus, already at the Charles Taylor trial, it was proposed that "conjugal slavery" better described what elsewhere had been labeled "forced marriage."[24]

Contestations over terminology were in part centered on its euphemistic and nonspecific nature: "The difficulty with labeling what is otherwise sexual slavery, rape, enslavement, and torture as 'marriage' is that it distorts

MARIANE C. FERME

and conceals the nature of the victim's experience."[25] Put another way, for those criticizing the introduction of "forced marriage" as an article of indictment, the very terminology that for its proponents captured the totality of harms suffered by victims ended up masking them. In the arguments presented at the ICC to add sexual slavery to the roster of crimes against humanity (and their subsequent deployment at the ICTY), many critics saw more solid legal foundations for prosecuting gender crimes committed in Sierra Leone. Already, they pointed out, the debates and jurisprudence around the criminalization of sexual slavery had moved away from the moralizing tone of earlier legislation against "enforced prostitution" in war, in which offenses against "human dignity" loomed large. Instead, at the ICC and ICTY, the central concepts in debates over sexual slavery were consent, personal freedom, and the exercise of elements of ownership by perpetrators over victims.[26] Among other things, my objection to the use of marriage terminology to describe this complex of crimes had in part to do with the ambiguous meanings of the word *wife* among Mende speakers.

ARRANGED AND FORCED MARRIAGES AND THE QUESTION OF CONSENT

One of the reasons for the discursive weakness of forced marriage in the setting of international humanitarian criminal institutions of the twenty-first century is that for most of its history, forced marriage was not clearly distinguished from arranged marriage. This historical slippage perhaps contributes to the mimicry observed by legal experts and practitioners in the SCSL setting, who nonetheless point to the fact that even though a wife's consent is not necessary in customary marriages, sometimes "the parties consent to the parents' choice."[27] Thus, forced and arranged marriages overlap partly because of the historical displacement of the former term by the latter. For some scholars, arranged marriages may have different connotations than for human rights advocates. For the former, the matter of consent may rest with the extended family, even though it ideally involves the wife's assent—a more appropriate term (normally associated with the limited consent of jural minors) because most women have no legal standing in customary courts and male relatives must "speak for them." But since this search for assent is optional, it hardly constitutes a robust distinction from a marriage to which contracting parties have not consented. This also suggests that practices violating individual but not familial rights are somehow less harmful to the person affected than those that violate both.

The issue of consent and agency emerges from the testimony in court of victims of forced marriages. A witness identified as TF1-016, who testified in the RUF trial, insisted on the illegal nature of her being "given to a man" because she was already married.[28] Other witnesses also used the objectifying, passive language of "being given" to combatants but described more complex experiences; one such witness, TF1-023, at the AFRC trial was only sixteen when she was "handed over" to a rebel combatant and forced to have sex with him. However, she refused to perform other domestic duties, such as cooking, and she could demand services from her captor's subordinates and their female captives.[29] In most women's testimony, the terms in which they referred to themselves as objects being given or handed over mirrored those attendant to marriage transactions in peacetime, when members of the groom's patrilineage would beg the family of a prospective bride to "give" her to them. Thus, part of what emerged from court testimony about forced marriage was the subjection of women in a manner consistent with their position in customary marriage negotiations.

The SCSL's position with respect to the consent of families and other forms of "community" appears to contradict the increasing focus on rights-bearing individuals, often to the detriment of rights-bearing collectivities that is a distinctive feature of the expansion since the 1990s of humanitarian jurisprudence and international criminal institutions.[30] Concurrently, there also has been a tendency to individualize responsibility for war crimes, even when this contradicted situations where violence and abuses in war were experienced as collective phenomena. One of the consequences of this focus on "personal responsibility" and narrower definitions of individual accountability higher up in chains of command in war crimes tribunals was that those targeted for prosecution were less likely to be the actual perpetrators of brutalities. Part of the reason for this was that—unlike the international tribunals of the 1990s—the "hybrid" tribunals encompassing the SCSL were supposed to have a complementary relationship with national courts, where perpetrators further down the chain of command could be prosecuted. This had not happened in Sierra Leone when these debates took place.

Feminist activists and legal scholars had great hopes for the SCSL, feeling that its unique, hybrid structure "and its location in-country could have potentially huge implications for the rights of Sierra Leonean women."[31] This was because crimes against women, such as domestic violence and

rape, were sometimes weakly prosecuted in local and national Sierra Leonean settings, and the exemplary performance of their prosecution in a
tribunal supported by international structures such as the United Nations
was seen as a possible model for reforming enfocement and legal norms
at the national level. Instead, the SCSL did not immediately have this impact although sexual crimes did come to be prosecuted more vigorously.
Although accusations of rape, sexual enslavement, and eventually forced
marriage were listed as articles of indictments, these did not always result
in convictions.[32]

LOST IN TRANSLATION: THE VARIETIES OF MARRIAGE

Testimony at the SCSL and other reports on violence against civilians confirmed that women of all ages were subjected to brutal rapes, forced conscription as fighters, and forms of enslavement—particularly between 1997
and 1999. This period coincided with the May 1997 coup carried out by
the RUF rebels allied with rogue members of the military comprising the
Armed Forces Revolutionary Council, bringing them to power until their
defeat some nine months later. Though pushed back at that time from the
capital city, the AFRC-RUF junta remained in control of other parts of the
country, and it attacked Freetown in January 1999. During this time, there
were reports of women being taken as "wives" by combatants or allocated
by them to their subordinates.[33] In one instance, witness TF1-016 testified
that she was "given" by an RUF commander to his local palm wine tapper,
who kept her and raped her for fifteen months; this suggests that noncom-
batants, too, took advantage of the war to perpetrate sexual crimes.[34]

These forced unions with nonconsenting women were sometimes referred to as "bush marriages," and "bush wife" became a common way to
refer to the women trapped in them in the reports of expert witnesses to
the SCSL, in proceedings of the Truth and Reconciliation Commission
(TRC), and in other documents.[35] Yet the expression was not used nearly as
much among the wider population in Sierra Leone, including combatants,
as it was in postconflict transitional institutions and in English-speaking
circles. Witness DBK-113 testified at the Special Court that he had never
heard the expression "bush wife" during his time as an AFRC captive, and
the prosecution's key expert witness in this trial admitted that only in 1999
did she become aware that combatants abducting women and taking them
as so-called wives was "common practice."[36]

In Sierra Leone, the bush is secondary forest growth, as distinct from a human settlement, cultivated farm, or mature forest. The bush is, for humans, an interstitial, liminal place that is crossed when traveling between village and farm or visited in order to hunt animals or harvest wild foods. Even in the daytime, the boundaries between bush and town are places governed by social norms.[37] Some activities associated with settled town life are proscribed in the bush—among them sexual relations including extramarital ones carried out during the daytime. The combination of location and temporality—the bush, which offers more privacy than the village, and the daytime, when people are supposed to engage in productive farm labor rather than dally in sexual liaisons—made this one of the circumstances in which customary law intervened to punish transgressors.[38]

In ordinary rural parlance before the civil war, referring to something as being "bush"—for instance, clothing or the solution to a problem—meant that it was makeshift and temporary, lacking the resources one might have in the village. In this sense, then, securing a bush wife or husband was similarly temporary, in a time when all social norms were disrupted by war.

Some witnesses at the SCSL testified to having been taken as what was translated as wives by male combatants, and the fact that female victims themselves used this terminology was key to arguments for criminalizing forced marriage.[39] However, the term translated as "wife" carries even more ambiguous connotations than "bush." In Mende, *nyaha* means "woman" as well as "wife." It also signals the fact that a person has been initiated into the women's Sande (or Bundu) society and is thus a social adult—ready for marriage and childbearing.

Children in Sierra Leone become adults through initiation into the Sande society, for women, and the Poro society, for men. Both are secretive (for the opposite sex and the uninitiated) and hierarchical institutions that cut across familial and other social groupings. Sande rituals transform girls into marriageable, fertile, and adult members of the society, and the women responsible for this transformation gain lifelong control over the marriage prospects of their initiates; historically, they have turned their position to political advantage.[40] In discussions at the SCSL, the legitimacy of arranged marriages was linked to family participation, but in fact, other institutions, such as secret societies, were equally important. Consequently, when one breaks down the ill-defined "community" whose legitimacy and consent were invoked by the court, one finds among its components powerful, hierarchically organized religious institutions whose political

MARIANE C. FERME

and economic interests crosscut those of secular institutions and of the family. These competing demands on members of collectivities are exercised in a context in which the young and unmarried of either sex—and women throughout their lives—are most fully embraced when they are "for" somebody—when they are tied by relations of dependence to a "big" person who, among other things, speaks for his or her dependents in customary courts.[41]

Historically, slavery was a key element in this system of interdependence, and marriage mediated relations between the free and the enslaved. Though domestic slavery was outlawed in Sierra Leone in 1927, the discourse of domestic and debt enslavement still haunts and potentially stigmatizes contemporary prewar rural and urban social relations. In particular, such discourse is used in connection with marriages that were supposed to "ransom" individuals from certain forms of indebtedness; therefore, it is at the core of a politicized perspective on marriage as an institution mediating but also potentially emancipating individuals from relations of inequality.[42] This is in part why I hold that the crime of sexual slavery "translates" much better than the more euphemistic forced marriage in the broader Sierra Leonean context, and thus offers more robust legal, historical, and socio-cultural grounds from which to mobilize on behalf of women's rights in Sierra Leone.

Ultimately, the context in which gender and intergenerational relations in Sierra Leone must be understood is one in which the (unequal) interdependence of members of familial, social, and political collectivities is valued—and even the powerful are beholden to those who depend on them. Individuals who seek autonomy from webs of mutual obligations usually do so in favor of alternative ones. In marriage, this means that family authorities tend to want some indication that their female relative is interested in a potential match before finalizing arrangements and accepting bridewealth, for if she dislikes her prospective husband, she might in future seek a divorce with the support of other kin. This, in turn, would force the wife's family to return marriage payments at a time when financial circumstances might make that a hardship. Though the collectivity is valued, then, and the language of hierarchical familial bonds is paramount in social and political rhetoric, the group's hold on any individual is, in some ways, quite fragile without a measure of explicit compliance. Individual agency is not eclipsed by familial interests: it hovers on the margins and is continually enlisted. In general, prewar and postwar conjugal arrangements tended to increase the possible range of unions that went under the rubric of "marriage," rather than drawing sharp distinctions. And the range of familial relationships women or men could draw upon to legitimate the preference of certain affective bonds and residential patterns over others was rather expansive, so as to offer alternatives to individuals who found themselves trapped in unhappy affinal, kin, or other relations.

The question of consent and violence in some of the unions formed during the war is similarly ambiguous. In one instance, a young woman I knew, whom I will call Moinyaha, was taken during a rebel incursion in her home village. I was told that she was approached by a rebel who "liked her" and had not been seen since. The ambiguity of the language used did not exclude the possibility that Moinyaha had some voice in the matter. Though she was married when the war broke out, her husband had never been around much, and she was a relatively junior wife struggling to support an infant. Then, her child died, so by the time the rebel leader who "liked her" arrived in the village, Moinyaha was, in some ways, a single woman.

In discussing her departure, villagers focused on the fact that her abductor "said he liked her . . . [so] we gave her to him." I asked whether *she* had agreed, according to the formula customarily employed during marriage negotiations whereby relatives turn to a prospective bride, point to money and goods brought to the meeting by would-be in-laws, and ask her whether they should accept them. It is the moment closest to what one might define as consent in the SCSL's sense of the term, in which a prospective bride moves from being a subject defined by her ambiguous acquiescence with the proceedings to having a more active voice. On this score, the villagers' responses were vague.

Other stories of so-called bush wives were less ambiguous: for instance, trial transcripts told of the woman who was swept up in a raid, raped, and then offered the protection of an exclusive relationship with a particular fighter, whose "woman/wife" she thus became.[43] In cases where forced marriages resulted in pregnancy and childbirth, the relationships were more likely to last beyond the war, as fathers sought to regularize their position and hence their claim to their children.[44] In one case, a woman and her abductor sought to formalize their relationship after the war and secure his status as the father of their two children, but her family refused his marriage offer. Having opted for her family's support, the woman separated from her husband, only to have her suspicious relatives still shun and mistreat her, driving her into prostitution to support her children.[45]

Though horrible crimes were committed against women during the 1991–2002 civil war, the forced marriages that joined rebels to kidnapped women sometimes ended up being better matches than the equally forced marriages that had preceded them in peacetime, particularly because they tended to be between individuals who were closer in age than those selected by families to improve their socioeconomic prospects. But the homogeneous characterization of all such unions as "crimes against humanity" did not reflect the full range of wartime experiences, which included the transformation of an original violence into a familiar bond. This possibility was addressed by Judge Doherty in the AFRC opinion; she wrote that "a decision to remain in the forced marriage or its transformation into a consensual situation does not retroactively negate the original criminality of the act."[46]

Contrary to the SCSL, where gradations of violence and consent were subordinated to legal arguments for criminalizing forced marriage, the responses to this practice varied across the country at large. In Kailahun near the Liberian border, which was the last place where elements of the AFRC-RUF junta were demobilized, bush wives were less stigmatized. But in Pujehun District, where some of the earliest war violence had unfolded, they could be suspected of collusion with the enemy and often mistreated.[47]

A different perspective on forced marriage can be gained from Sierra Leonean representations of even the most ordinary marriage as a form of aggression. Among Mende speakers, wife-takers are called "splitters" (*mbela,* the literal translation of "in-law"), for taking a lineage's women and their future offspring. If a bush husband who was brought back by a woman from her war captivity sought to formalize their union, he would face "wife troubles" (*nyaha monε*), referring to the labor, expenses, and gift giving for in-laws that accompany marriages throughout their duration. Patrilineages remind in-laws of their residual hold on their women's progeny beyond the jural rights exercised by their fathers by participating in all major decisions affecting their lives, particularly through their brothers. Historically, mother's brothers had the power to place sisters' children in debt servitude, a condition avoided through matrilateral cross-cousin marriage. Indeed, the rhetoric of slavery and ransom colors matrilateral cross-cousin marriage negotiations to this day in Sierra Leone.[48] Thus, an overlooked aspect of customary marriage practices in debates at the SCSL is the extent to which they are informed by contentiousness and explicitly political negotiations even in ordinary times.

Mende speakers refer to wife troubles as an intrinsic aspect of the relationship between wife-takers and wife-givers, and they recognize that at marriage, a man enters a form of lifelong indenture to his in-laws, in exchange for his wife and her future offspring. In a sense, then, even ordinary customary marriage encompasses social transactions centered on reparation for losses. A more nuanced understanding of cultural constructions of marriage and of the political and social negotiations that accompany its arrangement—which is a continuous process rather than a single event—might provide insights into ways of dealing with at least some of the unions formed in wartime, by framing their aftermath within a different logic of punishment and restitution than the incarceration meted out at the SCSL.

SEXUAL CRIMES IN GENERAL AND CUSTOMARY LAW

Transitional justice institutions, particularly the SCSL and the Truth and Reconciliation Commission, became the main context in which Sierra Leonean women could openly testify to being raped, while often remaining silent about the occurrence of rape in ordinary life in local and national legal settings.[49] Outside the exceptional, conflict scenario of forced abduction—and the settings of the SCSL and TRC—denouncing sexual violence remained fraught with stigma and exposed the victims to further trauma. The fact that victims of forced marriage could testify to it in the RUF and AFRC trials but not in the CDF one made even the SCSL less than a model for changing local thinking about consent in marriage more generally, not to mention making rapists legally accountable.

So what is the status of sexual crimes in customary law? "Woman quarrels"—litigation cases involving women—have long been among the most common in rural Sierra Leone, taking up the bulk of the time and efforts of family and chiefly courts at various levels.[50] But these are not generally cases of sexual violence. Instead, most involve adultery charges made by husbands against other men, sometimes in collusion with their wives. Lodging such charges can be a strategy for older men to secure the labor and "judicial serfdom" of younger men, who, once found guilty of adultery, must pay heavy court fines or do farmwork until the debt is extinguished. Indeed, some have seen in this form of debt servitude an important source

MARIANE C. FERME

of intergenerational grievances that fueled the 1991–2002 civil war and—if not addressed—a potential source of future conflict in agrarian settings.[51]

In the context of marriage, sexual violence is not recognized in customary law, but in practice, it can become the basis for divorce proceedings. But customary courts do intervene in cases involving sex with an unmarried virgin, which in Krio—a national lingua franca—are known as "virginating" cases. These are described as rape cases, and during the 1991–2002 civil war, evidence emerged that some combatants deliberately preyed on young virgins.[52] But in the cases prosecuted in areas where I did research before the war, this charge could also apply to consensual sexual relations between a man and any girl or woman who had not been initiated into Sande. The fines in such cases were so exorbitant—because they affected the woman's marriage and bridewealth prospects—that one prominent member of the village where I was living left the chiefdom permanently to escape the jurisdiction of its courts.

Many of the crimes examined at the SCSL fell within the categories of sexual crimes that were familiar in the customary legal landscape of Sierra Leone. However, though the SCSL drew liberally on customary law regulating marriage in debates, the court did not analyze its treatment of marital and sexual crimes. Perhaps this was because cases involving damage to women as well as virginating cases appeared to essentially reproduce the status of women as objects in conflicts among men. Nonetheless, because this was not done in a "hybrid" court that sought to move international humanitarian law closer to its intended beneficiaries, the opportunity to translate for the broader population the implications of prosecuting sexual crimes at the SCSL was missed.

A HOLISTIC approach to the traumatic afterlife of forced marriage—one truly dedicated to understanding the totality of the experience for those affected by it—needs to go beyond seeking justice for its victims and accountability for its perpetrators in courts of law. The fact that after the war, some victims of forced marriage tried to remain with their captors suggests that, over time, an original act of violence could be transformed.[53] Labels such as Stockholm syndrome—the attachment traumatized victims form with their captors—are not especially helpful in a broader context where the lack of a woman's consent is the norm in marriage, even in peacetime.[54] Giving attention to temporality—to the aftermath of harms suffered in war—was among the signal contributions of the SCSL to international criminal jurisprudence, particularly the focus on the lasting stigma of sexual violence, including the ways in which so-called rebel babies could hamper future reintegration of forced marriage victims within communities of belonging. But even though the aggravating effects of time were explored, evidence of the mitigating force of the passage of time was elided; for example, some wartime abductions had given way to familial units that offered a possibility of alternative remedy. The case of the woman shunned and driven into prostitution by a family that refused to recognize her bush husband suggests that further harm may result from such elisions, just as much as they could from overlooking other aspects of the totality of wartime experiences.

The Mende discourse of wife troubles and ransom brides suggests, too, that prewar customary marriage could be fraught with tension, evoking as it does relations of indebtedness between in-laws, obligations imposed on husbands, and even the historical legacy of enslavement. In this, the Sierra Leonean case underscores the relationship, drawn by other contributors to this volume, among marriage, property transfers, debt, and slavery in African social history. The role of key members of extended families in mediating these relations, which entail labor burdens and the deprivation of freedom even as they forge alliances, is at odds with the SCSL's finding that this collectivity's consent legitimates marital unions even against the will of prospective spouses. Harm, restitution, and the balancing of gains (alliances) with losses (a lineage's woman lost to another)—more than love and romance—are part of the conceptual and affective apparatus of marriage in this context. For a woman, marriage choices often center around relative food security and respectful partnership at the margins of subsistence, especially in urban poverty or agrarian settings. In this setting, submitting a former abductor to the trials of in-law obligations and of wife troubles in the process of legitimating the union with his bush wife might offer more readily recognizable forms of justice to families touched by the war's violence.

At the same time, the case discussed earlier of a young abducted woman who could not refuse to have sex with her captor but did refuse to cook and wash clothes for him suggests that within the totality of experiences of sexual enslavement, there were also spaces where consent could be denied and minor forms of control exercised. In the end, forced marriage—as a war crime—is best understood under as "sexual slavery," given the ways in which its juxtaposition with peacetime unions that also lack women's consent raises paradoxical implications for women's rights.

NOTES

Participants in the Rochester Institute of Technology workshop in April 2013—especially the editors of this volume—gave productive feedback on earlier drafts of this chapter. Kamari Clarke, Sharika Thiranagama, and Ozlem Biner did so for an earlier iteration of some of this material. I bear responsibility for its final form. Rebecca Small and Heather Mellquist helped with research assistance. Saleem Vahidy, chief of the Witness and Victims Section at the SCSL, offered friendship and generous hospitality in Freetown in 2008 and 2012, and facilitated the research. I am grateful to all. This chapter is based on my own observations of court proceedings, conversations with lawyers and court staff, and trial transcripts.

1. On the role of anthropologists in mediating between such disparate terrains, see, for instance, Sally Engle Merry, "Transnational Human Rights and Local Activism: Mapping the Middle," *American Anthropologist* 108, no. 1 (2006): 38–51; and Richard Ashby Wilson and Jon P. Mitchell, "Introduction: The Social Life of Rights," in *Human Rights in Global Perspective: Anthropological Studies of Rights, Claims, and Entitlements,* ed. Jon. P. Mitchell and Richard A. Wilson (London: Routledge, 2003), 1–15.

2. Michael P. Scharf and Suzanne Mattler, "Forced Marriage: Exploring the Viability of the Special Court for Sierra Leone's New Crime against Humanity," *Case Western Research Paper Series in Legal Studies* 05-25 (17): 1–24 (2005); Prosecutor v. Alex Tamba Brima, Brima Bazzy Kamara, Santigie Borbor Kanu (henceforth cited as Brima, Kamara, Kanu), SCSL-2004-16-T, Joint Defence Disclosure of Expert Report on Forced Marriages by Dr. Dorte Thorsen (August 12, 2006); and Chris Coulter, *Bush Wives and Girl Soldiers: Women's Lives through War and Peace in Sierra Leone* (Ithaca, NY: Cornell University Press, 2009).

3. Valerie Oosterveld, "Gender and the Charles Taylor Case at the Special Court for Sierra Leone," *William and Mary Journal of Women and the Law* 19, no. 1 (2012): 7–33, 15. See the introduction to this volume for a historical perspective on the continuities between, for instance, the colonial discourse on slavery and that on "child marriage," centered on the lack of the capacity for consent in both institutions.

4. See Bridgette A. Toy-Cronin, "What Is Forced Marriage? Towards a Definition of Forced Marriage as a Crime against Humanity," *Columbia Journal of Gender and Law* 19, no. 2 (2010): 576; Micaela Frulli, "Advancing International Criminal Law: The Special Court for Sierra Leone Recognizes Forced Marriage as a 'New' Crime against Humanity," *Journal of International Criminal Justice* 6, no. 5 (2008): 1033–42; and Jennifer Gong-Gershowitz, "Forced Marriage: A 'New' Crime against Humanity?" *Northwestern Journal of International Human Rights* 8, no. 1 (2009): 53–76.

5. David Crane, phone interview, March 8, 2011. On the SCSL's advances in sensitizing court staff to gender crimes and establishing new standards for handling witnesses and victims in international law, see Rebecca Horn, Simon Charters, and Saleem Vahidy, "Testifying in an International War Crimes Tribunal: The Experience of Witnesses in the Special Court for Sierra Leone," *International Journal of Transitional Justice* 3 (2009): 135–49, 137.

6. Beginning in June 2004 with the CDF case in trial chamber I, trials unfolded over nine years, concurrently and in staggered order in two chambers in Freetown,

Sierra Leone. Judgments were handed down in the CDF and AFRC trials in 2007 and in 2009 for the RUF. More information on the sequencing is available on the SCSL website. In 2007, the Charles Taylor trial was relocated to the premises of the International Criminal Court at The Hague, and proceedings were streamed live to the SCSL in Freetown over the following years. All trial judgments were followed by sentencing and appeals phases.

7. Oosterveld, "Gender and the Charles Taylor Case," 14.

8. Human Rights Watch, "'We'll Kill You If You Cry': Sexual Violence in the Sierra Leone Conflict," *Human Rights Watch Reports* 15, no. 1 (2003): 41.

9. Binaifer Nowrojee, "Making the Invisible War Crime Visible: Post-conflict Justice for Sierra Leone's Rape Victims," *Harvard Human Rights Journal* 18 (2005): 100–101.

10. Michelle Staggs Kelsall and Shanee Stepakoff, "'When We Wanted to Talk about Rape': Silencing Sexual Violence at the Special Court for Sierra Leone," *International Journal of Transitional Justice* 1 (2007): 355–74, 362.

11. One notorious case was that of the "laughing judges" at the callous, inept questioning and cross-examination of a rape victim in the Butare trial at the ICTR, discussed in Binaifer Nowrojee, "'Your Justice Is Too Slow': Will the ICTR Fail Rwanda's Rape Victims?" Occasional Paper 10 (Geneva, Switzerland: United Nations Research Institute for Social Development, 2005), 24.

12. Toy-Cronin, "What Is Forced Marriage?" 539–90, 572.

13. Bangura discussed by Presiding Judge Julia Sebutinde in her "Separate Concurring Opinion" to the Brima, Kamara, Kanu Judgment, June 20, 2007, 577. Zainab Bangura's testimony about the stigmatizing aspects of forced marriage can be found in Brima, Kamara, Kanu, October 3, 4, and 13, 2005.

14. See Karine Bélair, "Unearthing the Customary Law Foundations of 'Forced Marriages' during Sierra Leone's Civil War: The Possible Impact of International Criminal Law on Customary Marriage and Women's Rights in Post-conflict Sierra Leone," *Columbia Journal of Gender and Law* 15, no. 3 (2006): 565–69, 569. The chapter by Richard Roberts in this volume explores the emergence of the distinction between arranged and forced marriages in early twentieth-century colonial policies in Africa and points to some of the reasons why, in practice, this is a difficult distinction to maintain. This chapter makes a similar argument for contemporary Sierra Leonean marriage practices.

15. See Mariane C. Ferme, "'Archetypes of Humanitarian Discourse': Child Soldiers, Forced Marriage, and the Framing of Communities in Post-conflict Sierra Leone," *Humanity: An International Journal of Human Rights, Humanitarianism, and Development* 4, no. 1 (2013): 49–71.

16. For a detailed analysis of the negotiations leading to the adoption of sexual slavery as a crime against humanity at the ICC in ways that speak to the enrichment of the jurisprudence discussed in this section, see Valerie Oosterveld, "Sexual Slavery and the International Criminal Court: Advancing International Law," *Michigan Journal of International Law* 25 (2004): 605–51. Annie Bunting, "'Forced Marriage' in Conflict Situations: Researching and Prosecuting Old Harms and New Crimes,"

Canadian Journal of Human Rights 1, no. 1 (2012): 165–85 gives a succinct analysis of the shift between considering forced marriage as a crime against humanity under the "other inhumane acts" versus the "sexual enslavement" articles.

17. Brima, Kamara, Kanu Judgment, June 20, 2007, 578.

18. Ibid., 591.

19. Brima, Kamara, Kanu Appeals Judgment Summary, February 22, 2008, 23–25.

20. Scharf and Mattler, "Forced Marriage," 17 (italics in the original).

21. Valerie Oosterveld, "Forced Marriage and the Special Court for Sierra Leone: Legal Advances and Conceptual Difficulties." *International Humanitarian Legal Studies* 2, no. 1 (2011): 131; Brima, Kamara, Kanu Judgment, June 20, 2007, 580.

22. Brima, Kamara, Kanu Judgment, June 20, 2007, 591.

23. Oosterveld, "Gender and the Charles Taylor Case," 15.

24. Ibid., 20.

25. Toy-Cronin, "What Is Forced Marriage?" 577.

26. Oosterveld, "Sexual Slavery," 650–51.

27. Bélair, "Unearthing the Customary Law Foundations," 551–607.

28. Prosecutor v. Issa Sesay, Morris Kallon, Augustine Gbao, SCSL-2004-15-T, Trial Chamber I, October 21, 2004.

29. Brima, Kamara, Kanu, March 9, 2005, 44ff.

30. Kamari Clarke, *Fictions of Justice: The International Criminal Court and the Challenge of Legal Pluralism in Sub-Saharan Africa* (New York: Cambridge University Press, 2009), and Ferme, "'Archetypes of Humanitarian Discourse."

31. Eaton Shana, "Sierra Leone: The Proving Ground for Prosecuting Rape as a War Crime," *Georgetown Journal of International Law* 35, no. 4 (2004): 917.

32. See Kiran Grewal, "Rape in Conflict, Rape in Peace: Questioning the Revolutionary Potential of International Criminal Justice for Women's Human Rights," *Australian Feminist Law Journal* 33 (2010): 66–68, on the history of unsuccessful prosecutions, sometimes due to the perceived "unreliability" of female witnesses— which mirrored the failure to bring rapists to justice in domestic courts, for instance in Rwanda and Yugoslavia.

33. Human Rights Watch, "'We'll Kill You If You Cry,'" 26.

34. Prosecutor v. Issa Sesay, Morris Kallon, Augustine Gbao, 14–17.

35. See, for instance, Truth and Reconciliation Commission, *Witness to Truth: Report of the Sierra Leone Truth and Reconciliation Commission*, vol. 3B (Accra: Graphic Packaging Press, 2004), 131.

36. Brima, Kamara, Kanu, October 4, 2005, 3, and October 13, 2005, 90.

37. Mariane C. Ferme, *The Underneath of Things: Violence, History, and the Everyday in Sierra Leone* (Berkeley: University of California Press, 2001), 72.

38. Henry Joko-Smart, *Sierra Leone Customary Family Law* (Freetown: Fourah Bay College Bookshop, 1983), 127.

39. Bélair, "Unearthing the Customary Law Foundations," 565–69.

40. Carol Hoffer, "Madam Yoko: Ruler of the Kpa Mende Confederacy," in *Woman, Culture, and Society*, ed. M. Z. Rosaldo and L. Lamphere (Stanford, CA: Stanford University Press, 1973).

41. See Ferme, *Underneath of Things,* 81–111, 171–76, and Mariane C. Ferme, "The Violence of Numbers: Consensus, Competition, and the Negotiation of Disputes in Sierra Leone," *Cahiers d'Études Africaines* 38, nos. 150–52 (1998): 571–73.

42. Ferme, *Underneath of Things,* 84–88.

43. Coulter, *Bush Wives and Girl Soldiers,* and Human Rights Watch, "'We'll Kill You If You Cry,'" 25–50.

44. Brima, Kamara, Kanu, October 3, 2005, 57–61.

45. Coulter, *Bush Wives and Girl Soldiers,* 1–2.

46. Brima, Kamara, Kanu, Judgment, June 20, 2007, 590.

47. Brima, Kamara, Kanu, October 3, 2005, 74.

48. Ferme, *Underneath of Things,* 86–87.

49. Nowrojee, "Making the Invisible War Crime Visible," 85–105, 88.

50. Kenneth Little, *The Mende of Sierra Leone: A West African People in Transition* (London: Routledge, 1951), 152.

51. Esther Mokuwa, Maarten Voors, Erwin Bulte, and Paul Richards, "Peasant Grievance and Insurgency in Sierra Leone: Judicial Serfdom as a Driver of Conflict," *African Affairs* 110, no. 440 (2011): 339–66.

52. Human Rights Watch, "'We'll Kill You If You Cry,'" 24–30.

53. For a similar point about the ways in which violent abductions of women at India's partition in 1947 led to the formation of viable families and of the suffering caused by the Indian state in its insistence on breaking them up many years later, see Veena Das, *Critical Events: An Anthropological Perspective on Contemporary India* (Delhi: Oxford University Press, 1995), 82–83.

54. Prashina Gagoomal, "A 'Margin of Appreciation' for 'Marriages of Appreciation': Reconciling South Asian Adult Arranged Marriages with the Matrimonial Consent Requirement in International Human Rights Law," *Georgetown Law Journal* 97, no. 2 (2009): 589–620.

CHAPTER TEN

Between Global Standards and Local Realities

Shari'a and Mass Marriage Programs in Northern Nigeria

JUDITH-ANN WALKER

KANO STATE has an estimated population of 11.4 million, making it the largest of Nigeria's states. Yet it currently receives the lowest per capita share in federal government allocation to states, and 58 percent of the population lives in poverty.[1] Though famous for its precolonial history as the center of the Saharan kola, indigo-dyed textile trades, and Islamic scholarship, more recently the state has gained notoriety for ethnoreligious conflict, an Islamicist insurgency, and the disproportionate burden of poverty borne by women and children.[2]

Hausa and Fulani cultural traditions and an Islamic value system that permeates every facet of life deeply shape social reality in Kano State. The social value system has its roots in historical alliances between the state and the religious/traditional authority structures dating back to the colonial period, which conspire to exercise direct and complete control over the lives of youth, the working classes (or *talakawa*), girls, and women. Whereas the working classes emancipated themselves through the revolution of the Northern Elements Progressive Union and the People's Redemption Party of the 1960s, the youth rebellion engulfing current-day northern Nigeria is largely due to young males struggling to claim space and chart a separate course; the vicelike grip of control over women and girls is still intact in this region.

The fact that women and girls in the north remain under the control of the state, socioreligious, and familial power structures and are still compelled to fulfill cultural expectations as tolerant cowives and fertile mothers of large, servile, and faithful families is noted in the literature on women in northern Nigeria.[3] Much is known about the impact of the subordinate status of women and girls on their reproductive health, political participation, landownership, employment opportunities, and educational status, but few in-depth studies explore the complicit role of the state in their subordination.[4]

When governments in northern Nigeria do make policies restricting the agency of women and girls, it is worthy of in-depth exploration. A case in point is the 2005 Road Traffic Law, enacted by the Shekarau government, that banned women from riding commercial motorcycles, the main form of affordable public transportation in the state. The closed nature of shari'a governments in northern Nigeria makes it difficult for researchers to study the policy debates informing such decisions. Thus, little is known about the processes that take place within the state as male politicians and bureaucrats debate problems and justify policies that circumscribe and, in some cases, violate the rights of women and girls. This chapter examines one such case, whereby Kano State government's attempt to solve a perceived social problem—namely, the proliferation of poor and vulnerable single, widowed, and divorced women—set the stage for "state-sponsored" marriages through a provincial statutory policing authority, the Hisbah Board (or, alternatively, Hisbah Commission or Kano State Hisbah Corps).

The Kano Hisbah Board was established by the state government in 2003 with the institutionalization of formerly local and privately maintained Hisbah security units.[5] Hisbah, an Arabic word meaning an act performed for the good of the society, conveys an Islamic religious concept that calls for "enjoining what is right and forbidding what is wrong on every Muslim."[6] The Kano board operates as a virtual Islamic government, with responsibility for upholding morality, social norms, peace, and justice in the state in accordance with the tenets of the shari'a criminal code.[7]

The Kano board's marriage program is widely regarded in northern Nigeria as a success story and a model for addressing poverty among women and girls. Between 2011 and 2012, delegations from state governments in Gombe, Zamfara, and Sokoto visited and studied the Kano Hisbah Board's mass marriage "solution," and they have replicated similar programs in their respective states. The "Kano model" has also come to the attention of the global media.[8] This chapter examines the extent to which global norms on the rights of girls (and women) and the responsibility of the state to protect their welfare shaped the decisions when implementing the mass marriage program. From my perspective as a practitioner with several decades of experience in the region, I examine how the structure of the mass marriage program responds to global standards and local realities and employs a public policy-making framework to explore the competing influences in shaping governments' actions on issues of age of marriage and consent.[9] To make sense of the puzzling situation wherein forced and child marriages persist in modern-day northern Nigeria—despite the existence of international human rights standards and in spite of the fact that states are subordinate to the constitutional and legal framework of the Nigerian state as a federal entity—it is helpful to reflect on the colonial policy on girls in the northern region.

HISTORICAL PATTERNS IN THE TREATMENT OF GIRLS AND WOMEN IN THE NORTHERN REGION

Some historians and political sociologists present the situation in Nigeria's northern region as a classic case of a political system where global colonial civilizational values gave way to an alternative local reality, in the interest of maintaining the political status quo. In what Paul Lovejoy refers to as the "accommodation" between the British and the Sokoto Caliphate, indirect rule served to maintain the status quo and consolidate traditional authority over women and girls under colonialism.[10] Missionaries and mission schools between 1842 and 1888 expanded educational opportunities for girls in southern Nigeria by teaching arts and crafts and developing a female labor force to support a menial role in the colonial economy, but in Northern Nigeria, they were prohibited from implementing similar programs.[11]

The deep-seated historical practices in the Sokoto Caliphate and in Maliki madhab Hausa society broadly—practices that marginalized women and girls and minimized consent and autonomy, as described by Kari Bergstrom among others—were perpetuated by colonial rule.[12] Decisions related to the lives of girls and women remained firmly under the control of the political establishment.[13] Against a background of marginalization, the expansion of education for girls in the north was minimal and selective; this was part of a broader process, described by Catherine Coles and Beverly Mack, whereby women balanced the demands of Islamic expectations and emerging ideas of choice as Hausa society transitioned from Maliki precoloniality via British colonialism to the inclusivity of the modern Nigerian nation.[14] Though some colonial officials lamented the conditions of women and girls under "Mohammedan Marriage Custom in the Northern provinces," the colonial administration stopped short of advancing solutions that would shake the tight grip of Hausa tradition and Muslim ideology.[15] Not surprisingly, despite the prolific debates that took place under colonial rule about the age of marriage for "Mohammedan infant-brides," colonial deliberations over the special circumstances of the Muslim religion resulted in ratification of a very early minimum age of marriage—nine years—for northern girls in the early twentieth century.

The colonial position at times even trailed behind some emirs calling for legislation to prohibit this practice. According to the colonial secretary of the northern provinces,

> The argument adduced by the respectable Moslem in support of
> child marriage, as of purdah, is that it is the only way to protect
> a girl's chastity in the present atmosphere of sexual promiscuity
> amongst the youth of the country. . . . The Emir of Gwandu recently
> brought a case for the notice of the Divisional Officer in which
> a girl-bride was prematurely forced and died of the resultant
> hemorrhage: her parents considered this an act of God calling for no
> human retribution. The Emir asked for legislation prohibiting infant
> marriage. . . . A minimum age, say 14 years, for lawful marriage
> would require to be fixed by Nigerian legislation since such does not
> at present appear in the laws.[16]

In 1954, the British colonial administration in Northern Nigeria enacted a law that gave Native Authorities the power to legislate issues related to "regulating child betrothal" and regulating and controlling the movement of children and young females from or within the area.[17] Renee Pittin, who has written extensively on the historical roots of state/traditional institution accommodation to explain the conditions of girls, argues that the state "whether pre-colonial, colonial or post-colonial, has never been neutral. . . . Thus, for example, the state has tended to support continued control over women via marriage."[18]

Public policy making may be viewed as a dynamic process of decision making, which aims to address a public policy problem in which the state is the central actor. The decisional space of the state to select one policy option over another is a political process that involves multiple actors from the private and public sectors, as well as from the local and global domains.[19] As important as the policy content may be, it is the context of policy making that engages scholars in comparative public policy and administration, challenging them to explain competing influences of global and local forces as they shape the decisions of states.[20] The policy context consists of environmental factors including comparative and historical precedent and knowledge, which impinge on the definition and understanding of the policy issue and shape policy options considered by decision makers. Notions of the decisional space of governments are underpinned by assumptions of an autonomous state that is free to choose among competing policy options from local or global contexts, subject only to technical dictates of policy making and political considerations from lobbyist groups. This ideal liberal pluralist notion is far removed from the reality of policy making in the developing world, where the state is often embedded in traditional power structures within civil society and is unable to consider policy options from both local and international contexts when they come into conflict with the roots of state power.

Policy demands from the global policy environment are particularly difficult to entertain to the extent that they are often based on universal values, norms, and standards that conflict with the value system of powerful local interests. With regard to questions of forced and early marriage, global standards emerge from international conventions and guidelines, whereas the local realities embodied in tradition, custom, and in many cases customary laws may or may not be codified. This plurality of legal systems creates a parallel context, components of which governments sometimes seek to balance in making decisions related to girls and women. Global conventions on forced marriage that appear to impinge on national and local-level decisional space include, among others, the Convention on the Rights of the Child (CRC), the Universal Declaration of Human Rights, and the Convention on the Elimination of All Forms of Discrimination against Women (CEDAW).[21] African regional standards shaping the decisional space of national governments and substate entities include the African Charter on Human and Peoples' Rights, the African Charter on the Rights and Welfare of the Child, and the Protocol to the African Charter on Human and Peoples' Rights on the Rights of Women in Africa (also known as the Maputo Protocol).[22]

Research on the persistence of forced marriage practices in the Global South routinely explains a government's capacity or lack thereof to make and enforce minimum marriage age as a reflection of a balance between local cultural forces and normative orders with global norms and conventions. A 2006 United Nations Population Fund (UNFPA) study noted, for example, that

> governments are often either unable to enforce existing laws, or rectify discrepancies between national laws on marriage age and entrenched customary and religious laws. This is because of the "official tolerance of cultural, societal and customary norms that shape and govern the institution of marriage and family life." In general, there is seldom political will to act when it comes to women's and girls' human rights.[23]

When customary laws—or in the case of shari'a, religious laws—exist side by side with international law, some see a type of legal pluralism extending into the political and judicial realms.[24] But regardless of how we might classify the complex legal terrain of Maliki Hausa culture in Kano, much like the situations in Sierra Leone and South Africa discussed in this volume by Mariane Ferme and Elizabeth Thornberry, respectively, the human rights of girls—their freedom to choose a marriage partner, their right to access education, and their right to be protected from harmful traditional practices such as forced marriage—are circumscribed by contested customs and by the existence of distinct and equally powerful legal practices at community and state levels.[25]

THE STATE AND THE ISSUE OF FORCED AND EARLY MARRIAGE IN NIGERIA

Forced marriage practices are difficult to characterize and generalize in the Global South. Geetanjali Gangoli, Khatidja Chantler, Marianne Hester, and Ann Singleton, along with the authors in this volume, call into question the simple legalistic explanation of forced marriage as marriage without consent of the intended spouses, where duress is exercised over free and full will, leading to the violation of a number of international human rights instruments and standards. These authors interrogate the concept of consent, citing studies "where it is argued that women's ability to consent can be mediated by factors such as poverty," and they raise the issue of context

JUDITH-ANN WALKER

in the coercion/consent debate.[26] Sundari Anitha and Anisha Gill call for an awareness of "the socio-historical, political and cultural context of women's lives, and their location at the intersection of several vectors of inequality," arguing that this is "crucial to understanding the relationship between consent and coercion."[27] This formative scholarship and activism on forced marriage, elaborated in the introduction to this volume, provoke us to rethink global standards and the definition of forced marriage.

Research on the persistence of forced and early marriage of girls and women in Nigeria points to the complicity of the state in general and male political officeholders in particular, as they fail to enact, uphold, and enforce laws that treat these practices as violations. They opt instead for the silence of inaction and the preservation of tradition and customary laws.[28] In this regard, the Nigeria NGO Coalition on CEDAW notes:

> Under customary law, women do not have rights to enter into marriage, decide freely and responsibly on the number and spacing of their children. There still exist cases of forced marriage, child betrothal, wife inheritance, and widowhood practices across Nigeria. In Nigeria, the man is viewed as the "head of the family" and as the provider of food, shelter and clothing for the family. This gives the man greater rights to exert authority in the family even where he fails to provide or the woman earns a higher income.[29]

In northern Nigeria, where the median age of first marriage is fifteen years—the lowest in Nigeria and virtually unchanged over the past sixteen years—forced marriage is seen as coterminous with child marriage.[30]

A recent study by the Zaria-based Centre for Islamic Legal Studies acknowledged that

> it is true that some parents force their children to marry husbands of their parents' choice. This practice still persists in some parts of northern Nigeria. Parents who do this rely on the jurisprudential ruling of Imam Malik to the effect that a father may compel his previously unmarried daughter to marry a man he chooses for her. The right of compulsion, where it exists, can only be exercised by the father, who is also qualified to be a guardian on the assumption that his care and compassion for his daughter are ordinarily taken for granted. This fatherly power is known as *ijbar*. Public morality and the individual's own integrity take priority over personal freedom when they come into conflict.[31]

The military regime of General Ibrahim Babangida took the first step to protect women and girls in 1991, with the ratification of the United Nations Convention on the Rights of the Child. The CRC was domesticated in the form of the Child Rights Act (CRA), passed into law in September 2003 under President Olusugun Obasanjo. The CRA represented a brave attempt by the Obasanjo administration to harmonize existing laws and provide clarity on the minimum age of marriage, as well as issues of consent, coercion, and the illegality of forced marriage. The act improved upon the existing laws, such as section 3(I)(e) of the Matrimonial Causes Act of 1970, which rendered a marriage void where either of the parties was found to be not of "marriageable age" but failed to define the term *marriageable age*.

Under the CRA, eighteen was mandated as the minimum legal age of marriage, with no allowances being made for parental, guardian, or community leaders' consent for marriage under that age. Two sections in part III read as follows:

> [Section] 21. No person under the age of 18 years is capable of contracting a valid marriage, and accordingly, a marriage so contracted is null and void and of no effect whatsoever.

> [Section] 22. (1) No parent, guardian or any other person shall betroth a child to any person.

> (2) A betrothal in contravention of Subsection (1) of this section is null and void.[32]

Since the passage of the federal CRA in 2003, efforts of the Federal Ministry of Women's Affairs, the United Nations Children's Fund (UNICEF), the Gesellschaft für Technische Zusammenarbeit (GTZ), and the Canadian International Development Agency (CIDA) to domesticate this law in the northern states have been frustrated: eleven of the twelve states in Nigeria that have yet to pass the complementary state CRA are in the north. Despite the efforts of UNICEF to build consensus for the act by organizing study tours for Islamic scholars to Egypt and despite the initiatives of German funding agencies in Borno State to present the benefits of the act in terms of its potential to halt child trafficking, northern officials continue to reject statewide domestication.

The Kano State speaker of the House of Assembly describes that act as being "against the wishes of Kano and the entire Northern part of the country as it is against our religion and culture."[33] Similarly, the president for the Supreme Council of Shar"a in Nigeria, Dr. Ibrahim Datti Ahmed, described the act as "a conspiracy against Islam . . . and a direct attack on Islam," adding, "no Muslim will obey this law. It doesn't matter who passes it."[34] The sticking point for northern political and traditional leaders relates to sections 21 and 22 of the act, which outlaw consent to marriage by family members and only recognize spousal consent. This is widely viewed as being an affront to Hausa and Muslim marriage customs.

MARRIAGE AND CONSENT IN HAUSALAND

Several factors limit the extent to which girls are able to exercise free will and give consent to marriage in Hausa society. The ideal standard for Islamic marriage is a union in which consent is a mandatory requirement and without which any such marriage is void or voidable. However, in Hausa culture coerced marriage is the prevailing practice, whereby the father or even a wealthy elder male relative decides on behalf of the child bride without or against her consent or choice. Even in cases where the marriage is voluntary and possibly based on love, the father is the one to communicate consent. Thus, the father has a significant and undue influence on the girl's "choice." The paternal power to give consent or select a husband for his daughter is mostly legitimated using the Maliki doctrine of *ijbar* (fatherly authority). According to this Islamic principle, the father has the power to choose a husband for his "virgin daughter."[35] Though women do have great autonomy to marry a partner of their choice in second, third, or subsequent marriages in Hausa culture, the younger the girl is, the greater the likelihood that she will be married without or against her consent. Luigi Solivetti explains thus:

> Hausa tradition . . . gives the father authority over his daughter's first
> marriage, whatever her age; he does not even have to consult her.
> The essential social fact is clear: marriage is a manifestation of the
> families' will, not of the will of the couple getting married.[36]

With close to 60 percent of Kano's population living in poverty, the father's consent for marriage serves as an important mobilization strategy for the family and community to provide financial support for wedding festivities.

The poverty of Kano in particular and the northern zone in general has been widely cited ever since a landmark study by the World Bank in 1993.[37] Using largely quantitative methods, this and other subsequent studies stopped short of exploring the causes of female poverty, however. It was left to ethnographic studies, mapping high-risk behaviors of vulnerable women and girls in northern Nigeria, to examine the female experience and implications for public health. Family Health International (FHI) commissioned two studies between 2000 and 2008, and research was conducted by the Kano-based nongovernmental organization (NGO) known as the development Research and Projects Centre (dRPC). A 2004 Poverty Knowledge and Practice study, funded by the Institute of Development Studies (IDS) and conducted by the dRPC, also explored the meaning of poverty in Jigawa State.[38]

The FHI studies revealed the abject nature of poverty for widows and divorcées in northern Nigeria and showed how women were forced to engage in commercial sex work for cash and in-kind consideration simply to feed themselves and their children. This situation was particularly troubling in the traditional cities of Kano State. It was not surprising that a local NGO, the Voice of the Widows and Divorcees of Nigeria (VOWAN), with a membership of poor females, sought to alert policy makers to the plight of women. The group called on the government of Governor Ibrahim Shekarau, to enact a law that would "stipulate [a] heavy penalty on any man found to have unjustifiably divorced his wife."[39]

VOWAN constituted the first significant challenge to the then popular Shekarau administration, which came to power in April 2003. That administration displaced the progressive regime of Governor Rabiu Musa Kwankwaso, which was widely regarded as vacillating on the important question of shari'a. The masses, the traditional institutions headed by the emir and the Emirate Council, and the *ulama* (those recognized as scholars or religious authorities) class embraced the new governor, who himself was also regarded as an ulama. By the time of his reelection in 2007, Shekarau had consolidated a new elite power base, comprising traditional and modern Islamists, an Islamically oriented bureaucracy, and the Kano Royal House. With the exception of the Muslim Sisters Organization (MSO), most women's groups and even the women's wing of the ruling party were excluded from this inner circle. Conflict between the Shekarau administration and the VOWAN came to a head with the group's decision to hold a Million Women March in 2009. VOWAN abandoned the march after the intervention of the Kano State Hisbah Board, the provincial Islamic machinery for policing morality. Kano's Hisbah Board was established under Edict No. 4 of 2003, as amended in 2004. The board was constituted as a virtual Islamic government with responsibility for upholding morality, in accordance with the shari'a criminal code. The Hisbah Board has powers of enforcement, adjudication, and incarceration.[40]

THE ADMINISTRATION OF GOVERNMENT-SPONSORED MASS MARRIAGE

A new Kwankwaso administration, reelected to office in 2011, replaced the Shekarau-led All Nigerian Peoples Party (ANPP). Kwankwaso maintained the Hisbah Board as an agency of government but expanded its moral policing functions to include social welfare, child protection, and marriage counseling. Kwankwaso's win was secured with the strong support of youth and women, especially grassroots women's groups. Immediately upon taking office, the second Kwankwaso administration initiated policies viewed as prowomen, including women's economic empowerment programs, girl child education support initiatives, conditional cash transfer projects, and microfinance. The mass marriages program was envisioned as one of these prowomen interventions. To what extent was the state government's policy response on mass marriages guided by global standards or dictated by local factors of culture, religion, and tradition?

The political nature of this program may be viewed as a legacy project of the executive governor and a form of payback to the women of the state for their political support. The state government and the Hisbah Board allocated public revenues and mobilized funds and in-kind contributions from rich merchants to pay the bride-price, finance wedding ceremonies, provide brides with equipment for their economic survival, supply foodstuffs to the married couples, and offer pledges of postmarriage payments. Bridewealth items included cloth, beds, bed linens, sewing machines, and victuals such as rice and eggs (see Figures 10.1, 10.2, 10.3, and 10.4). Against this backdrop, the mass marriages program transmuted into a popular poverty-reduction strategy and grew beyond the initial focus on widows and divorcées.

FIGURE 10.1. Former Kano State governor (now federal senator) Rabiu Musa Kwankwaso talks to unidentified bride as Hajiya Amina Sambo, former second lady, and other women look on. June 2014. *Photo credit: Hassan A. Karofi © 2014.*

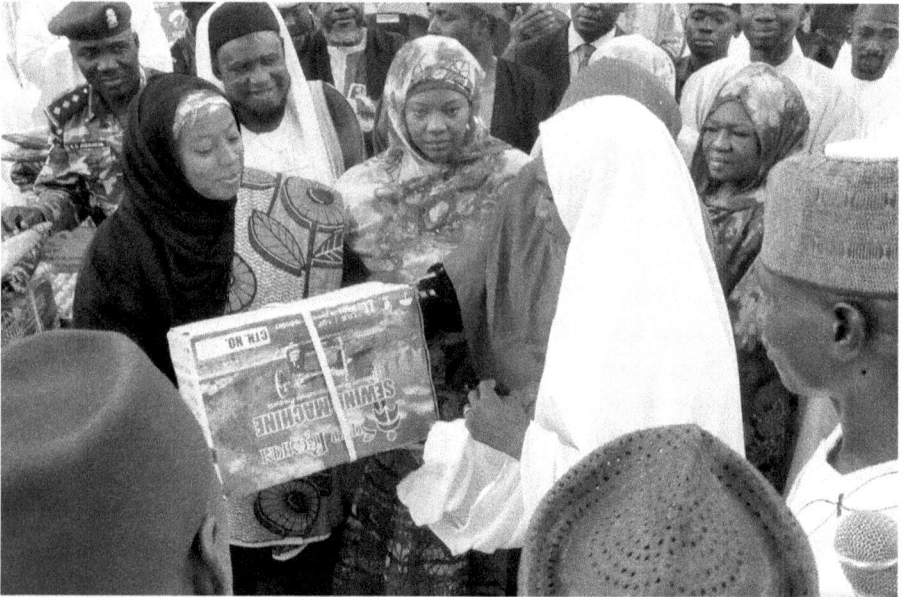

FIGURE 10.2. Hajiya Amina Sambo, former second lady, hands sewing machine to unidentified brides. Hajiya Baraka Sani, special adviser on school agriculture to former president Goodluck Jonathon and former Kano State women's affairs commissioner, and scholar Sheikh Aminu Abubakar look on. June 2014. *Photo credit: Hassan A. Karofi © 2014.*

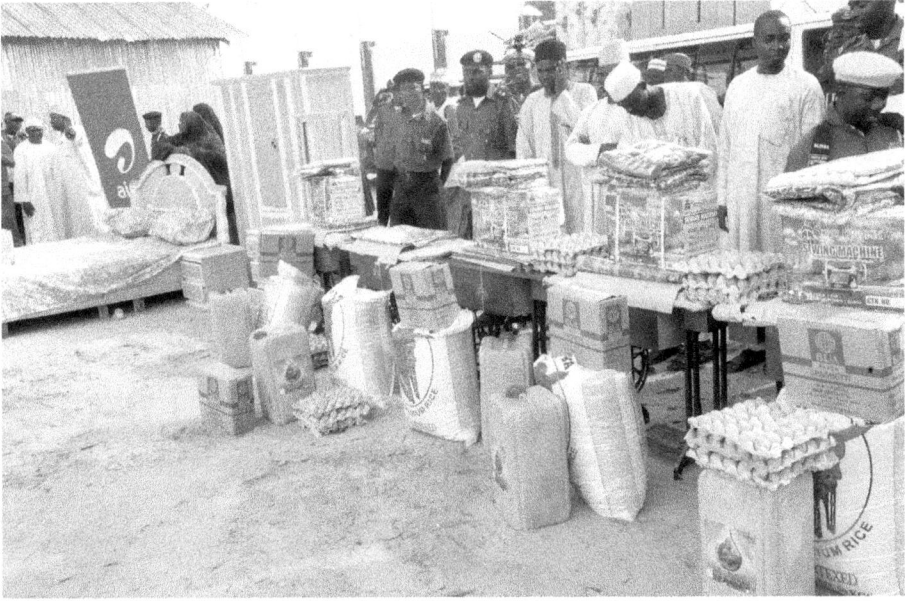

FIGURE 10.3. Kano State Hisbah Board delivering furniture, sewing machines, and victuals as bridewealth for mass wedding, outside Kano Government House. June 2014. *Photo credit: Hassan A. Karofi © 2014.*

FIGURE 10.4. Grooms inspecting bridal trousseau donated by Kano State government. Kano, 2013. *Photo credit: Aisha V. Hashim © 2013.*

A total of 2,461 women and girls were matched with husbands in the mass marriage program, in several cohorts between May 15, 2012, when the first one hundred brides were married, to the end of 2014. The first cohort consisted mainly of mature, divorced, and widowed women, spanning a wide range of ages, with most aged twenty to thirty.[41] By July 2012 when a second cohort was married, the state government responded to pressure from parents of younger girls who could not afford to marry off their daughters, and the cohort included previously unmarried girls. The second cohort therefore consisted of a disproportionately larger number of younger and previously unmarried girls, rather than widows and divorcées. Brides I interviewed at the time of the mass marriages admitted to being as young as sixteen years, although they had no evidence of their dates of birth because the majority of female births are not registered in Kano State. With the third cohort—comprising one thousand couples married in April 2013—equal numbers of young girls, widows, and divorcées were married. To be sure, many of the divorcées were also under the minimum legal age for marriage.

By August 2013, when preparations were being put in place for the fourth cohort of mass marriages, the Hisbah "commandant general," Sheikh Aminu Ibrahim Daurawa, revealed that 1,111 couples were to be married (see Figures 10.5 and 10.6) and that 50 slots were reserved for Christians. In his words:

> We decided to include Christians in the state since we are living together in the same environment. And just as we do not want to see our children engage in prostitution, we also do not want theirs to engage in it . . . we will allow them to go and do their weddings in their churches. We will only share the marriage bouquet (*walima*) together.[42]

In all cohorts, elaborate administrative procedures were put in place by the Hisbah Board to ensure strict compliance with the regulations and rules of the mass marriages program.

Administrative procedures covered screening for pregnancy, HIV/AIDS, and other sexually transmitted diseases, as well as background character checks and investigations to determine the marital status of the bride and groom. These measures were ostensibly to ensure that brides and grooms were disease free, that the bride was not pregnant and was legally unmarried at the time of the screening, and that both bride and

FIGURE 10.5. Unidentified brides and grooms, among 1,111 couples, sitting under canopies at the Kano State Government House compound on December 19, 2013, as part of a mass wedding for divorcées and widows organized by the Kano State Hisbah Board. *Photo credit: Aminu Abubakar © 2013.*

FIGURE 10.6. Unidentified brides and grooms exit Kano State Government House on December 19, 2013, after a wedding feast. *Photo credit: Aminu Abubakar © 2013.*

groom were known in the community. There was no rule against a married man being considered as a suitable groom for a new wife in a polygynous union; indeed, the desire to take another wife was seen as evidence of the husband's sense of responsibility and maturity. Hisbah Board members were among the grooms taking brides as second and third wives. There was also no requirement for Christians participating in the mass marriage program to convert to Islam.

No explicit rule set a minimum age for participation in the mass marriage program. The first step in the long administrative process of the program occurred at the community level, where the ages of the bride and groom had to be provided on an application form. In most cases, however, date of birth information was either left incomplete or provided but not verified.[43] Moreover, in the screening process that followed, the Hisbah Board did not use age as a criterion to disqualify girls under eighteen years. Indeed, in Hausa-language newspapers reporting on the second cohort of marriages, cases of underage marriage were discussed. For example, one item read: "Shafa'atu Ibrahim Gaida is a 17 year old and she has never been married. She said the person she just got married to is the one who took the form to the Hisbah Board . . . this is not his first marriage."[44]

The process of the state-sponsored marriage involved several steps. With respect to consent, interviews with community members at the local government level and at the Hisbah Board revealed that formal provisions were put in place to register the consent of both bride and groom insofar as both were expected to sign separate application forms.[45] It reality, however, field interviews revealed that it was often a male head of household, a literate community member, or the prospective husband who completed and signed the forms for the prospective bride, often without her knowledge. By the time of the third cohort, prospective husbands were increasingly taking over the responsibility of fathers by filling out and signing application forms for younger brides. Once complete, the forms were acknowledged and in some wards formally approved by the religious or traditional leader; they then moved upward to the central Hisbah office. The next step was for the potential bride and groom to undergo medical screening and counseling; the marriage was subsequently contracted if the outcome of these processes was successful. When this process was complete, executive consent for the sponsored marriages was given from the governor.

It is difficult to gauge public attitudes to the phenomenon accurately. Interestingly, though the foreign media has remained silent on the issue of coercion it has been hotly debated in the local media, causing the Hisbah Board to explain its procedures in detail. Analysis of news reports and interviews with brides revealed that despite their ages, prospective brides were generally happy to be married and were not troubled about whether or not they signed their application forms personally. What was of concern to them was that they should not be matched randomly: that is, they should be married to the same men who identified them, completed their forms, moved them through the system, and had begun bringing gifts to them. The future husbands' willingness to negotiate the Hisbah Board bureaucracy may be consider a de facto expression of consent by girl brides and their families. Brides who were rematched with different grooms were most dissatisfied with the particular husbands chosen for them. This was especially true when some prospective brides were rematched as a result of the screening panel's rejection of a first or second choice of a husband. In such cases, the Hisbah Board was accused of being a party to forced marriage.

The Hisbah Board addressed the allegation that girls were being forced into marriage in the official organ *Hisbah Today,* stating that "Hisbah is not going to harm or force anyone but is going to enlighten according to the Sharia."[46] In support of its claims, members of the board gave examples of how they prevented forced marriages on a daily basis in Hausa communities. The Hisbah Board documented one such case in the local Hausa newspapers:

> This couple brought themselves to the Board seeking support as
> the bride's parents refused to marry her to the person she loves. . . .
> After carrying out investigations, the commander of the Hisbah
> Board Mallam Aminu Ibrahim Daurawa agreed with the couple and
> married them. . . . An official of the Board Mallam Musa Tanko said,
> they have witnessed many of such problems and have solved them
> successfully.[47]

However, on the issue of age of marriage, the Hisbah Board members defended their practices by explaining they were simply responding to the requests of parents to marry off their daughters. They pointed out that it is the parents who actually initiate the decision to marry their daughters. As the Hisbah Board explained, "Parents come to us for assistance concerning their children's marriages. . . . This is because some girls at fifteen years have been exposed; their eyes are opened."[48]

In its assessment of the Kano State mass marriage program, the Gombe State Ministerial Committee reached a similar conclusion:

> The successful implementation of two phases of Zawarawa (divorcées) and Spinsters marriages in Kano state has endeared other states in the north worthy of emulation. . . . Parents and guardians with low income earning are eager to get their wards married through the program.[49]

The Gombe State committee concluded its report with the recommendation that the Kano State program be replicated but with the proviso that

> emphasis be placed in building consensus between parents and their child/wards in selecting spouses particularly, choice of a husband. . . . This is in realization of the fact that the practice of forced/unilaterally, arranged marriages (Hausa: *auren dole*) is a major cause of broken marriages in the North.[50]

THE FUTURE OF MASS MARRIAGE

In implementing its mass marriages program, Kano State seems to have been guided by the local reality of poverty that propelled parents to marry off fifteen-year-old girls. The government was working within a cultural context in which male authority figures, not the girl brides in question, were expected to give consent to marriage. However, we must not too hastily conclude that the mass marriages program reinforced the patriarchal value system of the local environment and rejected global standards. It is important to note that the conservative ulama class in Kano strongly opposed the program for its attempt to introduce "innovation" into Islamic obligations associated with marriage.

The ulama iterated a number of concerns, including the state government's insistence that the prospective bride and groom be tested for sexually transmitted infections (STIs), that the bride be examined and determined not to be pregnant, that a marriage certificate be issued to the couple, that the procedures for divorce be formalized and made to conform with Islamic precepts, and that the Hisbah Board would monitor the marriage to ensure that the new bride was happy and not abused. Moreover, the dates set for the marriages were troubling to the ulama class, as they coincided with global reproductive health days rather than locally preferred days that were significant in the Islamic calendar. For instance, the first cohort was married on May 15, which coincided with the International Day of the Family, and the second cohort was married on April 7, coincidentally World Health Day.

The experience of the mass marriages program of Kano State suggests that notwithstanding the constraints posed by culture and poverty on the decisional space of governments (and families), decision makers are able to select from among a menu of global prescriptions that protect women and girls and adopt initiatives despite resistance from local custodians of culture. To conclude that the mass marriages program in Kano State is yet another example of state complicity in the violation of the rights of girls and women in the Global South is to fail to appreciate the influence of socioeconomic context as well as to undervalue the power of state agency in advancing the rights of women and girls through incremental and unorthodox initiatives. It is this potential that must be exploited as development impact investors seek to encourage states in the Global South to act to protect girls and women.

NOTES

1. World Bank, *Nigeria Economic Report* (Washington, DC, May 2013), 27–29.

2. Jamila M. Nasir, "Sharia Implementation and Female Muslims in Nigeria's Sharia States," in *Islam in Africa South of the Sahara: Essays in Gender Relations and Political Reform*, ed. P. Badru and B. M. Sackey (Toronto: Scarecrow Press, 2013), 76–117.

3. Babara Callaway and L. Creevey, *The Heritage of Islam: Women, Religion and Politics in West Africa* (Boulder, CO: Lynne Rienner, 1994), and Barbara M. Cooper, "Gender and Religion in Hausaland: Variations in Islamic Practice in Niger and Nigeria," in *Women in Muslim Societies*, ed. L. Bodman and N. Tohidi (Boulder, CO: Lynne Rienner, 1998), 21–37.

4. Centre for Reproductive Rights and Women Advocates Research and Documentation Centre, *Broken Promises: Human Rights, Accountability and Maternal Deaths in Nigeria* (New York and Lagos: Center for Reproductive Rights and Women Advocates Research and Documentation Centre, 2008); Luigi M. Solivetti, "Family, Marriage and Divorce in a Hausa Community: A Sociological Model," *Africa: Journal of the International African Institute* 64, no. 2 (1994): 252–71.

5. Rasheed Olaniyi, "Hisbah and Sharia Law Enforcement in Metropolitan Kano," *Africa Today* 57, no. 4 (2011): 70–96.

6. Fatima Adamu, "Gender, Hisbah and Enforcement of Morality in Shariah Implementing States of Zamafara and Kano in Northern Nigeria," http://web.uct.ac.za/org/gwsafrica/african%20feminist%20thinkers/adamu/adamu%20publication.htm, accessed January 5, 2016.

7. Shari'a and Islamic Administration of Justice Reform Law 2000, signed into law on February 24, 2000, gazetted as No. 2 of 2001, *Kano State of Nigeria Gazette* 33, no. 3 (November 15, 2001). See Ibrahim Na'iya Sada, "The Making of the Zamfara and Kano State Sharia Penal Codes," in *Sharia Implementation in Northern Nigeria, 1999–2006: A Sourcebook,* ed. P. Ostien (Ibadan: Spectrum Books, 2007), vol. 4, chap. 4, pt. 2, pp. 22–32.

8. See http://www.bbc.com/news/world-africa-18072118, accessed December 2, 2014.

9. Annie Bunting and Sally Engle Merry, "Global Regulation and Local Political Struggles: Early Marriage in Northern Nigeria," in *Youth, Globalization, and the Law,* ed. Sudhir Alladi Venkatesh and Ronald Kassimir (Stanford, CA: Stanford University Press, 2007), 321–53.

10. Paul E. Lovejoy, "Concubinage and the Status of Women Slaves in Early Colonial Northern Nigeria," *Journal of African History* 29, no. 2 (1988): 245.

11. For a discussion of forced marriage in colonial Igboland, see Olatunji Ojo's chapter in this volume.

12. Kari Bergstrom, "Legacies of Colonialism and Islam for Hausa Women: An Historical Analysis, 1804 to 1960," WID Working Paper 276, Women and International Development, Michigan State University, East Lansing, 2002.

13. See Peter K Tibenderana, *Education and Cultural Change in Northern Nigeria, 1906–1966* (Kampala: Fountain Series in Education Studies, 2003), and Barbara Cooper, *Marriage in Maradi: Gender and Culture in a Hausa Society in Niger, 1900–1989* (Portsmouth, NH: Heinemann, 1997).

14. Catherine M. Coles and Beverly Mack, *Hausa Women in the Twentieth Century* (Madison: University of Wisconsin Press, 1991).

15. Nigerian National Archives, Confidential, Mohammedan Marriage Customs: 12/1938/8: Resident, Sokoto Province to the Secretary, Northern Provinces, Kaduna, 25 December 1938.

16. Nigerian National Archives No. 35927/41, Confidential, Child Prostitution and Child Marriage: Secretary, Northern Provinces, H. S. Bridel to The Honourable, The Chief Secretary to the Government, Lagos, 22 June 1946.

17. Aminu Hassan Gammawa, "Law and Policy to End Child Marriage in West Africa," ed. Judith-Ann Walker, forthcoming with the Ford Foundation.

18. Renee Pittin, "Selective Education: Issues of Gender, Class and Ideology in Northern Nigeria," *Review of African Political Economy* 48 (1990): 7–25.

19. Merilee S. Grindle and John W. Thomas, *Public Choices and Policy Change: The Political Economy of Reform in Developing Countries* (Baltimore: Johns Hopkins University Press, 1991), 43.

20. Eric Welch and Wilson Wong, "Public Administration in a Global Context: Bridging the Gaps of Theory and Practice between Western and Non-Western Nations," *Public Administration Review* 58, no. 1 (January–February 1988): 40–49.

21. Judith-Ann Walker, "Early Marriage in Africa—Trends, Harmful Effects and Interventions," *African Journal of Reproductive Health* 16, no. 2 (June 2012): 231–40.

22. Jewel Amoah, "The World on Her Shoulders: The Rights of the Girl-Child in the Context of Culture and Identity," *Essex Human Rights Review* 4, no. 2 (September 2007): 1–23.

23. UNFPA, *Ending Child Marriage: A Guide for Global Policy Action* (IPPF, UNFPA, and the Global Coalition on Women and AIDS, 2006), 6.

24. E.g., A. B. Yusuf, "Legal Pluralism in the Northern States of Nigeria: Conflict of Laws in a Multi-ethnic Environment" (PhD diss., University of Buffalo, 1976), and Ahmed Beita Yusuf, *Nigerian Legal System: Pluralism and Conflict of Laws in the Northern States* (New Delhi: National Publishing House, 1982).

25. See Allan Christelow, "Islamic Law and Judicial Practice in Nigeria: An Historical Perspective," *Journal of Muslim Minority Affairs* 22, no. 1 (2002): 185–204, for an extended discussion.

26. Geetanjali Gangoli, Khatidja Chantler, Marianne Hester, and Ann Singleton, "Understanding Forced Marriage: Definitions and Realities," in *Forced Marriage*, ed. Aisha K. Gill and Sundari Anitha (London: Zed Books, 2011), 27.

27. Sundari Anitha and Aisha K. Gill, "Reconceptualising Consent and Coercion within an Intersectoral Understanding of Forced Marriage," in Gill and Anitha, *Forced Marriage*, 58. See the introduction to this volume by Annie Bunting, Benjamin N. Lawrance, and Richard L. Roberts.

28. CLEEN Foundation and World Organization against Torture, *Rights of the Child in Nigeria*, Report on the Implementation of the Convention on the Rights of the Child, June 2004; available at http://www.cleen.org/nigeria_ngo_report_OMCT .pdf, accessed January 5, 2016.

29. Nigeria NGO Coalition on CEDAW, *CEDAW and Accountability to Gender Equality in Nigeria: A Shadow Report*, supported by the Henrich Boll Foundation, 2008, 63; available at http://tbinternet.ohchr.org/Treaties/CEDAW/Shared%20Documents /NGA/INT_CEDAW_NGO_NGA_41_9726_E.pdf, accessed January 5, 2016.

30. Judith-Ann Walker, "Scan of Early Marriage in West Africa," Ford Foundation, New York, September 2013. Also see Annie Bunting, "Stages of Development: Marriage of Girls and Teens as an International Human Rights Issue," *Social and Legal Studies* 14, no. 1 (2005): 17–38.

31. Centre for Islamic Legal Studies, Ahmadu Bello University, Zaria, with support from DFID Nigeria's Security, Justice and Growth Program, *Promoting Women's Rights through Sharia in Northern Nigeria* (DFID implemented by the British Council: Nigeria, n.d.), 10.

32. Child Rights Act, 2003, available at http://www.unicef.org/nigeria/ng _publications-Child_Rights_Act_2003.pdf, accessed December 2, 2014.

33. Ibrahim Shuaibu, "Nigeria: Child Rights Act's Anti-North, Says Kano Speaker," *This Day Online*, October 2, 2008.

34. As quoted in Nkoyo Toyo, "Revisiting Equality as a Right: The Minimum Age of Marriage Clause in the Nigerian Child Rights Act, 2003," *Third World Quarterly— The Politics of Rights: Dilemmas for Feminist Praxis* 27, no. 7 (2006): 1299–1312.

35. Gamawa, "Law and Policy," forthcoming.

36. Solivetti, "Family, Marriage and Divorce," 258.

37. See also Yahaya Hashim, "Report of Core Welfare Indicators Survey for Jigawa State, to the Federal Office of Statistics," Department for International Development (UK) funded project, 2003.

38. Yahaya Hashim and Judith-Ann Walker, "Religion, Politics, Poverty Knowledge and Policy in Jigawa State of Nigeria," in *Unpacking Policy: Knowledge, Actors and Spaces in Poverty Reduction in Uganda and Nigeria,* ed. K. Brock, R. McGee, and J. Gaventa (Sussex, UK: Institute of Development Studies, 2004).

39. "VOWAN Calls for Penalty for Unjustifiable Divorces," *New Nigerian,* September 14, 2005, 11.

40. Phil Ostein, *Sharia Implementation in Northern Nigeria, 1999–2006: A Sourcebook* (Ibadan, Nigeria: Spectrum Books, 2007).

41. Field interview notes, July 2012.

42. Kano to include Christians in state sponsored mass weddings, *Contra Culture E-Magazine,* August 23, 2013; http://contraculturemag.com, accessed December 12, 2013).

43. Northern Nigeria has very low rates of birth and marriage registration.

44. *Issue* (Hausa language newspaper), June–July 2012, 27.

45. Field interview notes, June 2013.

46. *Issue.*

47. *Leadership Hausa,* July 20–26, 2012, 27.

48. Women's Leader, Kano State Hisbah Board, interview by Federation of Muslim Women Organization of Nigeria, Kano, Nigeria, July 2013.

49. Report of the Ministerial Committee on the Zawarawa Marriage Scheme, Government of Gombe State (Government Publication, Gombe State), May 2013.

50. Report of the Ministerial Committee, Recommendations, 2013, 3.

CHAPTER ELEVEN

Dreams of My Mother

Good News on Ending Early Marriage

MUADI MUKENGE

With the heightened attention on the rights of the girl child globally, the conversation about early marriage as a human rights violation is also growing louder within and outside of the academy. Since 2011, at least three international conferences have examined the problems of early marriage. Outside of academia, as discussed in the introduction to this volume, the prevention of early marriage has been a priority in sectors such as public health, maternal health, international development, child rights advocacy groups, and the women's rights movement. This chapter will highlight the actions of women's rights associations that have organized to reform social practices that lead to early marriage, one of the key drivers of deaths among adolescent mothers.[1] The analysis adds the dimension of mothers who act to give their daughters the opportunities they themselves did not have, partially by delaying marriage, extending formal education, and promoting vocational training that can offer livelihood options. The "dreams of my mother" are, therefore, the twin dreams of acquiring an education and being married in a context where the union bestows greater status upon the woman. Efforts to enlist mothers as allies in program interventions are crucial to changing long-established social practices.

The recent focus on forced and early marriage among governments, international organizations, and funders has tended to take place at the level of UN resolutions, foreign policy discussions, and high-level advocacy such as the Girls Not Brides campaign. This chapter and the examples contained herein offer an important reminder that local organizations in Africa have been wrestling with this problem for a long time, and they have extensive expertise and experience in programming to address issues of age and consent in regard to marriage. Although it is beyond the parameters of this chapter to delve deeply into the sociopolitical history of each of the four countries discussed, the case studies offer the reader a novel view from the perspective of an informed funder in the area of women's and children's rights. Further, this chapter supports the thesis that low levels of socioeconomic development along with other social norms that are barriers to the investment in girls' human capital are decisive risk factors in early and forced marriage. With programs to mitigate these factors, the organizations described in this chapter are engaged in promising community-based initiatives.

Global Fund for Women (GFW) has been a major funder since the mid-1990s to African women's organizations working to increase the age at first marriage in their countries. Through an analysis of the grantees' programs, we are able to see some of the promising programs in communities—programs that empower girls, engage parents and community leaders, and try to address underlying causes of early and forced marriage such as poverty and limited livelihood options for young women. These examples are interesting contemporary comparisons to the colonial social engineering projects discussed in earlier chapters of this volume. As we have seen in other contexts and in other time periods, legislation alone does not change behavior and attitudes. Further, some programs may change behavior without necessarily changing minds; an example can be found in cases of direct transfers of school fees to schools for specific girls. This may in fact keep girls in school and delay the age of marriage without changing the parents' beliefs about marriage, age, and consent. Other programs, however, may change both behavior and attitudes, such as empowerment programs through girls' empowerment organizations and other peer support groups.

I begin this chapter with a brief survey on the prevalence of early marriage in sub-Saharan Africa, followed by an overview of legal frameworks and global campaigns that address early marriage in an attempt to curb the practice. Next, I examine several examples of the work of grassroots women's organizations in Benin, Burkina Faso, Uganda, and the Democratic Republic of Congo (DRC) that are working at multiple levels to address the complex factors that combine to perpetuate the practice. I end the chapter

MUADI MUKENGE

with a range of recommendations directed at government, donors, civil society, and families to reflect on their potential roles to make sustainable contributions that would enable strong economies to emerge—economies in which young girls can reach their potential, consider complementary life choices, protect their health, delay the age of marriage, and form healthy families as adult women. I invite practitioners and advocates for child rights to focus more significant attention on the structural factors that cause deep inequalities and chronic poverty in communities, thereby limiting economic options. In these settings, such as northern Nigeria (as discussed by Judith-Ann Walker in the previous chapter), child marriage continues to be the most pronounced.

EARLY AND FORCED MARRIAGE IN AFRICA

Sub-Saharan Africa has the second-highest rate of early and forced marriage in the world, and more than one-third of girls in this region are married before they reach eighteen.[2] Some countries in Africa are among those with the highest proportion of early marriage in the world, including Burkina Faso, Niger, Chad, Mali, Guinea, Central African Republic, Mozambique, and Malawi. In the countries where the rate of early and forced marriage exceeds 70 percent—Niger, Chad, and Mali—adolescent fertility and maternal mortality rates are also very high. (See table 11.1.)

TABLE 11.1 COUNTRIES WITH THE HIGHEST PROPORTION OF GIRLS AGES 15 TO 19 WHO MARRIED BEFORE AGE 15 **(M)** AND PROPORTION WHO GAVE BIRTH BEFORE AGE 15 **(B)**, OF THOSE WITH SURVEYS

	M (%)	B (%)		M (%)	B (%)
Sub-Saharan Africa			**South Asia**		
1998 Niger	27	4	2004 Bangladesh	26	6
1999 Guinea	20	7	1999 India	14	2
2001 Mali	19	5	2001 Nepal	9	0
2004 Chad	18	6	Afghanistan	Probably high	
2003 Nigeria	16	3			
1995 Central African Rep.	16	4	**Central America**		
2000 Ethiopia	14	1	2002 Dominican Republic	10	3
2001 Mauritania	13	3	2001 Nicaragua	9	2

Source: Demographic and Health Surveys, USAID DHS Program, available at http://www .measuredhs.com, STATcompiler.

Numerous research studies suggest there is a strong correlation be-tween additional education for girls and a delayed age of marriage.[3] In fact, this variable seems to be the strongest factor distinguishing rates of early marriage in developing versus developed regions, as sub-Saharan Africa and Asia lag behind North America and Europe in girls' educational at-tainment. Urbanization and expanded roles for women are additional factors that enable this shift to occur in a sustainable manner.[4] Gordon Dahl documents the socioeconomic developments that compelled the law in the United States to evolve from allowing marriage at age twelve for girls before the twentieth century to increasing it to the ages of fifteen to twenty-one in the early twentieth century.[5] Dahl argues that the combi-nation of compulsory education, marriage laws, and labor laws played a role in decreasing early marriage prevalence rates. As the country grew economically, women had more employment options. The United Na-tions Population Fund (UNFPA) documents that though the prevalence of early marriage in Africa has not changed dramatically since the mid-2000s, countries such as Cameroon, Zimbabwe, Ethiopia, and Tanzania have witnessed marked declines—but with significant variations between urban and rural areas.[6]

NORMS ON EARLY MARRIAGE

Scholars of marriage as an institution must recognize both the statutory and the customary norms regulating marriage. Particularly in sub-Saharan Africa, marriage holds significant importance and bestows sta-tus on women. Not being married is a stigma in some respects: a never-married woman stands out in societies where the family structure is deeply revered.[7] Statutory norms about marriage emerged with the colonial pe-riod but have collided with customary norms, some of which have their origins in strong traditions that govern human behavior across the African continent, and which were later influenced by colonial administrations.[8] A number of contributors to this volume discuss the conflicting concepts of personhood, subjectivity, and responsibility found in colonial and cus-tomary ideologies of consent, as well as contemporary local and interna-tional norms. Over time, as statutory norms have increasingly evolved to raise the minimum age of marriage, customary norms, by contrast, some-times allow girls to marry while still adolescents. The section that follows provides an overview of legal frameworks on marriage at international,

national, and customary levels, including descriptions of advocacy campaigns that have aimed to raise the visibility of early marriage as a human rights violation.

International Conventions Relating to Early Marriage

The Universal Declaration of Human Rights is one of the most significant documents, globally recognized as extending inalienable rights to all individuals—rights that supersede cultural norms and have relevance across all traditions. Theoretically, this declaration and the two international covenants that make up the International Bill of Rights should protect girls around the world facing early marriage. Other conventions that are more specific to the rights of women and children include the Convention on the Elimination of All Forms of Discrimination against Women (CEDAW), the United Nations Convention on the Rights of the Child, the African Charter on the Rights and Welfare of the Child, and the African Union Protocol on the Rights of Women in Africa. Developed to provide global protections and to set international and regional standards, these conventions appear to have little resonance in communities where economic pressures and social norms collide to perpetuate the marriage of girls who are fifteen to eighteen years old.

National Laws Relating to Early Marriage

In countries where the legal age of marriage differs by sex, the age for women is always lower. In Benin, Cameroon, Gabon, Mali, Niger, and the Democratic Republic of Congo, the legal age of marriage is eighteen for males and only fifteen for females. In recent years, women's rights coalitions have worked to reform the family legislation that regulates many social relations, including marriage. Mali failed to reform its Family Code in 2009 in the face of massive conservative protest, only to pass a regressive version in 2012. The DRC continues its efforts to harmonize its discriminatory Family Law with the more progressive 2006 Sexual Violence Law, but enforcement remains problematic. And it is premature to appreciate the impact of the promising Children's Law of Liberia, enacted early in 2012. Nevertheless, the introduction of national laws is vital to demonstrate that states recognize the need to regulate certain aspects of social behavior. It often takes years for pressure groups to succeed in their campaigns to pass laws, particularly those on the rights of women and girls, and there are many lessons to learn regarding the complexity of strategies employed over the years to bring the concerns of women onto the national stage. Even with national laws regulating the age of marriage, social practices often disregard these legal requirements, and enforcement remains elusive.

Customary Norms Relating to Early Marriage

Customary norms, particularly in sub-Saharan Africa, place a heavy emphasis on marriage as a woman's ultimate destiny, but more significantly, they recognize the family as the most "important institution."[9] Though girls themselves may dream of establishing a family and having children via marriage, the pressure for early marriage is exerted by elders. Such elders usually express a desire to preserve certain values by promoting marriage when a girl reaches fourteen or fifteen. These values include a desire to maintain the family honor by assuring that pregnancies do not take place outside of marriage.[10] This proclivity to "protect" girls by placing them in marriages is a strong one, particularly in settings where young people have few life options and where economic constraints do not enable parents to afford to pay school fees for their children, as in the northern states of Nigeria, discussed by Judith-Ann Walker, or in the Gambia, as analyzed by Bala Saho. In many African settings, the choice is to educate boy children and to assure that daughters get married.[11]

Strategies to curb early marriage must address the fact that in such cultures, marriage has a higher priority than the education of girls. How does one present alternatives that offer girls and communities choices for their future? An additional factor that is common in communities where early marriage is prevalent is women's economic dependence on male partners. In contexts where marriage enables economic security and family stability, early marriage becomes an incentive to mitigate poverty for current and future generations.[12] This reality makes the enforcement of legal statutes on the age of consent for marriage challenging. In fact, exceptions to legal statutes are often made for religious laws or customary practices.

Even without the parallel systems, laws regulating minimum age at marriage may be ignored or avoided. In many African settings, it is the traditional ceremony that formalizes a union and that holds the most importance. Couples almost always participate in a traditional marriage ceremony, and they may or may not register with civil authorities.[13] Furthermore, the lack of state services (especially in rural areas) or the minimal influence of formal state services assures that traditional norms persist. Indeed, the power of traditional norms over the state must not be

MUADI MUKENGE

underestimated. Elected leaders across the African continent thus often hesitate to interfere with traditional practices.

US Advocacy

Building on the existence of international conventions, significant advocacy efforts are under way to end early marriage. US legislation signed into law on March 7, 2013, renews and strengthens an almost twenty-year-old law designed to prevent and respond to violence against women—the Violence Against Women Act (VAWA). However, the 2013 version reaches beyond the American population to the world community in an attempt to prevent the marriage of children under eighteen. The new provisions of VAWA compel the secretary of state to develop and implement a plan to prevent child marriage, promote empowerment of girls at risk of early marriage, and target countries where a high prevalence of child marriage is known to occur. Advocacy groups such as the Center for Health and Gender Equity (CHANGE) applaud VAWA as it mainstreams ending violence against women best practices into all foreign assistance programs and clearly defines early marriage as a form of violence.[14] Unfortunately, a separate bill uniquely identified to end child marriage overseas died in committee.[15] Other countries, including Canada, have added child, early, and forced marriages as priorities in their foreign policy portfolios.

UN Advocacy

In 2012, the United Nations launched a global campaign to abolish child marriages. Led by the UNFPA, the launch also marked the first International Day of the Girl Child—October 11—as designated by the General Assembly in order "to recognize girls' rights and highlight the unique challenges girls face around the world."[16] A unique way to engage participation around the world was to set up the virtual Girls' Summit—by which girls' empowerment groups around the world could organize their own activities and share them online globally.[17] Of note is the elaboration of the Girl Declaration—a declaration drafted by girls around the world, with the support of twenty-five development organizations, to give input into the next iteration of the Millennium Development Goals, with the intent to prioritize girls' human rights. Another strategy is the 11 Days of Action—a commemoration of the International Day of the Girl Child that invites focused activities over eleven days by communities around the world.

Girls Not Brides is a global partnership founded in 2011 to end child marriage, bringing together governments, multilateral organizations, and nongovernmental organizations (NGOs) that work to tackle child marriage at the grassroots, national, and global levels.[18] Girls Not Brides now has over three hundred members across more than fifty countries, devoted to leveraging research, public education, advocacy, and community mobilization to create public conversations about child marriage as a human rights violation. Innovative strategies are included in the campaign, such as inviting girls to write about their future aspirations, asking them to interview their mothers about their experiences as adolescent brides, or focusing on families by extolling the benefits of supporting a girl through her secondary education. Girls Not Brides has a heavy online presence and has engaged high-profile sponsors such as Archbishop Desmond Tutu and several heads of states. In partnership with the campaign, the Ford Foundation has pledged $25 million over five years for interventions in India, Nigeria, Egypt, Central America, and broader West Africa.[19] The aims of these global initiatives are encouraging, but they must link with the change efforts grounded in communities through the initiative of local women's groups. The next section will explore this level of work, which is most closely linked to girls facing early marriage.

EARLY MARRIAGE AND GIRLS' HEALTH

According to the International Women's Health Coalition, child marriage is the major cause worldwide of pregnancies before age fifteen. In most developing countries, 90 percent of girls who give birth before age eighteen are married. Because the bodies of young brides (bone structure, pelvis, and reproductive organs) are not yet fully developed, girls who are fourteen and younger run a very high risk of complications in pregnancy and childbirth compared with older adolescents.[20] Prolonged and obstructed labor, which is common among pregnant young adolescents, can lead to hemorrhage, severe infection, and maternal death. Those who survive may suffer from obstetric fistulas, which cause chronic incontinence; as an example, the Fistula Hospital in Addis Ababa, Ethiopia, operates on twelve hundred girls per year to correct fistulas.[21] Girls who give birth between the ages of fifteen and nineteen are twice as likely to die from pregnancy and birth-related causes than women in their twenties, and for girls under the age of fifteen, the risk is five times higher.[22] In fact, according to the International Center for Research on Women, pregnancy is the top cause of death for females between fifteen and nineteen.[23] One may well ask why early marriages continue to persist in the face of this reality.

DREAMS OF MY MOTHER

Women's rights organizations have engaged thoughtfully with customary leaders and influential community members to exert pressure toward preventing early marriage. Economic deprivation on the continent, the lack of economic opportunities for women, and the reality of paying fees for secondary school often combine to cause families to sacrifice girls' education in exchange for the perceived economic security of marriage. As educational opportunities have increased across the African continent, parents have recognized the livelihood options available to girls with an education. Yet even though mothers dream of giving their daughters a better life than they have had, the pressures for marriage often compete with access to education. Furthermore, the considerable prevalence of pregnancies among female students provokes a high rate of school abandonment and limited livelihood options as a result. Indeed, school is not always a safe environment for teenaged girls.

Nevertheless, the following examples of intervention program successes are worth noting as ways to decrease factors that have led to generations of feminized poverty across Africa. I would recommend that these community-based initiatives be integrated into the broader regional and global campaigns that have gained stronger profiles and seek to bring about transformation in the everyday lives of girls.

Burkina Faso

Many families in Burkina Faso pay for their sons to study but believe that the consequences of not educating a daughter are not serious, given her assumed role as a mother-to-be and not someone who will be involved in substantive roles outside the home. In fact, girls are taken out of school to provide labor on family farms, contributing to the reality that only about 13 percent of girls enroll in secondary school. Early marriage is the norm for over half of Burkinabé adolescent girls.[24] The majority of marriages across the country are polygynous unions. Interestingly, Burkina Faso has progressive laws on marriage rights, women's land rights, and criminalization of violence against women. It is also a CEDAW signatory. The government has established structures such as the Women's Bureau to ensure women's development, and the country has a gender policy to express a high priority for gender equality. Yet these measures fail to bring women and girls out of their current status of marginalization and subordination, including vulnerability to early marriage. These laws have also not translated into significant changes in attitudes and practices that can make a difference in women's everyday experiences.

Across the country, 85 percent of the population is engaged in subsistence agriculture as the primary economic activity. Women do not own or inherit land but instead are permitted to till land belonging to male relatives. Women produce crops for household consumption, in a region that is susceptible to recurrent drought and famine. Growing food is therefore about survival, and women are beholden to male relatives for the land on which to grow the food they eat. Burkinabé women's lack of secure access to land, capital, and state services, along with their low literacy rates, continue to fuel the feminization of poverty and undermine the realization of women's rights. When families are worried about survival, a girl's education takes a back seat to economic security, such as that expected within marriage.

One of the earliest key platforms that emerged to encourage stakeholders to address the negative consequences of early marriage in Burkina Faso was the Forum on Marriage and the Rights of Women and Girls, held in 1998. One outcome of this forum was the Ouagadougou Declaration on Early and Forced Marriage, signed by Burkina Faso, Ghana, the Gambia, Mali, Nigeria, and Sudan in 2003. This declaration calls upon African governments to end child marriage. The host organization for this initiative was the Foundation for Women's Health, Research and Development—FORWARD—an African diaspora women's charity registered in the United Kingdom. FORWARD was formed in 1983 to advance sexual and reproductive health and rights, particularly in regard to female genital mutilation (FGM). In 2003, it incorporated other issues allied to FGM, especially fistulas and child and forced marriage. FORWARD was instrumental in launching the Forum on Marriage and the Rights of Women and Girls in November 1998, to share research and program work on forced and early marriage. Through a global network, the forum aims to promote best practices and develop common strategies. FORWARD has programs in several African countries to address violations of the rights of girls and contributors to child marriage. In northern Nigeria, it has established clinics to treat girls and women with obstetric fistulas, and it runs income-generating projects and other initiatives to improve their social and economic status. Lessons learned from this program have highlighted the importance of a holistic approach to addressing child marriage, necessitating integrated education, health, economic, and participatory community development efforts.[25]

In 1998, the group Pugsada, a Global Fund for Women grant recipient, launched its "support centers for girl brides" in Burkina Faso. As a local NGO, Pugsada works with three Catholic religious centers that shelter girls who have run away from forced or early marriages. Pugsada, in conjunction with the centers, provides the girls with vocational training and mediates between the girls and their families. The engagement with mothers is key, as they can become stronger advocates to protect the rights and dreams of their daughters.

Association Dawla Séno was established in Dori, Burkina Faso, in 1992 to increase rural women's economic development, civic participation, and literacy rates. Its activities also aim to eliminate gender-based violence and harmful traditional practices such as FGM and early marriage. The group provides literacy classes in French and local languages via ten literacy centers; workshops in improved animal husbandry, agricultural methods, and health; and microcredit for women entrepreneurs.

Association Dawla Séno works in Burkina Faso's northeastern Sahel region where desertification, conservative cultural norms, and lack of infrastructure combine to leave few options for the empowerment of women and girls. As of 2011, Dawla Séno has provided over eight hundred women with literacy training, and it has supported a cadre of its members to become certified literacy trainers. The group received GFW support in 2001 and 2002 to finance its literacy classes and seed its microcredit program. It also received GFW funding in 2009 for literacy classes and reproductive health campaigns in fifty-three villages. Over 92 percent of students graduate from the class. Dawla Séno received renewal funding to expand its literacy program in 2011. Its students include adolescent girls, some married and some facing pressure to marry. Literacy skills have provided a tool for women to use in negotiating their rights and pursuing livelihood options that were previously closed to them. This development enables girls to dream of a life that was not available to their mothers—a new life where economic dependence does not drive one into early marriage.

The Association pour la Promotion Féminine de Gaoua (APFG) was created in 1990 and works in seventy villages in southwestern Burkina Faso. With four hundred members, its overall objective is to combat ignorance, economic dependence, and female subjugation. APFG's work has made a significant dent in the areas of women's access to land, enhancing food security, expanding women's citizenship rights by accessing administrative documents such as identification cards and marriage certificates, and reducing female genital mutilation. It has also created a women's leadership forum to lobby for gender-sensitive practices in customary and civil law.

APFG brings together chiefs, circumcisers, religious leaders, local authorities, and NGOs to develop strategies to end harmful practices. This strategy is critical in a context where the Burkinabé fiercely hold on to their traditions, even if they discriminate against women. APFG broadcasts radio programs and performs community theater to raise awareness on human rights issues and highlight the negative implications of certain customary practices on women. It combats early marriage, widowhood rites, and wife inheritance, and with the help of eighty paralegals, it ensures that women have a thorough understanding of legal instruments such as the Burkinabé Family Code. To expand livelihood options for women, it conducts training in business management skills and provides support and loans for the implementation of business projects, such as the soap-making business where women transform shea butter into various skin care products. APFG also runs an Internet café and provides training and subsidized equipment to enhance farming and animal husbandry and to promote food security, including via composting. It also negotiates for farmland to enable rural women to plant a range of vegetables. With recent GFW funding, APFG has undertaken food security programs and trained fifty community-based organization leaders who then become community trainers on women's rights, family planning, and ending early marriage. With this range of program offerings, young women can acquire skills that lessen their dependence on men, thereby giving them some leverage to use in resisting early marriage. APFG has become very influential in its community, enabling women to turn into advocates for their daughters, and creating opportunities for women to earn income to pay for their daughters' education.

L'Association KOOM pour l'Auto Promotion des Femmes du Burkina (AKAFEM/BF) was established in Ouahigouya, Burkina Faso, in 1999 to promote rural women's empowerment, enhance HIV/AIDS awareness, and eliminate female illiteracy. With a membership of over three thousand rural women spread over four provinces, AKAFEM/BF provides business development training for women, organizes campaigns against harmful traditional practices such as forced marriage and FGM, and mobilizes communities for reforestation campaigns. It also engages in policy advocacy for women's empowerment.

Accomplishments of the group include providing over fourteen thousand women with literacy training and/or skills training; promoting adolescent girls' access to education; and organizing comprehensive advocacy campaigns on harmful traditional practices, HIV/AIDS, women's reproductive health, gender-based violence, and women's civic rights. In 2008, the group received GFW funding to support the building of its first literacy center, which also serves as a community center to conduct workshops, and to organize conferences and meetings. The center also serves as a space to provide vocational trainings to school dropouts and girls fleeing forced marriages. In 2010, AKAFEM/BF received renewal funding to promote women's citizenship rights via assisting two thousand women to obtain national identification cards and marriage licenses; organize a community civil marriage for rural women; and cover administrative costs. Civil marriages lead to rights for children and opportunities for schooling, including possibilities for girls to develop their potential by delaying marriage. In essence, Association KOOM's programs enable girls to expand their horizons and explore other options besides marriage.

Burkina Faso ranks among the world's poorest countries (173 out of 175 on the United Nation's Human Development Index). Few women have birth certificates or marriage certificates, and few obtain birth certificates for their children. Consequently, women remain outside the reach of public services, their children cannot attend school, and they are excluded from electoral processes. AKAFEM/BF provides literacy training and obtains formal identification for women, which enhances their citizenship rights, allows greater access to social services, and protects them from losing their inheritance upon becoming widows. Widowhood without inheritance represents another risk for women, whose female children are the first to be taken out of school and become susceptible to early marriage.

Lastly, it is important to note interventions undertaken by multilateral partners. These include the UNFPA and United Nations Children's Fund (UNICEF) campaign from 2008 to 2011, with the Ministry of Social Affairs and National Solidarity. That campaign leveraged $1.6 million in twenty-four villages, targeting girls from the ages of twelve to nineteen in an intervention called "Eliminating Child Marriage in BF: A Plan for Protection, Empowerment and Community Action"—a multisectoral approach to social change. The campaign goals were to build a culture of human rights and respect for women rights via engagement with one hundred community leaders; to give 50 percent of girls the opportunity to stay in school or access economic resources; and to offer peer education and vocational training for married adolescent girls and improve maternal health services. At the end of three years, the initiative realized the following outcomes: (1) it trained leaders and reached two hundred thousand via film screenings, drama, and radio to create enabling environments; (2) it supported five hundred at-risk girls with school fees and employment (thirteen literacy centers were built); and (3) it created a support network of "mother educators" for married adolescent girls and improved maternal health services.[26] These outcomes are significant, given the desire to space the future deliveries of first-time mothers such that they can develop other capacities and not put their health or the health of a newborn at risk by another birth while the mother is still an adolescent.

Because this chapter makes reference to structural reforms as pivotal factors in reducing early marriage in Burkina Faso, it is worth mentioning that the country's recent national development strategy, the Strategy for Accelerated Growth and Sustainable Development 2011–15 (SCADD), includes promising focus areas such as diversifying the economy, intensifying cotton exports, and increasing budget allocations in priority sectors such as health and education. Added to the community-based interventions described earlier, it is hoped that an analysis of early marriage in the next decade would yield favorable trends due to an enabling environment for a strong economy and social development options that can create opportunities for girls.[27]

Benin

According to UNICEF, about 50 percent of girls in Benin enroll in primary school, and only 11 percent continue on to secondary school. It is therefore not surprising that only 30 percent of Beninese women ages fifteen and older are literate.[28] Women's rights groups report that a considerable number of girls choose to drop out of school because they are sexually harassed by teachers and are unaware of ways in which to address this violence. Women's rights groups have succeeded in drafting a family code that could improve the status of women and children under the law. However, it has not been enforced. As sexual harassment perpetuates truancy and dropping out, it makes female school-leavers vulnerable to early marriage.

The Beninese NGO SIN-DO works in rural communities to promote women's rights, improve women's literacy, build the entrepreneurial skills of women, and facilitate access to financial resources for poor women. It defends the rights of the girl child through its antitrafficking program and sexual harassment prevention initiative in schools.

Over the course of a decade, SIN-DO received GFW support to gradually develop an initiative that combines women's literacy and economic empowerment with girls' education. Over several years, SIN-DO undertook a GFW-funded grant supporting women's literacy and microfinance and girls' education. The first phase of the latter component included payment of school fees and produced results such as boosting the rate of girls' enrollment from 31 percent to 39 percent, decreasing the dropout rate from 51 percent to 21 percent, and increasing girls' passing rate from 55 percent to 78 percent. In the second phase, beginning in 2004, GFW awarded SIN-DO a larger grant to conduct a comprehensive initiative addressing sexual harassment in two pilot schools by developing preventive and punitive measures to protect the psychological and physical well-being of girls. The grant enabled the documentation of cases of violence, as well as the formation of girls' clubs designed to build self-confidence and knowledge in human rights and reproductive health. A committee at the community level brought attention to cases of gender violence, including early marriage, rape, and child kidnapping. The advocacy strategy included radio programs and meetings with police, elected officials, courts, school officials, and local chiefs.

SIN-DO received a final grant of $25,000 in 2009 to expand the sexual harassment initiative to eight schools and challenge a pervasive climate of abuse against girls. The program aimed to implement a 2006 law criminalizing sexual harassment and to raise awareness about its existence in rural communities. The group was able to obtain important results in girls' enrollment between 2000 and 2009 in six of twelve districts of the country. Results revealed that

1. More than 2,000 girls were supported with school fees via credit extension to 1,351 women (a total of 8,022 girls were reached via awareness workshops, girls' clubs, school fees, and other assistance);

2. In some districts of the project, primary school graduation rates climbed from 45 percent to 79 percent over six years;

3. More than 400 teachers were trained on preventing gender violence;

4. There was a fivefold increase in girls' reporting of sexual harassment in some districts; and

5. Local governments now contribute financially to girls' empowerment via offering girls' scholarships and summer classes for girls.

There is more work to be done, but these strategies are important to further develop girls' intellectual capacity and stem the pressure to "protect" them via early marriage. The initiative also demonstrated to the community that, with the appropriate support and enabling environment, girls can succeed academically on an equal level with boys and have additional life possibilities outside of marriage. Such improvements develop life skills and lessen female dependence on males, while also decreasing rates of early marriage. The country case studies cited earlier are informed by grantees' self-reporting and communications with GFW staff. However, GFW commissioned a formal evaluation of SIN-DO by an external evaluator, who presented the detailed analysis shared here.

Democratic Republic of Congo

In a country where 50 percent of young people do not attend school, it is not surprising that a high rate of early marriage exists. Poor school enrollment is a direct consequence of Congo's protracted war, and some local traditions have encouraged early marriage as a means to avoid out-of-wedlock pregnancies and also to affirm social ties and economic security. The urban areas of the Congo have witnessed an increase in girls' marriage age, but in rural areas, early marriages are more pronounced. As the women's movement has evolved in the Congo, women's groups have therefore begun to tackle this phenomenon. Débout Fille de Fizi (Stand Up, Girls of Fizi [DFF]) was formed in Fizi, in eastern Democratic Republic of Congo, in 2005 to promote girls' rights and to prevent gender-based violence and harmful traditional practices such as early marriage. It aims to address all violations facing girls in rural communities and to raise awareness of girls' legal rights. DFF challenges sexual harassment in schools, forms girls' clubs, and provides assistance in cases of rape within schools.

The group provides public education in an effort to change attitudes and behaviors and to enable women to overcome their subordinate status. It promotes girls' education as a human right and organizes girls' clubs (Girls' Parliaments) that champion girls' human rights. It has held awareness campaigns and workshops on early marriage prevention, reproductive health, the complications associated with unsafe abortion, and the prevention of gender-based violence (GBV) in multiple communities, directly reaching thousands of in-school and out-of-school rural adolescent girls. DFF has received two GFW grants since 2009. In 2009, GFW support facilitated the establishment of girls' clubs to combat sexual violence in thirteen high schools and to train seventy-eight student peer educators, who then offered regular update sessions. The Girls' Parliaments are also mechanisms to support girls in the continuation of their studies by building self-confidence and providing career advice and leadership experience. A renewal grant from GFW in 2010 enabled a scaling up of the initiative.

To further develop its approach, DFF received renewal support in 2012 for its reproductive health and GBV initiative for adolescent girls in twenty schools, designed to break the taboo on sexuality education for adolescent females. Activities included training thirty adolescent peer educators on sexual and reproductive health and women's rights, offering reproductive health and women's rights education in schools, and organizing teachers and parents to train other parents. Sexuality education goes a long way in providing girls with tools to manage their sexuality and avoid unplanned pregnancies. As an unplanned pregnancy is often a precursor to early marriage, this strategy is paramount. In fact, to avoid the shame that comes with an out-of-wedlock pregnancy, some communities in Congo force the young couple to immediately marry. Upholding the family "honor" is a constant refrain when relatives discuss girls' early entry into family life.[29]

Uganda

The Pastoral Women Alliance to Break Cultural Chains (PWABC) was created in 2003 in Kiboga District about 100 miles northwest of Kampala, Uganda. With a membership of over two thousand women organized into thirteen village groups, the network advocates for pastoralist women's socioeconomic and political rights by reforming cultural practices and traditions that discriminate against women. The group works with male community leaders and elders to advocate for women's rights and cultural reform. It links with lawyers, law enforcement, and local government offices to enhance its community education work.[30]

PWABC pursues three main objectives: to increase awareness among pastoralist communities of women's human rights; to enable grassroots women's groups to raise their voices and demand their rights; and to influence government officials, elders, men, and policy makers to develop and support legislation and practices advancing pastoralist women's rights. Examples of its activities include forming ten school clubs to address human rights and cultural reform, training seventy-five human rights defenders to provide support at the community level, providing urgent assistance through its Village Alert Rescue Committee to women and children needing either counseling for domestic violence and HIV/AIDS or rescue from abduction into marriage by male suitors, offering adult literacy classes, performing live theater on women's reproductive rights, and airing radio shows on women's rights issues.

With GFW support in 2006, PWABC launched its community initiative to end forced marriage and other harmful traditional practices; it also facilitated community awareness workshops for ninety people. Similarly, in 2009 PWABC received a GFW renewal grant to train fifty-eight women's rights paralegals, train thirteen community groups and eleven school management committees on the importance of girls' education, produce media programs in local languages on the need for cultural reform, and conduct skills training for HIV-positive and disabled women. The strategy of empowering community members to become advocates for social change is a significant one to assure sustainability of any cultural reform process.

PWABC received a third grant in 2011 to (1) conduct a three-day legal rights training session for fifty police, local authorities, church leaders, and youth representatives of school clubs to build an understanding of constitutional law, especially around women's rights and GBV, and (2) produce radio programs on women's rights in local languages.

Pastoral communities typically reside in dry regions of Uganda and regularly move around in search of water for their animals. PWABC states that such a lifestyle has relegated women to a status below that of valued animals. PWABC describes a range of practices in the local culture that treat women as sexual objects and violate their rights, including preventing girls from attending school and instead using them as commodities to exchange for cows, in order to pay the dowries that enable male children to marry; promoting forced and early marriage; practicing wife inheritance;

and denying inheritance rights for women. The training in legal rights by community groups such as PWABC introduces constitutional norms such that women have tools to defend their rights, for instance, by delaying marriage and by insisting on a civil marriage when they are ready to wed.

RECOMMENDATIONS

An African Women's Decade (AWD) 2010–2020 was declared by African governments through the African Union and aims to enforce the regional and global commitments on gender equality and women's rights. In the AWD era, the women's movement has several tools at its disposal to make a case for challenging entrenched patriarchy and to enhance the human rights of women and girls. The chapter has discussed the legal frameworks that women's groups are seeking to leverage so that they can exercise their rights. Here, I will briefly present additional recommendations at both the local and national levels to enable further structural change—change that will enable the dreams of mothers across Africa to become sustainable.

Community-Based Initiatives

Programs by local groups reach girls who are most impacted by social norms that determine their future options. The contributions of women's groups have revealed the importance of holistic, community-based, bottom-up approaches to ending early marriage. Women leading efforts from these communities know how to engage with parents and elders in a culturally appropriate way. Local groups have also successfully lobbied schools and school districts to reverse expulsions of pregnant girls. There is a need to expand policies that enable teen mothers to reenroll in school and reach their potential.

With the cost of secondary education beyond the reach of many parents in Africa, rather than pushing out-of-school adolescent girls into marriage the emphasis should be placed on enhancing the recruitment of girls into national vocational training programs. There is an opportunity to advocate for the funding of programs that expose girls to nontraditional careers that can offer them economic independence so they will not have to revert to marriage for economic security.

With regard to legal options, activists can promote a greater investment in training paralegals who can conduct local awareness-raising programs on new laws that relate to social norms and human rights. Paralegals play an important part in efforts to simplify complex texts and popularize them, and they often accompany clients who need formal legal support. However, practitioners and the government must develop a deeper understanding of the effects of harsh legal measures that may push early marriage and other customary practices underground. This reality has been observed with the punitive measures taken against FGM—measures that have driven the practice underground, sometimes pushed it across borders, and even extended it to babies—all of which make such practices harder to detect.

Finally, community-based initiatives must reach mothers in order to build their capacity to advocate on behalf of their daughters. The SIN-DO case study and other programs across the continent reveal the effectiveness of this method.

National and Regional Advocacy

Positive trends at the national and regional levels and across the African continent create space for an enabling environment to address ending early marriage in strategic ways. Civil society groups, including women's groups, have experienced some successes in calling for citizenship rights for women who previously held no identification papers. Strategies that remove financial barriers for obtaining identification documents are very significant in that they are a prerequisite for accessing public services, including education in public schools. This leads us to another level of structural reform that will propel the continent to new heights, given the requisite political will. Expanding free secondary education will liberate parents from having to pay school fees, much like parents in the United States and Europe, so that they do not have to neglect schooling for their daughters due to a lack of funds. The current wave of state-sponsored free primary education is not enough for Africa to make significant development gains and prepare the next generation for productive roles in society.

Another recommendation to the women's movement and other human rights coalitions is to take advantage of the opportunity to conduct advocacy with African governments to meet obligations to which they have signed (the African Union Protocol on the Rights of Women, the Convention on the Elimination of All Forms of Discrimination against Women, and so forth). The African Union has recently appointed a goodwill ambassador on child marriage, and the Committee on the Rights of Women has seized on the topic. The conventions contain language on the rights of girls and, in particular, on ending early marriage. Stimulated by increasing public discussions of these issues, there is new momentum for the implementation of these conventions, and pressure is building to compel influential actors to ally with women's rights coalitions and enforce these rights. In much the same way, activists can raise the visibility of campaigns such as the International Day of the Girl Child and the African Women's Decade to pressure governments to meet their obligations.

I am convinced that a systemic shift is necessary in order to complement the important efforts to end child marriage. By continuing foreign debt forgiveness initiatives and thereby enabling state savings to be allocated to free public education, this policy shift can benefit girls facing early marriage stemming from family poverty. The availability of free secondary education will present an opening for girls to pursue further studies en masse instead of being pulled out due to their parents' lack of income to pay school fees.

In addition, activists may conduct advocacy with donors to allocate a greater percentage of their annual budget to women's rights groups in rural communities. The groups that champion ending child and forced marriage do so with very modest funding but a great deal of passion. Financial support to meet their institutional needs will provide critical resources to maintain qualified staff, conduct outreach efforts in hard-to-reach communities, and cover communication and other operating costs. Donors must commit to support groups working in rural communities where the majority of early marriages take place.

Finally, ending early marriage requires promoting donor support for economic growth initiatives that benefit African communities and enable job creation that will also benefit women. Increased economic options for women open opportunities in the labor force that provide livelihoods for economic security, thereby removing a driver of early marriages in many parts of the continent.[31] This final recommendation is an invitation for stakeholders to think big on supporting an enabling environment where girls can grow into adulthood and have meaningful educational and livelihood options.

NOTES

1. I thank Global Fund for Women for sharing documentation on its grantees for this chapter.

2. UNICEF, "Child Marriages: 39,000 Every Day," 2013, available at http://www.UNICEF.org/media/media_68114.html, accessed December 21, 2013.

3. Susheela Singh and Renee Samara, "Early Marriage among Women in Developing Countries," 1996, *International Family Planning Perspectives,* available at http://www.guttmacher.org/pubs/journals/2214896.pdf, accessed December 21, 2013.

4. Singh and Samara, "Early Marriage."

5. Gordon Dahl, "Early Teen Marriage and Future Poverty," *Demography* 47, no. 3 (August 2010): 689–718.

6. UNFPA, "Marrying Too Young: End Child Marriage," 2012, New York, pp. 24–26, available at http://www.unfpa.org/public/home/publications/pid/12166, accessed December 21, 2013.

7. Global Press Institute, "Uganda: Women Choose to Delay Marriage," posted March 4, 2013, in *African Farm News in Review,* no. 237, Past Issues, available at http://weekly.farmradio.org/2013/03/04/uganda-women-choose-to-delay-marriage-global-press-institute/, accessed December 21, 2013.

8. Mojbol Olfnk Okome, "Domestic, Regional, and International Protection of Nigerian Women against Discrimination: Constraints and Possibilities," *African Studies Quarterly* 6, no. 3 (2002), available at http://www.africa.ufl.edu/asq/v6/v6i3a3.htm, accessed December 21, 2013.

9. Peter C. W. Gutkind, "African Urban Family Life," *Cahiers d'Études Africaines* 3, no. 10 (1962): 149–217. See Richard Roberts's chapter in this volume.

10. "Early Marriage Adds to Socioeconomic Woes, NGOs Say," available at http://www.irinnews.org/report/81667/nigeria-early-marriage-adds-to-socioeconomic-woes-ngos-say, accessed October 21, 2013.

11. For a discussion of socioeconomic factors contributing to early age at marriage, see Annie Bunting, "Stages of Development: Marriage of Girls and Teens as an International Human Rights Issue," *Social and Legal Studies* 14, no. 1 (2005): 17–38.

12. UNICEF, "Child Marriages."

13. See IWHC, http://www.iwhc.org/index.php?option=com_content&task=view&id=3487&Itemid=629, accessed December 21, 2013.

14. See https://www.change.org/petitions/end-violence-against-women-and-girls-worldwide-pass-the-international-violence-against-women-act-2, accessed December 21, 2013.

15. See https://www.govtrack.us/congress/bills/112/hr6087, accessed December 21, 2013.

16. See http://dayofthegirl.org/about/, accessed December 21, 2013.

17. See http://dayofthegirlsummit.org/, accessed December 21, 2013.

18. See www.girlsnotbrides.org, accessed December 21, 2013.

19. See http://www.fordfoundation.org/newsroom/news-from-ford/678, accessed December 21, 2013.

20. UNFPA, "Marrying Too Young."

21. Linda Osarenren, "Tradition at the Heart of Violence against Women and Girls in Africa," *Pambazuka News,* 2008-03-06, iss. no. 351, available at http://pambazuka.org/en/category/comment/46520, accessed December 21, 2013.

22. See International Center for Research on Women, available at http://www.icrw.org/child-marriage-facts-and-figures, accessed December 21, 2013.

23. See H.R. 6087 (112th Congress): International Protecting Girls by Preventing Child Marriage Act of 2012, available at https://www.govtrack.us/congress/bills/112/hr6087, accessed December 21, 2013.

24. UNICEF, available at http://www.UNICEF.org/infobycountry/burkinafaso_statistics.html, accessed December 21, 2013.

25. See http://www.forwarduk.org.uk/key-issues/child-marriage, accessed October 21, 2013.

26. See https://docs.unocha.org/sites/dms/HSU/Outreach/Burkina%20Faso/049/Burkina%20Faso%20Summary.pdf, accessed December 21, 2013.

27. IMF, Country Reports—Burkina Faso: Strategy for Accelerated Growth and Sustainable Development, 2011–2015 (2012).

28. World Factbook, 2012, available at https://www.cia.gov/library/publications/the-world-factbook/geos/bn.html, accessed December 21, 2013.

29. Rita Mutyaba, "Early Marriage: A Violation of Girls' Fundamental Human Rights in Africa," *International Journal of Children's Rights* 19 (2011): 339–55.

30. See Pastoral Women Alliance to Break Cultural Chains, available at http://pastoralwomen.wordpress.com/, accessed December 21, 2013.

31. Singh and Samara, "Early Marriage."

CHAPTER TWELVE

"To Be Taken as a Wife Is a Form of Death"

The Social, Military, and Humanitarian Dynamics of Forced Marriage
and Girl Soldiers in African Conflicts, c. 1990–2010

STACEY HYND

> Even though the relationship was generally framed in terms
> of bush "wife" and "husband" or even "lover," the actual
> relationships had little in common with the notions of a
> traditional relationship between consenting adults.
>
> —*Republic of Liberia, Truth and Reconciliation*
> *Commission Final Report*[1]

Forced marriages have been documented within armed groups in many recent African conflicts, most notably in Sierra Leone, Liberia, Rwanda, and northern Uganda. These coercive relationships, formed without the valid consent of the female and her family, encompass the forcible ascription of conjugal status and usually involve the provision by the female of domestic labor, sexual relations, and sometimes reproduction. These "marriages" are not recognized under civil or customary law. Significantly, the majority of these forced marriages occurring in modern African conflicts involve girls as so-called wives: figures for Sierra Leone's Truth and Reconciliation Commission (TRC) indicate that 50 percent of "sexual slaves" with documented ages were fifteen or under; in northern Uganda among Joseph Kony's Lord's Resistance Army (LRA), some 27 percent of abducted girls became "bush wives," and most were between eleven and seventeen years old.[2] Forced marriage within modern warfare is an issue of children's rights as well as women's rights, and it is closely linked to the mobilization of children as combatants in African conflicts.[3]

This situation is a product not only of military strategies and patterns of violence but also of gendered and generational tensions within African societies. Over 120,000 children are estimated to have fought in recent African conflicts, and studies suggest that girls constitute some 30 to 40 percent of these child combatants.[4] Surveys indicate that 2,000 to 3,000 girls were recruited into armed groups in Sierra Leone, and the LRA has abducted some 25,000 child recruits, with girls constituting around a third of that number.[5] The figure of the child soldier has often been taken as evidence of the depoliticization and criminalization of modern warfare in Africa, of the "new barbarism" and extreme violence that apparently marks contemporary civil conflict.[6] It is also linked to the "civilianization" of contemporary warfare, whereby ordinary civilians, male and female, have been the targets of military violence and are increasingly drawn into fighting themselves.[7] Forced marriage, from this perspective, is part of the wider militarization of girls'—and women's—lives and labors during contemporary conflict.[8] However, "new war" theories do not accurately depict the logics of violence behind children's involvement in warfare or the forced marriage of girls. The social, legal, and humanitarian structures that shape girls' experiences of conflict and how these are reported and tackled on a world stage also need to be taken into account.[9]

The mobilization and exploitation of children in African conflict emerge out of the crisis of the postcolonial state and the youth revolutions facing African societies.[10] Marriage has proven to be a key site of social tension through which disenfranchised young men and women seek to attain adult status, on one hand, and adults look to control youth status and labor, on the other, with such struggles played out in war zones.[11] Socially marginalized and vulnerable children are often the first to be drawn into conflict, and girls are no exception to this pattern; some enter armed groups after fleeing potential early marriage or domestic violence at home, and others are forcibly recruited as potential wives.[12] Although histories of girls' experiences of conflict were previously marked by "silences and empty spaces," girls are now well represented in child soldier narratives.[13] Academic studies have consequently shown that girls participate in almost every facet of military life, with many individuals fulfilling multiple positions, sometimes simultaneously: fighters, sex slaves, mothers, porters, cooks.[14] Sixty percent of girls involved with fighting forces in Sierra Leone, for instance, acted as wives, a role that involved sexual, military, and domestic labor.[15] Girls' experiences in war, however, have predominantly entailed "victimisation, perpetration and insecurity," with their bodies used as figurative and literal sites of combat.[16] Sexual abuse and exploitation seem to be pervasive and nearly systematic across Africa's conflicts—for both civilian and combatant girls.[17] Rape and sexual violence should not, though, be read as a material fact of women's lives but as a "grammar of violence" that is shaped by particular contexts of conflict and society.[18] Consequently, the questions this chapter explores regard what function the practice of forced marriage serves for various armed groups and individuals and how this type of marriage relates to other forms of sexual violence and gender inequality.

Debates on forced marriage demonstrate the intersection of local and global gender norms and constructions of childhood. Childhood is not a universal category but rather a historical and cultural construct.[19] The twentieth century saw the imposition of middle-class Western concepts of childhood—which read children as innocent, nonsexual beings who should be protected from labor and a too rapid transition to adulthood—onto colonial and global societies, creating new globalized notions of the "child," notions that bear little resemblance to the lived realities of many African youths.[20] Girls, in particular, are taken symbolically as the quintessential victims.[21] In transnational political discourses, these constructions of the child have served as a global disciplinary tool and moralizing practice, aiming to impose Western liberal norms on the developing world.[22] The emergence of the girl soldier is therefore a product not only of shifting patterns of warfare and African societies but also of liberal humanitarianism and its entanglement with international political and legal discourses of rights. Historians must question how far discourses and descriptions of forced marriage have changed over the past decades and how far actual practices have shifted. Campaigns by organizations such as Child Soldiers International, the United Nations Children's Fund (UNICEF), and Human Rights Watch have pulled child combatants into the international spotlight.[23] Although these campaigns have crafted boys' participation in physical violence into a narrative discourse that lends weight to their accounts, girls' experiences of war are primarily recounted through narratives of sexual abuse and exploitation, foregrounding their victim status.[24] Following this focus on sexual violation, many commentators have argued that girls' abduction, exploitation, and rape comprise a form of sexual slavery.[25] The concept of forced marriage, which combines sexual abuse with domestic labor and inverts the socially desirable status of marriage and motherhood, presents a more complicated picture of girls' experiences, highlighting the clash between local and global attitudes to girls' sexuality and sexual violence.

Testimonies drawn from TRCs, humanitarian reports, memoirs, and academic investigations form the main body of evidence here. Wider empirical research is needed on historical and contemporary patterns of girls' experiences in conflict to present an accurate comparative pattern of forced conjugality. Nonetheless, this chapter offers a preliminary discussion of forced marriage and its relationship with child soldiering in humanitarian discourses, as well as of the rationales for its practice in contemporary African conflicts. Some studies have suggested that the incidence of forced marriages in conflict seems to be highest in Africa—if this is indeed the case, then why is this so?[26] Is this related to patterns of warfare, structural gender violence, customary patterns of marriage, and/or histories of forced labor and slavery? Is forced marriage in conflict part of a wider militarization of female labor and sexuality driven by the civilianization of conflict in Africa? This chapter suggests that forced marriage emerges from historical patterns of structural gender violence that have shaped generations of girls' lives, as well as immediate military instrumentalities. It is molded by patriarchal desires to control girls' (and women's) bodies to impose a certain version of social order; further, it is a tactic geared toward military survival and victory.

LEGAL AND HUMANITARIAN DISCOURSES OF FORCED MARRIAGE IN CONFLICT

The prosecution of gendered and sexual offenses as war crimes or crimes against humanity is a recent development in international humanitarian law, with the 1998 *Akayesu* case at the International Criminal Tribunal for Rwanda establishing the first conviction for rape as a war crime.[27] Driven by a growing focus on women's victimhood in civil war, charges of sexual slavery and forced marriage have increasingly appeared in lists of war crimes.[28] In 2001, the International Criminal Tribunal for the Former Yugoslavia became the first court to recognize forced marriage as a prosecutable crime in armed conflict.[29] Within Africa, the Special Court for Sierra

Leone recognized forced marriage as a crime against humanity in the 2004 Armed Forces Revolutionary Council (AFRC) case, as described in Mariane Ferme's chapter in this volume. However, the focus has been on the gendered dimensions of these crimes, and their relationship to child combatant experience is yet to be rigorously explored. Outside the legal arena, the systematic analysis of forced marriage has been slow to emerge. The 1996 report on children in armed conflict prepared by Graça Machel for the United Nations, a foundation text in the study of children in contemporary warfare, investigated sexual exploitation and gender-based violence. But its primary focus was on rape, prostitution, and sexual exploitation during war and in refugee camps and disarmament, demobilization, rehabilitation, and reintegration (DDRR) camps rather than on sexual abuse within armed groups.[30] There was no explicit discussion of forced marriage or sexual slavery apart from a passing reference to "bush wives," which is perhaps surprising considering that field visits for the report included Angola, Sierra Leone, and Rwanda.[31] Nonetheless, there was sufficient international concern about the abuse of girls in coerced relationships that forced marriage was explicitly detailed in the definition of *child soldier* outlined by the 1997 Cape Town Principles:

> [A child soldier is] any person under 18 years of age who is part of any kind of regular or irregular armed force or armed group in any capacity, including but not limited to cooks, porters, messengers, and those accompanying such groups, other than purely as family members. It includes girls recruited for sexual purposes *and forced marriage.*[32] (my emphasis)

This shift in the late 1990s was driven by a confluence of emerging concerns about child rights, child soldiering, women's rights, and sexual violence in international political, humanitarian, and human rights discourses, alongside the aforementioned developments in international humanitarian law and the prosecution of gendered war crimes. Graça Machel's 2000 review on children in armed conflict notably engages more explicitly with questions of forced marriage than its predecessor had, and a growing number of humanitarian and feminist studies have highlighted sexual violence and forced conjugality in Africa's wars.[33] But despite these discussions, forced marriage and sexual slavery have, until recently, been surprisingly sparsely reported in general accounts of conflict, and most frequently they are referenced as symbolic markers of the "barbarity" of

African conflict rather than analyzed in detail. Part of the problem is the compartmentalization of humanitarian discourses and campaigns—one recent report on forced marriage and gender inequality in postconflict South Sudan barely mentions the country's long-running civil war and its impact on gender relations and incidences of sexual violence.[34] The issue of forced marriage also presents a complexity that existing humanitarian and legal narratives struggle to account for effectively. As this volume argues, existing legal debates have focused on whether these offenses are better prosecuted under existing crimes against humanity such as sexual slavery or under a new heading such as forced marriage, without fully analyzing the experiential differences encompassed within these terms.[35] Moreover, international humanitarian norms and postconflict reconstruction are both highly gendered and based around an idea of conjugal order that seeks to return girls and women to the "correct" spaces and family structures based on liberal norms. In such structures, marriage is supposed to be the solution to girls (re)integration into society, not the problem.[36] Forced marriage corrupts and perverts the social institution of marriage, creating a form of conjugal disorder that threatens society. Although international humanitarian discourses have brought the issue of forced marriage to a global audience, there is much that still needs to be done to contextualize and facilitate understanding of the rationales underpinning this practice, as well as the wide variety of girls' experiences that have been categorized under this heading.

FORCED MARRIAGE AND THE LOGICS OF VIOLENCE

In order to combat forced marriage effectively, we must analyze it as a social and military, as well as legal, category. It has been suggested that the militarization of girls' labor and sexuality can be read as part of the civilianization of contemporary conflict. But women have always played a significant role in African warfare, as victims, fighters, logistical support, and commentators.[37] With conceptions of marriage, consent, gender roles, and women's rights shifting over time, it is difficult to trace historically the category of forced marriage. Yet as Sierra Leonean legal expert Joko Smart notes, "There was, in the olden days, marriage by capture. . . . Such a wife was, however, regarded as a slave."[38] Early colonial militaries also awarded captured women as wives to their African soldiers, including forces in Sudan, Uganda, and the Congo Free State.[39] Forced marriage is not simply a tactic of barbaric new wars; rather, it is a result of particular "logics and modalities of violence," with contemporary conflict bearing striking similarities to precolonial patterns of total economic warfare in terms of its appropriation and exploitation of female labor and bodies.[40]

Forced marriage is neither a straightforward form of sexual violence nor a substitute for rape: some groups, such as the Revolutionary United Front (RUF) of Sierra Leone, used mass and gang rape as well as forced marriage, whereas others, such as the LRA, do not systematically use rape as a military weapon against their opponents.[41] The institution of forced marriage is about power, the enforcement of masculine control, and the logics of violence within an armed group rather than simply about sex. In some conflicts, the evidence suggests there is an instrumental use of forced marriage by senior commanders and leaders of armed groups. Forced marriage appears to function as a tactic of warfare to terrorize populations, maintain discipline, and secure the necessary labor and logistical support to sustain the war effort, especially for nonregularized, mobile forces. As well as tearing apart local communities, the abduction and forcible marriage of young girls also quickly increases the numerical strength of an armed group, as girls tend to be more vulnerable and less able to escape after abduction.[42] In Angola alone, some thirty thousand girls may have been abducted during the civil war.[43] The RUF notably increased its coercive recruitment of so-called wives after it was nearly wiped out in 1993.[44] According to Zoe Marks, within the RUF marriage was promoted as an antidote to the destabilizing effects of mass and gang rape on the armed group: "marriage" allowed men a socially legitimate form of sexual access, at least in the eyes of the RUF, and aimed to prevent competition between fighters for women.[45]

In northern Uganda, forced marriages have been an integral aspect of Joseph Kony's attempts to discipline and develop the LRA, described as an effective tool for building control and discipline in an "ideologically committed (essentially charismatic) armed force."[46] Analysis of the group suggests that coerced relationships have been highly regulated and controlled by the LRA's top leadership, with senior commanders selecting wives for themselves based on their physical and educational attributes, drawing on cultural norms that encouraged polygamy by powerful men as a marker of high status. Commanders have then dictated the "marriage" of remaining girls to lower-ranking fighters.[47] The LRA is a highly mobile force that cannot rely on popular support from within its locales.[48] Thus, discipline was essential to the operation of mobile units, and it was maintained through the screening and socialization of recruits, harsh punishments, strict codes of behavior, and a puritanical creed. The centralized distribution of wives assisted discipline by acting as a system of privilege and remuneration within the group.[49] Wives were distributed as compensation and status markers for soldiers in the absence of material goods, and families were fabricated to create bonds among soldiers while fostering dependence on the LRA.[50] Children born of these relationships would then themselves become fighters for the group. On a more prosaic level, the recruitment of wives facilitated the provision of essential logistical support and domestic services, such as porterage, locating food and water, and cooking, to keep the group functioning. The selection of sexually inexperienced adolescent girls and "virgins" also served the purpose of limiting the transmission of sexually transmitted diseases, which became a concern after a number of senior commanders died of HIV/AIDS.[51]

In addition to immediate military instrumentalities, the political economy of forced marriage must also be considered. With historical structures of child labor, domestic slavery, and forced/coerced labor in many areas of Africa, both gender dynamics and labor patterns can predispose armed groups toward the use of sexual slavery and forced marriage.[52] As Meredith Turshen argues, the "control of women's productive labor is one of the gains from rape and abduction in civil conflicts," not just for the armed group but also for the individual "husbands" involved.[53] Young men who are unable to pay bridewealth and find legal marriage partners may also be attracted to insurgency as a way of gaining access to women. Recent research from Sierra Leone has highlighted that "woman damage" (adultery) became a divisive issue in agrarian communities in the years preceding the conflict. Poorer young men who were unable to enter into formal marriage contracts, due to an inability to pay bridewealth or because polygyny limited the availability of girls, would often enter into "girl friend" relationships with the young wives of elder men. The elder in such an arrangement would then demand labor from the paramour; if this was not paid, he would take the paramour to court and sue for "woman damage." In this context, the RUF's practice of forced marriage offered young men a new source of marriage partners, allowing them "to break free from a restrictive customary institution."[54]

During the Rwandan genocide in 1994, thousands of Tutsi girls endured forced marriages to Interahamwe members. A 1996 Human Rights

Watch report described these girls not as wives but as "captives, looted possessions of the militiamen, held in slavery."[55] In some instances, Rwandan militias used these forced relationships to disguise rape as sanctioned intercourse between husband and wife; the purported marriage was then used to legitimate the seizure of land, which was a significant point of tension during Rwanda's civil war due to the high population density.[56] A wife's labor, however, varied according to her status and where she was held. Though some females were forced to farm and cook, others were "women of the ceiling" and were hidden to avoid being targeted by other Hutu *génocidaires* (persons who committed genocide) and to provide sexual services for their captors. One girl, "Nadia," who was eleven years old at the time of the Rwandan genocide, recounted how her family was hacked to pieces in front of her before she was taken as a wife by one of the militiamen. "He only came to rape me, he never brought any food. He came about five times. He would say, 'lie down or I'll kill you.' So I was afraid. I would just go to the bed."[57] For many wives in Rwanda, the relatively short duration and the static nature of these marriages limited the domestic services entailed and meant that sexual violence dominated their experiences. In other testimonies from former bush wives, the interconnection of their sexual and domestic labors is clear. Grace Akallo, one of the 139 Aboke schoolgirls infamously abducted by the LRA in October 1996, recalls in her memoirs how Kony gave her to one of his commanders, "a man older than my father. His eyes were so hard that my sweat made a pool. He seized me and forced me to bed. I felt like a thorn was in my skin as my innocence was destroyed."[58] But Grace's account of her captivity appears to suggest that what affected her at least as severely at the time was the physical hardship she experienced in marching, going on raids, and searching for food, followed by the fear of severe punishment if she did not perform her labors adequately: "I didn't know what he would tell me now that I had come back with nothing from the raid. He might be the one to kill me that day."[59]

Still, the question remains: why do armed groups choose to pursue the particular strategy of forced marriage? Their instrumental military, logistical, and sexual requirements can be met through forced labor and sexual slavery, so why do they introduce the element of conjugality? Forced marriage is a form of symbolic warfare in seeking to control female bodies and their reproductive labors, but it can also be an aspect of armed groups' political desire to "reorder" society. During the Rwandan genocide, the forcible marriage of Tutsi women to Hutu men was part of efforts to establish Hutu dominance of the nation at both micro- and macrolevels; similarly, the LRA's use of forced marriage for reproduction has been identified as part of a larger plan to "populate a new Acholi nation."[60] According to Krijn Peters, many wives were held in the RUF's bush camps—spaces where a youth underclass tried to forge a new meritocratic Sierra Leone.[61] These attempted reorderings of society were based on strictly patriarchal power structures. Marks argues that RUF laws governing gender relations were "strident perversions of pre-existing social norms," reconfigured to socially alienate women and limit their agency within marriage, building dependence on husbands and the armed group.[62]

In Somalia, al-Shabaab instituted forced and early marriage as part of the group's efforts to impose its version of shari'a. A recent Human Rights Watch report argues that these marriages were not simply the actions of individual fighters but a more organized practice by which al-Shabaab preached marriage of fighters to schoolgirls and abducted and detained girls under the group's auspices for this purpose.[63] As a seventeen-year-old boy from Mogadishu pointed out: "Usually they [al-Shabaab] were in town and when they would see girls from school they would find one, confront her, say they want to marry her. Sometimes they would go to the parents but if the parents refuse they just take her. I saw it all the time."[64] The line between forced marriages and "arranged marriages" was sometimes blurred, but it is clear that girls or families who refused marriages faced considerable reprisals: "Girls were taken at gunpoint and forced to become wives of combatants. One parent who protested was killed. One girl said she could not go and al-Shabaab shot her in the forehead in front of my class."[65]

Recent humanitarian efforts to combat rape and sexual violence in the Democratic Republic of the Congo (DRC) have highlighted that early and forced marriages among civilian populations are common in some areas.[66] Numerous accounts of sexual enslavement have been reported in Goma, Bukavu, and Uvira in the DRC, with girls and young women abducted by combatants and taken to bases in the forest where they were forced to provide sexual services and domestic labor, sometimes more than a year. But these situations were apparently not initially termed "forced marriages" in humanitarian reports.[67] It was noted that some girls joined armed groups to escape arranged marriages at home.[68] Maï-Maï forces tended to hold girls in common; other groups more frequently allocated abducted women to individuals, although the designation of these captive women as wives in a "bush marriage" did not routinely occur.[69] In these regions, rape was also widely used as a weapon of terror to maintain control over the civilian population, so perhaps the forced relationships there lacked more overtly conjugal elements and were closer to sexual slavery because they were more focused on meeting the immediate sexual, domestic, and labor requirements of armed groups, many of which appear to have had no clear political aim of ruling local populations or establishing new social orders. In contrast, former girl soldiers from the Tigrayan People's Liberation Front (TPLF) in Ethiopia have reported that rape or sexual abuse was rare and severely punished, stressing that within their units, "there was no forced sexual relationship with males. The male fighters did not force us to do anything without our interest. The male had no feeling of superiority over the female"—a situation they contrasted starkly with civilian life. Marriage and children were seen as distractions from the goal of overthrowing the Derg and were therefore rejected by the TPLF's hierarchy.[70] In this situation, a combination of Marxist-Leninist political ideology, clear military goals, and close cooperation with local communities, with the ultimate aim of controlling the nation, appear to have limited the use of sexual violence and coerced relationships within the TPLF.

Girls' experiences of conflict are shaped by wider long-term patterns of structural gender violence as well as patterns of warfare. West and Central Africa, where wartime forced marriage seems to have been most common, also have some of the world's highest rates of early marriage, with 74 percent of girls being married before the age of nineteen in the DRC and just under half of the girls in Sierra Leone and Uganda being married by age eighteen.[71] In many societies, unmarried women and unattached girls have long been regarded as a destabilizing force and a "social evil."[72] This context helped forced marriage to become a socially normalized institution. Across Africa, there are also historically high levels of domestic violence and rape.[73] In Mozambique, "rape and the use of slave-wives is rather seen by Renamo soldiers as simply the rights of access to women, and a key perk of the job, not a direct tactic of war."[74] A former girl soldier from the Sudan People's Liberation Army (SPLA) in South Sudan felt that her three "marriages" were conducted to justify and legitimate the rapes she suffered within local social and moral codes.[75] There are examples of girls joining armed groups to escape an arranged marriage or domestic sexual abuse, only to find themselves drawn into similar structures of violence within the group. "Josephine" from Masisi, DRC, stated that she chose to join the National Congress for the Defense of the People (Congrès national pour la défense du peuple, CNDP) to escape an arranged marriage. "I joined the CNDP to avoid revenge from [the man who was to be] my husband, [it] would give me protection," she recalled, but she left the group after being raped by several commanders and giving birth to a child.[76]

One question that requires further research involves the relationship between early and arranged marriage in peacetime, and forced marriage in conflict. The chapters in this volume demonstrate that "customary" practices of marriage contained varying levels of coercion and were historically highly contested, so there is no simple link between early marriage, customary marriage, and forced marriage in conflict. Vivi Stavrou notes that in Angola, girls were drafted into the Revolutionary Youth of Angola (Juventude Revolucionário de Angola, JURA), the youth wing of the National Union for the Total Independence of Angola (União Nacional para a Independência Total de Angola, UNITA), at adolescence, when it was permissible for them to be involved in regulated sexual activity and enter into marriage.[77] The Sierra Leone TRC suggested that forced marriages were customary marriages in extreme situations, but the Special Court for Sierra Leone refuted these claims, highlighting the dangers of "making straightforward links between complex social practices of arranging marriages between kin groups, international conceptualizations of forced marriages and the coercion of women into being 'bush wives.'"[78] The Special Court drew a clear distinction between the customary practice of early marriage and bush marriage, the difference lying in familial and individual consent, as well as adherence to recognized religious ceremonies sanctifying and validating the union.[79]

Although humanitarian narratives tend to stress girls' victimhood, recent academic investigations have emphasized the "constrained" or "tactical agency" that many individuals display in their navigation of wartime environments.[80] Chris Coulter notes that in Sierra Leone, "as the idiom of marriage was applied to intimate relations between men and women in the bush, perhaps sexual coercion in this context was considered by the girls and women, if not normal, then to be expected."[81] Some wives saw forced marriages as a strategy for minimizing sexual violence and thus condoned it.[82] "I wouldn't say that I was taken by force," one wife said, "I did it to save my life. He was my husband . . . we call these men our husbands. But they were not a true love. I hated this man."[83] For some girls, accepting the status of wife offered a form of limited protection:

> At the beginning I was raped daily. At least one person would come to me for sex . . . I was every man's wife. But later, one of them, an officer, had a special interest in me. He then protected me against others and never allowed others to use me. He continued to [rape] me alone and less frequently.[84]

It should be noted that women's use of the term *wife* does not necessarily denote acceptance of their status but rather its normalization.

Blurring the boundaries between consent and coercion, some former girl combatants from UNITA in Angola who were forced to become the "war wives" of elders in their units noted that marriage allowed them to avoid forced labor and marches:

> Some, when they look at the others, who are pregnant or have children, then they begin to think that if I do that then perhaps the suffering will be less because the others who are pregnant or who have children do not go anywhere. They do not go to the marches to collect food. . . . I accepted the father of my child because of that suffering.[85]

Stavrou demonstrates that sex work was regarded as a routine part of their labor during the war, but girls frequently distinguished between forced unions with elders, rape, strategic unions for protection, and free sexual relations for love:

> Well some were forced, they tell them, and from now on you must marry this man. Others are the girls themselves who decide, they see an old man, even really old, but because he has a little bit (food, clothes) and she doesn't have to go on missions, she accepts to live together with him.[86]

The duties and treatment of a wife depended on her status and that of her husband, as well as the nature and location of the armed group. One woman explained:

> On our arrival we were assigned to the wives of commanders and later given to commanders or fighters to be their bush wives. As a bush wife, my duties were to provide for him anything he requested, including sex at any time of the day. I was used as a sex slave for

each commander when they came to our camp, especially because my bush husband was not a senior commander.[87]

Forced marriage was also shaped by interfemale dynamics rather than simply by victimhood. Some marriages were polygynous, raising tensions between the elder wife and the new war wives.[88] Wives of senior officers or those who gained status as fighters themselves could "adopt" other, younger children to carry out domestic duties. The experiences of girl wives were shaped not just by luck, chance, individual agency, and their husbands' or cowives' personalities but also by the structure of the armed group and the nature of the conflict.[89] Girls' experiences of forced marriages are also shaped by their postconflict lives. Although submitting to these forced marriages was perhaps the only available strategy of survival for many of these young women, devastated communities subsequently interpret their "marriages" as signs of collaboration. As Justice Teresa Doherty stressed in her dissenting opinion in the Special Court for Sierra Leone, the crime of forced marriage is not simply the sexual violence and labor exploitation experienced by the victim but also the "mental and moral suffering" imposed by the forced conjugal status—a status that has long-term repercussions for the girls as they attempt to reintegrate into their communities, particularly in cases where they are rejected by their families or encouraged to formally marry their husbands.[90]

FORCED MARRIAGE is not a monolithic category: it varies in its instrumentality and symbolic function between different conflicts and armed groups and also by individual experiences within those groups—the experiences of a bush wife and girl soldier in the RUF are not necessarily the same as those of a young war wife within Renamo, or those abducted by Boko Haram from schools in Chibok in Northern Nigeria. More research is needed into the internal dynamics of armed groups, comparative assessments of "marriage" across different groups, and historical patterns of women's involvement in warfare in order to fully analyze the development of forced marriages as a tactic of war and as a crime of war.[91]

Different forms of sexual violence in war have varying purposes, but the logic behind forced marriage is shaped by the normalization of gender violence, sexual abuse, and the exploitation of labor in contemporary African conflicts. It facilitates instrumental gains for armed groups in terms of providing regulated sexual release for male combatants, creating internal loyalties to the group, providing logistical support and domestic duties through girl labor, creating dependence among forcibly recruited girls, social reproduction, and terrorizing civilian populations. Such factors are particularly significant for mobile, armed groups that lack strong civilian support, stable supply lines, and forms of material remuneration for the troops.

It is significant that forced marriage also seems to be more common where existing cultural norms support or allow early marriage, as young girls are more easily controlled and retained. However, sexual slavery could just as well supply these military gains, so why is the element of conjugality introduced? The enforcement of so-called marriages and the resultant creation of new family units speak to a desire to reorder society, enforcing patriarchal control and providing access to key avenues of social maturation for young, disenfranchised fighters who were controlled by older generations in peacetime. Social tensions as well as military tactics drive the practice of forced marriage. Moreover, given the way forced marriage has been presented in international humanitarian and legal debates, it is clear that a more nuanced understanding is needed in regard to both local African concepts of marriage (and consent) and local constructions of girlhood if the practice is to be effectively combated in the future.

NOTES

This title is taken from Human Rights Watch, *Shattered Lives: Sexual Violence during the Rwandan Genocide and Its Aftermath* (New York: Human Rights Watch, 1996), interview by HRW/FIDH, Birenga, March 31, 1996. Human Rights Watch and other NGO reports cited in this chapter are available online and are accessible through a search of the title.

1. Republic of Liberia, Truth and Reconciliation Commission Final Report (hereafter cited as LTRC), vol. 3, app. 2—"Children, the Conflict and the TRC Agenda," 50.

2. Sierra Leone, Truth and Reconciliation Commission Final Report (hereafter cited as SLTRC), vol. 3B, chap. 4—"Children and the Armed Conflict in Sierra Leone," 125; Jeannie Annan, Christopher Blattman, Dyan Mazurana, and Khristopher Carlson, "Civil War, Reintegration and Gender in Northern Uganda," *Journal of Conflict Resolution* 55, no. 6 (2011): 877–908.

3. The dominant legal and humanitarian narratives follow a "straight-18" position whereby all females under the age of eighteen are defined as girls. This chapter works within that framework, but I will differentiate between prepubescent girls and adolescents or youths where the evidence allows. Customary law does not recognize forced marriages.

4. Susan McKay and Dyan Mazurana, *Where Are the Girls? Girls in Fighting Forces in Northern Uganda, Sierra Leone and Mozambique—Their Lives during and after War* (Montreal: Rights and Democracy, 2004).

5. See Coalition to Stop the Use of Child Soldiers, Global Report 2008, available at http://www.childsoldiersglobalreport.org/, accessed December 19, 2011; McKay and Mazurana, *Where Are the Girls?*

6. P. W. Singer, *Children at War* (Berkeley: University of California Press, 2005), 30.

7. Adam Roberts, "The Civilian in Modern War," in *The Changing Character of War*, ed. Hew Strachan and Sibylle Scheipers (Oxford: Oxford University Press, 2011), 357–80.

8. Cynthia Enloe, *Maneuvers: The International Politics of Militarizing Women's Lives* (Berkeley: University of California Press, 2000).

9. Stathis Kalyvas, "New and Old Civil Wars: A Valid Distinction?" *World Politics* 54, no. 1 (2001): 99–118.

10. Jon Abbink, "Being Young in Africa: The Politics of Despair and Renewal," in *Vanguards or Vandals: Youth, Politics and Conflict in Africa*, ed. Jon Abbink and Ineke Van Kessel (Leiden: Brill, 2005), 1–34; Alcinda Honwana, *Child Soldiers in Africa* (Philadelphia: University of Pennsylvania Press, 2007). As children under fifteen years of age now constitute half the population in some countries, their involvement in military and civilian affairs has become increasingly significant.

11. Krijn Peters, *War and the Crisis of Youth in Sierra Leone* (Cambridge: Cambridge University Press, 2011).

12. United Nations, "Promotion and Protection of the Rights of Children: The Impact of Armed Conflict on Children—Report of the Expert of the Secretary-General, Ms. Graça Machel, Submitted Pursuant to General Assembly Resolution 48/157," A/51/306, August 26, 1996 (hereafter cited as the Machel Report).

13. Carolyn Nordstrom, *Girls and Warzones: Troubling Questions* (Uppsala: Life and Peace Institute, 1997), 5; Yvonne Keairns, *The Voices of Girl Child Soldiers: A Summary* (New York: Quaker United Nations Office, 2002); Senait Mehari, *Heart of Fire: From Child Soldier to Soul Singer* (London: Profile Books, 2006); China Keitetsi, *Child Soldier* (London: Souvenir, 2004); Faith J. H. McDonnell and Grace Akallo, *Girl Soldier: A Story of Hope for Northern Uganda's Children* (Grand Rapids, MI: Chosen Books, 2007).

14. Angela Veale, *From Child Soldier to Ex-fighter* (Pretoria: Institute for Security Studies, 2003), 25–26, 64–65; Virginia Bernal, "Equality to Die For? Women Guerrilla Fighters and Eritrea's Cultural Revolution," *Political and Legal Anthropology Review* 28, no. 2 (2000): 72–73; Harry G. West, "Girls with Guns: Narrating the Experience of War of Frelimo's 'Female Detachment,'" *Anthropological Quarterly* 73, no. 4 (2000): 180–94.

15. McKay and Mazurana, *Where Are the Girls?* 92; Human Rights Watch, "'We'll Kill You If You Cry': Sexual Violence in the Sierra Leone Conflict," *Human Rights Watch* 15, no. 1(A), January 16, 2003.

16. Myriam Denov, "Girl Soldiers and Human Rights: Lessons from Angola, Mozambique, Sierra Leone and Northern Uganda," *International Journal of Human Rights* 12, no. 5 (2008): 813.

17. See Nordstrom, *Girls and Warzones,* 51; Honwana, *Child Soldiers in Africa,* 88; Susan Shepler, "Les filles-soldats: Trajectories d'après-guerre en Sierra Leone," *Politique Africaine* 88, no. 4 (2002): 49–62; Chris Coulter, *Bush Wives and Girl Soldiers: Women's Lives through War and Peace in Sierra Leone* (Ithaca, NY: Cornell University Press, 2009).

18. Sharon Marcus, "Fighting Bodies, Fighting Words: A Theory and Politics of Rape Prevention," in *Feminists Theorize the Political,* ed. Judith Butler and Joan W. Scott (New York: Routledge, 1992), 392; Doris E. Buss, "Rethinking Rape as a Weapon of War," *Feminist Legal Studies* 17, no. 2 (2009): 288–349; Liz Kelly, "Wars against Women: Sexual Violence, Sexual Politics and the Militarized State," in *States of Conflict: Gender, Violence and Resistance,* ed. Susie Jacobs, Ruth Jacobson, and Jennifer Marchbank (London: Zed Books, 2000).

19. Philippe Ariès, *L'enfant et la vie familiale sous l'ancien régime* (Paris: Plon, 1960); Allison James, Chris Jenks, and Alan Prout, *Theorizing Childhood* (Cambridge: Polity Press, 1998); Peter N. Stearns, *Childhood in World History,* 2nd ed (London: Routledge, 2011).

20. Paula S. Fass, "Children and Globalization," *Journal of Social History* 36, no. 4 (2003): 963–77.

21. Jacqueline Bhabha, "The Child—What Sort of Human?" *PMLA* 121 (2006): 1526–35; Erica Burman, "Innocents Abroad: Western Fantasies of Childhood and the Iconography of Emergencies," *Disasters* 18, no. 3 (1994): 238–52.

22. Sharon Stephens, "Children and the Politics of Culture in Late Capitalism," in *Children and the Politics of Culture,* ed. Sharon Stephens (Princeton, NJ: Princeton University Press, 1995), 3–48.

23. David M. Rosen, *Armies of the Young: Child Soldiers in War and Terrorism* (New Brunswick, NJ: Rutgers University Press, 2005), 157.

24. There is a hypervisibility of gender and sexual violence in many accounts of conflict, although, unfortunately, such visibility has not translated into effective international intervention. See Nancy Rose Hunt, "An Acoustic Register: Tenacious Images and Congolese Scenes of Rape and Repetition," *Cultural Anthropology* 23, no. 2 (2008): 220–53.

25. See Karine Belair, "Unearthing the Customary Law Foundations of 'Forced Marriages' during Sierra Leone's Civil War: The Possible Impact of International Criminal Law on Customary Marriage and Women's Rights in Post-conflict Sierra Leone," *Columbia Journal of Gender and Law* 15 (2006): 557.

26. Lisa Alfredson, Coalition to Stop the Use of Child Soldiers, "Sexual Exploitation of Child Soldiers: An Exploration and Analysis of Global Dimensions and Trends," report published on ReliefWeb.Int, 1 January 2001.

27. Prosecutor v. Jean Paul Akayesu, ICTR-96-4-T. See Nicola Henry, *War and Rape: Law, Memory and Justice* (London: Routledge, 2010).

28. Amy Palmer, "An Evolutionary Analysis of Gender-Based War Crimes and the Continued Tolerance of 'Forced Marriage,'" *Northwestern University School of Law Journal* 7, no. 1 (2009): 133–59; Augustine S. J. Park, "'Other Inhumane Acts': Forced Marriage, Girl Soldiers and the Special Court for Sierra Leone," *Social & Legal Studies* 15, no. 3 (2006): 315–37.

29. Prosecutor v. Miroslav Kvocka et al. (Trial Judgement), ICTY-98-30/1. 30. See the Machel Report. The investigation into sexual and gender-based violence was not in the original remit for the study but was added by Machel.

31. Prosecutor v. Brima, Kamara and Kanu (AFRC case), SCSL-04-16-T, available at http://www.refworld.org/pdfid/467fba742.pdf, accessed December 15, 2015.

32. UNICEF and the NGO Working Group on the Convention of the Rights of the Child, Cape Town Principles and Best Practices, adopted at the Symposium on the Prevention of Recruitment of Children into Armed Conflict and on Demobilization and Social Reintegration of Child Soldiers in Africa, April 27–30, 1997, available at http://www.unicef.org/emergencies/files/Cape_Town_Principles(1).pdf, accessed July 16, 2013.

33. Office of the Special Representative of the Secretary-General for Children and Armed Conflict in collaboration with UNICEF, *Machel Study Ten-Year Strategic Review: Children and Conflict in a Changing World* (New York: UNICEF, 2009).

34. Human Rights Watch, *"This Old Man Can Feed Us, You Will Marry Him": Child and Forced Marriage in South Sudan* (New York: Human Rights Watch, 2013). The report was written by Agnes Odhiambo, Africa researcher in the Women's Rights Division.

35. See Annie Bunting, "'Forced Marriage' in Conflict Situations: Researching and Prosecuting Old Crimes and New Harms," *Canadian Journal of Human Rights* 1, no. 1 (2012): 165–85.

36. On conjugal order and humanitarian intervention, see Megan H. Mackenzie, *Female Soldiers in Sierra Leone: Sex, Security and Post-conflict Development* (New York: NYU Press, 2012).

37. John Laband, ed., *Daily Lives of Civilians in Wartime Africa* (Westport, CT: Greenwood, 2007); Richard J. Reid, *Warfare in African History* (Cambridge: Cambridge University Press, 2012).

38. H. M. Joko Smart, *Sierra Leone Customary Family Law* (Freetown: Fourah Bay College Bookshop, 1983), 28–29.

39. David Killingray, "Gender Issues in African Colonial Armies," in *Guardians of Empire: The Armed Forces of the Colonial Powers c. 1700–1964,* ed. David Killingray and David Omissi (Manchester: Manchester University Press, 1999), 226.

40. Elizabeth Wood, "Variation in Sexual Violence during War," *Politics & Society* 34, no. 3 (2006): 307–41; Reid, *Warfare in African History,* 7.

41. Zoe Marks, "Sexual Violence inside Rebellion: Policies and Perspectives of the Revolutionary United Front of Sierra Leone" *African Affairs* 15, no. 3 (2013): 359–79; Sophie Kramer, "Forced Marriage and the Absence of Gang-Rape: Explaining Sexual Violence by the Lord's Resistance Army in Northern Uganda," *Journal of Politics and Society* 5, no. 1 (2012): 11–49.

42. On general child recruitment, see Bernd Beber and Chris Blattman, "The Logic of Child Soldiering and Coercion," *International Organization* 67, no. 1 (2013): 65–104.

43. Vivi Stavrou, "Breaking the Silence: Girls Forcibly Involved in the Armed Struggle in Angola," Christian Children's Fund Angola Research Project (2005).

44. Marks, "Sexual Violence."

45. Ibid.

46. Jeannie Annan, Christopher Blattman, Dyan Mazurana, and Khristopher Carlson, "Women and Girls at War: 'Wives,' Mothers, and Fighters in the Lord's Resistance Army," working paper, 2009.

47. Ibid., 12; Elizabeth Laruni, "From the Village to Entebbe: The Political Mobilization of Acholi Identity, c. 1950–85" (PhD diss., University of Exeter, 2014).

48. See Tim Allen and Koen Vlassenroot, eds., *The Lord's Resistance Army: Myth and Reality* (London: Zed Books, 2012); Sverker Finnström, *Living with Bad Surroundings: War, History and Everyday Moments in Northern Uganda* (Durham, NC: Duke University Press, 2008).

49. Annan et al., "Civil War," 7.

50. Kramer, "Forced Marriage."

51. Annan et al., "Civil War," 8.

52. See Loretta Elizabeth Bass, *Child Labor in Sub-Saharan Africa* (Boulder, CO: Lynne Rienner, 2004); Benjamin N. Lawrance and Richard L. Roberts, eds., *Trafficking in Slavery's Wake: Law and the Experience of Women and Children in Africa* (Athens: Ohio University Press, 2012).

53. Meredith Turshen, "The Political Economy of Rape: An Analysis of Systematic Rape and Sexual Abuse of Women during Armed Conflict in Africa," in *Victims, Perpetrators or Actors? Gender, Armed Conflict and Political Violence,* ed. Caroline O. Moser and Fiona C. Clark (London: Zed Books, 2001), 55–68.

54. Esther Mokuwa, Maarten Voors, Erwin Bulte, and Paul Richards, "Peasant Grievance and Insurgency: Judicial Serfdom as a Driver of Conflict," *African Affairs* 110, no. 440 (2011): 343.

55. Human Rights Watch, *Shattered Lives.*

56. Turshen, "Political Economy of Rape," 55–56.

57. Human Rights Watch, *Shattered Lives,* interview by HRW/FIDH, Rusatira, 23 March 1996.

58. McDonnell and Akallo, *Girl Soldier,* 110.

59. Ibid., 112.

60. Civil Society Organisations for Peace in Northern Uganda, *Nowhere to Hide: Humanitarian Protection Threats in Northern Uganda* (Kampala: Civil Society Organisations for Peace in Northern Uganda,), 5.

61. Krijn Peters, *War and the Crisis of Youth in Sierra Leone* (Cambridge: Cambridge University Press, 2011).

62. Marks, "Sexual Violence."

63. Human Rights Watch, *No Place for Children: Child Recruitment, Forced Marriage and Attacks on Schools in Somalia* (New York: Human Rights Watch, 2012). The report was written by Laetitia Bader, Zama Coursen-Neff, and Tirana Hassan.

64. Ibid.,, interview with "Baashi M.," June 4, 2011.

65. Ibid., interview with "Dahnay K.," June 3, 2011.

66. UN Office of the High Commissioner for Human Rights, *Report of the Panel on Remedies and Reparations for Victims of Sexual Violence in the Democratic Republic*

of Congo to the High Commissioner for Human Rights, March 2011, available at http://www.refworld.org/docid/4d708ae32.html, accessed December 15, 2015.

67. See Human Rights Watch, *The War within the War: Sexual Violence against Women and Girls in Eastern Congo* (New York: Human Rights Watch, 2002), report written by Joanne Csete and Juliane Kippenberg. Local accounts have spoken of forced marriage after this date; many thanks to Annie Bunting for this information.

68. Austrian Centre for Country of Origin and Asylum Research and Documentation (ACCORD), *Democratic Republic of the Congo: 1) Situation of Persons Fleeing Forced Marriages; 2) Situation of Victims of Sexual and Gender-Based Violence; 3) Situation of Street Children in Kinshasa,* October 3, 2011, a-7764, available at http://www.refworld.org/docid/4ea14f372.html, accessed December 15, 2015.

69. Human Rights Watch, *War within the War,* 60.

70. Veale, *From Girl Soldier to Ex-fighter,* 32.

71. Judith-Ann Walker, "Early Marriage in Africa—Trends, Harmful Effects and Interventions," *African Journal of Reproductive Health* 16, no. 2 (2012): 231–40.

72. See Mariane C. Ferme, *The Underneath of Things: Violence, History, and the Everyday in Sierra Leone* (Berkeley: University of California Press, 2001), 81–111.

73. See Richard L. Roberts, Elizabeth Thornberry, and Emily S. Burrill, eds., *Domestic Violence in Africa: Historical and Contemporary Perspectives* (Athens: Ohio University Press, 2010).

74. Kenneth Wilson, "Cults of Violence and Counter Violence in Mozambique," *Journal of Southern African Studies* 18, no. 3 (1992): 536.

75. "Rose," cited in Christine Ryan, *Children of War: Child Soldiers as Victims and Participants in the Sudan Civil War* (London: I. B. Tauris, 2012), 75.

76. Institute for War and Peace Reporting, "Grim Prospects of DRC's Female Child Soldiers," April 28, 2011, https://iwpr.net/global-voices/grim-prospects-drcs-female-child-soldiers, accessed December 15, 2015.

77. Stavrou, *Breaking the Silence,* 87.

78. SLTRC, vol. 3B, chap. 4, 164.

79. *AFRC Case,* SCSL-04-16-T, concurring and partly dissenting opinions, 574–96.

80. Honwana, *Child Soldiers in Africa;* Mark Drumbl, *Reimagining Child Soldiers in International Law and Policy* (Oxford: Oxford University Press, 2012).

81. Coulter, *Bush Wives and Girl Soldiers,* 227.

82. Marks, "Sexual Violence."

83. Human Rights Watch, *Shattered Lives,* interview in Shyanda commune, Butare prefecture, April 2, 1996.

84. Myriam Denov and Richard MacLure, "Engaging the Voices of Girls in the Aftermath of Sierra Leone's Conflict: Experiences and Perspectives in a Culture of Violence," *Anthropologica* 48, no. 1 (2006): 77.

85. Stavrou, *Breaking the Silence,* interview EM2, Huambo, 38.

86. Ibid., interview EM16, Luanda, 47.

87. SLTRC, vol. 4, Children and Armed Conflict, TRC confidential statement recorded in Moyamba Town, Kaiyamba Chiefdom, June 14, 2003.

88. Stavrou, *Breaking the Silence,* 47.

89. Marks, "Sexual Violence."

90. *AFRC* Case, SCSL-04-16-T, Doherty dissenting opinion, 592, para. 52.

91. A lack of perpetrators' voices also limits current analyses of sexual violence. See Maria Eriksson Baaz and Maria Stern, "Why Do Soldiers Rape? Masculinity, Violence and Sexuality in the Armed Forces of the Congo," *International Studies Quarterly* 53, no. 2 (2009): 495–518.

Historicizing Social Justice and the
Longue Durée of Forced Marriage

EMILY S. BURRILL

At the time of this publication, we find ourselves working with a height-ened awareness of scholarly topics that elicit stressful affective and psy-chological responses from our readers and students, particularly topics dealing with trauma. Such topics are often referred to as trauma stressors or trauma triggers. The topic of forced marriage, like human trafficking and sexual violence, is a potential trigger. This increased sensitivity to trig-gers partially reflects the scholarly community's growing awareness of the silencing and destructive power that academic topics exploring suffering and violence may have on an audience. As a result, the trigger that ap-pears in the classroom or on the written page often comes with a warning, preparing the reader or student to look away or disengage as an act of self-protection or even self-preservation. This is a good thing, to my mind. But triggers and their attendant warnings also require some of us to ap-proach and engage, the way some might rush into a fire, in order to make sense of trauma, often with an eye toward preventing the trauma from occurring again. This is an act of scholarly social justice. Similarly, when we take a long view of trauma in society, we see that actors emerge along the historical landscape who may have "named the problem" and situated it within a milieu, identifying causes and suggesting correctives. Tracing such engagements with trauma over time tells us something about how actors and institutions perceived different forms of inequality as problems to be solved, rather than elements of normative social order. This is the work of historicizing social justice. What makes this interdisciplinary volume so valuable is that it does both: it performs social justice in a scholarly realm, while also historicizing social justice as an enduring yet changing phenomenon. Forced marriage on the African continent is thus taken up as something to be situated and understood as a present-day predicament, but it is also a unit of analysis that helps us understand long-standing trends in gender-based inequality and the uses and abuses of conjugality.

NO DISCRETE MOMENTS: THE *LONGUE DURÉE* OF FORCED MARRIAGE

Far too often, stories that trigger, such as stories about forced marriage, are read as spectacular narratives or episodes that stand apart from what is normal or socially sanctioned. This spectacular quality pulls readers and listeners in, but it also suggests that the narrative stands alone, untethered to any enduring dynamic or normative pattern. In this way, the problem at the core of the spectacular story might be seen as exceptional, in a social sense ("we don't do this"), a historical sense ("this has never happened before" or "this is unprecedented"), or both. One might be inclined, for example, to isolate stories such as the 2014 Boko Haram abduction of schoolgirls in Chibok, Nigeria, for the declared purpose of forced marriage as an anomaly or a singular episode, something that cannot be explained by structural or processual analysis. The result is that stories such as these become spectacles without a history, moments that garner attention but eventually drift away as outliers. It can therefore be difficult to situate such predicaments within the fabric of humanity, so to speak, and apply analytical and theoretical lenses in order to understand how conditions develop to make such things possible. This is a challenge familiar to social justice scholars and to feminist historians in particular.[1]

Literary scholar Debali Mookerjea-Leonard, in her analysis of scholarship on the wide-scale gendered violence that occurred in the aftermath of the Partition of India and Pakistan, makes a case for the use of a *longue durée* (long term) approach to understanding episodes of gendered and sexual violence. The longue durée, an approach to understanding historical change offered by French historians of the Annales school (otherwise known as Annalistes), de-emphasizes event-based history in favor of long-term structural change. Annalistes maintained that such a focal

EMILY S. BURRILL

point would shine light on old attitudes and resistant frameworks, revealing sites of conservation and enduring mores. Inspired by this approach, Mookerjea-Leonard shows that tracing legislative reform on the status of women over time throughout India's colonial history reveals that laws on the status of Indian women (often anchored to "spectacular" problems, such as widow burning and child brides) were not "discrete moments" but rather points on a continuum that, when taken together, tell us much more about "women's bodies as sites for discourse [and] . . . also sites of patriarchal constraint and violence" in the struggle for colonial and nationalist narratives and anticolonial resistance.[2] The longue durée analytic, then, flies in the face of the spectacle without a history, and it presses us to see the entrenched and even mundane elements of the stories that trigger.

I find Mookerjea-Leonard's suggestion that there is a longue durée of gender-based oppression useful because it emphasizes the fact that power has a practice that changes over time—it is both entrenched and socially constructed, on the one hand, and contingent, on the other. Here, I propose that there is a longue durée of forced marriage, a continuum of plotted episodes that are linked and embedded in their own social milieu. The longue durée of forced marriage that we see in this particular volume is not all that long in Braudelian terms, but it helps us sketch out transformations over time that point to slowly evolving structures. Moreover, it indicates an even longer-term history that extends further back than the contributions to this volume suggest. This challenges the idea that African history over the past two hundred years was a period of accelerated changes—in many ways, it was, but in other ways, perhaps it was not.

Uneven relationships of obligation and exchange underpinned marriage in all of the African case studies examined here. This interwoven thread holds many of the observations in this book together. It is in this changing yet enduring dynamic of obligation and exchange where we locate forced marriage. This is not specific to African marriages, though—arguably, it is something that describes the nature of global marriage in broader historical perspective, and more to the point, it describes one of the cornerstones of patriarchy. However, in this volume some chapters make very strong cases for the contextual specificity of the longue durée of forced marriage at work. For example, Ann McDougall argues that present-day discussions about the causes of forced marriage in Mauritania fail to fully acknowledge the deeper history of concubinage that connected the families of *bizan* (masters) and *hratani* (freed slaves). Unraveling family histories in Mauritania reveals a localized Islamic legal interpretation of obligation and uneven exchange that perpetuated both poverty among hratani families and a notion of paternalistic privilege and obligation to provide for former slave families. This dynamic promotes the persistence of forcible marriage that stems from a longer history of concubinage.

One factor that sets the uneven relationships of obligation and exchange in marriage apart in this book is the shared historical experience of European colonization. As many of the chapters show, the early colonial encounter troubled practices of marriage and sexuality in Africa, in part because of the trappings of consent. In addressing consent, I am not talking about agreement in the simplest terms—certainly, agreement and mutual understanding underpinned exchange and marital arrangements in a number of different legal and customary frameworks—but rather, the specific post-Enlightenment, new liberal category of consent that applied to legal and political action and philosophy. Here, consent was tied to the sovereignty of the individual and the disavowal of preordained rights to governance and rule. It was not that European powers fully upheld this philosophical and political ideal in the colonies (or in the metropole, for that matter), but that it determined how regimes would measure African societies. However, at times colonial regimes themselves relied upon new forms of forced labor, though this was when the colonial regimes themselves were not necessarily invested in promoting a notion of democratic ideals at home. As we see in Francesca Declich's chapter, forced marriage emerged as an element of the Italian empire in Somaliland, arguably giving men a certain type of freedom—but a freedom tied to labor in a colonial-capitalist context. Mariane Ferme describes how long histories of slave-based marriage in Mende societies in present-day Sierra Leone reveal a background of nonconsensual marriage that persisted well into the colonial period, which partially accounts for the emergence of "bush wives" in the Sierra Leonean civil war in the early 1990s. In most colonial contexts, however, consent was a bureaucratic and ideological guidepost for critiquing African masculinities as either too childlike or too brutish; it also became a way to measure the degree to which African women were in need of rescue.

As the chapters in this book show, the evidence of forced marriage was quite often the spectacular story, which emerged from the record in some form of first-person testimony (oral narrative, life history, or court testimony) or as an outsider's account of an observed event (ethnography,

EMILY S. BURRILL

travelogue, or journalistic reporting). In this sense, we still see the spectacular story emerging from both the historical record and the present-day accounts. What each of the contributions in this book show us is that social justice actors frequently tried to make sense of these stories of trauma and wrongdoing by situating them within a larger social problem to be solved or addressed through political negotiation, legislative reform, or direct intervention. However, this is not to argue that social justice always comes from a position of unadulterated altruism. Certainly, much of what we see is the development of justice within the context of colonial paternalism and maternalism—social justice as the white woman's and white man's burden. This is not specific to Africa; for instance, this European, liberal dream of consent was at the core of what Gayatri Spivak was talking about when she wrote that in colonialism in India, "white men are saving the brown women from brown men."[3] We can thus understand consent as a defining tool of gender making and marriage reform of the nineteenth and twentieth centuries.[4]

In historicizing social justice with an eye for long-term trends, the chapters in this edited volume sketch out a framework for an epochal history not only of forced marriage as practice but also of the social justice that developed around the practice of forced marriage. Though the book itself is organized in three parts, all of which correspond to a chronological order, there are also thematic "ages" that emerge in the history of social justice on forced marriage in colonial and postcolonial Africa: an Age of Contract that bleeds into—and overlaps with—an Age of Consent and ultimately an Age of Convention. This is not to argue for a whiggish or teleological interpretation of the history of forced marriage; rather, it is to suggest that there is a transformational history of a debate that emerges in the history of forced marriage. Arguably, these ages are not monolithic, and in fact, they have blurred edges. This is particularly the case when we consider the relationship between consent and contract. However, these ages tell us something about how the political stakes of forced marriage changed over time and how they were often tied to visions for colonial statecraft, postcolonial sovereignty, and present-day membership in a human rights community—the last of which is unfolding within a postcolonial context as well.

Despite the fact that bridewealth was regarded as problematic by early colonial administrators in French and British colonial Africa, colonial administrators at times privileged marriages based on bridewealth exchange over other forms of marriage. In my own work on the French Soudan in French West Africa, I discuss the Senufo practice of exchange marriage, which involved two families exchanging girls or young women from their families for marriage to men in the opposing families. This type of local marriage fell under heavy scrutiny in the early colonial period. The benefit of exchange marriage for Senufo families was that it tied them together in social and familial bonds and eliminated the exchange of labor or material bridewealth. However, in late 1905 the commandant in Sikasso, within the colony of the French Soudan, recommended that this practice be eradicated and that Senufo families should instead "pay a bridewealth in currency, and renounce this practice." He further stated that "such practice is sensitive, and in fact touches upon political issues as well."[5] Attempting to shift the practice of exchange marriage touched upon political issues because administrators risked undermining relationships with local men of authority by potentially destabilizing a man's wealth in people by emphasizing the value of material wealth and currency. Interfamilial relationships of obligation and exchange were based on a certain economy of marriage, and changing the currency of that economy risked upending the flow of power and resources. Administrators on the ground understood this, but they were also keen on attending to a broader politics of the civilizing mission, which rested on both respecting local practice and eradicating practices that were "contrary to civilization," as Richard Roberts's chapter explains. This was a concern in French colonial contexts and in British colonial contexts as well.

Early forms of social justice, then, attempted to disaggregate bridewealth-based marriages from non-bridewealth-based marriages. So, even though ambiguity existed around the exchange of bridewealth in early colonial Africa, it was more desirable than other forms of marriage rooted in customary practice—such as sister exchange; *isinmo*, or the forcible claiming of a woman, as we see in Olatunji Ojo's chapter; and, as Elizabeth Thornberry shows us later in the volume, *ukuthwala*, or bride abduction. This was because bridewealth could be standardized and formalized so that it appeared to be a contractual agreement. In this way, we see the Age of Contract emerging as a foundational stage of social justice and colonial marriagecraft in Africa.

In part 1 of the volume, entitled "Colonial Struggles," the authors all address a common confusion that troubled colonial administrators and court assessors in the initial years of the colonial encounter in Africa. In the early twentieth century throughout different parts of colonial Africa, administrators were concerned about bridewealth: they were unsure of whether or not they were observing the sale of young women and girls or if such transactions associated with marriage were rooted in the consent of the individual woman in question. In chapter 3, Brett Shadle explores this when he shows us how debates over early marriage in colonial Kenya—although they did not yield legislative outcomes—tell historians something about the effort to define early marriage in the first place. Shadle argues that even though colonial lawmakers and politicians were hesitant to interfere in matters of African marital customs, he can track a "language of girlhood" developing in the archive, which revealed a shifting consciousness concerning acceptable marriage and ideas of force. Early marriage was identified as a problem to be solved beginning in the 1920s, but by 1950, it was apparent that there was no clear sense of how early was too early. Of the many different elements that contributed to the construction of a notion of early marriage, one involved the question of whether or not a girl could consent. Ability to consent was determined by a few things: not only age and ability to reason in a mature way but also the obligation of a girl or woman to uphold her end of a marriage agreement when significant resources had been given to her family as gifts tied to her transfer to a new household in marriage. Here is where we see a linked concern over bridewealth exchange and forced marriage. Indeed, what the part 1 chapters by Roberts, Shadle, Ojo, and Declich show us is that quite often, discussions of the nature of bridewealth developed alongside questions about whether or not a marriage was forced or arranged. That is, arranged marriages, particularly those brokered while the betrothed woman was still a young girl or a baby, reflected the interests and desires of the two families rather than the marital choices of the girl herself, apart from her family. In many ways, it was this lack of clarity over the difference between marriage by force and marriage by arrangement that animated early social justice efforts to codify marriage practices, including the transactions that underpinned bridewealth and gift giving, or prestation. Obligation between families—that is, the cultivation of social indebtedness—is what ensured social harmony, which was often manifested in arranged marriages. The social justice effort that we see in these four chapters rested on the predicament of establishing consent, while at the same time maintaining customary practices and values within indigenous societies. In this way, we see the Age of Consent emerging in the history of forced marriage.

The Age of Convention unfolded in the late colonial period, marking the emergence of a self-conscious human rights community that is dependent upon state membership but that also sees itself as a watchdog or gatekeeper for rogue or compliant members. The Age of Convention emerged from the Age of Consent, and this is no better illustrated than in the 1962–64 United Nations Convention on Consent to Marriage. As I have written elsewhere, it is not a coincidence that the Convention on Consent to Marriage was ratified on the heels of postcolonial independence for the majority of African states. Postcolonial sovereignty and membership in the international community were measured in part by a state's investment in liberal marriage forms and the role that consent-based marriages would play in defining a postcolonial citizenry, at the very least in ideological terms.[6] African states that are signatories to international conventions at times integrate certain ideals of postcolonial era conventions into their constitutions. Some of the chapters in this volume show us how the 1979 Convention on the Elimination of All Forms of Discrimination against Women (CEDAW) and the 1990 Convention on the Rights of the Child have been particularly influential on postcolonial state constitutions. Bala Saho explores how the Gambian Constitution and the Domestic Violence Bill reflect some of the core values of consent, self-determination, and freedom from gender-based discrimination that stemmed from these conventions, but he also points out that there are limits to the effectiveness of such instruments and language. All of these documents emphasize the enduring importance of custom, which, Saho argues, becomes a legal and ideological loophole that allows for forced marriage. However, what is encouraging to Saho is the fact that many local women's and human rights groups in Gambia have successfully incorporated the language of international rights as we know it through conventions in local action—what Sally Engle Merry refers to as the vernacularization of rights and justice.[7]

However, just as possibilities emerge in the Age of Convention, there are also limitations to both the concept of the convention and the convention's reach. Benjamin Lawrance and Charlotte Walker-Said, in their chapter, point out that the 1951 Refugee Convention and the 1967 Protocol do not include gender as a category of persecution, and there is no precedent for using forced marriage as an example of persecution that qualifies a person for refugee status. As a result, complainants are required to repackage their own spectacular stories in such a way that new stories of trauma emerge that adhere to the standards of refugee conventions and asylum

EMILY S. BURRILL

qualifications. In this way, the promotion of standardization and best practices—and worst practices—in marriage defines the Age of Convention, largely as an effort to identify and eradicate abuse—a social justice move, arguably—but it also creates the grounds for the erasure of intimate and individual experiences of forced marriage, which is a new layer of trauma altogether. As a result, some policy advocates and scholars, such as Lawrance and Walker-Said, argue for the creation of a new category of persecution that highlights "networked obligations," to be applied in asylum cases for victims of both forced marriage and violent homophobia. The emphasis on networked obligations in contemporary human rights laws and conventions brings us back to the longue durée of forced marriage: what policy workers and social justice advocates in cases of forced marriage need today is an understanding of the deeply entrenched social practices of exchange and obligation that underpin marriage. As Muadi Mukenge notes in her chapter, "some programs" initiated to combat early marriage "may change behavior without necessarily changing minds."

Political, social, and economic changes come with the Age of Convention and result, paradoxically, in new forms of forced marriage. Stacey Hynd describes how forced marriage in contemporary conflict zones, especially Sierra Leone and northern Uganda, form a central part of a militarized strategy of social control and discipline of young—and often forcibly conscripted—soldiers. Here, then, we see a deliberate strategy on the part of some warlords to draw on older connections between forced marriage and militarism. Indeed, the battles of colonial conquest throughout Africa—a period that defined the Janus face of the Age of Consent in the history of social justice outlined here—were fought on the backs of forcibly conscripted African soldiers and the women who accompanied them in conjugal arrangements.[8] The rise of so-called bush wives and forced marriage in militarized zones within Africa is modern and postcolonial, but it is also anchored in a longue durée structure of gender-based oppression and militarization, manifest in forced marriage. In a different iteration of this longue durée, Judith-Ann Walker writes of the 2011–13 state-sanctioned mass marriage program in Kano, Nigeria, an effort deployed ostensibly for the protection of poor and unmarried girls and women. The Kano case was framed as a stabilizing reform, with marriage serving as a cornerstone of social harmony, but it was widely criticized by local Islamic authorities as a perversion of marriage. Here, we see men of influence engaged in a struggle over the meaning of marriage and the deployment of righteous paternalism. The Kano case of mass marriages emerged within the context of the Age of Convention, and it is therefore another example of the limitations of the top-down convention approach to social justice efforts to combat forced marriage.

In returning to Mookerjea-Leonard's analysis, we are reminded that women's bodies occupy the discursive and physical sites of patriarchal constraint and violence, factors that mark nationalist struggles and state-craft. It is here that intervention is critical: contested political transformation and struggles over material and human resources almost invariably accompany forcible marriage. Critical engagements with the past will aid in the creation of new policy categories that acknowledge the cultural embeddedness of marriage, as well as the ways forced marriage emerges from other types of debts and obligations.

NOTES

1. See, in particular, Judith M. Bennett, *History Matters: Patriarchy and the Challenge of Feminism* (Philadelphia: University of Pennsylvania Press, 2007).

2. Debali Mookerjea-Leonard, "Quarantined: Women and the Partition," *Comparative Studies of South Asia, Africa, and the Middle East* 24, no. 1 (2004): 35.

3. Gayatri Spivak, "Can the Subaltern Speak?" in *Marxism and the Interpretation of Culture,* ed. Cary Nelson and Lawrance Grossberg (London: Macmillan, 1988), 271–313. And it is also important to note the context in which Spivak wrote this now-famous truism: a critical assessment of the published literature and colonial archive on *sati,* or widow burning, in India. Spivak's 1988 observations inform Mookerjea-Leonard's point, cited earlier in this essay.

4. I address this to a further extent in a French colonial and West African context in Emily S. Burrill, *States of Marriage: Gender, Justice, and Rights in Colonial Mali* (Athens: Ohio University Press, 2015). For a thoroughgoing analysis of consent as a legal category in a British colonial context, see Elizabeth Thornberry, "Colonialism and Consent: Rape in South Africa's Eastern Cape, 1847–1902" (PhD diss., Stanford University, 2011).

5. "Justice indigène, troisième trimestre," Cercle de Sikasso, 1905, Archives Nationales du Mali (Bamako, Mali), Fonds Anciens (FA), 2M 93.

6. Burrill, *States,* 185.

7. Sally Engle Merry, "Transnational Human Rights and Local Activism: Mapping the Middle," *American Anthropologist* 108, no. 1 (2006): 38–51.

8. Sarah Zimmerman, "*Mesdames Tirailleurs* and Indirect Clients: West African Women and the French Colonial Army," *International Journal of African Historical Studies* 44, no. 2 (2011): 299–322.

About the Contributors

Annie Bunting is Associate Professor in the Law and Society program at York University in Toronto and teaches in the areas of social justice and human rights. She is the author of numerous articles in *Social and Legal Studies, Journal of Law and Society,* and *Canadian Journal of Women and the Law* and of chapters in various book collections. She has served on the editorial boards of *Law and Social Inquiry, Transnational Human Rights Review,* and the *Muslim World Journal of Human Rights.*

Emily S. Burrill is Associate Professor of Women's and Gender Studies and History and Director of the African Studies Center at the University of North Carolina, Chapel Hill. She is the author of *States of Marriage: Gender, Justice, and Rights in Colonial Mali* (Ohio University Press, 2015) and the coeditor of *Domestic Violence and the Law in Colonial and Postcolonial Africa* (Ohio University Press, 2010), with Richard L. Roberts and Elizabeth Thornberry.

Doris Buss is Professor of Law at Carleton University and teaches international law and human rights, women's rights, global social movements, and feminist theory. She is author (with Didi Herman) of *Globalizing Family Values: The International Politics of the Christian Right* (University of Minnesota Press, 2003), coeditor (with Ambreena Manji) of *International Law: Modern Feminist Approaches* (Hart, 2005), and coeditor (with Joanne Lebert, Blair Rutherford, and Donna Sharkey) of *Sexual Violence in Conflict and Post-conflict Societies: International Agendas and African Contexts* (Routledge, 2014).

Francesca Declich is Associate Professor of Socio-Cultural Anthropology in the Department of International Studies at the University of Urbino Carlo Bo. She researches and teaches refugee studies, Western Indian Ocean peoples, and the relationship between narrative and identity. She is the author of numerous articles and book chapters, and has published three books, among them *Sul genere dei diritti umani. Riflessioni sull'impunità dei crimini contro le donne: Il ruolo della Corte Criminale Internazionale* (Il Paese delle Donne, Roma, 2000).

Mariane C. Ferme is Associate Professor of Anthropology at the University of California Berkeley. Her research focuses on materiality and everyday life in rural Sierra Leone, the political imagination, and humanitarian institutions and practices, ranging from war crimes prosecution at the Special Court for Sierra Leone to the Ebola epidemic. She is author of *The Underneath of Things* (University of California Press, 2001). She is completing a book on the 1991–2002 civil war that reimagines figures and sites of the political. Her work has appeared in *Cahiers d'Études Africaines, Politique Africaine, Anthropological Quarterly, Humanity: An International Journal of Human Rights,* and in various edited volumes.

Stacey Hynd is Senior Lecturer in the Department of History at the University of Exeter. Her work explores the histories of law, crime, and punishment in Africa, particularly capital punishment in British Africa and criminal law in the British Empire and the Judicial Committee of the Privy Council. Her forthcoming book is entitled *Imperial Gallows: Capital Punishment, Violence and Colonial Rule in British Africa, c. 1908–68.*

Benjamin N. Lawrance is the Hon. Barber B. Conable, Jr. Endowed Professor of International Studies, and Professor of History and Anthropology at the Rochester Institute of Technology. He has published ten books, including *Amistad's Orphans: An Atlantic Story of Children, Slavery, and Smuggling* (Yale University Press, 2014). *African Asylum at a Crossroads,* coedited with Iris Berger, Tricia Hepner Redeker, Joanna T. Tague, and Meredith Terretta (Ohio University Press, 2015), examined asylum, refugee issues, and expert testimony, and *Trafficking in Slavery's Wake* (Ohio University Press, 2012), coedited with Richard L. Roberts, explored contemporary trafficking in women and children in Africa.

E. Ann McDougall is Professor of History and the founding director of the Middle East and African Studies Program at the University of Alberta. She is author of over fifty articles and book chapters on the social and economic history of the Moroccan and Mauritanian Sahara. Her recent research is a comparative study of *haratine.* In Morocco, they are client-cultivators and self-employed small-scale merchants; in Mauritania, they mostly self-identify as former slaves or descendants thereof. An edited collection from this project, *The Invisible People*, is under review with Karthala Press.

Muadi Mukenge is Program Director for Sub-Saharan Africa at Global Fund for Women. Her professional and education background is in women's health, African politics, and economic development. She has served on the boards of the African Studies Association and New Field Foundation. She is the author of articles and book chapters on women's rights and African development and is active in Congolese and Africa-focused advocacy groups.

Olatunji Ojo is Associate Professor of History at Brock University, where he teaches African, slavery, economic, and women's history. His research interests include slavery, ethnicity and identity formation, religion, and gender, and center on the history of social and economic change. He has published essays in the *Journal of African History, African Economic History*, the *International Journal of African Historical Studies*, and *History in Africa*.

Richard L. Roberts is the Frances and Charles Field Professor of History and Ford Dorsey Director of the Center for African Studies at Stanford University. He is the author of twelve books, including *Litigants and Households: African Disputes and Colonial Courts in the French Soudan, 1895–1912* (Heinemann, 2005), *Two Worlds of Cotton: Colonialism and the Regional Economy in the French Soudan, 1800–1946* (Stanford University Press, 1996), and *Law in Colonial Africa* (Heinemann, 1991), with Kristin Mann.

Bala Saho is Assistant Professor of African History at the University of Oklahoma. He is currently working on a book exploring the legal and judicial traditions and practices in colonial Gambia. He was previously the Director General of the National Centre for Arts and Culture in the Gambia, and Director of the Oral History Archive.

Brett L. Shadle is Associate Professor of African History at Virginia Tech. His current research is on the history of refugees in Africa. He has published two books, *"Girl Cases": Marriage and Colonialism in Gusiiland, Kenya, 1890–1970* (Heinemann, 2006), and *The Souls of White Folk: White Settlers in Kenya, 1900–1920s* (Manchester University Press, 2015).

Elizabeth Thornberry is Assistant Professor of African History at Hobart and William Smith Colleges, where is she affiliated with the Department of Women's Studies and the Program in Africana Studies. She is also an affiliated researcher with the Centre for Law and Society at the University of Cape Town. Her work focuses on the history of gender, sexuality and the law in Southern Africa, comparative women's history, the history of British colonialism, and gender and development in postcolonial Africa. Her new book analyzes changing conceptions of sexual violence in South Africa's nineteenth-century Eastern Cape. She is the coeditor of *Domestic Violence and the Law in Colonial and Postcolonial Africa* (Ohio University Press, 2010), with Richard L. Roberts and Emily S. Burrill.

Judith-Ann Walker is a nonresident fellow at the Brookings Institution, and a development practitioner with nineteen years' experience working in Nigeria, where she supports several international development programs as an independent advisor and evaluator. She is a founding member and the current coordinator of the indigenous nonprofit, the development Research and Projects Centre (dRPC). She is the author of *Development Administration: Women's Education and Industrialization* (Palgrave, 2005) and *Why Ending Child Marriage Needs to Be an Education Goal* (Brookings Institution Press, 2013).

Charlotte Walker-Said is Assistant Professor of Africana Studies at John Jay College of Criminal Justice, City University of New York. Her work explores transnational Christianity, gender politics, family law, and human rights in Africa. She is the coeditor of *Corporate Social Responsibility? Human Rights in the New Global Economy* (University of Chicago Press, 2015) with John D. Kelly.

Index

abduction: by Boko Haram, 83, 305, 314; as custom, 14, 26, 31, 71, 137–38, 140, 142, 147, 149, 150, 318; forced, 240; in Gambia, 185; of girls, 11, 13, 295, 298, 314; raids for, 69; rescue from, 286; in Somalia, 114–15; in South Africa, 137; wartime, 11, 242, 299, 301–2. *See also* kidnapping; *ukuthwala*
abolitionism, 73
abortion complications, 285
Abubakar, Animu, 258
abusers, controlling behavior of 24. *See also* domestic violence
activism and activists: antislavery, 3, 4; feminist, 234; on forced marriage, 19, 90–91, 93, 154, 200, 253; gender equity, 2; human rights, 20, 28, 167, 183, 287; South African, 139; women's rights, 137, 183, 192, 289
adultery, 77, 79, 240; woman damage, 299
adulthood, 103, 104n2
advocacy and advocates: asylum, 201, 206, 321; child rights, 269, 271; community-based, 287–88; early and forced marriage, 1, 3, 5, 12, 29, 31, 269–70, 273, 275–76, 283; gender equity, 29, 189; on harmful and traditional practices, 281; national and regional, 288–89; on women, 281, 285–86, 288–89
AFRC. *See* Armed Forces Revolutionary Council (AFRC) of Sierra Leone
Africa: colonial conquest of, 321; early and forced marriage in, 271–72; postcolonial, 2, 17, 19, 27, 34, 165–66, 199, 293, 317, 320–21; social practices in, 43. *See also* Central Africa, map; East Africa, map; Southern Africa, map; sub-Saharan Africa; West Africa; *individual African countries by name*
African Charter on Human and People's Rights, 6–7, 182, 252

African Charter on the Rights and Welfare of the Child, 252, 273
African Union, 6, 287–88
African Union Protocol on the Rights of Women in Africa, 6–7, 252, 273, 288
African Women's Decade (AWD), 287, 289
age of consent, 4, 20, 22, 25, 26, 32, 65, 73, 75, 91–93, 95, 104n11, 180–82, 190, 193, 274; in Nigeria, 83. *See also* consent to marriage
age of contract, 317–18
age of convention, 317, 320–22
age of majority, 20, 167
age of marriage/marriageable age, 17, 30, 75–76, 84n5, 92–94, 104n11, 104n14, 140, 183, 190, 203, 250, 254, 263, 270, 273, 284; arguments against setting, 95–96; attempt to determine, 103; in Kenya, 89; legal, 273; minimum age, 6–7, 44
age of maturity, 6
age of reason, 20, 60
agency, 37n47, 227: and forced marriage, 23, 201, 211, 227, 234; of girls, 23, 49, 59, 248, 305; individual, 17, 21, 237, 305; of refugees, 201; of women, 60, 119, 248, 301
Ahmed, Ibrahim Datti, 254
AIDS. *See* HIV/AIDS
Aissatou (Cameroonian asylum seeker), 205–7
Akallo, Grace, 300
Akayesu case, 295
Alberti, Ludwig, 144
Al-Hadrami (Mauritanian elder), 159, 160, 162, 164, 166
Ali (asylum seeker from Ghana), 215–17
All Nigerian Peoples Party (ANPP), 257
Allain, Jean, 2, 4
Allman, Jean, 78, 83
al-Shabaab, 301
Ama-Xosa, The (Soga), 146

Angola, 296, 298, 303, 304
Anitha, Sundari, 190, 253
Annales school (Annalistes), 314
anthropologists and anthropology, 2, 3, 18, 45, 56, 76, 109, 167, 228
Anti-Slavery International, 5
antislavery laws and policies, 13, 32, 72–73
antitrafficking programs, 283
Appeals Chamber of the Special Court for Sierra Leone (SCSL), 7, 43. *See also* Special Court for Sierra Leone (SCSL)
Armed Forces Revolutionary Council (AFRC) of Sierra Leone, 7, 10, 11, 13, 43, 228, 230–31, 235, 239, 296
Armstrong, W. W., 95
arranged marriage: arrangement by kin, 15, 17, 45, 56, 70, 84, 205, 230; in colonial Africa, 65, 319; consensual model of, 14; contemporary, 109; debate over, 43, 65; defined, 180; economic justification for, 184–85, 191; vs. forced marriage, 13–15, 45, 60, 68, 109, 230, 233–35, 244n14; as forced marriage, 189–92; in Gosha, 128; and social networks, 110–11; in Somalia, 26, 113; study of, 182; as tradition/custom, 14–15, 184–85; among the Xhosa, 26, 138, 139, 141–44. *See also* early marriage; forced marriage; *isinmo*
assault, 140; sexual, 26, 150, 200, 209
as-sirriyya. *See* marriage: secret
Association for the Promotion of Women & Girls Advancement, 195n14
Association pour la Promotion Féminine de Gaoua (APFG), 280
asylum claims, 13, 28, 34, 207; tribunals for, 32
asylum narratives, 202
asylum seekers: fleeing forced marriage, 24, 28, 203–10; and gender-based persecution, 109, 320–21; LGB 28, 199–201, 210–19; mobilities of, 34
Aubert, Alfred, 48, 51
Australia, laws against slavery in, 13
authority, patriarchal, 17, 19, 203. *See also* patriarchy
autonomy: and forced marriage, 22–23, 201; individual, 111, 183, 201, 219, 232, 237; of women, 22, 60, 62n24, 122, 154, 197n48, 199, 218, 249

Baba of Kano, 56–57
Babangida, Ibrahim, 254
baby dumping, 196n32
Bagayogo, Moussa, 54

Baldeh, Awa, 186
Baldeh, Konkon, 186
Bamakana, Faraba, 53
Bambara people, 45, 48–49, 51, 52
Bangura, Zainab, 230, 231
Basden, George, 66
Basoga people, 57
Beavon, Eric, 95
Benadir, 116–17. *See also* Gosha; Somalia
Benin: early and child marriage in, 28, 32, 182, 282–84; forced marriage in, 71, 202, 205; grassroots women's organizations in, 270; legal age for marriage, 273; women fleeing from marriage in, 83
Bennett, T. W., 140
betrothal. *See* child betrothal
Beyruk, M'barek ould, 166–67
bisexual individuals, 28, 199, 202. *See also* sexual minorities
Biya, Paul, 212
Bledsoe, Caroline H., 181
Boko Haram abduction, 83, 305, 314
Bokwe, John Knox, 143
bondage, 2, 209. *See also* slavery
Bourouillou (administrator), 59
boys: preferential treatment of, 183; sexual violence against, 229. *See also* children
Brevié, Jules, 48
Bricchetti, Luigi Robecchi, 117
bridal contracts. *See* contract(s)
bridal payments. *See* bride-price; bridewealth
bride abduction. *See* abduction; *ukuthwala*
bride-price, 18, 51, 67, 175n13; increase in, 75–76. *See also* bridewealth; gift exchange
Bride Price, The (Emecheta), 71–72, 77
brides: ransom, 242. *See also* girls; wives; women
bridewealth: in Africa, 3, 4, 15, 17–18, 25, 32, 184–85; change in value of, 18; in colonial Africa, 75, 191, 317–19; and the conferral of rights, 67–68; debate over, 103; financial dependence on, 72; government-sponsored, 257–59; in Igboland, 67; impact on capacity to consent, 45–47; limits to, 87n39; preconjugal payments, 27; repayment of, 46–47, 58–59, 77, 78, 80, 191; lack of resources for, 31; and the rights of children, 52–54, 56; and the transfer of rights in persons, 22, 44, 48; in Xhosaland, 146. *See also* contract(s)
British Commonwealth League, 90

Children's Law of Liberia, 273
child rights, 3, 6, 32, 35n1, 53–54, 173, 182, 251–52, 254, 269–71, 273, 293, 296, 320
Child Rights Act (CRA), 254
child slavery, 60, 63, 69, 73, 103, 208–9, 239, 254
child soldiers, 10, 32, 293–4, 296, 302, 305, 307n10
Child Soldiers International, 294
child trafficking, 254. *See also* human trafficking
Christelle (asylum seeker from Douala), 211–13
Christianity in Africa, 17, 191, 212, 260, 262
Christian missions and missionaries, 3, 19, 30, 60–61, 67, 72, 74, 75, 81, 89, 90, 93, 95–97, 100, 101, 103, 145, 151–52, 249
Church Missionary Society (CMS), 67, 97
circumcision: female, 101 (*see also* female initiation practices); male, 97
citizenship rights, for women, 280, 281, 288
Civil Defense Militia (CDF), 229
clans, patrilineal, 45–46, 111–12, 115
coercion: and betrothal, 66; and consent 15, 23, 33–34, 190, 253, 304; labor, 25–26; into marriage, 2, 10, 15, 20, 25, 28–29, 31, 33, 34, 65–67, 70, 71, 73, 76, 111, 184, 190, 213, 218, 254, 263; and mass marriage program, 262–63; moral, 107n50; sexual, 147, 303; in traditional practices, 154, 180, 184, 303; as violence against women, 15
Coles, Catherine, 250
colonial maternalism, 317
colonial paternalism, 317
colonialism: British, 72–84; and the economy, 74; European, 316; French, 43–44, 47–52; Italian, 110, 117–29; and marriage custom, 17, 19, 50, 145–50; in Nigeria, 75
Colucci, Massimo, 114
Comaroff, John, 146
Commission for Human Rights and Administrative Justice (Ghana), 216
Commission on the Status of Women (CSW), 182
Committee on the Elimination of Discrimination against Women (CEDAW), 182, 183, 231, 251, 253, 273, 288, 320
Committee on Traditional Practices (GAMCOTRAP), 195n14
community. *See* networks and alliances; kinship relations
community-based initiatives, 287–88

Compendium of Kaffir Law and Custom (Maclean), 142
concubinage, 27, 164, 166, 175n15, 315–16
concubines, 55, 120, 159, 161. *See also* slave wives: Islamic
conflict situations. *See* warfare
Congo Free State, 117, 297
Congo. *See* Democratic Republic of the Congo (DRC)
Congress of Traditional Leaders of South Africa (CONTRALESA), 138, 141
conjugal slavery. *See* slavery
consent to marriage: vs. coercion, 15, 23, 33–34, 190, 253, 304; and the concept of freedom, 21; in conflict situations, 229, 292; constrained, 51–52; debates over, 43; familial, 141, 150–54; and forced marriage, 66, 201, 227, 254, 270, 319; free and full, 6–7, 15, 60, 183; French opinions regarding, 32, 44; influenced by bridewealth, 45–47; lack of, 3–4, 72, 125, 141, 144, 191, 292; and marriage reform, 317; by parents or guardian, 21, 48, 67; spousal, 72, 78; tacit, 51. *See also* age of consent
contraceptive injections, 181
contract(s): *as-syrriyya*, 168–69; farming, 124; *fatiha*, 173; legal aspects of, 4, 20–22, 35n11, 47, 219, 230, 233, 254, 317–18; liberal theories of, 21; marriage, 22, 26, 51, 71, 77, 81, 89, 100, 110–11, 117, 122, 125, 162, 170, 182, 193, 202, 203, 206, 210, 299; oral, 168; pawning, 50, 77; stipulating monogamy, 161, 167, 174
control: of Africans, 119; over children, 21, 75, 145, 253, 255, 274; colonial, 34, 117; familial, 143–45, 151–54, 184, 236; over labor, 17, 19, 24–27, 45, 60, 110, 116, 118, 293, 299–300; over men, 110; political, 112, 235, 302; of slaves, 21, 68, 118, 122, 163; of tradition, 188; over women, 19, 24, 30, 47, 60, 110, 115, 122, 188, 192, 242, 247–48, 250, 298–300; of young girls, 188, 247–48, 295, 306. *See also* power
Convention on Consent to Marriage, Minimum Age for Marriage and Registration for Marriage (1962), 6
Convention on Elimination of All Forms of Discrimination Against Women (CEDAW), 6, 182, 183, 231, 251, 253, 273, 288, 320
Convention on the Rights of the Child (CRC), 6, 180, 182, 251, 254, 320

Dumbia, Kaniba, 55
Dundas, Charles, 103

early marriage: advocacy against, 269, 275–76, 280, 283, 285, 286; in Benin, 283; consequences of, 20, 27, 192; customary norms, 271–75; defined, 180; in DRC, 284–85; factors perpetuating, 32–33; and girls' health, 276–77; as human rights violation, 269, 273; international conventions, 273, 283; in Kenya, 30; mothers' worry about, 189–90; national laws, 273–74; question of, 319; in Sierra Leone, 302; as slavery, 3, 69; as tradition, 69, 73, 181; in Uganda, 285–87, 302; underlying causes of, 270; in West Africa, 182. *See also* child marriage; early marriage in Kenya; forced marriage
early marriage in Kenya: Archdeacon Owen (1930s), 97–100; on the coast (1949–50), 100–103; difficulty in defining, 89–90; imperial context, 90–93; Nyanza province (1926–28), 93–97
East Africa, map, 9. *See also* Ethiopia; Kenya; Tanzania; Zanzibar
Eastern Cape Province, abductions in, 31, 137
Eastern Nigeria Limitation of Dowry Law (1956), 84n5
Eastern Nigeria Marriage Law (1956), 83
economic factors, 23, 33–34; in arranged marriage 184–85, 191; in child betrothal/marriage, 173, 174, 179–80
education: of children 184, 257, 274; for girls, 23, 28, 183, 192, 272, 274, 277–78, 281, 282–88, 289; literacy classes, 279, 286; mission schools, 74, 249; sexuality education, 285; vocational training, 269, 279, 287
Egungun, 209
elders, in African society, 27, 48, 52, 81, 102–3, 112, 179, 188–89, 206, 218, 274, 285–87, 304
Elements of Crimes (ICC), 12
11 Days of Action, 275
"Eliminating Child Marriage in BF: A Plan for Protection, Empowerment and Community Action", 282
elopement, 75, 77, 79, 80, 81, 113, 146
Emecheta, Buchi, 71
enslavement: of children, 69; for debt, 70, 237; domestic, 237; through forced labor, 11; through forced marriage in wartime, 231–32; in the Rome Statute, 12; ritual, 209. *See also* slavery

epochal history, 317
Eritrea, 118
Ethiopia, 118, 272, 302
eugenics, 95, 106n36
European Union, forced marriages in, 15
Evans, M. N., 101
Extraordinary Chambers in the Courts of Cambodia, 7

face, saving, 189, 197n38
Fallers, Lloyd, 57, 59
family: arrangement of marriage by, 15, 17, 45, 56, 70, 84, 205, 230; control by 143–45, 151–54, 184, 236; consent to marriage by, 141, 150–54; role of, 15, 71. *See also* fathers; mothers; parents
Family Code: Benin (2004), 209; Mali, 273; Togo, 204
Family Health International (FHI), 256
Family Law (DRC), 273
Farage, Loubna, 183
fatalism, 51
fathers: authority of, 17, 167; control over daughters' marriages, 102, 144–45, 148, 151–54, 169, 178, 189, 191–92, 204, 253, 255. *See also* men
fatiha marriage, 173
Federal Ministry of Women's Affairs, 254
female initiation practices, 97, 115–16, 236; female excision, 97, 101, 107n53; female genital cutting (FGC), 101, 115, 183; female genital mutilation (FGM), 131n28, 193, 200, 278, 280, 288, 291; female labia cutting, 115, 131n28
Female Lawyers Association–Gambia (FLAG), 179, 180, 181, 195n14
female maturation: debate over, 91–103; liminal period for, 91–92, 104n7; racial differences in, 92, 94, 95 104n9
female religious bondage, 209
Ferrandi, Ugo, 121
fertility rates, adolescent, 271
FGC. *See* female initiation practices: female genital cutting
FGM. *See* female initiation practices: female genital mutilation
Fingo people, 152
fistulas, obstetric, 276, 278, 279
food security programs, 280
forced conjugal associations/forced conjugality, 10, 203, 295, 296, 305. *See also* forced marriage
forced impregnation, 11, 43, 200, 220n5, 231

forced marriage: advocacy against, 192–94, 269, 278, 281, 286; arranged marriage as, 189–92; vs. arranged marriage, 13–15, 45, 60, 68, 230, 233–35, 244n14; and asylum applicants, 209–10, 320–21; in colonial archival records, 29–30; and colonial social engineering, 3–4; consent issues, 14, 15, 80; as continuing crime, 23–24; and control over labor, 25, 34, 109, 110; criminalization of, 12, 33, 83, 227–33, 239; critique of term, 11; debate over, 34, 103; decreasing instance of, 151; defined, 180; as economic decision, 23, 33–34, 173–74, 179–80, 184–85, 191; in the European Union, 15; examples and interviews, 185–87; and human rights, 1, 43; in immigrant communities, 15; as inhumane act, 7; and interfemale dynamics, 305; justifications for, 217–18; in law and politics, 3–7, 10–13, 33–34; *longue durée* (long term) approach to, 314–15, 321; and the mass marriage program, 263; *nikaax talyiani,* 126–68; as persecutory harm, 202; political economy of, 299; postindependence transformations, 34; as a power issue, 298; present-day practices, 34; protest against, 74; public awareness of, 28–29; and public policy, 251–52; role of the family in, 15, 71; scholarship on, 24, 182; to settle debts, 14, 69–70; as slavery, 3, 4, 5, 11–12, 65, 99, 100; sociocultural habitus of, 29; sociohistorical context of, 34; as tradition/custom, 1, 33–34, 181, 179–80, 184–85, 206, 218, 271–72, 317; as trauma trigger, 313; underlying causes of, 270; and the use of amulets, 186; and violence, 25; vulnerability to, 34; women fleeing from, 24, 25, 28, 34, 75, 83, 109, 200–203, 281, 293. *See also* coercion; forced marriage by country/culture; forced marriage during conflict; marriage; *ukuthwala*

Forced Marriage Act (UK), 29

"Forced Marriage: A Wrong, Not a Right" (UK Foreign and Commonwealth Office), 14

forced marriage by country/culture: Benin, 205; Cambodia, 7; Cameroon, 203, 205; Cape Town, 296; Gambia, 14–15, 30, 179; Global South, 252; Igbo, 83–84; Sierra Leone, 10, 301; Somalia/Somaliland, 301, 316; Togo, 203–5; West Africa, 205

forced marriage during conflict, 7, 11–14, 32–33, 228, 292–3, 295–8, 302–3; as crime against humanity, 7, 14, 228, 296; as crime of war, 27, 295, 305; as form of protection, 304–5; legal and humanitarian discourses, 295–97

forced pregnancy, 11, 43, 200, 220n5, 231

forced sterilization, 200

Ford Foundation 276

Fortier, Corinne, 167

Forum on Marriage and the Rights of Women and Girls, 278

Foundation for Women's Health, Research and Development (FORWARD), 278

Free the Slaves, 5

French Soudan, 25, 31–32

French West Africa: consent vs. coercion in, 23; exchange marriage in, 318; forced marriage issues in, 43; marriage arrangements in, 45–7; native courts in, 47–48; women's conditions in, 47–52

Frye, Poppy, 152

Fulani people, 185, 205, 247

Gabon, 273

Gaida, Shafa'ato Ibrahim, 262

Gallaway, Barbara, 187

Gambia: 1997 Constitution, 183, 320; arranged marriage in, 184–85; forced marriage in, 14–15, 27, 30, 179, 184–85; and the Ouagadougou Declaration, 278; on women's and children's rights, 182–3

gang rape, 298. *See also* rape

Garden, T. W., 73

Gautherot, Gustave, 49

gay men, 28, 199, 202

gender: as category of persecution, 200, 320; discrimination based on, 183; and the social construction of personhood, 16

gender-based violence (GBV), 10, 183, 193, 200, 281, 284, 296. *See also* gendered violence; gender violence

gender crimes, 229, 232, 235

gender discrimination, 204, 320. *See also* discrimination

gendered crime, 11, 295–96. *See also* war crimes

gendered violence, 2, 15, 203, 314. *See also* gender-based violence (GBV); gender violence

gendered war crimes, 295–96

gender equality, 278, 287

gender equity, 189, 200

gender inequality, 23, 66, 294, 297

gender relations, 66, 75

Lugard, Frederick, 73
Luo Union, 96, 103

Mabandla, George, 152
MacDonad, Claude, 70
Machel, Graça, 296
Mack, Beverly, 250
Maclean, John, 142
Mahmood, Saba, 111
Mahmoud, Hamody ould, 164
Maigari, Malam, 56, 57
Makua (Somali), 115, 116
Malawi, 115, 271
male circumcision, 97
male household heads. *See* fathers
Mali, 271, 273, 278
Mandela, Mandla, 141
Mandel Decree, 44
Mandinka people, 178, 185
manumission papers, 121–22
maps: contemporary Central and Southern
    Africa, 8; contemporary East Africa, 9;
    contemporary West Africa, 7
Maputo Protocol, 6–7, 252, 273, 288
Marakong, Alhagi Sunkare, 189
Mariama (forced marriage victim), 180, 181
Marie-André (soeur du Sacré-Coeur), 50,
    51, 60
marital consent. *See* consent to marriage
Marks, Zoe, 298
marriage: abuse and exploitation in, 66; in
    African society, 15; age disparity in, 23,
    79–80, 96, 99, 107n49, 174; as alliance,
    47, 66; civil, 193; coerced, 2, 4–5, 10,
    15, 20, 25, 28–29, 31, 33, 34, 65–67, 70,
    73, 76, 111, 184, 190, 213, 218, 254, 263;
    changes under colonialism, 72–75, 182,
    272; collective, 114; without consent, 4,
    5, 11, 12; cross-cousin, 56, 173, 185, 239;
    delayed, 269, 272; in the diaspora, 34; as
    economic transaction, 109; exchange,
    318; exogamic, 112; fatiha, 173; as form
    of persecution, 200; incapacitous, 29;
    intercommunity, 205–6; as investment,
    45; irregular forms of, 142; and Islamic
    law, 23, 30, 172, 180, 191, 192–93, 253–55;
    monogamous, 7, 26, 30, 123, 125, 161;
    parental control over, 102, 144–45, 148,
    151–54, 169, 178, 189, 191–92, 204, 253, 255;
    patrilineal, 46; and personhood, 184; and
    the place of women, 50–51; and political
    power, 184; polyandric, 110, 119, 123;
    polygamous, 90, 99, 101, 107n49, 123, 170,
174, 203, 205, 298, 305; polygynous, 3, 52,
    73, 79, 99, 119, 123, 203, 204, 207–8, 217,
    262; same-sex, 15; second and subsequent
    marriages, 46, 56–58, 60, 169, 205, 216–17;
    secret, 27, 167–73; and slavery, 10, 97,
    175n15; and social networks, 192; in
    Somalia, 112–16; "state-sponsored", 248,
    249; tradition in, 187–89; victimization
    in, 69; virilocal, 46. *See also* abduction;
    age of marriage; arranged marriage;
    child marriage; coercion; consent to
    marriage; customary marriage; divorce;
    early marriage; forced marriage; mass
    marriage program
marriageability: debate on, 105n14; physical
    vs. emotional considerations, 94–99. *See
    also* age of marriage/marriageable age
marriage age/marriageable age. *See* age of
    marriage/marriageable age
marriage by capture, 72, 297. *See also*
    abduction; forced marriage; *ukuthwala*
marriage contracts. *See* contracts
marriage customs: in Benin, 28, 32, 71, 182,
    202, 205, 282–84; in Burkina Faso, 27–28,
    32, 182, 271, 277–78; in Gambia, 14–15,
    27, 30, 179, 184–85; Igbo, 70–71, 80–81,
    83–84; in northern Nigeria, 30, 75–76, 253,
    271; Xhosa, 26, 138, 139, 141–44. *See also*
    tradition(s)
marriage in absentia. *See* forced marriage
Marriage Ordinance (Gambia, 1862), 182
Marshall, M. H. F., 79, 80
Martha (victim of abduction), 149–50
Mashhour, Amira, 192
mass marriage program, 30–32, 248–49,
    257–65, 321–22
mass rape, 298. *See also* rape
Matanzima, Nangomhlaba, 141
maternal health, 269, 282
maternalism, colonial, 317
maternal mortality, 23, 271
Matomela, David, 152
Matrimonial Causes Act, 254
maturity: age of, 6; attainment of, 75, 95,
    97, 102, 104n9, 207, 209; emotional, 92,
    93, 102; of husbands, 262; legal, 204, 207;
    psychological, 92, 102; sexual, 30, 90, 102
Maupoil, Bernard, 48, 59
Mauritania, 27, 160, 164, 174, 315–16
Mbilinyi, Marjorie, 83
McDougall, Gay J., 10
McElwane, P. A., 95
Meillassoux, Claude, 184, 188

men: control over daughters' marriages, 102, 144–45, 148, 151–54, 169, 178, 189, 191–92, 204, 253, 255; sexual violence against, 229. *See also* fathers

Mendela (Fingo headman), 152

mental health treatment, 216, 224n51

Merry, Sally E., 183

Mgbeke, Diribeofor, 68

Mgbocha (from Kwale), 65

Mgbolie (Igbo woman), 76–77

Mhaka, Msitshana, 153

Miers, Suzanne, 68

Millennium Development Goals, 275

Million Woman March, 257

Ministry of Women's Empowerment and the Family, 203

misogyny, 203

mission schools, 74, 249. *See also* education

missionaries. *See* Christian missions and missionaries

Mitchell, Sally, 91

Mnongerwa, Mame Nthukano, 126

Mnongerwa, Mze, 126

Mnxeba (plaintiff), 153

Moinyaha ("bush wife"), 238

monogamy, 7, 26, 30, 123, 125, 161

Mookerjea-Leonard, Debali, 314–15

mothers: as advocates for daughters, 269, 279, 280, 282, 288; single, 30. *See also* women

Mozambique, 115, 271, 302

Muslim communities, 61. *See also* Islam

Muslim Hausa. *See* Hausa

Muslim Sisters Organization (MSO), 256

musu suñaa, 185, 187. *See also* abduction

mysogyny, 210

Nadia (Rwandan rape victim), 300

National Congress for the Defense of the People (Congrès national pour la défense du people, CNDP), 303

National Union for the Total Independence of Angola (União Nacional para a Independência Total de Angola, UNITA), 303

Native Catholic Union (NCU), 93–94, 96

networked obligations, 219, 321

networks and alliances, 66, 71, 109–11, 128–29, 190, 192. *See also* kinship relations; social networks

"new war" theories, 293

Ngwu, Jack, 68

Niger, 18, 271, 273. *See also* Hausa

Niger Coast Protectorate, 70

Nigeria: age of consent in, 83; British imperialism in, 72–73; child betrothal in, 253–54; clinics for obstetric fistulas, 279; marriage coercion in, 31; marriage courts in, 74; marriage customs in, 30, 75–76, 253, 271; marriage disputes in, 31; NGO Coalition on CEDAW, 253; and the Ouagadougou Declaration, 278; slave trade in, 65; subordination of women in, 248; women fleeing from marriage in, 83. *See also* mass marriage program

nikaax talyiani, 123, 125–29

Njanua (Mozambique and Malawi), 115, 116

Nomini (Pieter Soldaat's victim), 150

nongovernmental organizations (NGOs), 33, 141, 181, 182, 256, 276, 279, 280, 283

Nontozonke (rape victim), 146

Notoyi (Nomini's intended husband), 150

Ntsabo (putative husband), 146

Nyangori Mission, 95

Obasanjo, Olusugun, 254

obstetric fistulas, 20, 276, 278, 279

Ogada Mission, 96

Okpani (buyer-husband), 68–69

Okronkwor (accused abductor), 68

Onor, Romolo, 124

Oosterveld, Valerie, 10, 11

oppression, gender-based, 91, 192, 199, 315, 321

Organisation Mondiale Contre la Torture, 221

orphans, female, 62n24

Other Inhumane Acts, 7, 10, 11, 231, 244–45n16

Ouagadougou Declaration on Early and Forced Marriage, 278

Ouattara, Mariam, 182

out-of-wedlock pregnancy, 23, 274, 284

Owen, Walter E. (Archdeacon), 93, 97–100, 107n49

Pakistan, partition of, 246n53, 314

panyarring, 65, 73

paralegals, 280, 286, 287–88

parents: attitude toward education, 270, 274, 277, 285, 287–89; authority of, 204, 255; bridewealth payments to, 5, 67–68, 74, 76, 170, 184–85, 187; complicity in abductions, 71, 137–38, 185, 187, 196n24; consent for marriage by, 26, 146, 153, 182; control over children, 21, 66, 68, 75, 184;

control over marriage, 75, 102, 144–45,
148, 151–54, 169, 178, 189, 191–92, 204, 253,
255; decisions made by, 15, 68, 71, 113, 264;
labor of groom benefitting, 27, 68, 115, 185;
marriages arranged by, 56, 65, 66, 70, 71,
81, 84, 137, 144, 178, 180–81, 184–85, 190,
193, 207–8, 233, 253, 263; obedience to, 84,
113, 144, 189; pawning of girls by, 70; and
questions of custody, 52; refund of bridal
payments by, 46–47, 58–59, 74, 77, 78, 80,
191; rights of, 103; sale of children by, 73;
support for mass marriages by, 32, 260,
264. *See also* fathers; mothers
Parker, J. (Justice), 29
Partition, of India and Pakistan, 246n53, 314
Pastoral Women Alliance to Break Cultural
Chains (PWABC), 285–86
Pateman, Carole, 60
paternalism: colonial, 317; righteous, 321–22
paternity acknowledgement, 161, 174n4,
175n16
patriarchy, 24–26, 28, 43, 60, 71, 190, 192–93,
202–4, 287, 306; authority of, 17, 19, 203;
resistance to, 202, 203–10, 217
patrilineal clans, 45–46, 111–12, 115
patrimonialism, 24, 33, 201
Paul, Ncedisa, 141
pawning and pawnship (*igba ibe*), 25, 44, 49,
65–67, 69–70, 72, 73, 84
Pemba islands, 122
persecution in asylum claims, 14, 24, 28,
109, 199–200, 202, 207–9, 211, 213–15, 217,
320–21
personhood: in Africa, 15–16, 129; and
consent in marriage, 21; culture and,
16–17; gender and, 16; and marriage, 184.
See also identity
Peters, Krijn, 301
Pittin, Renee, 250
Pollera, Alberto, 109
polyandry, 110, 119, 123
polygamy, 90, 99, 101, 107n49, 123, 170, 174,
203, 205, 298, 305
polygyny, 3, 52, 73, 79, 99, 119, 123, 203, 204,
207–8, 217, 262
Pombani (headman), 152
Ponty, William, 57
Popular Front, 44, 50
Poro society, 236
poverty, 242, 247, 252, 255–56, 265, 271; and
early marriage, 196n31; female, 17, 248,
256, 278
Poverty Knowledge and Practice study, 256

power: of chiefs, 75, 83; to consent, 81;
economic, 25; familial, 248, 253, 255;
and forced marriage, 24, 110, 125, 128,
154, 218, 228, 298; of ownership, 4, 11, 12;
paternal, 30, 46; political 25, 184, 235, 256;
reproductive, 18, 60; social, 25, 188, 205,
248; of women, 145, 151, 154; over women,
25, 68, 75. *See also* control
pregnancy: complications in young mothers,
20, 276; forced, 11, 43, 200, 220n5, 231; out-
of-wedlock, 23, 274, 284; unplanned, 285
premarital sex, 23, 143
Prevention and Combating of Trafficking in
Persons Act (2013), 140
private investment, 118
prostitution, 121–22, 239, 242, 256, 296
Protocol Relating to the Status of Refugees
(1967), 200, 320
Protocol to the African Charter on Human
and Peoples' Rights on the Rights of
Women in Africa (Maputo Protocol), 6–7,
252, 273, 288
psychological harm and suffering, 20, 43
puberty (first menses), 6, 20, 21, 30, 49, 60,
68, 84, 90, 92–98, 105n12, 113, 115, 116, 126,
131n34, 181, 191
public health, 256, 269
public opinion, 101, 102, 106n34, 107n53
Pugsada, 279
Puntland, 111. *See also* Somalia

Queen v. Tang, 13
Quirk, Joel, 12
Qur'an, on marriage, 162. *See also* Islam;
Islamic (shari'a) law

Radcliffe-Brown, A. R., 45–47
Raitt, W. S., 100–101
Ramatoulie (abduction victim), 185–86
Ranger, Terence, 179
ransom brides, 242
rape: and abduction 26, 31, 72, 140, 146–47,
150, 155n11; as crime against international,
220n5; and early marriage, 96, 283; and
forced marriage, 32, 69, 71–72, 146, 200;
legal issues of, 22; of lesbians, 213; as
persecution, 200, 208–10, 213, 215, 217; in
schools, 284; of slave wives, 69; during
war, 7, 10, 11, 43, 229–32, 234–35, 238,
240–41, 294–96, 298–304
rapists, marrying victims, 14
Rathbone, Eleanor, 91
rebel babies, 230

wife inheritance, 72, 264, 280, 286. *See also* levirate

wife stealing, 196n24. See also *ukuthwala*

wife troubles, 242

Wilson, F. R., 100

wives: fugitive, 77, 83; and Islamic law, 159; multiple, 99; secondary, 79. *See also* bush wives; slave wives; wife inheritance

Wokocha (accused abductor), 68

Wolof people, 185, 197n49

woman damage (adultery), 299. *See also* adultery

"woman quarrels," 240

women: abuse of, 127–28; access to independent sources of income, 74; and African warfare, 297; agency of, 301; autonomy of, 22, 60, 62n24, 122, 154, 197n48, 199, 218, 249; benefits from colonialism, 75; business support for, 280–81, 283; "of the ceiling", 300; challenges to traditional marriage customs by, 77–78 ; citizenship rights of, 280, 281, 288 ; conscription of, 235 ; control over, 19, 24, 30, 47, 60, 71, 110, 115, 122, 188, 192, 242, 247–48, 250, 298–300; crimes against, 234–35; discrimination against, 182–3, 194n5; divorced, 28, 30, 59, 60, 248, 256, 257, 260, 264; emancipation of, 26, 60; empowerment of, 203, 257, 270, 276, 279–84; enslavement of, 11, 73, 227–42; exploitation of, 298; fleeing forced marriages, 24, 25, 28, 34, 75, 83, 109, 200, 201–3, 281, 293; in the household order, 50–51; Igbo, 76–78; in India, 315; inheritance of (levirate), 5, 48, 99, 204, 205, 209, 210; lack of input in forced marriage decisions, 186; legal status of in Gambia, 179; literacy training for, 279, 281, 282, 283; marginalization of, 249, 278; obedience to men, 144, 184, 192, 197n49, 248; oppression of, 91; pawning of, 72; in poverty, 28, 30, 256, 257, 260, 264, 265; practices impinging on the freedom of, 72; as property, 5, 49–50, 72, 78, 109, 110, 122, 286; remaining with captors, 238, 239, 241; scarcity of, 119; as sexual objects, 286; single, 78, 248; single mothers, 30, 78; state control over, 247–9, 250; subjection of, 234; subjugation of, 110, 188, 280; subordination of, 22, 248; victimhood of, 32, 295; victimization of, 78; violence against, 15, 182, 203, 215, 220n11, 275, 278; widowed, 28, 30, 248, 256, 257, 260, 281. *See also* abduction; girls; marriage; wives

women's movement, 21

women's grassroots organizations, 32, 257, 286

women's rights, 3, 33, 90–91, 183, 192, 209–10, 248, 249, 269, 278, 279, 281–3, 285–6, 293, 296; to freely consent to marriage, 6–7; inheritance, 287; and South African custom, 138–43; and *ukuthwala*, 137–43

women's rights organizations, 182, 277

Xhosaland, 143–46

Xhosa marriage customs, 26, 138, 139, 141–44

Yao (Somalia), 116

Yoruba, 209

Yorubaland, 83

Young, Samuel, 145

Zanzibar, 122

Zarewa, Dabo, 56

Zarewa, Sarkin, 56

Zigula (Somali), 115, 116, 126

Zimbabwe, 272

Zuma, Jacob, 139

www.ingramcontent.com/pod-product-compliance
Lightning Source LLC
Chambersburg PA
CBHW072047020426
42334CB00017B/1422